The Book of Klezmer

The Book of

Klezmer

•

THE HISTORY
THE MUSIC
THE FOLKLORE

YALE STROM

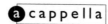

Library of Congress Cataloging-in-Publication Data
Strom, Yale.
    The book of klezmer : the history, the music, the folklore /
Yale Strom.—1st ed.
        p. cm.
Includes bibliographical references (p.   ) and index.
Discography: p.
    ISBN 1-55652-445-5 (hardback : alk. paper)
    1. Klezmer music—History and criticism. 2. Jews—
Music—History and criticism. I. Title.
    ML3528.8 .S77 2002
    781.62'924—dc21   2002002701

Jacket and book design by: Lindgren/Fuller Design

Published by A Cappella Books
an imprint of Chicago Review Press, Incorporated
814 North Franklin Street
Chicago, Illinois 60610
1-55652-445-5

Printed in the United States of America
5 4 3 2 1

To all the Jewish klezmorim *and Rom musicians who perished in the Holocaust, and who took their brilliance with them.*

Contents

◆

A Note on Yiddish Spellings

As with any foreign language that does not use Latin letters in its alphabet, Yiddish has often been spelled the way the user deems closest to its sound. For example, Poles might write *sznajder* (tailor), while Americans, relying on German spelling, would write *schneider*. There are many spelling land mines in Yiddish because it is a language derived from several others (German, Hebrew, Polish, Russian, and French), all of which are in use today. There are even spelling discrepancies for Yiddish words that have crossed over into English. For example, the word *Chanuka*, originally a Hebrew word, can be spelled *Chanukah*, *Hanukah*, or *Hannuka*. But according to the academic guidelines set up by the YIVO Institute, the Yiddish word for the Festival of Lights is spelled *Khanike*.

Since this is a book about the *klezmer* and his world in Central and Eastern Europe, where Yiddish was the lingua franca, all the Yiddish and Hebrew words herein are spelled according to the YIVO standard—even those that have crossed over into everyday English usage like *Hasid, Rosh Hashanah, Shabbes, Torah,* etc. The first time each word appears, the more common spelling follows in parentheses.

Acknowledgments

•

I began writing this book in the summer of 1999, but I had been researching and collecting archival material, field recordings, and oral histories since 1981. Along the way many people have helped me and given freely of their time; while I'd like to personally thank them all, it all began with my parents: Phyllis and David Strom. They gave me love, supported all my artistic endeavors, and taught me the attributes that assisted me in writing this book: from my father, I learned the importance and richness of my East European Jewish roots and acquired my *khasidic yikhes* and my love of history. From my mother, I learned to be inquisitive, talkative, personable, and respectful with everyone I meet. In addition, she taught me the importance of setting goals and persevering until they are attained. And I thank them both for providing me with the violin lessons that began in Detroit with my first violin teacher, Mrs. Baker.

Over the years I have had the opportunity to perform with and learn from many fine musicians in both my *klezmer* bands. They include Fred Benedetti, Ismail Butera, Marty Confurius, Matt Darriau, Adam Del Monte, Damian Draghici, Mark Dresser, Marty Ehrlich, Lou Fanucchi, Amir Halfon, Misha Heitzler, Dave Hofstra, Benny Koonyevsky, Gene Perry, David Rozenblatt, Sprocket J. Royer, Seido Salifoski, Tripp Sprague, Norbert Stachel, Peter Stan, Andy Statman, Bertram Turetzky, Alon Waisman, Greg

Wall, and Robert Zelickman. Then there is Jeff Pekarek, with whom I have been playing music since I was fourteen years old and who helped me start my first *klezmer* band. His friendship and musical talents have guided and helped me immensely over the years.

While going to undergraduate and graduate school I learned from many excellent professors and teachers, but there are a few I want to especially thank for their encouragement and scholarly input when I first began my research into *klezmer:* Dina Abramowicz, Barbara Kirshenblatt-Gimblett, Jack Kugelmass, Lucjan Dobroszycki, Peysakh Fishman, Laurin Raiken, Hillel Schwartz, Kay Shelemay, Ita Sheres, Mark Slobin, and Sheva Zucker.

During the twenty years of my serious involvement in *klezmer,* I have met a number of other fine *klezmer* proponents, many of whom have become good friends. Their musicianship, support, and knowledge of *klezmer* helped me when it came time to write this book, and without them, the task would have been much more difficult. They are: Michael Alpert, Moshe Berlin, David Buchbinder, Leo Chelyapov, Bob Cohen, Adrienne Cooper, Zev Feldman, David Krakauer, Margo Leverett, Frank London, Zalman Mlotek, Hankus Netsky, Ron Robboy, Michael Schlesinger, Deborah Strauss, Alicia Svigals, Josh Waletzky, Jeff Warschauer, and John Zorn.

I also want to thank the celebrated artists Theodore Bikel, Joel Grey, Arthur Hiller, Dick Hyman, Tony Kushner, Leonard Nimoy, and Joan Micklin Silver, who gave so generously of their time and insights into the world of Jewish art.

I feel deep gratitude to all those people who gave of their time at the YIVO Institute, where I spent many hours researching the archives, and all the other people who helped me with the various language translations and archival research: Aviva Astrinsky, Archie Barkan, Erica Blankenstein, Eric Canepa, Luca Comisso, Dariusz Czwojdrak, Gregory Diamant, Naomi Fatouros, Paul Glaser, Alfred Gruenspecht, Sam Guncler, Bogdan Kaczorowski, Benny Koonyevsky, Herbert Lazarus, Yeshaya Metal, Chana Mlotek, Yale J. Reisner, Robert Rothstein, Mel Solman, Harold Strom, Ruth and Abraham Taigman, Marek Web, and Helen Winkler.

Then there are all the informants I interviewed over the years in Central and Eastern Europe. They opened their homes, minds, and hearts and made me always feel welcome when I visited them. Their music and memories into the *klezmer* world of pre–World War II Central and Eastern Europe gave this book its special *heymishe* characteristic. There were too many informants to list them all here, but some of those who were most generous were: Paul Babici, Dimitru Bughici, Berko Gott, Izu Gott, Leopold Kozlowski, Ludmilla Pollack, Nikolai Radu, Cili Goldenzweig Svarṭ, Itzik Kara Svarṭ, Aron Tinichigiu, Shani Virag, Asher Wainshteyn, and Simkhe Wajc.

I had wanted to write a book on the history of *klezmer* music for many years; it took the help and friendship of my agent, Mary Jack Wald, to bring it to A Cappella Books. At A Cappella, I have had the good fortune to have Yuval Taylor as my editor. With his friendship, editorial input, and persistence in quality he helped guide me during the sometimes arduous writing process.

I owe my deepest gratitude and feel most indebted to my wife, Elizabeth. Without her constant encouragement, artistic and editorial input, and endless patience, I would not have been able to finish this book. She has always been there when I needed her. Finally, I want to thank my dear daughter Tallulah. She taught me there is more to life than just writing a book, and I treasure every time she asked me, "*Tate,* why are you sitting in front of the computer? Let's go out and play."

Introduction

◆

It was midnight when the congregants, all fifteen of them, went outside to the synagogue courtyard to bless the new moon. These mostly elderly men, holding their prayer books, gathered around Rabbi Grossman as he began to softly chant the prayers. The ambient noises from the surrounding streets were muffled by the high thick walls of the courtyard, which had been built in the eighteenth century. Just as they finished their prayers, in marched two musicians: a violinist and a bassist. They played a Jewish melody that sounded like a Khasidic *nign* (Yid.: song). As the two musicians moved closer to the congregants, suddenly one of them began to dance, then another, and another, and another, until all the men were dancing and singing at the top of their lungs.

I stood to the side so as not to disturb them, photographing this incredible sight. Here I was in the middle of a synagogue courtyard in Košice, Czechoslovakia (today, Slovakia), watching Jewish men pray, sing, and dance to the new moon on a balmy late August night. Although I knew it was 1981, it was easy to pretend it was 1931. All of these men, any of whom could have been my great-uncle or grandfather, had survived the Holocaust. Most of them were wracked with the infirmities of old age but seemed to have found the elixir of youth. Their *taleysim* (Heb.: prayer shawls) fluttered in the breeze as they danced. This was only my third week on the road researching remnants of Jewish life, specifically *klezmer* music, in Central and Eastern Europe. Before this night, I had only come across some old sheet music and met and recorded a few Jews who sang Yiddish songs for me. But here I was, celebrating *Rosh Khoydesh Elul* (Heb.: the first day of the sixth month) in a town lying at the foot of the Carpathian Mountains, with *klezmer* music provided by two Rom musicians. It felt appropriate that it was Elul, the month in which Jews prepare themselves for *Rosheshone* (*Rosh Hashanah*), the Jewish New Year, a time of repentance for the past year's transgressions and a time of renewal. Despite the heavy memories they carried with them daily, these men were celebrating Jewish life. At this moment, my faith that that life would continue in Central and Eastern Europe was restored.

Rabbi Grossman later told me, "Yitskhak, Jewish music has been part of the Jewish Nation since the beginning, when Jubal played his flute and violin in the Garden of Eden. It is the language that is purest in the ears of God."[1] Indeed, since biblical times our forefathers and -mothers have chanted when they prayed, sung songs of sorrow and happiness, and played on instruments in praise of God. In Jewish lore, it is said that when these ancient instruments (e.g., lyre, psaltery, oud) were played, the sound they emitted was that of angels singing, and was heard throughout the heavens. At that moment in Kosice in 1981, while the musicians played and the congregants sang, this little courtyard felt like the Garden of Eden.

Klezmer music in Central and Eastern Europe was only one branch of the Jewish Tree of Life that had been severed by the Holocaust; but here was living proof that it had not disappeared from the cultural landscape. For the Jews of the Austro-Hungarian, Czarist, and Ottoman empires in the last half of the nineteenth century and the early twentieth, *klezmer* was an essential component for all life-cycle rituals, so important that it was said, "A wedding without *klezmer* is worse than a funeral without tears."

In the United States, the American musicians who rediscovered *klezmer* in the mid-to-late 1970s set the example for us to follow. But none of

---

[1] Interview with Shimshon Grossman, December 13, 1981.

them had gone outside the country to build their repertoires and educate themselves about *klezmer*'s relevance to Jewish culture. When I first became interested in *klezmer*, I wondered about this. Why hadn't anyone gone to Central and Eastern Europe to see what remained after the Holocaust? And what, if anything, had remained? The idea of recycling these already recycled (from old 78 LPs and published manuscripts) *klezmer* tunes wasn't interesting or challenging to me. As a musician and scholar, and also as a Jew separated from Eastern Europe by only two generations, I wanted to connect with the source. I bought a one-way ticket to Vienna and worked my way from Central Europe to Ukraine over the next ten months. I have since been back over fifty times. The research and experiences I've gathered on these sojourns through archival sources, oral histories, and interviews are collected in this book.

In the following pages, you will read how Ashkenazic instrumental Jewish music was born a twin to the Yiddish language at approximately the same time and following the same journey, from Western and Central Europe through the golden age of Prague (in the seventeenth and eighteenth centuries) to Eastern Europe. This music evolved into the sound we recognize today as *klezmer* (a term adopted by Jews in the eighteenth century). *Klezmer* was brought to America and transformed by the Jazz Age, but diminished to almost nothing by the early 1950s. Near the end of the book, through interviews with noted artists and celebrities, I examine the reasons and zeitgeist behind the resurgence of this popular musical form over the last thirty years. I've also included three appendixes: the first is the first fully translated and annotated bibliography of *klezmer* music in the *yizker bikher* (Yid.: memorial books), accounts of life before the Holocaust from first-person sources; the second is a glossary of *klezmer loshn,* the *klezmer*'s secret argot; and the third collects some *klezmer* melodies from field recordings.

This book is a window into the *klezmer* world that until the mid-1970s was virtually unknown to the non-Jewish public and only nostalgically remembered by a small number of American Jews. Perhaps this world was best described in a memorial book:

Every Jewish *shtetl,* even the one in Ostrolenka, had its own *klezmorim* and other entertainers who would play for all the Jewish weddings. They would play... at the wedding feast for the father and mother, grandfather and grandmother, guests and relatives from both sides, and especially for the bride and the groom—a bride and groom taking the first precarious steps in their unclear life.... The music stirred the public, and especially the young couple, who were moved to reflect on the tenor of the past and their long life ahead. The townspeople believed in an old saying: "As the *klezmorim* played, so it went in life."[2]

---

[2] Yitzhak Ivri, "Klezmorim," *Sefer Kehilat Ostrolenka,* ed. Y. Ivri (Tel Aviv: Assoc. of Former Residents of Ostrolenka, 1963), pp. 92–93.

The Book of Klezmer

Fun David Ha-Melekh biz Duvid der Klezmer

•

(FROM KING DAVID TO DUVID THE *KLEZMER*)

Jewish Instrumental Music from Biblical Times to 1800

Origins

What is the origin of *klezmer*[1] music? Who were these enigmatic Jewish folk characters? Why did they have such a strong influence on *shtetl* social life?

Today's *klezmorim* are often asked such questions, and all too often they base their answers only on what they know about the last three hundred years of Eastern European Jewish history—that is, on the most accessible written archival material. Before the eighteenth century (the Age of Enlightenment), very little was written about the Jewish folk musician, and only since the late seventeenth century was he known as a *klezmer*.

---

[1] *Klezmer.* The word comes from two Hebrew words: *kley-zmer: kley* means vessels or tools and *zmer* means melody. In Yiddish, the word *klezmer* literally means "vessels of the music." Before the seventeenth century in Central and Eastern Europe, *klezmer* meant a musical instrument. By the mid-seventeenth century the word had begun to be used to denote the Jewish musician. And by the eighteenth century it meant the Jewish folk instrumentalist. His music was primarily Ashkenazic folk dance music. Today the definition has broadened to include Ashkenazic dance, vocal, and melismatic instrumental music.

But to fully understand his origins and the music he played, we have to first look at the earliest Jewish historical writings: those of the *Toyre* (Torah).[2]

Music has been a vital part of Jewish culture since biblical times. The first Jewish musician appears in the bible as early as the fourth chapter of Genesis: Jubal, son of Lamech, played the harp and flute.[3] Later, the Levites are mentioned as the only musicians allowed to perform at the Temple in Jerusalem. Their music not only emotionally heightened the religious symbolism of the sacrificial services, it actually performed miracles. The ancient Jews, like their neighbors, believed that music held magical powers: it could inspire ecstasy, foretell the future, and treat mental illness. "And it came to pass, when the evil spirit from God was upon Saul, that David took the harp, and played with his hand; so Saul found relief, and it was well with him, and the evil spirit departed from him."[4]

While the Levites were specifically trained to perform only sacred music in the Temple, other Jews played secular music. The most common instruments for both were the *kinor,* a lyre-type instrument which some musicologists believe is related to the Greek kithara, with ten vertical strings plucked with a plectron; the *nevel,* a psaltery-like instrument with ten to twelve vertical strings plucked with the fingers; the *khalil,* an oboe-like double-reed instrument; the *uggav,* a flute-like single-reed instrument; the *khatsotserah,* a trumpet-like instrument with a long cylindrical body ending in an expansive bell; the *shoyfer* (shofar, the only Biblical instrument still used in the synagogue), a ram's horn; various percussive instruments, including frame drums, cymbals, bells, and timbrels; and the *magrephah,* a pneumatic pipeorgan-like instrument. Interestingly enough, many generations of Jews, referring to the *magrephah,* claimed that the pipe organ had been invented by their ancient ancestors. But when organ music became indispensable to the church in Europe in the twelfth century, rabbinical authorities adamantly forbade its use in the synagogue.

---

[2] *Toyre* (Heb.): the Hebrew bible of the Jewish people. Sometimes referred to as *The Five Books of Moses.*

[3] Genesis 4:21.

[4] I Samuel 16:23.

After the destruction of the Second Temple in 70 C.E., the Jews were dispersed throughout the world, and the Levites' sacred Temple services were no longer needed. The rabbis then banned all instrumental music with the explanation that their congregants should be in mourning for Zion. This self-imposed mourning was to be lifted only once the messiah came and rebuilt the Temple. The rabbis associated any kind of secular music with the decadence of Greek culture. "It became synonomous with obscenity and was chiefly used for carnal purposes at frivolous occasions. No wonder then that Judaism opposed 'profane' music."[5] Unfortunately, these extreme attitudes persisted through the seventeenth century, and helped create a negative stance towards the Jewish folk instrumentalist among the community.

The earliest musical influence on Jewish instrumentalists was the melismatic sound of synagogue chants. Some of these melismas and melodies had been written, but most were handed down orally to be interpreted personally by each musician. The few music manuscripts available were jealously guarded by the *khazn* (Heb.: cantor),[6] because, besides his musical knowledge and vocal abilities, his worth depended on the demand among his congregants for his compositions for specific prayers. For several centuries the *nusekh*[7] and the *trop*[8] were the only constant musical elements among the myriad synagogue chants in Western and Central Europe. The *trops* used in the *Toyre* were composed between the sixth and ninth centuries B.C.E., and recomposed by Ezra and Nehemiah and the *Sanhedrin*.[9]

---

[5] Abraham Zvi Idelsohn, *Jewish Music: Its Historical Development* (New York: Henry Holt, 1929), p. 93.

[6] The *khazn* became a permanent synagogue position in the Middle Ages. The earliest known notation of the *Toyre* cantillation is from Johannes Rochlein's manuscript (Hagenau, 1518), which shows that the *khazonim* used four-part harmony.

[7] *Nusekh* (Heb.): musical version. There were several accepted *nusekhs* for the singing of the *Toyre*.

[8] *Trop* (Heb.): musical accent. *Trop* markings indicate how to cantillate the *Toyre*.

[9] *Sanhedrin:* the supreme Jewish political, religious, and judicial body in ancient Israel during the Roman period until c. 425.

The other great influence on the *khazn*'s repertoire was the relationship between the Jews and their gentile neighbors in Western and
Central Europe. As A. Z. Idelsohn, the father of Jewish musicology,[10]
wrote,

> The close relations between Jews and Gentiles in early centuries and
> especially during the reign of Charlemagne and his son Louis the Pious
> brought about a cultural reciprocity in which at first the Jews were
> more frequently those to exert the influence than those to be influ-
> enced. We learn this fact from the campaign which Bishop Agobard
> of Lyon in his letters to Louis the Pious started in 825 against the Jew-
> ish influence upon the Christians, which in his opinion endangered
> the Christian faith. He complains that... Christians attend Jewish
> services and prefer the blessings and prayers of the Jewish rabbis; that
> Christians attend Jewish meals on Sabbaths and that Christians rest
> on Sabbath.... In view of this fact, Agobard demanded that a prohi-
> bition should be issued to the effect that no Christian man or woman
> should attend Jewish services, nor observe the Sabbath, nor participate
> in Jewish festal meals, and that Christian people should stay away from
> the Jews.[11]

By the end of the Middle Ages, Christian liturgical music had moved
from plainsong to rich polyphonic melody, while secular music and song
became more accessible to the masses. And although Jews were forced to
live in ghettos, these changes influenced them too. Among the Christians,
secular music and song were represented by wandering troubadours, min-

---

[10] Abraham Zvi Idelsohn (1882–1938) was born in Russia and settled in Jerusalem in 1906,
where he was a cantor and music teacher. In 1922 he started teaching Jewish musicology
at Hebrew Union College in Cincinnati. He wrote extensively on ancient Jewish prayer
and biblical music; his book *Jewish Music: Its Historical Development* (op. cit.) became the
cornerstone of Jewish musicology. His other major book was the ten-volume *Thesaurus of
Hebrew Oriental Melodies and Jewish Music.*
[11] Idelsohn, op. cit., p. 130.

strels, *minnesingers,*[12] *spielleute,*[13] and *jongleurs,*[14] who entertained both at the courts of the aristocracy and in market squares across Europe. But two of the most famous Provençal troubadours of the thirteenth century were Jews: Bonfils de Narbonne and Charlot le Juif. Among the German Jews, the *minnesinger* Süsskind von Trimberg (born around 1220 in Trimberg, near Würzberg) was the best known, often satirizing in song the gentiles' anti-Semitism. Traveling from town to town and castle to castle, these wandering minstrels endured hardships and abasements. One gets a sense of Süsskind's pain from a song he wrote:

> I want to grow a beard,
> Long must it be, its hair quite gray.
> And then I'll go through life the way
> The Jews have always gone:
> Wrapped in a cape, billowy and long;
> Deep under the hat hiding my face;
> Meek and with a humble song;
> Bare of God's grace.[15]

The lyrics of these itinerant entertainers were written in the vernacular, and their themes were taken from the bible and *medresh* (midrash).[16]

The early Jewish minstrel, called *shpilman* (Yid: gleeman), helped preserve not only Jewish folksongs but German ones as well. In the early Middle Ages, the church had taught that individual musical notes and the ways they formed melodies held certain spiritual powers. Thus the knowledge

---

[12] *Minnesinger:* an itinerant German lyric poet and singer of the twelfth to the fourteenth centuries.

[13] *Spielleute* (Ger.): playing person. Itinerant German musician.

[14] *Jongleur:* itinerant French musician, eleventh to thirteenth centuries. *Jongleurs* traveled throughout France and Norman England singing lyric songs and reciting epic stories, often accompanying themselves with the lute or cittern.

[15] Paul Nettl, *Forgotten Musicians* (New York: Philosophical Library, 1957), p. 30.

[16] *Medresh* (Heb.): homilies consisting of biblical exegesis and rabbinic literature.

of writing music was kept secret from secular musicians. But around 1450 appeared perhaps the first German songbook with vocal polyphony, and its author is believed to be the Jewish minstrel Wölffle von Locham.[17]

These early Jewish minstrels acted as go-betweens, disseminating popular gentile melodies (even dance melodies) that the local *khazonim* then incorporated into the Sabbath services. They also took the musical fashions of the ghetto to the outside world. For most Jews during the thirteenth and fourteenth centuries, life in these ghettos was difficult and depressing. Jews were governed by strict regulations, especially when they worked (often in hostile conditions) outside the ghetto walls. After a hard week, they sought respite in the synagogue service and, to the great dismay of the rabbis, often demanded that the *khazn* sing his prayers to the gentile tunes they had heard outside the ghetto walls. Quarrels and sometimes fistfights would break out among the congregants—and even with the rabbi—during services if the *khazn* was not satisfactory. Fearful that the singing and playing of gentile music was contaminating not only the synagogue service but the ethics and morals of Jewish life, the rabbis in Western and Central Europe one by one began to ban the playing of any kind of music and the singing of Christian melodies in the synagogue. They further forbade the male congregants to listen to female singing. Some *khazonim* followed these strict rules; others were persuaded not to by their congregants; still others were permanently banished from the community and forced to wander from city to city leading prayers and concertizing wherever they could.

Here we see just how early in our history—long before the advent of the itinerant *klezmer*—the rabbis made it hard for the Jewish musician to ply his trade among his brethren without social castigation. Even Idelsohn, centuries later, held a low opinion of itenerant musicians, writing: "This abnormal condition developed the type of the wandering *khazn* with all the bad habits of the wanderer. These, in addition to the artistic strain, gave the *khazn* a minstrel-like character, resembling that of the wandering

---

[17] Paul Nettl, *Alte Jüdische Spielleute und Musiker* (Prague: Dr. J. Flesch, 1923), p. 33.

Italian musicians of that time who overran Central Europe."[18] From the Middle Ages on, the itinerant Jewish musician would constantly struggle for legitimacy and acceptance.

Despite strict rabbinical edicts against the playing of instrumental music for any happy occasion (religious or secular), the rabbis (often reluctantly) allowed it at weddings, which were generally celebrated by the entire Jewish community.[19] The Maharil of Mainz (Jacob ben Moses Möllin, ?1360–1427) was a reknowned *khazn* and rabbi who performed at many Jewish weddings, and whose rabbinical authority at this time carried the strongest weight. He believed that the *mitsve* (Heb.: good deed) of making the wedding couple happy with song and music was a biblical command that overruled even the most zealous rabbis. Once in one of the smaller German principalities the wife of the ruling prince died; a year of mourning was declared and music was forbidden. So the Maharil took the wedding party to another city outside the district, where the local Jewish musicians were allowed to play. He felt so strongly about the importance of this *mitsve* that he would hire gentile musicians to play on the Sabbath for the bride and groom (Jewish musicians were not allowed to play on the Sabbath, not even for a Jewish wedding). And eventually, because Jewish instrumental folk music was such an emotional necessity in the crowded, unsanitary, dank Jewish quarters, it became an essential ingredient in most celebrations for the Jews of Central and Eastern Europe.

---

[18] Idelsohn, op. cit., p. 179.

[19] The Jewish communities in the Middle Ages (c. 500–1450) varied in size but were not so large to exclude anyone from a Jewish wedding celebration, whether inside or outside a synagogue. For example, in the thirteenth century there were fifty-four Jewish homes in Mainz. In the mid-fifteenth century the largest Jewish community was in Frankfurt and comprised approximately nine hundred Jews, roughly 10 percent of the total population. In 1546, 976 Jews lived in Prague, and by the end of the sixteenth century there were some twelve hundred. "The Jewish communities were rather small then. This is seen by the size of the old synagogues which remain in Prague and Worms." M. Gidman, *Yidishe Kultur-Geshikhte in Mitlalter: Yidn in Daytshland dos XIV un XV Yahrhundert* (Berlin: Klal Verlag, 1922), p. 89.

Jewish Music in Italy

In Italy, meanwhile, the nobility's more liberal treatment of the Jews encouraged development of the arts, especially music. And, unlike the rest of Europe, there the rabbinate was not as exacting in the renunciation of music in the community. Exiles from the Iberian peninsula, the Middle East, and Central Europe made Italian Jewish communities the most cosmopolitan in all of Europe. Several Jewish artists were known throughout Italy, including Wilhemo Ebreo Pisarraisa, who hailed from Pisa and was known by his Hebrew name, Binyomin. A dance teacher who performed at many courts in Milan, Binyomin invented a number of new dances and wrote a book on Italian dance.[20] And from 1555 to 1577 a Jewish family of musicians known as Efram performed in the court of prince Giosaldo Divanusa in Naples, later working with Monteverdi at the court of the Duke of Mantua.[21] The majority of Jewish musicians in Italy, however, were not able to work at the courts and therefore traveled from town to town, playing for both Jews and gentiles.

At the Casale Monferrato, the most famous cantorial school in Italy at the end of the sixteenth century, synagogue music proliferated under the leadership of Salomone Rossi (ca. 1565–ca. 1628). Rossi came from an old and well-respected Jewish family and benefited from the encouragement of the local rabbis and the patronage of Duke Vincenzo I of the Gonzaga family, who ruled in Mantua. Rossi's orchestra at the Duke's court included several Jewish members; he was also the director of the violin academy, where he taught a generation of instrumentalists whose accomplishments made them world famous. As a conductor, violinist, composer, and teacher, Rossi's status was such that in 1606 he was given a rare exemption from having to wear the degrading yellow badge on his clothing denoting his Jewish faith. Besides his court music, Rossi wrote many instrumental and choral pieces

---

[20] Joachim Stutschevsky, *Ha-Klezmorim: Toldotehem, Orakh-Hayehem, v'Yezirotehem* (Jerusalem: Bialik Institute, 1959), p. 26.

[21] Ibid., p. 27.

for the synagogue, including his famous *Ha-Shirim Asher L'Shlomo* (The Songs of Solomon, 1622). This music was generally conservative in style and melodically similar to the madrigal church music of the time. Rossi and his fellow Jewish composers helped to make Jewish music more acceptable to the Jewish establishment; but they also may have helped usher in a process of assimilation that sacred Jewish music underwent in Europe, a process that ended only in the nineteenth century. Rossi's sister also achieved national fame as a singer, garnering the nickname "Madame Europa"; Monteverdi admired her so much that he had her sing in the first performance of his last opera, *Arianna.*

When Mantua fell to Kaiser Ferdinand II's Austrian army in 1630, many of the Jews (including the musicians) sought refuge in Venice. One of them was Leone Modena, a faithful supporter of Rossi's. A rabbi, *khazn,* and choral conductor, Modena helped establish the first music academy in the Venice ghetto in 1629; it gave weekly concerts and attracted Jewish and gentile visitors. Many of its musicians also performed in the Sephardic synagogue's orchestra, which, stretching the goodwill of the rabbis even further, used an organ on *Simkhes Toyre* (Simchat Torah).[22] "This created such a sensation that Christians and Jews came in multitudes to hear this extraordinary performance. There was such a tumult at the doors that police were called upon to prevent a turmoil. To avoid further disorders, the organ was removed... and the experiment was never again repeated, though the orchestra remained."[23]

Jewish instrumental music flourished during the Italian Renaissance, with even women participating: playing lute or clavichord, they taught the synagogue hymns to their sisters. Jewish musicians, considered to be the best teachers, taught the children of many aristocratic families. But by the mid-seventeenth century, the church's permissiveness ended. Gentile musicians were angry about having to compete with Jewish musicians for church

---

[22] *Simkhes Toyre* (Heb.): rejoicing of the *Toyre.* See discussion of holidays below.
[23] Alfred Sendrey, *The Music of the Jews in the Diaspora Up to 1800* (Cranbury, New Jersey: Thomas Yoseloff, 1970), p. 333.

and secular functions; the priests were worried about the influence their music would have on their parishioners, and how they interpreted the Catholic church's music. Consequently, the church levied heavy taxes upon Jewish musicians and severely restricted who could play, when, where, and for how many hours.

The high level of musical training would serve these musicians well in the seventeenth and eighteenth centuries, as they began to leave Italy and travel to Jewish communities in Central Europe in search of employment. From the archives in Breslau (Wrocław, Poland), we know of some Italian Jewish musicians that came to Silesia as early as 1564. Because of their accomplishments and ability to read music, their Polish Jewish counterparts did not welcome them. But the lutenists Giovan Maria and Jacopo Sansecondo were so well liked by the Christian people of Brieg that they petitioned Pope Leo X to grant them permission to stay there. Eventually they were given a large parcel of land and the title of *graf* (Yid.: count).

Jewish Music in Germany

Though most German Jewish instrumentalists did not reach the level of musical proficiency of their Italian counterparts, the German synagogue music of the fourteenth through sixteenth centuries equaled that of Italy. German historian Johannes Rochlein wrote that four-part harmony was sung in the synagogue in Hagenau in 1518 and that the singers were sophisticated enough to sing both parlando and rubato.[24]

Because German Jews were unable to openly express themselves in religious life, Jewish dance became very popular. Unlike the calm and dignified dance of the Jews of Italy, the Jews of Germany[25] danced by hopping in circles, furiously swinging their arms, and sometimes jumping over chairs

---

[24] Stutschevsky, op. cit., pp. 18–19.
[25] When I refer to Germany during the Middle Ages, I am referring to some three hundred principalities that constituted the German lands until their unification in 1848.

or people. The rabbis prohibited mixed dancing, fearful it would lead to licentious behavior, so men danced only with men and women only with women. The Christians derided these unbridled displays of *Judentantz* [26] and disapproved of the mockery these Jewish dances seemed to make of their own dances. Very few of these early Jewish dance melodies have survived, since the majority of this music was never written down: most Jewish musicians were musically illiterate. Those who had some musical education wrote their melodies down in tablature form (the common way to notate music prior to the eighteenth century). One of the oldest preserved Jewish dances can be found in Heckel's *Lautenbuch* (1562);[27] it was a simple dance, called *Judentantz,* written for lute accompanied by either a drone bass or *dudlezack.*[28] Another example is in Hans Newsidler's book *Ein neu kunstlich Lautenbuch* (A New Artistic Lute Book; 1544; Newsidler was a well-known lutenist of the period).[29] Paul Nettl described it as follows:

> This piece, entitled *Der Juden Tanz,* has a naive humorous inscription. It says you have to play it quickly and loudly otherwise it does not sound good. But even if you play it as well as you can it will never sound pleasant. The unpleasant tones are attributed to the accompaniment of the *dudlezack* or sometimes the *Judenleier,* a very old, primitive instrument which characteristically played an important role in Jewish music. The poor playing of the Jewish musicians I would say is a kind of *katzenmusik.*[30]

The remarkable thing about this description is not the derogatory characterization of early German Jewish instrumental folk music as simple "cat music," but which instruments were used to play it. Of the three Nettl

---

[26] *Judentantz* (Ger.): Jewish dance; the word was used by Medieval Christians to derogate Jewish folk dances.

[27] Nettl, *Alte Jüdische Spielleute,* p. 41.

[28] See discussion below.

[29] Sendrey, op. cit., p. 325.

[30] *Katzenmusik* (Ger.): cat music. The quote is from Nettl, *Alte Jüdische Spielleute,* pp. 41–42.

mentioned, only the bass is still used among *klezmorim*. Jewish folk musicians from the Middle Ages through the seventeenth century in Germany, Bohemia, Moravia, and Silesia played a variety of instruments, including the cittern, lute, zither, shawm, harp, flageolet, harpsichord, *dudlezack*, *Judenleier, postiv, Judenharfe, zink,* and *hackbrett.* A word about each of these instruments is in order.

1 The *dudlezack* (Ger.: tootle sack) was a sheepskin or goatskin bag that had a chanter (melody pipe) which one blew into; it was similar in size to the French bagpipe (*musettet*) that was a favorite in aristocratic circles.

2 The *Judenleier,* or Jewish hurdy-gurdy, was, by the sixteenth century, a lowly instrument associated with blind beggars, making it an option for the poorer Jewish musicians.

3 The *positiv,* a fixed organ also called *postive* in English, stood on the floor or a table; the keys were close together. There was also the *portative,* whose straps the musician slung over the shoulder: it was used in processions and chamber music and was popular through the nineteenth century. Like the accordion, it was blown with one hand and played with the other.

4 The *Judenharfe* (Jew's harp or *guimbard*), was played quite extensively in the Middle Ages, usually accompanying singers. The public often called the itinerant Jewish Polish musicians of the eighteenth century who played it *kharpe-shpilers* (shameful players) because they played such a lowly, unpleasant sounding instrument; it was a play on words, as *kharpe* (instead of *harfe*) meant *shameful* in Hebrew. It was rarely played in a *klezmer* ensemble.

5 The *zink* (Ger.: tusk) was a kind of cornet, a slender curved instrument made from a goat's horn, usually with six bored holes, wrapped in black leather, with a trumpet mouthpiece. It was not an easy instrument to master because the player's lips had to do much more to focus the pitch and give equality to the notes than with other wind and brass instruments. But with experience the player could produce a beautiful sound without equivalent today, mixing the qualities of the trumpet with the

sweetness and agility of the oboe. It was popular from 1500 to 1650, after which the finest *zinkenisten* (cornetists) were attracted to the rapidly developing techniques of the violin.

6 Lastly, the *hackbrett* (Ger.: cutting board), sometimes called *holzhar-monika* in German (or *hakbreydl* in Yiddish), was similar to the hammer dulcimer, or *tsimbl* (Yid.: cymbal), that *klezmorim* in Central and Eastern Europe in the eighteenth century used widely. Sixteenth-century Italian Jews called it *dulce melos* (sweet melody). The most famous *hack-brett* player was the Polish *klezmer* Mikhl Joseph Guzikov (1806–1837); he played a Belorussian folk instrument called the *shtroyfidl* (Yid.: straw fiddle) similar to the *hackbrett,* which he modified by increasing its range to two-and-a-half octaves so that it was closer to today's xylophone. This portable instrument consisted of a set of solid wooden bars tuned diatonically and laid horizontally across a bed of cylindrically wound straw, which created the sound cavity. It was played by striking the bars with small wooden sticks.

These instruments are rarely if ever used in *klezmer* performances any more. Today's instruments—like the violin, clarinet, and accordion—date from later: the violin appeared in the second half of the sixteenth century in Italy but was not in vogue until early in the seventeenth century, and did not reach the Jewish ghettos in any significant numbers in Germany and Bohemia until late in the seventeenth century; the clarinet was invented in 1690 and was not used regularly by the *klezmorim* until the mid-nineteenth century; and the accordion was invented as late as 1852. The instruments played by early Jewish itinerant musicians and, later, by the *klezmorim,* fell out of favor because they could not compete tonally (like the viola da gamba, displaced by the violin), because they were difficult to play (like the shawm and *zink*), because they produced discordant tones (like the *dudle-zack* and *Judenleier*), or because when they were played in an ensemble or on festive occasions they were too soft to be heard (like the lute, flageolet, and *hackbrett*). Some instruments (like the kettledrums) were simply too heavy to carry. There are other reasons that *klezmer* bands no longer play the repertoire of the Central European Jewish itinerant musicians of the Middle Ages: very few music manuscripts from the period survive; and the public for the last twenty-five years has been familiarized with a sound more reminiscent of the late nineteenth and early twentieth centuries. A few bands, however, have preserved the East European *klezmer* repertoire and playing style of the nineteenth century in as authentic a presentation as possible, including Budowitz, the Joel Rubin Jewish Music Ensemble, and Khevrisa.[31]

Jewish dance was on full display on four primary occasions. *Simkhes Toyre* is the last day of the festival of *Sukes* (Succoth), when the annual reading of the *Toyre* is completed and recommenced; its celebration is replete with singing, dancing (while holding a *Toyre* scroll), and drinking. In the Middle Ages Jewish musicians would sometimes play for those dancing in the synagogue, even though the rabbis were against this practice. *Purim*[32] originated in ancient Persia and its story is written in the Book of Esther, which is recited in synagogues throughout the world on the evening and morning of the festival. It celebrates the deliverance of the Jews from Haman, who plotted to kill them, by Queen Esther and her uncle Mordkhay (Mordecai). During the Middle Ages the festival acquired some of the customs (dancing, playing music, and drinking) that the gentiles used to celebrate carnival in March. Jewish musicians were hired to perform at many dances and to accompany local performances of the *Purim Shpil. Khanike* (Chanukah)[33]

---

[31] Budowitz was led by expatriot Joshua Horowitz, who lived in Graz, Austria; he plays *tsimbl* (see chapter 2) and has written extensively about its use in nineteenth-century East European *klezmer* music. The Joel Rubin Jewish Music Ensemble is led by the eponymous expatriot clarinetist, who lives in Berlin and has done extensive research on *klezmer* music, particularly on the *klezmer* tradition in Israel and the research of Soviet ethnomusicologist Moshe Beregovski. Khevrisa, an ensemble of violins and *tsimbl,* is led by *tsimbler* and ethnomusicologist Walter Zev Feldman, who has researched the repertoire and style of Ottoman Turkish and *klezmer* music; Feldman and Andy Statman (mandolin, clarinet) helped initiate the *klezmer* revival in the mid-1970s, and Khevrisa has reintroduced a style that was popularized by the violin-and-*tsimbl* ensembles of the mid-nineteenth to early twentieth centuries in Galicia, Belarus, Moldavia, Bessarabia, and southern Ukraine.

[32] *Purim* (Heb.): lots.

[33] *Khanike* (Heb.): dedication.

lasts eight days and commemorates the victory of Judas Maccabee and his followers, who recaptured Jerusalem after defeating the Assyrian-Greeks. Like *Purim, Khanike* is considered a festival, as opposed to a holiday, which meant it was not governed by the Talmudic rules that prohibited most instrumental music on the holidays established by the *Toyre—Peysekh, Shvues,* and *Sukes* (Passover, Shavuot, and Succoth).

But the most important occasion for dancing was the wedding feast. Sometimes the weddings would last for a week, even including a Sabbath, or would immediately follow a Jewish holiday. It was common among German Jewish musicians to mix serious and light music at a wedding ceremony held outside of a synagogue. Often *Kol Nidre*[34] was played for the groom while he solemnly walked to the wedding canopy. Then the musicians played a light piece for the bride as she approached the groom, the richest wives in town dancing around her. This mix of the profane and frivolous displeased the rabbis and elders of the community, because the synagogues were becoming more entertainment centers than houses of worship. Forced out by the rabbis' displeasure (and because the synagogues and private home were becoming too small), Jews built their own dance halls, known as *Tanzhäuser* in German. These halls, where people also played cards and watched theatrical performances, became a fixture in many of the Jewish ghettos of Germany, France, Holland, and Switzerland. One of the earliest known Jewish dance halls was in Augsburg, Germany (1190).[35] In Frankfurt am Main in 1390 a guild of Jewish musicians were hired to play weekly dances at both Jewish and gentile dance halls.[36] On Jewish holidays gentile musicians were hired to perform at the dance halls, which greatly angered the rabbis. As the popularity of the halls grew, the rabbis

---

[34] *Kol Nidre* (Aramaic): all vows. This prayer, the declaration of annulment of vows to God made unwittingly or rashly by the worshipper, is one of the most reverent in the synagogue liturgy; it begins *Yom Kiper,* the day of atonement and most solemn holiday and fast day in the Jewish calendar. The Ashkenazic melody to *Kol Nidre* is so famous that when it is sung or played it automatically creates an atmosphere of seriousness and awe.

[35] Stutschevsky, op. cit., p. 35.

[36] Nettl, *Alte Jüdische Spielleute,* p. 41.

were forced to relax their ineffective prohibitions against women singing in public, playing instrumental music, and dancing with men. Gradually the *Juden Tanzhäuser* attracted Jewish and gentile itinerant musicians from out of town, who would introduce new tunes for the dances; and as the music became more important than the dancing, these halls began to be also called *Juden Spielhäuser* (Ger.: Jewish playhouses).[37] Their wide repertoire of melodies inspired new dances, including:

1. May Day Dance, in pairs, like a polonaise. Taken from the Germans who danced around the maypole. This custom still exits in the Rhineland district.
2. Marching Dance, a dance similar to court dances.
3. Springing Dance, a robust peasant dance.
4. Judentanz, a parody of the dance of the Jews.
5. Dance of the First Man (or in Hebrew sometimes called *Adam ha-Rishon*), a pantomime of biblical content imitating primitive man.
6. Doctor Foist (Faust) Dance, of German origin.
7. Fish Dance, of which the origin and form are not known.
8. Death Dance, where the dancer pantomimed various classes of society: the prince, cardinal, archbishop, rabbi, and others each fighting off the figure of death and its embrace. The Christians performed this dance in parades while the Jews used it at weddings and other family festivals. In German-Jewish annals we find it mentioned in the famous memoirs of Glückel of Hameln,[38] where she says that at a wedding of a relative "they concluded their performance with a truly splendid Dance of Death."[39]

---

[37] Some were called *Tanz-un-Spielhaus* (Ger.: dance and playhouse).

[38] Glückel of Hameln (1645–1724) was born in Hamburg; her Yiddish memoirs are an important source for German Jewish history (especially about women), culture, and Yiddish linguistics.

[39] Sendrey, op. cit., pp. 327–28.

Sometimes the Jewish musician had no choice but to follow the orders of the local rabbis, because they were backed by the gentile police. In Strassbourg in 1547 the Jews were forbidden to have a dance hall, and for "those Jews who received permission to marry their children, the wedding music had to be provided by Christians." In Hagenau the prefect ordered that no Jew could have a wedding on a Friday or Saturday. Laws such as these, dating from 1613, 1658, 1700, and 1706, were also enforced by the Jewish councils in Hagenau, who wrote "when such Jewish weddings are made there will be no public dancing so that they should not dance together with the Christians."[40]

Most Jewish weddings, however, were on Fridays before sundown. After synagogue services the following day, the big wedding feast took place. Since Jews were forbidden to play music on the Sabbath, they hired non-Jewish musicians; the Jewish musicians would play during the rest of the week. Some sources mention that even Jewish women sometimes formed their own bands and would travel to weddings to "present their artistic abilities and contribute to the festivities."[41] But traveling the roads between towns in those times was dangerous for all travelers, and for none more than itinerant Jewish musicians, who faced the twin perils of anti-Jewish violence and robbery, with the added threat of rape for the occasional women among them. Once a band of Jewish women had traveled to a town to entertain at a Jewish wedding, but the non-Jewish authorities would not let them return to their hometown unless they converted to Christianity. Some of the women tried to escape and were killed. A few others agreed to be converted but returned to Jewish practices when they returned to their homes. The Christian authorities in this town found out, went after them, and murdered them. This is an extreme example, of course; the number of itinerant Jewish women musicians was quite small and became even smaller by the seventeenth century.

---

[40] Albert von Wolf, *Mitteilungen zur Jüdische Volkskunde* (Leipzig, 1908–09), vol. 27, pp. 90–91.

[41] Ibid., p. 92.

The Klezmer*'s Antecedents: The* Lets *and the* Marshalik

About one hundred years before the creation of the Jewish dance halls, the itinerant Jewish *shpilman* (like his German prototype the *spielleute*) was generally only a musician. But as this wanderer, like the Christian merry-andrew, began to incorporate other light and serious forms of entertainment into his act, German Jews began to refer to him as a *lets* (Heb.: clown, jester, buffoon), *possenreiser* (Ger.: jester, buffoon), and sometimes even *nar* (Yid.: fool, clown).[42] In addition to playing music, the *letsim* (pl.) would create merriment through magic tricks; tumbling; clowning; comical dancing; singing humorous, satirical, and epic songs;[43] telling doggerel jokes and riddles; giving short dramatic soliloquies; and even trick horseback riding. The *Toyre,* Talmud,[44] and daily synagogue prayers provided much of the material the *lets* drew from. Here is an example of a humorous *Khanike* song the *letsim* would sing:

> *Moaus zur Jeschuosi,*
> *ich hab' kein Geld was tu' ich hie?*
> *Geh ein Stuckle weiter,*
> *begegnet mir ein Reiter,*
> *der Reiter will mich schlagen usw.*[45]

---

[42] The earliest written references to the *letsim* are found in the writings of Talmudist Rabbi Elijah ben Isaac Lattes of Carcassonne, France, in the thirteenth century. See Ezekiel Lifschutz, "Merrymakers at a Jewish Wedding," in *YIVO Annual Jewish Social Science,* Vol. VII, 1952, p. 44.

[43] Just like the *minnesingers* and *jongleurs,* the *letsim* performed popular epic songs of the day. They were written in Yiddish in the typical *ottavarima* (a stanza of eight lines with the rhyme scheme *ababababcc*) style.

[44] *Talmud* (Heb.): study or learning. The Talmud, which was completed circa 500 C.E., contains the oral commentaries, interpretations, history, and teachings of the rabbis on Jewish law and customs. One Talmud was compiled in Jerusalem and the other in Babylonia.

[45] Wolf, op. cit., p. 22.

> How strong is the rock of my salvation;
> I have no money—what shall I do?
> I will continue a little farther,
> Where I will encounter a rider,
> The rider will hit me.

These itinerant jesters became so popular at Jewish weddings they became fixtures despite the great disapproval of the rabbis and *khazonim*. "The main objective at a wedding was to bring joy, and it was not always clean. Furthermore, the merrymaker's actions often led to troubles for the community's religious elders. However, the merrymaker's great popularity assured them their place for generations."[46] The *lets*'s singing at a wedding often duplicated the *khazn*'s duties. And because the *lets* was not a member of the clergy (unlike the *khazn,* who led the synagogue prayers), he was allowed to sing even ribald songs (often his own compositions). Sometimes the *khazn* was able to convince the rabbis to bar the *lets* from entertaining at a local wedding; such requests were usually economically driven. Unsurprisingly, a strong rivalry between *lets* and *khazn* arose.

Over time the profession of *lets* evolved into that of *marshalik* (Yid.: marshal), a wedding jester or master of ceremonies, and *batkhn* (Yid: wedding bard; originally from the Aramaic *bada,* to make merry). To complicate matters, these terms were sometimes interchangeable with *lets.* From the written evidence, it appears that these various occupations gradually melded into that of the *klezmer* (a term popular from the eighteenth century through today). "The name *lets* meant not only a merrymaker, a comic, a satirist, or a *jongleur* who had the task of entertaining the public at a wedding (or other happy occasion). Often this word meant simply that he was a *muzikant*."[47] In 1580 and in 1590, in two different *Purim* plays, the *letsim* are referred to as the *muzikantn* (pl.) rather than merrymakers.

---

[46] I. Lifschitz, "Batkhonim und Letsim bay Yidn," in *Arkhiv far der Geshikhte fun Yidishn Teater un Drama,* ed. by Dr. Jacob Shatsky (Vilna–New York, 1930), Vol. I, pp. 33–34.
[47] *Musikant* (Yid.): musician. By the nineteenth century in Eastern Europe the Jewish musician was either referred to as a *musikant* or a *klezmer.* See Lipshitz, op. cit., p. 40.

There is a great deal of confusion about when the term *klezmer* began to be used to denote the Jewish musician rather than the instrument being played. The following example from the Maharil of Mainz's book of marriage law uses the word *klezmer* to denote musical instruments and *lets* to denote the musician: "Then the Rabbi led the groom before him. Afterwards all the people followed by the light of the torches with *klezmer* to the synagogue courtyard. Then he returned to bring the bride with her attendants."[48] According to Jewish historian Isaac Rivkind,[49] even the Polish and Lithuanian Jews who emigrated to Holland in 1542 referred to those playing Jewish music as *letsim*.[50] And in 1562, Rabbi Yosef Yosefa wrote, in reference to the laws of *Tishebov* (Tisha b'Av),[51] "It is forbidden for the children of the wealthy to study or play *klezmer*,"[52] the word again clearly denoting musical instruments.

But by the eighteenth century, *klezmer* could also mean *musician*. In the first Yiddish songbook, Rabbi Elkhanan Kirchen's *Simkhat HaNefesh* (The Happiness of the Soul; Fürth, 1707), Kirchen refers to the Jewish musician as a *klezmer*: "Here is the music I've written. It is for dancing with the *klezmorim*.... Even if you can't read music, there are musicians who can, and they will be able to read it for you."[53] A few years earlier in Hesse, Rabbi Khaiyim Yair wrote a statute (1690) that limited the entertainers one could have at a wedding: "The *letsim* are a necessary part of the wedding, as are the servers, but the luxury of having *klezmorim* is forbidden."[54]

---

[48] Isaac Rivkind, *Klezmorim: Perek b'Toldot ha'Amanot ha'Amamit* (New York: Futuro Press, 1960), p. 12.

[49] Isaac Rivkind (1895–1968) was born in Lodz (Łodz), Poland and became the head of the Hebrew department at the Jewish Theological Seminary in New York. He wrote on many Jewish subjects, including a significant pamphlet on the *klezmorim*.

[50] Rivkind, op. cit., p. 14.

[51] *Tishebov* (Heb.): the ninth day of *Av*. After *Yom Kiper*, this is the second most solemn day in the Jewish calendar, a day of fasting and mourning commemorating the destruction of the first and second Temples in Jerusalem.

[52] Rivkind, op. cit., p. 12.

[53] Ibid., p. 15.

[54] Lifshitz, op. cit., p. 40.

From these and other sources it seems that the term *lets* was used fairly exclusively to denote the Jewish musician in Central and Eastern Europe as late as the sixteenth century. By the seventeenth century there are written sources that used the term *klezmer* instead of *lets*. But it was not until the nineteenth century that the word *klezmer* or *musikant* was used fairly exclusively to represent the Jewish folk musician, while the word *lets* now meant only the wedding jester.[55]

Whether called a *lets, muzikant, shpilman,* or *klezmer,* the Jewish musician still inspired animosity in the rabbis. For example, the Christian historian Johann Jacob Schudt[56] wrote that in Frankfurt in 1716, the rabbis issued a statute that read, in part: "There could be no more than four *letsim* playing at a wedding and they could not play past midnight. If they played past midnight then they were banned from playing in that city for a year."[57] Schudt goes on to explain that the rabbis would not call the musician a *shpilman* or *muzikant* because in the time of the first and second Temples musicians played serious music for the Levites. Now when the *letsim* played they did a "bad imitation" of the former Temple musicians. "They were considered no better than 'beer fiddlers,' common tavern musicians, who deserved the name *letsim.*"[58]

A great deal of what we know about German and Bohemian Jewish ghetto life in the late sixteenth and early seventeenth centuries is from Schudt's writings. But at the same time, one must be careful when reading

---

[55] Rivkind, op. cit., p. 13. In a book called *Letsonim,* written by Reb Moshe Shimshon in the eighteenth century, the author referred to those musicians who entertained the bride and groom as *bale zemer* (Heb.: owners or masters of the music). This term never became part of the Yiddish vernacular though it describes the musician and his unique place in Jewish European life better than any other term besides *klezmer.* Until one paid for the services of the *klezmer* he owned his tunes outright and was the master of his instrument.

[56] Johann Jacob Schudt (1664–1722) was a German historian whose specialty was the Levant. He wrote a four-volume work about the history and culture of the Jews of the German lands in his times. Since he was from Frankfurt, he specialized in the social history of the Jews in his city and environs. The book was entitled *Jüdische Merkwürdigkeiten* and printed in Frankfurt and Leipzig in 1715.

[57] Wolf, op. cit., p. 153.

[58] Nettl, P. *Alte Jüdische Spielleute,* p. 34.

his book, which is sometimes anti-Jewish (common in history texts of the time). He wrote that the *letsim* would travel with their violins, hurdy-gurdies, citterns, and celli from town to town and from courtyard to courtyard, telling jokes, acting as jesters, and begging for money. And, just as the *klezmorim* of the 1940s, '50s, and '60s followed their Jewish patrons to the resort colonies of the Catskills, their seventeenth- and eighteenth-century counterparts followed their patrons to vacation spas in Moravia and Bohemia, performing there for wealthy Jews and non-Jews alike. Schudt wrote about his visit to the spas of Hesse and seeing a group known as the *Badekapelle* (spa orchestra) from a town near Nitra, Bohemia:

> In 1716 there was a Jew in Ems, who asked the trumpet and French horn player to play for him while he sat in the hot mineral water. And when I was in Schwalbach Am Brunnen every morning near the fountain were four to five *spielleuter* playing. Afterwards they passed a plate around for the guests to put some money in for their efforts. I regularly made fun of them by asking them to play for me on their Sabbath, knowing they would not accept money on that day.[59]

Schudt also gives a more positive account of a Jewish wedding in Altona. "Dancing, jumping, and hopping is the young people's biggest pleasure at a Jewish wedding. While the prominent men danced the *mitsve tants*[60] with the bridegroom and the women did the same with the bride, the others

---

[59] Ibid., p. 36.

[60] *Mitsve tants* (Heb.): good deed dance. This dance was the highlight of the wedding celebration. Jewish law prohibits the dancing of men and women together but the *mitsve tants* was the one special exception to this rule. Usually the first man to dance with the bride was her father (sometimes the rabbi or father-in-law), who would hold one corner of a handkerchief while the bride held another as they danced in a stately circle. Then all the important male guests, one at a time, would take turns holding the handkercheif with the bride, who kept her eyes lowered out of modesty all the while. The dance was also known as the *tikhl tants* (Yid.: handkerchief) or the *kosher tants*. However, the *kosher tants* also meant that the bride was *kosher* (Heb.: fit, proper, valid)—in other words, she was not menstruating, thus clean and able to dance with men.

enjoyed the dance they called *'Abraham sein Pferd.'* The cadence was graceful."[61]

In addition to the *shpilman*, the *lets*, the *muzikant*, and the *klezmer*—who were also called *freyd-bashafers* (Yiddish: joy creators)—some Jewish musicians in the late seventeenth century could trace their heritage to the *marshaliks*, who emerged during the German Renaissance in the late sixteenth century, when the *Purim* play the *Akheshveyrosh shpil*[62] and other plays based on biblical stories became popular among German and Polish Jews. These Purim plays (*Purimshpil* in Yiddish) were the earliest expressions of Yiddish theatre. They reenacted the Book of Esther, read on the festival of *Purim*. The tradition began in Central Europe in the sixteenth century and reached its aesthetic peak and popularity in the seventeenth and eighteenth centuries in Eastern Europe. Though the *Akheshveyrosh shpil* was the most-performed play, there were others that derived their themes from the *Toyre* and other Jewish religious texts, e.g., *The Sacrifice of Isaac, The Selling of Joseph, Wise King Solomon, Sodom and Gomorrah,* etc. Though *Purim* was the most common time to present these plays, they were also done at other times in the year, particularly during *Khanike* and *Peysekh*. The *Purim* play provided work for the *klezmorim*, who accompanied the actors on stage, as they paraded through town, and when they were invited to private homes. Jewish musicians also often performed during and after the play, which was presided over by the *marshalik*, the master of ceremonies (and probably also sometimes the author of the play). Wearing a cap with bells and the garish clothes of a jester, he would escort the actors on and off stage while entertaining the audience with comical faces. Both during intermissions and the play itself, he would make satirical comments on the characters' motives and perform doggerel rhyming songs, often accompanying himself on the hurdy-gurdy. At weddings he would make sure that the entire wedding celebration (sometimes lasting a week)

---

[61] Wolf, op. cit., p. 92.

[62] *Akheshveyrosh shpil* (Yid.): Ahashuerus play, an alternative term for the *Purim shpil*, named after the king of Persia who married Esther and made her his queen.

was done according to both local Jewish tradition and the specifications of the bride's and groom's families. He also made sure that the various events were concluded in a timely manner and that the *lets* (or *batkhn*) and the *klezmorim* were doing their jobs.

By the late seventeenth century the defined duties of the *marshalik* were, like those of his fellow wedding entertainers, rather ambiguous. A dictionary (Prague, 1660) in Hebrew, Yiddish, Latin, and Italian defined the *marshalik* as a merrymaker. Another in French (Amsterdam, 1701) defined him as a buffoon. Finally, in Lithuania in 1673, a rabbinical statute limited the kinds of luxuries one could have at a wedding and stated that the *marshalik* could only play music at the wedding canopy, not during the meal. One thing is clear: the local or provincial prohibitions against hiring wedding entertainers determined if the *lets*, *batkhn*, or *marshalik* was bard, merrymaker, master of ceremonies, or just musician. Whatever function these entertainers performed, the rabbis did not change their negative attitude toward them. "These wandering entertainers, the *klezmer*, the card player, the dice player, the *lets*, and *marshalik* are all part of the same crowd engaged in nonreligious pursuits."[63]

Political Upheavals

As the *klezmer* developed from itinerant *shpilman* to significant *shtetl* musical personality during these centuries, a number of catastrophic social and political forces outside the Jewish community came to affect his music. The hysterical religious hatred fomented at the time of the First Crusade in 1096 was soon given official sanction by the church, and over the centuries caused the murders of thousands of Jews; even more fled German lands and sought refuge in Poland. In the sixteenth century Martin Luther

---

[63] Max Erik, *Geshikhte fun der Yidishe Literatur* (Warsaw: Pinkas Farlag, 1928), p. 149.

said, "If it is a mark of a good Christian to hate Jews, what excellent Christians all of us are!"[64]

During Polish King Casimir III's reign (1331–1370), Jews were officially protected by the Polish crown, because of their much-needed educational and craft skills and economic resources and contacts. This protection was especially valuable during the Black Plague of 1348–49, which killed thousands of Christians and Jews in Western and Central Europe, when the Jews were promptly blamed for poisoning the wells. Jews again fell victim to religious politics during the Thirty Years' War (1618–1648), when Protestants and Roman Catholics fought in Germany and the surrounding countries. Finally, in 1648–49 *Hetman*[65] Bogdan Chmielnicki (1595–1657) led the cossacks and the Tatars in a revolt against the Polish nobility, whom they regarded as exploiters of the Ukrainian peasants. Even though most Jews were at the mercy of the Polish nobility and were treated accordingly, Ukrainian and Polish peasants looked upon them as bitter enemies. The Chmielnicki massacres were the worst tragedy to happen to the Jews prior to the Holocaust: some historians claim that more than 200,000 Jews were murdered and 300 Jewish communities destroyed. Thousands of Jews headed south, seeking refuge in the Wallachia region of Romania or in Turkey; others went west to Slovakia and the Carpathian mountains; and still others went even further west, back to Italy and Germany. Of those Jews living in Lithuania and Poland who managed to escape the marauding cossacks, many fell victim to the Swedish army in the area, who were fighting the Poles in another devastating war (1650s–1690s) known as the Deluge.

Some of the Jewish musicians who fled south to the territories of the Ottoman Empire (Wallachia, Greece, and Turkey) teamed up with Rom (Gypsy) musicians and toured the Balkan peninsula and Black Sea regions, ending up as far as Odessa and Istanbul. The new music they composed— with its Turkish modalities, its different tuning and playing styles—

---

[64] Nathan Ausubel, *The Book of Jewish Knowledge* (New York: Crown, 1968), p. 272.

[65] *Hetman* initially meant a Polish military officer, then came to mean a cossack chief or leader.

influenced the *klezmer* style and repertoire to such a degree that it is now some of the most popular *klezmer* performed. The ethnomusicologist Zev Feldman traced the path this "Bessarabian *klezmer*" took: "The Greeks in particular formed a lively market for Jewish and Romanian music, and the Romanian *klezmorim* returned home with new Turkish and Greek melodies that soon found their way north to Galicia and Ukraine."[66]

The myriad upheavals of the seventeenth century had a lasting musical influence on the Jewish musician. During the Thirty Years' War many Jews served in the music corps of the various warring armies, playing primarily military music on woodwind and brass instruments. When they left the army they continued to perform many of the same tunes on the same instruments, thus influencing the Jewish repertoire.

After the debilitating Thirty Years' War and the cataclysmic Chmielnicki pogroms, the rabbis of Central and Eastern Europe imposed even stricter ascetic edicts on the Jewish community. The consensus was that the Jews were partly to blame for these tragedies, because they had strayed too far from the moral values and teachings of the *Toyre* and Talmud. Pious asceticism spread and influenced all aspects of Jewish life. Subsequently, many Jews, particularly in Poland, were in no mood for the jesting and singing of the *letsim* and *marshaliks*.

The Batkhn *and the Jewish Wedding*

Among these musicians was a folk bard who concentrated on song and story: the *batkhn*. Like the *klezmer*, the *batkhn* often inherited the job from his father, grandfather, or uncle. He consoled the people by reading passages of the *Toyre* and Talmud and by singing moralizing songs. His often semi-improvised rhyming poems were called *batkhones* or *shtey-gramen* (Yid.:

---

[66] Walter Zev Feldman, *Khevrisa: European Klezmer Music* (Washington D.C.: Smithsonian Folkways Recording, 2000 [compact disc liner notes]), p. 3.

stand-up rhymes), in which he combined the waggery and witticism of the *lets* with the leadership of the *marshalik* and the sharp intellect of the Talmudic scholar. He often recited or sung his *batkhones* unaccompanied, but sometimes was accompanied by a *klezmer* or accompanied himself. Because the *batkhn* was able to quote by heart from learned texts, he merited a more dignified position in the eyes of some rabbis.

The *batkhn* was also adept at poking fun at the wedding guests, using *Toyre* and Talmudic references, doing impersonations and dances, and telling ribald jokes about them. Of course, the rabbis complained about this offensive, shameful humor; one, David Levi, wrote: "A sin most grievous is to engage *batkhonim* [pl.] to amuse guests with jests built on verses from the Holy *Toyre* and other sacred writings. Happy is the man who keeps away from such blasphemers!"[67] This complaining led to barbed exchanges between rabbis and *batkhonim,* such as this one from Lissa (Lezno, Poland): " 'Such a shame that you found such a good wine in a terrible barrel,' said the Rabbi, and the *batkhn* replied, 'Better to have good wine in a terrible barrel than terrible wine in a good barrel.' "[68]

The *batkhn*'s craft was honed and most requested at Jewish weddings, where he was the master of ceremonies and played an integral part in preparing the bride for her wedding vows during the prewedding ceremonies, moving both the wedding party and guests from sober melancholy to exultation.

First came the *mikve* (Heb.: ritual bath),[69] to which the *klezmorim* often accompanied the bride and waited for her outside, playing music. For example, in Chelm, at the end of the nineteenth century, on the night before the wedding, the bath attendants would enjoy some cake inside while the

---

[67] Ausubel, op. cit., p. 280.
[68] Lifshitz, op. cit., p. 58.
[69] Jewish women went to the *mikve* in the bath house to cleanse themselves after menstruation and on the eve of the Sabbath and Jewish holidays.

klezmorim played music and the *batkhn* sang *muser* (Heb.: moralizing)[70] rhymes.[71]

During the *bazetsn* (Yid.: seating), the bride sat on a large stuffed chair made especially for her, where her closest female friends and relatives would come to solemnly pay their respects. Here the bride would often have her beautiful long braids cut, which invariably caused her and her female guests to cry, thus giving this process the name *baveynen* (Yid.: crying). Jewish married women did not go in public with their hair uncovered, as it was immodest, so they wore either a kerchief over their shorn hair or a *sheytl* (Yid.: wig). At the same time was the *bazingen* (Yid.: singing), in which the *batkhn* would sing an unaccompanied, long, poignant rhyming poem that exhorted the bride to cry along with her female guests. (Sometimes the *klezmer* violinist played an improvised, rubato, sad melody emphasizing certain sung refrains along with the *batkhn*.) Using quotes from the *Toyre,* Talmud and other religious texts, the *batkhn* sang about how her beautiful hair was being cut and how her friends would never see it again; how she was leaving her carefree youth for the difficult years of marriage; how she would have the heavy work of raising her many children while her husband studied all day in the *yeshive;* how she should remember all those who had died tragically in a pogrom or from disease and could not be at her wedding or never had the opportunity to be wed. These and other exhortations about burdensome responsibilities were sung in a deliberately melancholy tone. Then, while all the women were wailing, the *batkhn* changed his tone to one of rejoicing and sang to the bride about all the wonderful things awaiting her. He spoke glowingly about the groom; about the respect and love she would receive from her children; about the honorable *mitsves* she would garner by keeping a *kosher* home. After the *batkhn* was finished he had the *klezmer* play an upbeat melody.

---

[70] The study of *muser,* or strict ethical behavior according to Jewish law, began in the late nineteenth century. Its leading proponent was Rabbi Israel Lipkin Salanter, who introduced the study of ethical works into the *yeshives* of Lithuania. Eventually *muser* became an integral part of the Lithuanian *yeshive.*

[71] Lifschitz, op. cit., p. 55.

While the *batkhn* was officiating the *bazetzen* and *bazingen*, the groom and his closest male friends and relatives were busy at the *khosn's tish* (Yid.: groom's table). It was customary for the groom to give a *drash* (Heb.: sermon) based on a religious text pertaining to that week's *Toyre* portion. While he was preparing one, there would be singing, drinking, and music provided by the *klezmorim*. Sometimes the *batkhn* would split his duties and spend some time singing at the *khosn's tish* after he finished with the *bazingen*. Then he would accompany the groom and his male friends as they walked to the bride for the *badekn* (Yid.: veiling of the bride; originally from the Hebrew *badok*, to check, examine, inspect). The bride was usually being attended in her home or the home of a relative; the males would approach her, accompanied by the *klezmorim*. The groom would lift up the veil to see his bride and then cover her face once again. Most marriages were arranged, and the bride and groom had usually only seen each other once during their brief courtship. The tradition of *badekn* comes from the biblical story of Jacob, who had been promised Rachel, the youngest daughter of Laban, but instead was tricked into marrying the first-born daughter Leah, and had to work an additional seven years until he was granted permission to marry Rachel.

The *batkhn* was also an important component of the wedding entertainment during the party, working alongside the *klezmorim*, entertaining the wedding couple and guests with jokes, songs, and rhymes. And after the meal he would entertain everyone with rhyming and non-rhyming verse, both dignified and doggerel, during the *droshe geshank* (Yid.: announcement of the presents). The *batkhn*, sometimes with accompaniment from the *klezmorim*, would stand on a table and announce the names of each gift giver and what he or she had given. He would use all of his oratorical and improvisational skills to create short little rhyming verses, mixing metaphors and using material from the *Toyre*, Talmud, or liturgy. The guests were often at the mercy of the *batkhn's* sharp witticisms. For example, if a person who was known to be rather wealthy gave a gift to the newlyweds that the *batkhn* felt did not fit the stature of the giver, he would not hesitate to not-so-subtly embarrass him and exhort him to give some money in addition to the gift.

Here is an example of a *batkhn* entertaining for the bride and groom:

> *Oyb ir hat a tokhter a shlak,*
> *Tah kumt tsu undz in der yeshive,*
> *Ir vet patur veryn fun dem pak,*
> *On sheloshim un on sheva.*
> *Dah kent ir oysklaybn*
> *A bokher mit a ale meyles,*
> *Vos ken lernen un shraybn*
> *Un afile paskenen shayles.*
> *Koyft im nor shtivl mit kalashn*
> *Un git im nor smetene mit khale,*
> *Dertsu nokh a por groshn—*
> *Gefelt im shoyn di kale.*

If you have a daughter who's a nuisance, then come to us in the *yeshive,* you will dispose of this bundle without thirty and seven.[72] There you can choose a *yeshive* student with all the virtues, one who learns and writes and even rules on ritual questions. Buy him boots and galoshes and give him only sour cream on white *khale.* In addition a few *groshn*—now he's pleased with the *kale* (Heb.: bride).[73]

And here is an example of a *batkhn's* rhyming poem during a *bazetsn* of an orphan girl:

---

[72] Thirty and seven (Heb. *sheloshim* un *sheva*) refer to the seven days of sitting *shive* (days of mourning after a close relative or friend dies) and the first month after the death, when the mourner abstains from pleasure and entertainment.

[73] Lifschitz, op. cit., pp. 70–71. This *batkhones* was written by Yisroel-Issur Kosovitch, who lived in the environs of Minsk in the 1870s, and was performed at the wedding of his brother, who was marrying his first cousin. Kosovitch was accompanied by a *klezmer kapelye* from Minsk led by Sender the *Batkhn.*

Azind, lieb kind, darfst di vin dein Kopf kol hamakhshavos zros
   upkeren.
In wejnen var (hay-shin-yud-sav) mit hejsse Treren,
In sugen: Reboyne shel oylem, di host bei mir dem Taten zigenemen,
Ich hob sech nit zi wemen zi wenden in zi kehren,
Nur di, starker Gott, sollst mein Geschrej oishören.
Lo'mich chotsch dem zkhus hubn as mein Tate soll vin mein khupa
   gewahr were.
Wej geschrien oif die Kinder, wus Gott Barukh Hashem thit sej mit
   dem Wort yesoym oder yesoyme baklejden.
Lo'mir nur sejhen, a yesoym oder afiloo a yesoym in grössten nogid-
   schaft in in grösste Frejden.
Trugen sej oich in Harzen sejere groisse tsores in lejden.
Wurem sie hot kein Taten nit, zi wemen hot sie denn a gritreien
   Wort oiszirejden.
In der getreier Tate, wus er riht in lechtigen gan eyden.
Hot der vin oich kein nakhes in Frejden,
Wus me tot ihm gethin var des Zat vin seine Kinder upschejden.
Lo'mir nur sejhen, a yesoyme is bei der
Welt gor der mindster!
Kale getreie, kick sech nur arim oif dem Ort.
Wus der Tate darf san oif der khasone is dus khoshekh, finster.
Der Ort allejn thit oich derof jammern in klugen,
Wus hot wit derlejbt der Tate soll san oif der khasone,
wus hot dech oif seine Händ getrugen.
Wej geschrein, meine Frand, Wus stejhn bei mir hant!
Ich frejg: wi is mein Tate? in es enfert mir kejner.
Getreir Tate, wi wolgern sech (herumliegen) in der Erd deine hejlige
   Bejner!
Asoi schreit a kale var dem Nora allila:
Ejder asa elende yesoyme is glacher gur nit geboiren weren l'khatkhilah.
Wie men lost a Brejt oif dem groissen yom schwimmen,
Wus die Chwiljer (Wellen) losen sie nit zim Breg (Ufer) zikimmen,

Asoi host di mech gelost oif der groisser Welt-yom allejn.
Wej geschrien, ich bin gebliben oif der groisser Welt elend wie a Stejn.
Wi abin ich kick, in wuser an Ort,
Hob ich nit, wer es soll sugen far mir a git Wort.
Reboyne shel oylem ! kick nur oif mir b'eyna p'keeha
Nur oif dir is mein ganze smikhe, Reboyne shel oylem! Vernehm
*   meine Treren mit mein Gemejn*
In helf mir mit a git mazl mit mein zivig zi der khupa gejhn."
In ihr gite Frand, entfert amayne!

Dear child, clean out all the bad thoughts in your head by crying before
God with hot tears. Dear God, ruler of the universe, you took away
my father. I have no one to turn to for care. Only you, strong God,
can hear my crying. Let me at last have the honor that my father should
know that I waited for the *khupe*. The crying and the wailing of the
children, that God called them orphans—let us make them happy and
well-off. They carry in their hearts great troubles and suffering. She
has no father with whom she can talk. And this devoted father, who
is in the Garden of Eden, did not have much pleasure and joy from
you, God. Because you separated him from his children before his
time. Let me only say that the world considers the orphan the most
pitiful of beings. Faithful bride, look around here, where your father
should be at this wedding—but it is dark. Here there is only lamenting and complaining. If he had lived, he would be here for the wedding. He carried you in his hands. Cry and wail, my friends, who
remain with me today! I ask, where is my father? And there is no answer.
Dear father, where are your holy bones that are turning in the earth?
And so, screams the bride, woe is me! Rather than such an unhappy
salvation she would have been better off not born. She is like a piece
of wood drifting in the sea, and the waves won't let her come back to
shore. That is how you left me in this big world, this big sea. Crying
and wailing, I am left alone in this big world like a lonely stone. Wherever I look, in whatever place I turn, I have nobody to put in a good

word for me. God in heaven! Look at me with open eyes! I depend on you with all my honor, God in heaven! Take notice of my tears, of my whole being. Help me with good luck with my intended as I go to the wedding canopy. And you, good friends, answer *Omeyn.*[74]

For *batkhonim* who could double as *klezmorim,* weddings were very lucrative. Some led their own *klezmer kapelyes,*[75] which meant the family that hired the *batkhn* was forced to hire his band as well. Occasionally, this close relationship between the *batkhn* and *klezmorim* turned sour. Some- times, out of the amount paid to the *kapelye,* the *batkhn* would take a larger fee for his singing and playing duties; claiming that this was unfair, the *klezmorim* either physically took the extra money from the *batkhn* or fired him, even if he had been the leader of the *kapelye.* In his memoirs, Eli- akum Zunzer[76] wrote that when he first began working as a teenage *batkhn,* the *klezmorim* forcefully took his money after every job.

Most *batkhonim, marshaliks,* and *letsim,* however, had good relationships with the *kapelyes* they worked with, whether they performed solely as bards and jesters or also as *klezmorim.* In Minsk in the 1840s some *kape- lyes* were led by the *marshalik,* who wore several different masks during a wedding: improviser, singer, comic, juggler, and, most of all, merrymaker. During the wedding dinner the *klezmorim* performed pieces from operas and *nigunim* (Heb.: melodies)[77] from famous *khazonim.* Sometimes the

---

[74] S. Weissenberg, "Eine Jüdische Hochzeit in Sudrussland," *Mitteilungen zur Jüdischen Volkskunde,* Vol. XV, No. 1 (1905), pp. 66–67.

[75] *Kapelye* (Yid.): band. This term was used more often to describe the *klezmer's* band than any other. However, sometimes a band was called a *grupe* (Yid.: group), a *kumpanye* (Yid.: company), or, occasionally, a *khevrisa* (Yid.: bunch or gang; this word derives from the Hebrew *khevre,* a gang or group of friends).

[76] Eliakum Zunser was a *batkhn,* Yiddish bard, and dramatist born in Vilna in 1836. His song booklets were avidly read throughout Poland and America after he emigrated to the United States in 1889. He died in 1913 in New York, where a huge Jewish public memorial service was held in his honor.

[77] *Nigunim* were generally wordless melodies popularized by the *khasidim.* Instead of lyrics they sang made-up words like *ai, dai, yai,* etc., repeating them over and over until the song or dance was finished.

marshalik, with his *kapelye,* performed for Italian gangsters or for a cruel Zaparožher cossack, singing songs from Schiller and Schubert.[78]

Here are a few of the notable *batkhonim, marshaliks,* and *letsim* of this period, along with the activities they performed to entertain their public:

9 Merkish Friedland of Schwabia (1800–?) would lead the wedding party to the synagogue dressed as a harlequin, half his face covered in black, dancing and jumping while conducting his musicians with a baton.

10 Kheikel (1825–?) was a *batkhn* and *klezmer* in Poltava who entertained the wedding guests by dancing a *kozatshka,*[79] then getting up on the table and reciting *Toyre* while accompanying himself on the drum.

11 Berl Bass of Hundsdorf, Bohemia was considered a universal genius in the 1840s. During funerals he sang the prayers; he was the caretaker of the cemetery; he owned the Jewish poorhouse; and at weddings he was the *marshalik* and *klezmer.* When he recited rhymes for the bride he accompanied himself on the violin. His face was especially interesting: he could twist it like rubber, enabling him to make all sorts of grimaces, which was especially helpful on *Purim.*

12 In Amsterdam, the last *batkhn* and *lets* was Itzik Shlak (?–1875), who worked closely with the *klezmorim,* entertaining at weddings held in the dance hall he owned in the ghetto.

13 In 1870s Pinsk, the *batkhn* Schwartzer Yehuda was also a *klezmer* in a *kapelye,* and was the first violinist who showed off his skills by playing with gloves on or holding the violin behind his back. He was an exceptional *batkhn* and well known for his ardent singing of Eliakum Zunzer's songs.[80]

---

[78] Lipschitz, op. cit., p. 54.

[79] *Kozatshka* (sometimes *Kozatshok*): a Ukrainian male folk dance in 2/4 popularized by military border guards known as cossacks. Men performed this physically challenging dance to show off their skills; it was popular at Jewish weddings.

[80] Lifschitz, op. cit., pp. 49–74.

In Germany and Bohemia, the *batkhonim* (sometimes called *possen-makers,* or buffoons) were never held in the same esteem as their fellow *batkhonim* in Eastern Europe and were "often just like any of the other merrymakers using all the tools from the *lets*'s art."[81] Eventually the German *batkhn*'s lighter comic style influenced his compatriots in Poland, and they too declined in prestige. Despite the heavy moralistic hand of the rabbis, the majority of Jews in Germany, Poland, and Holland were clamoring for entertainment that distracted them from the sorrows of the ghettos. All the Jewish entertainers, and particularly the *klezmer,* had to contend with being pushed and pulled between the rabbinical and gentile authorities on one side of the fence and their adoring audiences on the other. The following quotes reveal the wide gulf between the rabbis and their constituency and how absurd the rabbis' regulations were:

14 Relief from our sorrows does not come from the songs, music, rhymes, or holy words that the *letsim* say; instead our sages tell us it comes from the *Toyre* and our wails to God. The *letsim*'s children play the violin, sing whorish songs, and speak obscenely [from the rabbinical authority *Etz Khayim,* Fürth, Germany, 1753]. [82]

15 When a scholar gives a sermon at a wedding everyone sleeps. But when the sermon is followed by impertinent songs (from the *marshalik*) and music...the feet knock and jump on the tables [from the Yiddish songbook *Simkhat HaNefesh*].[83]

16 Students, servants, maids, or strangers who were married in Württemberg in 1738 could not walk in the street and dance with the musicians. It was completely forbidden. The music could be in the synagogue.[84]

17 During Passion time in Frankfurt there were no Christian weddings, and at Jewish weddings there was no music. The people wanted Jewish

---

[81] Ibid., p. 46.

[82] Ibid.

[83] Ibid.

[84] Albert von Wolf, *Fahrende Leute bei dem Juden in Mitteilungen* (Hamburg, 1908–1909), vols. 25–32, p. 154.

music at the wedding so they performed it on a boat in Florsheim in the environs of Mainz. This was in March of 1713. On their way back they were stopped in Hochst and had to pay a large fine for breaking the law.[85]

18 In Mainz a law was revised in 1694 allowing music to be played on the eve of the engagement, on the day of the wedding, on the evening of the day after the wedding, and on the Saturday night after the wedding. But only three instruments could be played, and one of them had to be the flute or the whistle. Among the musicians, only one could be from outside Mainz.[86]

19 It may be that the Berliner *klezmorim* had to support themselves only through their art because there was a provincial law dating from the eighteenth century that stated that Jewish *shul-klapers*,[87] teachers, headmasters, gravediggers, and musicians could not change their professions. Once a gravedigger always a gravedigger.[88]

20 In Amsterdam we first hear about a dance hall in the Ashkenaz community in 1719; the following year the "High-German community" decided to lock it up. This obviously had no effect, since the rabbis had to formally make a decree in 1737 against the use of the dance hall by the *letsim* and musicians.[89]

21 In 1815 in Baden they did not want *batkhonim* and *klezmorim* at celebrations because their actions were harmful to the Jewish customs. The rabbinical authority did not like their general way of life and their style of clothing.[90]

---

[85] Ibid., p. 153.

[86] Ibid.

[87] *Shul-klaper* (Yid.): synagogue striker. This person, usually the *shames* (Heb.: sexton) of the synagogue, knocked on doors and windows to awaken worshipers for morning prayers.

[88] J. Shatsky, "Purim-Shpiln un Letsim in Amsterdamer Getto" *YIVO Bleter*, Vol. 19 (1942), p. 214.

[89] Stutschevsky, op. cit., p. 38.

[90] Rudolf Glantz, "Der Kamf Kegn Batkhonim un Klezmorim in Daytshland Onheyb 19tsn Yohrhundert," *YIVO Bleter*, Vol. 28 (1948), p. 394.

Despite the plethora of hindrances from the rabbis and Christian authorities, numerous wandering Jewish musicians in Poland and Germany managed to ply their skills. Occasionally they had legal protection. For example,
a document dated August 25, 1654,[91] stated that the local Jewish musicians
in Lublin could play at weddings and parties and were not to be disturbed
by the gentile musicians. At the end of the seventeenth century, the minister Bogusaw Leszczynski put the *klezmorim* from Lissa (Leszno, Poland,
near Posen) under his jurisdiction, and told the city council that they were
to be allowed to play at gentile weddings and baptisms. Another source
tells us of all kinds of Jewish entertainers (magicians, jugglers, balancers,
caperers, organ grinders with monkeys, dancers, and musicians) frequenting
the Leipzig fairs that were held once a year from 1668 to 1764. These musicians came from such cities as Amsterdam, Kraków, Lublin, Lvov (Lemberg),
Leszno (Lissa), Leipzig, Berlin, Dresden, Frankfurt am Main, Dessau, Breslau (Wrocław), Prague, and Fürth.[92] Despite the weight of Jewish custom
against women playing music in public, daughters and wives played with
their fathers and husbands and women performed on their own.[93]

Another reference to women *klezmorim* describes a Jewish wedding in
Elizabethgrad (Elizabetgradka), Ukraine in the early part of the twentieth
century that could only afford to hire *klezmorim* for the actual ceremony
and wedding party. So for the week of festivities that surrounded the wedding preparations, the *batkhn* sang songs in the bride's and groom's homes,
accompanied by older women who played percussion using rolling pins
on washboards.[94]

---

[91] M. Sh. Geshuri, "Warsaw: Klezmorim, Jew," in *The Encyclopedia of the Jewish Diaspora,*
ed. J. Grünbaum (Jerusalem, 1953–73), p. 474.

[92] In Fürth, the Jewish musicians were called *zinkenisten,* or cornetists. Wolf, *Fahrende
Leute bei dem Juden,* p. 154.

[93] Some of the more notable women were Khava Meyer from Dresden (1740 and 1742),
Mariana Meyer from Dresden (performed with her father, 1739), Mariana from Halberstadt (1741), and Sofia from Halberstadt (1741). I. Lifschitz, "Yidishe Favayler oyf di Leiptsiger Yaridim," in *Arkhiv far der Geshikhte fun Yidishn Teater un Drama,* ed. by Dr. Jacob
Shatsky (Vilna–New York, 1930), Vol. I, pp. 450–53.

[94] Weissenberg, op. cit., p. 62.

Jewish Music in Prague

By the middle of the nineteenth century the *batkhn, lets, marshalik,* and *klezmer* had nearly disappeared in Germany, Austria, Moravia, Bohemia, and Holland. However they continued to flourish in the Yiddish-speaking centers of Eastern Europe—Poland, Slovakia, Lithuania, Romania, Carpathian Hungary, Ukraine, Belarus, and Russia. The *klezmer* had become indispensable to all Jewish celebrations, particularly weddings, in Eastern Europe, a situation that lasted through the eve of World War II.

Outside of Mantua and Venice, Jewish musical life was most distinguished during the seventeenth and eighteenth centuries in Prague, the largest and most important Jewish ghetto in the Germanic lands. In the tenth century, Jewish merchants plied the trade routes from the Rhineland to the Near East; by 906 there was a settlement in Bohemia, and by 1091 a permanent Jewish community in Prague. In 1096 the First Crusade killed many Jews and forced others to be baptized, and in 1142, the Second Crusade drove the Jews out of the city. When they returned, they settled on the right bank of the Moldau River in what would become Prague's Jewish quarter. In 1270, the famous *Altneushul* [95] was built, and it soon became the central building of the ghetto. Other Jewish buildings were soon constructed, including guild halls, a Jewish town hall, and several synagogues still standing today. A Hebrew printing house was started and Jewish craft guilds (including the first *klezmer* guild, established in 1558 with a violin on its shield) added splendor to the vibrant community. The Prague Jewish community became a state within a state and had a great deal of autonomy, which attracted more Jews, so that by 1600 the community numbered two thousand, helping to spawn a golden age lasting into the mid-eighteenth century. There were thirteen synagogues in Prague, the smallest bigger than the largest in Frankfurt. Meanwhile, Bohemia, Moravia, and Silesia became part of Austria, linking the history of Prague's Jews with that country's.

---

[95] *Altneushul* (Yid.): Old-New Synagogue; built c. 1247, it is the oldest synagogue still in use.

Again, much of what we know about the Prague Jewish musicians comes from Schudt's detailed but uncharitable jeering. "The ability of the Jewish musicians of Prague in the seventeenth century cannot be compared to that of those gentile Mantua musicians. These profane *shpielleuter-letsim* were no better than mere beer fiddlers."[96] But even before Prague's golden age, Jews were musically active. At the turn of the fourteenth century, during King Wenceslas's reign, Jews wrote and sang *Einheitsgesänge* (Ger.: songs of oneness) in the vernacular. This display of the love of God made a tremendous impression on the Christians as they watched the Jews march through the streets. In 1512 there was another display of praise, this time for Ludwig II, the last Polish king of Bohemia, as they welcomed him into Prague. Hymns of praise were accompanied by violins, celli, trumpets, and percussion.

In Prague's Jewish cemeteries, the last names and engravings on the headstones of deceased musicians give further evidence of the importance of music and musicians to the community. Among them are Löb Harfner (harp), Efraim Fidler (violin), Löbel Bass (bass), Löb Klappzimmer (harpsichord), Lösser Zimbal (harpsichord or *tsimbl*), and Joachim Krummholz (lute: *krummhals* in German means curved neck).[97]

These musicians played for all the Jewish family celebrations and for Christian baptisms. The Christian musicians, because they were often competing for the same jobs, complained (often successfully) to the authorities. Between 1641 and 1651 they made five appeals to the archbishop of Prague, asking him to forbid the Jews to play at baptisms, Christian weddings, in Christian homes, on Christian holidays, and on Sundays. In a rare historical victory, on Oct. 1, 1651, the office of the archbishop renewed the Jews' privilege to be able to play on Sundays and all Christian holidays. Having

---

[96] Nettl, *Alte Jüdische Spielleute und musiker*, p. 37.

[97] The *klezmer*'s last name told what instrument he played and differentiated him from others in the town with the same first name. Here are some of the common last names of Jewish musicians in the eighteenth and nineteenth centuries: Arpe, Basadi (Italian); Bass, Geiger, Harpner, Shpielmann (German); Melodysta (Bohemian); Fidler, Skrypek (Russian); Fidelman, Zimbler, Zimbalist, Shpielberg, Shpielfidl, Muzikaski, and Strunen (Polish).

lost in Prague, the Christian musicians appealed, in vain, to the state government of Bohemia, writing, "They confuse the music and do not keep the tempo, and the pleasant music they play they perform jokingly. Furthermore, they do not have their own compositions, and when they play Christian music they play it in an alien way, depriving the noble and charming music of its esteemed quality."[98]

Despite the on again—off again restrictions, Jewish music flourished in Prague among Jews and non-Jews as well. The guild of Jewish musicians comprised a Jewish orchestra, consisting of nineteen trumpets, four French horns, eight violins, and four kettledrums. In the *Altneushul* on Friday evening, Jewish music was played on an organ built by Rabbi Maier Mahler to welcome the Sabbath. In other synagogues in Prague, *klezmorim* played cymbals, violins, and organ for the Sabbath eve celebration. The better violin players used a nonstandard tuning known as *scodatura*[99] to enable them to traverse several octaves quickly when accompanying the melismas of the singers.

The *klezmer* violinists were known for their skill and sought after by many gentile violinists for lessons. Franz Benda (1709–1786), one of the greatest classical violinists of his time, went through a period of depression due to his dissatisfaction with his playing. In 1766 he took a leave from concertizing in the Polish king's court and studied with an old *klezmer* known only as Leybl the Blind, whose repertoire consisted mainly of dances in the key of A. Benda was jealous of Leybl's ability because the latter had never studied the violin formally; he also admired the amazing tone this little old blind Jew was able to get out of his instrument. Eventually, after some time traveling with Leybl's *kapelye* throughout Moravia and Bohemia and living the life of an itinerant musician, Benda went to Prague. There he continued his violin lessons with a teacher Leybl had rec-

---

[98] Nettl, *Alte Judische Spielleute und musiker*, p. 38.

[99] *Scodatura* (It.): untuned. A large seventeenth- and eighteenth-century repertoire required the strings to be tuned differently in order to obtain larger intervals. The most famous *scodatura* pieces were those of H.I.F. Biber.

ommended and began to concertize, playing classical music once again. Years later, Benda wrote in his memoirs that the time he spent with Leybl was the happiest of his life.[100]

In Prague in 1678 we find one of the first written sources to use the word *klezmer* to describe instruments—in this instance those the Jewish musicians held as they paraded through the ghetto in honor of the coronation of the Emperor Leopold I of Austria (1658–1705). These *klezmer* included violins, clavicembalo, *positiv*, trumpets, French horns, and kettledrums; the women played cymbals.[101]

Klezmorim occasionally played in the synagogue when there was a special service honoring a dignitary or occasion. For example, on May 15, 1716, Graff von Isenburg of Offenbach visited the synagogue in Offenbach, and *klezmorim* played on the Sabbath eve. On November 26, 1785, Churfursten Wenceslas visited the synagogue in Koblenz, where the *klezmorim* accompanied the *khazn* as he sang psalms. In the Worms synagogue on September 17, 1790, *klezmorim* helped to celebrate the coronation of Kaiser Leopold II, and in 1802 Erzherzogin Marie Louise (wife of Napoleon I) wrote, "In Pressburg the synagogue was all lit up and the Jews were singing accompanied by trumpets and drums. After every psalm they yelled out loudly '*Vivat!*'[102] It gave me such a tick-tock in my breast."[103] When there were no *klezmorim* available, non-Jewish musicians were employed, as for the installation of the new synagogue in Königsberg, December 23, 1756.

---

[100] Wolf, *Fahrende Leute,* pp. 8–9. (Antonia Melis-Korschner, a Bohemian, wrote a novel in German, *Judith-Marie,* about Leybl the Blind.)

[101] Sendrey, op. cit., p. 350. The cymbals (*tatsn* in Yiddish) were very important in a *kapelye.* Since they were loud they could be heard over the din of the crowd and the other musicians. Along with the drums, they set the rhythm and tempo of the procession. A Yiddish saying, *gayn mit di tatsn* (go like the cymbals), affirms this.

[102] *Vivat* comes from the Italian *viva!* (long live!). Sometimes it was also used as a term for the Jewish dances *freylekhs* or *mazltov.* The *freylekhs* (from the Yiddish *frey,* or joy), also called *lebediks* (Yid.: lively), were the most common line dances at Jewish weddings in Eastern Europe, with an upbeat tempo and a 2/4 or 4/4 rhythm. When the *vivat* was played in Silesia, Bohemia, and parts of southern Ukraine, it was similar to the *mazltov* (Heb.: good luck).

[103] Wolf, *Fahrende Leute,* p. 96.

Finally, this vivid description of a sumptuous parade through the Prague ghetto in honor of the birth of Empress Maria Theresa's son Joseph Erzherzogs on March 15, 1741, shows how important the *klezmorim* were to community celebrations and how high was their social status among the Jewish and non-Jewish public:

> During the morning prayer-time the synagogues were full of Jews. Then they divided up all of the donations that had been collected and were to be given to the Jews and non-Jews, especially those who were in the prisons. In the evening they gathered in front of the town hall where musicians entertained them while they drank wine and beer.... During the afternoon they had closed up all their stores, locked the second-hand goods market, cleaned the streets, hung their carpets out of the windows, and, quite unusually, even the doors to the houses were taken down so that it would be easier for the people to go through the streets. On the main street they made special railings for the galleries in front of the houses. The three towers in the ghetto were decorated with ornamental candles and carpets. And every tower was furnished with an orchestra of trumpets and a drum to welcome all strangers. Then, at 3 P.M., the procession began in this order:

> 1. The Jewish postmen.
> 2. Two trumpeters.
> 3. Six well-dressed Jewish runners.
> 4. The *Rosh-Kahal* [104] Frankel, the first leader, in a peculiar Jewish costume, riding a horse wearing a red velvet embroidered cover. Next to him on both sides throughout the parade were two landowner *haidamacks*. [105]

---

[104] *Rosh-kahal* (Heb.): leader of the Jewish community.

[105] *Haidamacks* were Ukrainian and Polish paramilitary groups who wreaked havoc on towns in the eighteenth century, massacring and plundering everything and everybody in sight, including women and children. Their main victims were Jews. Eventually they were suppressed by Polish and Russian troops.

5. The second leader, David Lebl Kahave, riding a horse, and next to him six *haidamacks* on beautifully dressed horses.

6. The community's court reporter and synagogue herald dressed in distinctive synagogue clothing.

7. Two synagogue heralds, one who was eighty-eight years old and carried a pewter synagogue-hammer, and the other carrying a gold and wooden synagogue-hammer.

8. Then came the students and the head of the *yeshive* [106] in beautiful clothes, accompanied by trumpeters and French hornists.

9. Then more *yeshive* students riding horses while holding silver prayer books in their hands.

10. Then special students, with their principal, who could be told apart from the other *yeshive* students by their special school hats.

11. Then a host of riders led by Shimon-Aron Nayshtadle.

12. Then came the Jewish doctor Moshe-Shlomo Gumpert. Alongside of him ran two men dressed as Turks with long beards. Then came a boy carrying a diploma of medicine in his hand. Next to him was the Jewish pharmacist carrying a beaker in his hand, and next to him were the Jewish barbers.

13. Then came the *khazn* of the community, who carried a small pulpit from which he would from time to time stop to sing a prayer, accompanied by a man carrying a *positiv.* That evening this prayer was hung on a tablet next to the town hall and was illuminated for all to read. It was written in *Taytsh,* [107] Latin, and Hebrew.

14. Then came a host of poor orphans from the *Talmud-Toyre* [108] who were under the direct supervison of the *Rosh-Kahal* and lived only on donations. They sang psalm sixty-two.

15. Then came the Jewish *klezmorim* with large tin cups, wearing hats with a piece of paper on them reading *Vivat.* One of these *klezmorim*

---

[106] *Yeshive* (Heb.): academy. These were institutes for talmudic learning.

[107] *Taytsh:* The Yiddish version of the *Toyre.* It was traditionally read mostly by women.

[108] *Talmud-Toyre* (Heb.): study of the law. *Talmud-Toyres* were religious schools where the study of religious texts formed the curriculum.

was an eighty-year-old man who was dressed as a woman and played the bass trumpet.[109]

16. The Jewish *shokhtim*[110] with their flag. In front of them were elevated two bowls half-filled with oil.

17. Two Jewish comedians who walked on their hands and sometimes leaped about. On their breasts and eyes were clubs (cards).

18. Under the leadership of Shimon-Leybl came the furriers, who were carrying all their specific tools of the trade. They had two shields made of the best furs. One had the picture of her majesty the queen and the newborn prince; the other had a Star of David. Then came a cage of wild animals with a hunter who at times would shoot.

19. The butchers with their flag, dressed in their work clothes and shrouds. Reclining on the flag was a twelve-year-old boy who waved at the onlookers at their windows.

20. Then came the tailors' guild with music as they carried their scissors and ribbons.

21. Then came the lacemakers with music.

22. Then came the shoemakers with music. In front of them was a wooden boot.

23. Then there was a host of married Jewish couples on horses who wore expensive Hungarian costumes, carrying spears. In front of them was a pair of trumpeters and a runner.

24. Then a group of unmarried Jews on horses dressed as *Hussars*,[111] with a runner alongside of them as well.

25. Then came two Jews on horses. One of them was dressed in a precious costume like a woman. Jewish bystanders came up to him and kissed and caressed his clothes.

---

[109] I found two versions, one that said he was playing a bass trumpet, and one that said he was playing a *fagott,* or bassoon.

[110] *Shokhtim* (Heb.): slaughterers. The *shoykhet* was the person who slaughtered the animals according to the laws of *kashrut* under the strict supervision of the rabbi.

[111] A hussar was a member of any of the various European units originally modeled on the Hungarian light cavalry of the fifteenth century.

26. A *batkhn* who had wooden kitchen utensils hanging from all his sides. On his head he wore a wooden pot instead of a hat. He entertained the spectators with many quick short leaps.

27. A clown dressed all in green.

28. Several *narim*. One who was dressed as a young woman. Another old man dressed as a little girl with kasha stuffed in his mouth and another riding a fake horse making comedic poses.

29. A pair of savage-looking men.

30. Three fat stuffed gluttons.

31. A cook on a wagon making fun of the gluttons as he pretended to guzzle down liquor.

32. And at the end of the procession a happy farmer's wedding.[112]

Unfortunately, in 1745 the musical life of the Prague Jews came to an end: Empress Maria Theresa issued an order expelling all the Jews from Bohemia. Three years later, the Jews were allowed a ten-year reprieve. However, the damage had been done. Joseph II (in whose honor was the above parade), an admirer of Rousseau and Voltaire, ruled from 1765 to 1790, and abolished many of the limitations his mother had imposed on the Jews, opening schools and universities to them, and accepting them for military service. But he also forced them to adopt German family names, establish secular schools, and cease using Hebrew and Yiddish in all business transactions. These measures assisted in displacing Yiddish as the vernacular and encouraged assimilation; as a result, many facets of Jewish culture began to disappear. By 1854 there were only ten *klezmorim* left in Prague.[113]

---

[112] Rudolf Glantz, "A Berikht fun a Ben-Dor Vegn der Fayerlikher Protsesia fun dem Prager Yidn dem 24tsn April 1741," *Arkhiv far der Geshikhte fun Yidishn Teatr un Drama*, I (1930), pp. 77–84.

[113] Stutschevsky, op. cit., p. 45.

The Beginnings of Assimilation

The *haskole* (Heb.: enlightenment) movement was founded by the German Jew Moses Mendelssohn (1729–86), who believed that the Jews who
had been living for almost a thousand years walled in their ghettos should
free their education of its religious shackles and strive for full civil emancipation. He felt the Jews were languishing under the religious yoke of the
rabbinical authorities as well as the yoke of the Christian kings, feudal lords,
and church; so he resolved to lead "the Jews out of the narrow labyrinth
of ritual-theological casuistry onto the broad highway of human culture."[114]

Mendelssohn and his devotees decided that the vernacular of Jews living in German lands should be German rather than Yiddish. Almost everything associated with spoken Yiddish (including the songs and homilies
of the *lets, batkhn,* or *klezmer*) was to be suppressed to some degree. German *haskole* ideology viewed spoken Yiddish as "a badge, offensively rec-
ognizable to Gentiles, which advertised blatantly the cultural inferiority
and pariah role of the Jew."[115] Consequently, its proponents besmirched
Yiddish as a corrupt jargon, one they felt assisted in the continued abase-
ment of European Jewry. Their vehemence had a lasting effect: even on the
eve of World War II, many German, Austrian, Hungarian, Bohemian, and
Moravian Jews felt culturally superior to their Yiddish-speaking brethren
in Eastern Europe. Some of these German-speaking Jews turned away
entirely from religion but maintained an active interest and role in their
cultural identity, while many others, particularly among the wealthy, felt
that, to varying degrees, assimilation was the answer to being fully accepted
by the gentile public.

For thousands of these Jews, assimilation meant visiting the baptismal
font and converting to Christianity. In truth, conversion did allow them
to pursue vocations that had been denied to them in the past just because
they were Jews. As Jews began to supplant their traditional culture with a

---

[114] Ausubel, op. cit., p. 139.
[115] Ibid., p. 140.

more Germanic one, many of their ritual customs began to change. Synagogue worship took on more and more of the trappings of the Protestant church: some congregations used a bell to announce the time of prayers, some synagogues dispensed with the *khazn* and the traditional singing of the *Toyre* and Prophets in the ancient Semitic melismatic modes, replacing them with Christian compositions. Prayers were now sung in German rather than in Hebrew and were generally in major keys; German hymns were introduced, often with a mixed choir in four-part harmony; the organ replaced all other instruments; and many *klezmorim* were replaced by Christian musicians. As the Jews became less religious and more emancipated, the function and style of music that the *klezmer* performed at weddings, engagements, and other *simkhes* shrank in popularity. (Ironically, Moses Mendelssohn's grandson Felix [1809–47], who was brought up Protestant, wrote the famous "Wedding March" that became the standard tune for many Jews and Christians.)

It was becoming more and more difficult for the *klezmorim* to find work among their brethren. In Baden, for example, Jewish authorities had complained about the itinerant *batkhonim* and *klezmorim* for some time. But after six hundred years of *klezmer* music in Central Europe, the *haskole* succeeded where the rabbis' religious edicts did not. There was no more employment for these Jewish performers. "They are just simple beggars and charity rattlers.... They take comfort and charity from women when it should really go to our local poor.... Their art has a harmful influence on the public, particularly the youth... and their noise and immodest antics will only attract the gentiles' attention and provoke anti-Semitic feeling."[116]

In the end, some *klezmorim* changed their repertoire to reflect strong Christian influences, while others managed to eke out a living among those segments of the Jewish community who chose not to assimilate. Finally, many *klezmorim* traveled eastward into Galicia, Poland, Belarus, Lithuania, and Ukraine, where traditional *klezmer* music still thrived.

---

[116] R. Glantz, "Der Kampf Kegen Batkhonim un Klezmorim in Daytshland Onheyb 19tsn Yahren," *YIVO Bleter,* Vol. 28 (1948), p. 394.

Fun der Haskole biz dem Khurbn

·

(FROM THE ENLIGHTENMENT
TO THE HOLOCAUST)

Khasidim

In Eastern Europe at the end of the eighteenth century, Jewish daily life underwent major religious and cultural changes. After Poland was partitioned in 1772, 1793, and 1795 between Russia, Prussia, and Austria, the *haskole* movement spread quickly to Galicia, then the easternmost region of the Austrian empire, for the Jews were treated better by the Austrian ruler King Joseph II, who relaxed many restrictions and governed them rather mildly, than in the rest of partitioned Poland. In Galicia, the large Jewish populations in cities like Lvov, Kraków, Brody, Tarnopol, and Brest-Litovsk had commercial and cultural links with their brethren in Vienna and Berlin, with many Jews traveling from one city to another, thus helping to disseminate the German *haskole* among Galician Jews. (Some Jews even called Berlin "Jerusalem" because of their enthusiasm for German culture and language.)

As the *haskole* movement grew, two other Jewish philosophical movements attracted their fair share of adherents—as well as vitriolic opponents.

One group was known as the *misnagdim* (Heb.: opponents),[1] led by Rabbi Elijah ben Solomon Zalman—the Vilna Gaon[2] (1720–97). The other group, whom the *misnagdim* opposed, were the *khasidim* (Heb.: pious ones).

The Gaon stressed the values of *Toyre*, talmudic scholarship, and ascetic discipline, while remaining open to secular studies. He himself studied Hebrew grammar, biology, astronomy, trigonometry, algebra, and medicine. On his orders, *misnagdim* excommunicated *khasidim,* burned their books, vilified them publicly, and even ran them out of town.

The *khasidim* were devotees of the *khasidic* movement, founded by Israel ben Eliezer, the Ba'al Shem Tov[3] (c. 1700–c. 1760). Born in Mezritsh, Poland, in the Carpathian Mountains, the Ba'al Shem Tov was a healer, herbalist, and informal preacher who was able to have conversations with learned rabbis, simple Jews, and non-Jews. He never wrote anything down, but his teachings and folk tales were transcribed by his disciples, who helped to spread his philosophy, the complete opposite of the Vilna Gaon's. He found little solace in the caustic, regimented life many of the great *misnaged* talmudic rabbis lived. Instead, the Ba'al Shem Tov taught that there were no divisions between the sacred and the secular. God permeates everything: inanimate objects, plants, living creatures, and man. Rejecting asceticism, the Ba'al Shem Tov emphasized joyfulness: "Our Father in Heaven hates sadness and rejoices when His children are joyful. And when are His children joyful? When they carry out His commandments."[4] The most direct way one could communicate one's joy to God was through prayer, which removed any barrier between God and man if it was thorough and done with enthusiasm. With prayer, man slowly rose from this world into

---

[1] Later a *misnaged* referred to a non-*khasidic* Lithuanian Jew who disapproved of the miracle-like aura of the *khasidic* leaders known as *tsadikim,* and the way they infused too much singing into the daily prayers.

[2] *Gaon* (Heb.): genius.

[3] *Ba'al Shem Tov* (Heb.): master of the good name.

[4] Yale Strom, *The Hasidim of Brooklyn: A Photo Essay* (Northvale, New Jersey: Jason Aronson, 1993), p. xviii.

the world of God, and song and dance were the most potent aids in reaching this end. So prayer filled with *hislayvus* (Heb.: ardor) replaced melancholy prayer, whose very idea was anathema to *khasidim*. And prayer filled with song (and dancing during celebrations) became the most essential way of reaching *dveykes* (Heb.: adhesion) to God.

Thus the Ba'al Shem Tov's philosophy gave many poor and uneducated Jews the moral strength to endure their daily hardships, so much so that by the end of the nineteenth century there were between three and four million *khasidim*, living mainly in *shtetlekh* (Yid.: Jewish market towns), across Eastern Europe. At the same time, more and more urban Jews became attracted to various visionary *rabeim* (Yid.: Khasidic masters, teachers, rabbis), some becoming *khasidic*, others just neo-*khasidic* for sentimental or spiritual reasons.

The *rebe* was a mystic and wonder healer in the eyes of his followers, and many *nigunim* were composed and sung in his praise. He was the spiritual "vessel" from which his supporters, from the simplest to the brightest, drank to attain *dveykus* with God. Even Christians would come to the *rebe*, especially if they had a sick child that the non-Jewish doctors had failed to cure. The non-Jew would ask for a blessing even though he could not understand Hebrew. Sometimes the blessing was written on a small piece of paper and taken back to his home as an amulet. The *rebe* never promised a miracle, but only wished that, with God's help, something would happen.

Each *rebe* had his own interpretation of the *khasidic* way of life, forming a communal base centered around *hoyfn* (Yid.: courtyards), within which were the home of the *rebe*, his family, in-laws, and, depending how wealthy he was, his *gabe* (gabbai; Heb.: synagogue manager), *shames*, and important guests that came to visit. Also in the *hoyfn* were a *besmedresh* (Heb.: house of worship), the *shoykhet*'s workshop (where he koshered only fowl), a Talmud *Toyre*, and a *kheyder* (Heb.: class; daily religious school for boys under *bar mitsve* age). The walls that formed the courtyard also formed one of the walls of the main synagogue; in Eastern Europe it was common practice to build the synagogue so that its entrance faced the courtyard in order to minimize the presence of the synagogue, thus providing some measure of safety from anti-Semites.

During my travels in Eastern Europe I visited several *hoyfn* that were still in use to some degree. Two were in Miskolc, Hungary and Košice, Slovakia. Though these *hoyfn* were not as vibrantly active as they had been before World War II, activity centered in and around the kosher kitchens. These Jewish community restaurants were established after World War II and were funded by the American Joint Distribution Committee to serve those Jews (mostly elderly) who wanted to have one kosher meat meal every day of the year (except on religious fast days). It was in these two kosher *kikhn* (Yid.: kitchens), as well as in others, that I met and interviewed several former *klezmorim*.

Some *khasidim* borrowed folk melodies and songs from their non-Jewish neighbors and created *nigunim* with and without new text. Two of the more famous non-Jewish tunes that became part of the *khasidic* repertoire are the Lubavitch *nign* "Napoleon's March" (sung to the melody of the Marseillaise) and the "Kalever Nigun" (a Hungarian song called "Szol A Kakos Mar," or "The Rooster Is Already Crowing").

Interestingly enough, Rabbi Shneur Zalman (1747–1813; the founder of the Lubavitcher *khasidim*) aligned himself with the anti-French faction during Napoleon's march from France to Russia, seeing, like some other *rabeim*, Napoleon as a symbol of heresy and agnosticism. But many Polish Jews, including followers of the Lubavitcher *Rebe* and other *rabeim*, regarded Napoleon as a liberator, since Polish Jewry received little sympathy from their Russian rulers. This Lubavitcher melody is still sung during the High Holidays.

The Kalever *Rebe* (Rabbi Yitskhok Isaac Taub, 1751–1821) was the founder of Hungarian *khasidism* and was the rabbi in Nagykálló, Hungary for some forty years.[5] Legend has it that one day Rabbi Yitskhok was walking in the countryside when he heard a poor young shepherd sing a

---

[5] Rabbi Yitskhok was known as the Kalever *Rebe* because Nagykálló (Kálló) is just east of Nyiregyházá.

beautiful song of longing for his beloved. He asked him to teach him the song, and then paid him for his efforts. When the rabbi got home he wrote new words to the haunting melody, so that instead of a song about a rooster who will sing when the young man's beloved returns, the song is one of longing for the messiah. When will the rooster crow to tell us of his coming? "When the Temple will be rebuilt and Zion will be repopulated."[6] The *Kalever Nigun* is known, sung, and played among all Hungarian *khasidim* and many of the world's Hungarian Jews.

The first time I heard the *Kalever Nigun* I was traveling in eastern Slovakia near Velki Kapušany with a group of Hungarian Rom. To my astonishment they sang the song with the Hungarian and Hebrew words. I asked them where they had learned it, but all they remembered was that it was a "holy Jewish song from a healer." Another time, in Sátoraljaújhely in eastern Hungary, I met some Rom who knew the melody and words as well; they told me they had learned it while playing at Jewish celebrations before World War II.

Besides incorporating and re-creating indigenous folk tunes, *khasidim* also composed their own *nigunim,* some, such as the Belzer, Bobover, Buhusher, Bratslaver, Moditser, Vishnitser, Stefuneshter, and Stoliner *rabeim,* becoming well-known in the process. Others were famous for their musicianship, and a few even had their own *hoyf kapelyes,* which generally only played at *simkhes* for the *rebe* and their fellow *bale'batim.*[7]

The Stoliner Repertoire

I am partial to the Stoliner *nigunim* because I grew up going to the Stoliner synagogue in Detroit and heard the melodies there and at home. In

---

[6] Harry M. Rabinowicz, *Hasidism: The Movement and Its Masters* (Northvale, New Jersey: Jason Aronson, 1988), pp. 292–94.

[7] *Bale'batim* (Heb.): masters of the home: the men, women, and children who followed a specific *rebe* and his teachings.

addition to this, my *yikhes*[8] on my father's side stems from his parents, who were followers of the Stoliner *rebe,* and my paternal great-grandmother (Chava Weiner), who was a close friend of Rabbi Israel Perlow (1873–1921), the Stoliner *rebe,* known as the *Yenuka* (Heb.: baby) because he became *rebe* just after his *bar mitsve.*[9] While keeping with the Stoliner tradition of fervent *davenen* (Yid.: synagogue praying), the *rebe* was also a great lover of music and continued the musical tradition of Stolin by having music in his *hoyf* on a daily basis. He also employed noted composers as part of his *hoyf* to compose new *nigunim;* the two best-known were Rabbi Jacob from Telekhan (near Pinsk) and Rabbi Yossele Talner. The Stoliner *rebe* had two girls and four sons; three of the sons formed a *kapelye* to play music for *simkhes* in the *hoyf.* One son, Rabbi Asher, was such a talented cellist that he studied (much to the dismay of Rabbi Israel) at the conservatory of music in Berlin for a short time. The tradition of playing and singing these beautiful and passionate *nigunim* is still alive, for, as Rabbi Israel once said, "*As es brent, shrayt un zingt men*" ("When one is on fire, one shouts").[10]

My repertoire includes the music that Rabbi Israel Perlow's *kapelye* played. I had the good fortune to meet Asher Wainshteyn (1890–1983), a *khasid* from Stolin, in 1982 when he was living in Boro Park, Brooklyn. He was a violinist in a *klezmer kapelye* that also included a bassist, a *tsimbalist,*[11] a trumpeter, and a Belorussian drummer; they performed through-

---

[8] *Yikhes* (Heb.): pedigree, descent, lineage, parentage. Every Jew in Eastern Europe had some *yikhes*—even the orphan, whose, sadly, was low. Having better *yikhes* gave you higher social status even if you were of poor to average means. For example, a direct descendent of a famous rabbi had beneficial *yikhes* if he or she came from a poor family and were to be married. But if you were the son or daughter of a poor peddler your *yikhes* was quite low. Money was important in the *shtetl,* but education (particularly in religious Jewish texts) was even more so. Though most *klezmorim* did not have much *yikhes,* some were famous, adored for their personality and artistry, which gave their wives and children good *yikhes.*

[9] *Bar Mitsve* (Heb.): son of the commandment; a religious ceremony for a Jewish male of thirteen—he is called up to the *Toyre* for his first official *alie* (*aliyah;* Heb. rise, ascent; a reading from the *Toyre*) and formally becomes an adult member of the community.

[10] Rabinowicz, op. cit., pp. 250–54.

[11] A *tsimbalist* played the *tsimbl* (hammer-dulcimer).

out the Pinsk, Belarus region from 1906 to 1919, for Jews and non-Jews alike. Wainshteyn immigrated to New York after World War II. The *klezmer* manuscript he gave me contained ninety-four tunes and demonstrated the extensiveness of his repertoire: many of the tunes were not indigenous to the region, and these demonstrated how often the *kapelye* played for non-Jews. In the collection were *dobranotshes*, *fantazies*, *hopkes*, *khusidls*, *kozatshoks*, a *koyletch tants*, a *mazltov tants*, mazurkas, polkas, *padespans*, *shers*, *skotshnes*, *tish-nigunim*, waltzes, *zogekhts*, and even two cakewalks. This repertoire provides a good opportunity to enumerate the kinds of tunes *klezmorim* were performing at this time, along with their ritual functions:

- The *dobranotsh* (Rus.: good night)—also known as the *dobranots* (Polish), *a gute nakht* (Yid.: good night), *zay gezunt* (Yid.: be well), or *gezegen* (Yid.: farewell)—was a piece, generally in 4/4 time, played at the end of the wedding when the guests departed for home, often just before sunrise; afterward the *klezmorim* accompanied the newlyweds and their parents to their respective homes with a march or sometimes a *freylekhs*.
- The *fantazi* (Yid.: fantasy) was a nondance tune often played at the *tish* (Yid.: table) where the newlyweds and the parents sat and dined; like the classical music composition known as a fantasia, it had no fixed form, the structure being determined by the musician's or composer's fancy.
- The *hopke* was a lively Russian circle dance where one dancer danced within a bigger circle of dancers; it was very popular among non-Jews.
- The *khusidl* (Heb.: small *Khasid*) was both a solo and communal slow, dignified *khasidic* dance in 2/4 time that could be performed either in a circle or a line; however, in Galicia, Transylvania, and the Carpathian regions of Hungary, it was considered the same as a *freylekhs*.[12]
- The *koyletch tants* (Yid.: dance of the *khale*, or challah bread) incorporated a special twisted or ringed bread that was eaten on certain holidays

---

[12] In Berbești, Romania (south of Sigheta-Marației, or Sziget to the Jews), I met a former *klezmer* who played me a couple of pieces he called *khusidls* on the violin that were in 4/4 time and were exactly like *freylekhs*.

and celebrations; it was sometimes performed immediately after the *khupe* (Heb.: wedding canopy), and was thus also called the *khupe tants*. Usually the grandmother or another matriarch of the family danced in front of the bride and groom while holding the *koyletch* for all to see as the *klezmorim* accompanied them through the town to the wedding feast, all the while singing these words to the groom: "*Vos vilstu, di khale oder di kale?*" (Yid.: What do you want: the bread or the bride?).[13]

- The *mazltov tants* (Heb.: congratulation or good-luck dance) was similar to the *mitsve* dance, which was also known as the *kale tants* (Heb.: bride dance). It was performed several times in the course of the wedding ceremony: first, when all the bride's female friends danced with her at the *khupe* before the ceremony; again during the *bedekn* after the groom had veiled the bride, when the *batkhn* called out the women's names and each danced with the bride in turn in a stately circle while holding her hands and wishing her good luck; and again during the meal, when the *batkhn* called each of the honored guests by name to come up and congratulate the newlyweds, upon which the guests, in same-sex couples, danced to a melody in 3/4 or 3/8 time.

- The *mazurka* was an up-tempo Polish dance—in 3/4 or 3/8 time, often with a "B" or trio section, and usually in a major key—native to the Mazovia region; it was quite popular in western salons in the 1830s and '40s and was played as a sign of solidarity for partitioned Poland. It resembled the polka, but had two sliding steps in place of one.

- The polka was an up-tempo dance in 2/4 time and a major key that originated in Bohemia around 1830. The basic step was a hop followed by three small steps; it could have two or three sections, with the last part a trio.

---

[13] In and around Warsaw, the custom was to dance with lit candles in the *koyletch*. The other time the *koyletch* dance took place was at the *tish* of the newlyweds, just before the blessing over the bread, which meant the dining could begin. Again, it was the grandmother of the bride or groom who danced. Isaac Rivkind, *Klezmorim: Perek b'Toldot ha-Amanot ha-Amamit* (New York: Futuro Press, 1960), p. 31.

- The *padespan* (*pas d' espagnol,* Sp.: Spanish step) was a Russian waltz based upon Spanish themes.

- The *sher* (Yid.: scissors) was one of the most common Jewish dances. According to ethnomusicologist Moshe Beregovski, it probably came from the German melody "Der Sherer oder Schartanz," which dates from 1562. It was a contradance in which from four to eight couples formed two facing lines; the couples bowed their heads toward each other as they switched places, going under the gate formed by each other's arms. The *khasidim* called the dance *hakhna'a* (Heb.: submission) because bowing one's head was a gesture of respect. The music was often a *freylekhs* in 2/4 time in a minor key, with two or three sections.[14]

- The *skotshne* (Pol.: hop) was sometimes an instrumental display piece, but those Asher Wainshteyn played were like *freylekhs* in 2/4 time and a minor key, except more technically elaborate; when dancing to them, the *khasidim* incorporated hopping into their steps.

- The *tish-nign* (Yid.: table song) was a *khasidic* wordless melody sung with great spirituality, sometimes at the *rebe's tish,* when the *rebe* and his followers welcomed the Sabbath with songs on Friday night, and other times sung by the *batkhn* while the wedding guests were dining. The accompaniment was a solo instrument, usually violin, which played rubato.

- The waltzes that were in Wainshteyn's manuscript were arranged from popular classical melodies of the day as well as from Russian and Polish folksongs. One of the most popular waltzes Wainshteyn's *kapelye* was asked to play at both Jewish and non-Jewish celebrations was Tchaikovsky's Waltz Sentimentale (opus 51, number 6).

- The *zogekhts* (Yid.: say) was a display piece in which the *klezmer* utilized a synagogue prayer motif to compose an improvisational piece in rubato rhythm. Occasionally it segued into a *khusidl,* like the *zogekhts* in the Wainshteyn manuscript that was sung to the prayer "V'hi Sheyomda

---

[14] Mark Slobin, ed., *Old Jewish Folk Music: The Collections and Writings of Moshe Beregovski* (Philadelphia: Univ. of Pennsylvania Press, 1982), p. 534.

Lavosaynu" (Heb.: and he stood for us).[15] When the *zogekhts* was sung, the singer often used coloratura (trills, runs, scales), a vocal technique that the *khazn* also used.

- The cakewalk, an African American folk dance from the late nineteenth and early twentieth centuries, was a strutting dance step originally developed for competing for a cake. The two cakewalks in the Wainshteyn manuscripts had three sections, the first two in minor and the third, a trio, in a major key.[16]

One of the *tish-nigunim* in the collection was one that the present-day Stoliner *khasidim* had forgotten. It was such a beautiful tune that I went to the current Stoliner *rebe*, Rabbi Baruch Perlow, and played it for him; he was so impressed by the haunting melody that he told me to teach it to the Stoliner *bale'basim* the following week on *Purim*. *Purim* came and I took my place on a table in the back of the synagogue and began to play the melody on my violin. After I played it one time through, the *Khasidim* began to sing and dance along. Despite my bow arm cramping, I managed to play the melody on and off for four hours. Today Stoliners in Brooklyn and Israel sing this *tish-nign* every *Purim* and at other *simkhes*.

The Polish and the Russian Repertoire

Much of what we know about the repertoire the *klezmorim* played from the mid-nineteenth century to the eve of World War II comes from the few surviving collections, manuscripts, and single sheets of music (most *klezmorim* did not read or write music). The largest of these collections,

---

[15] We sang this tune at our *Pesekh sederim*. See Walter Zev Feldman, *Khevrisa: European Klezmer Music* (Washington, D.C.: Smithsonian Folkways Recording, 2000 [compact disc liner notes]), p. 27.

[16] Wainshteyn explained to me that a man from Pinsk (a friend of the *tsimbler's*) had visited America around 1910 and brought back some sheet music, including these two cakewalks.

consisting of more than 2,500 folk tunes, comes from the monumental field research Soviet ethnomusicologist Moshe Beregovski did from 1928 to 1936.

Moshe-Aaron Yakovlevich Beregovski (1892–1961) was the leading Soviet ethnomusicologist in the field of Jewish music. He was educated at the Kiev and Leningrad (St. Petersburg) conservatories, and from 1930 until it closed in 1948 he was the head of the Musical Folklore Department of the Institute of Jewish Proletarian Culture at the Ukrainian Academy of Sciences in Kiev. In 1944 he received his doctorate in the subject of Jewish instrumental folk music. From 1941 to 1949, he served on the Ukrainian Academy of Sciences as head of the Musical Folklore Section of the Institute of Literature's Department of Jewish Culture. There was a plan to open a similar institution that same year at the Belorussian Academy of Sciences, but it was not realized. During these difficult years under Hitler and Stalin, Beregovski tirelessly collected Jewish folk music in the field:

> During the summer of 1944 we received from our correspondents a number of ghetto songs, labor-camp songs and Jewish partisan songs.... We organized expeditions in 1944 in Chernovits...[and] in August 1945 in the Vinnista area.... In 1946 we visited Vilnius and Kaunas, where we collected material from the Vilnius and Kaunas ghettos. We prepared the book *Jewish Folklore in the Period of the Great Patriotic War* for publication.[17]

In 1937 Beregovski had written one of the seminal articles on *klezmer* music, entitled "Yidishe Instrumentale Folks-Musik."[18] Beregovski lamented the fact that "we know scarcely anything!" about the *klezmer*'s repertoire and how and where the *klezmer* was trained. He continued to exhort the reader:

---

[17] Joachim Braun, *Jews in Soviet Music* (Jerusalem: Hebrew University of Jerusalem, Research Paper No. 22, June 1977), p. 43.
[18] In *Kabinet far di Derlernen di Yidishe Sovietishe Literatur, Shprakh un Folklor* (Kiev: Folklor-Sektsye, 1937).

THE BOOK OF KLEZMER

If we know little about the average *klezmer,* are there perhaps descriptions of the talented, gifted ones? Also scarcely any! Can we perhaps say that *klezmer* music has not been taken up because it is too trifling to be interesting for purposes of collection and study? Because the mass of *klezmorim* was so gray and untalented, so artistically poor and untalented, so artistically poor and uninteresting, because we won't find any talented and interesting personalities among them? No! Even superficial acquaintance with the art of the *klezmer* and with the tens of talented artists produced by the mass of *klezmorim* is enough to convince us that it is worth taking up this neglected and overlooked area.[19]

At the end of the article Beregovski provided a special questionnaire that he hoped researchers would use as a guide in gathering data. In all there were four categories—1. The *Klezmer,* 2. *Klezmer* Bands, 3. The *Klezmer* Repertoire and Dances, and 4. Amateur Musicians—encompassing 110 questions. But the Holocaust began only two years after this article was published.

By 1946 his archives contained about seven thousand items (written music, photographs, and recordings), most of which he had collected himself. Much of what he wrote, though, whether in Russian or in Yiddish, went unpublished during his lifetime. The articles and the part of his five-volume study of Jewish musical folklore that was published and reached the United States went unnoticed except by a very few experts. Not until Mark Slobin's significant work of translating, editing, and publishing *Old Jewish Folk Music* in 1982 (which contained five essays: "Jewish Folk Music" [1934], "The Interaction of Ukrainian and Jewish Folk Music" [1935], "Jewish Instrumental Folk Music" [1937], "The Altered Dorian Scale in Jewish Folk Music" [1946], and "Jewish Folk Songs" [1962]) did researchers and exponents of *klezmer* music know of and have at their disposal such a treasure trove of music and information. As Slobin says: "Beregovski is a major and forgotten ethnomusicologist of Eastern Europe.... The song

---

[19] Slobin, op. cit., pp. 531–32.

anthologies presented here represent the chief corpus of accurately notated songs in Yiddish from oral tradition; there is not even a close runner-up.... Beregovksi's notations are meticulously detailed and annotated, and they hold up against the highest standards of his day and our own."[20]

The following is a list of dances and instrumental display pieces from the collections and manuscripts of Beregovski, Kostakowsky,[21] Wainshteyn, and from my own field research in Eastern Europe. These tunes were played between 1850 through the 1930s at weddings, social dances, and other celebrations. The instrumental dance pieces were: *bezem, broyges, bulgarish,* cakewalk, chaconne, *czardas, dobranotsh, dobridyen, dzhindobri, fandanca,* fox-trot, *freylekhs, gas-nign, gut-morgn, hakhna'a, honga, hopke, hora, korohod, khupe, khusidl, kosher, kolomeyke, koyletsh, kozatshok, kozattshka, krakówiak, krentsel, lancer, lebediks, mazltov,* mazurka, *mekheteneste, mignon mitsve, nign, oberek, padespan, patsh, pleskn,* polka, quadrille, *reydl, severs, sher,* shimmy, *shtiler, shtekn, shwer un shwiger, sirba, skotshne,* tango, *tikhl, vivat,* waltz, *wingerka,* and *zhok.* The display pieces were: *doyne, dveykele, fantazi, gaguyim-nign, taksim, terkisher gebet, tish-nign, vulekhl,* and *zogekhts.* Some of the pieces I have not described above are as follows:

• The *bulgarish,* also known as *bulgar* in English and *bulgareasca* in Romanian, became one of the most common dance tunes in the American *klezmer* repertoire. In fact, the saying "playing the bulgars" basically meant playing *klezmer freylekhs.* In 8/8 time, the *bulgarish* was danced either as a circle or line dance and was popular in Bessarabia and south Ukraine. The name probably refers to the Bulgarian minority in Bessarabia.

• The chaconne was a stately waltz, originating from an eighteenth-century Spanish dance, popular among the Polish and Russian upper class. It later became a 4/4 dance with an occasional trio section.

---

[20] Slobin, op. cit., p. 2.

[21] Nat and Wolff Kostakowsky's *International Hebrew Wedding Music* (1916) contains over two hundred dance tunes.

- The *czardas* was a Hungarian dance that started slow and gradually increased in tempo; it was especially popular among the Hungarian Jews of eastern Slovakia, Carpathian Ukraine, and Transylvania. It generally consisted of two to three sections in 4/8 with the last section being a trio in 2/4.
- The *dobridyen* (Rus.: good morning), also known as the *gut morgn* (Yid.) and *dzhindobri* (Pol.) dance, was played by the *klezmorim* to greet guests. Sometimes the *dobridyen* was performed after a *dobranotsh* or march in the wee hours of the night; and sometimes the wedding celebration lasted so long that when the newlyweds reached their home it was sunrise. The *dobridyen* welcomed the new day for the exhausted bride and groom and foretold of the further celebrations that evening, as the *sheve brukhes*[22] began.
- The *fandanca* was another lively Russian dance enjoyed by the upper-class Poles and Russians. It originated from the Spanish *fandango* and was rhythmically varied from slow to quick three-quarter time.
- The fox-trot was a popular dance in the 1930s among younger Jews and originated in the United States. It was danced with a variety of steps, both fast and slow, in 4/4 time.
- The *gas-nign* (Yid.: street song), in 3/4 or 3/8, was played for the newlyweds and their guests as they walked home in the evening after the wedding celebration through the streets of the *shtetl*. Sometime *klezmorim* played *gas-nigunim* for the guests each day of the *sheve brukhes* as they walked home. Moldavian Jews called the dance *zhok*.
- The *honga* was a Bessarabian line dance in 2/4 also known as *hangu* or *onga*.
- The *hora* was a popular Romanian Jewish dance played in a hobbling

---

[22] *Sheve brokhes* (Heb.): seven blessings. The *sheve brokhes* that were said under the *khupe* were repeated during the traditional seven days of wedding feasts, often at the newlyweds' or in-laws' home. After reciting the blessing, the celebration continued with *klezmer* music, dancing, drinking, and eating. This party could last the whole night, so during the week of the *sheve brokhes* the newlyweds did little more than sleep during the day.

3/8 gait. Often an upbeat *bulgar* followed it. Other names for it included *zhok, vulekhl, londre,* and *krimer tants* (Yid.: crooked dance).[23]

- The *korohod* (Yid.: round, circle, choral dance) danced at Jewish weddings came from the Ruthenian dance called *khorovod*. It was a women's dance that contained lyrics and movements from ancient Slavonic times. The melody was rather haunting and had walking and circle figures. The dance and lyrics described the greeting of spring, the death of winter, the celebration of the winter solstice, and the celebration of the fall harvest. The Jewish *korohod* was danced both by men and women who, while dancing, sang the praises of the newlyweds. Sometimes this dance was known as a *redl, redele* (Yid.: circle), or *igl* (Heb.: circle).

- The *kolomeyke*, a brisk circle dance in 2/4 time, originated in the East Galician Ukrainian town of Kolomyja. This was a folk melody popular among Poles, Ukrainians, and Ruthenians. Jews in the Carpathian Mountains customarily danced the *kolomeyke* in the mountain meadows during the Jewish festival of *Lagboymer* (*Lag B'Omer*). "When it was *Lagboymer* we use to go with our school to the meadows outside of town. There we celebrated with dance, music from our local *kapelye*, and a small play that the students put on. The play was about Rabbi Akiva and his students, who studied the *Toyre* while hiding from the Romans in forests and caves."[24]

- The *krakówiak*, a spirited dance in 2/4 time with syncopated rhythm, originated from the region near Kraków, which was the capital of Poland under the Piast and Jagiello dynasties. It became a popular ballroom dance in the mid-nineteenth century in Austria and France; in Parisian salons it was a symbol of solidarity with partitioned Poland.

- The *krentsl* (Yid.: group, gathering, huddle) was a circle dance in 2/4 time common among *khasidim*. It was sometimes danced without instruments on the Sabbath eve around the *rebe's tish* and on *Simkhes-Toyre*

---

[23] Interview with Michael Alpert, May 27, 2000.

[24] Interview with Shimon Rozner (originally from Bilki) in Beregove, Ukraine, August 23, 1997.

at the end of *Sukes*. (*Sukes* was the harvest festival, and *Simkhes-Toyre* celebrated the completion of the year's reading cycle of the *Toyre* and the renewal of the reading cycle that began that very night.)

• According to Beregovski, the *lancer* was first performed by the ballet in Berlin in 1857. It was similar to the quadrille, in 6/8 time, and popular among the upper class in Russia.

• The *mignon* was a French waltz, danced daintily, and popular among upper-class Poles and Russians (particularly the Francophiles).

• The *nign* was a popular, generally textless song in 2/4 time accompanied by either a line or circle dance at moderate tempo, although sometimes it accelerated to a presto, with spirited singing. Often these melodic forms of the *nigunim* were similar to the *freylekhs*.

• The *oberek* was a spirited, acrobatic circular Polish dance in 3/8 time, popular among the peasantry.

• The *patsh* or *pleskn* (Yid: clap) was a Jewish dance for the women, who stood in a circle with the bride in the middle. The women clapped during specific rhythmic passages celebrating the bride's marriage and her womanhood.

• The quadrille originated in early nineteenth-century France. It was a square dance in which four couples performed five complete movements. Like the *lancer*, it was in 2/4 time and popular among the Russian and Polish upper class.

• The *shtiler* (Yid.: quiet) was a kind of *patsh* dance, with clapping of hands and stomping of feet, but without music. It was popular among certain sects of *Khasidim*, who believed it taught the Jews how to worship God without noise and music.

• The *shtekn* (from the Yiddish *shtek*, stick) was created by the *batkhn* Eliakum Zunzer. The dance was similar to the game of musical chairs. A certain number of people would wave either a stick or broom in the air to the rhythm of the melody, around a group of chairs numbering one less than those who were dancing. When the music stopped, everyone ran to find a chair to sit in. The one left standing had to leave the dance. This continued until there was only dancer left. Rivkind remembered seeing the *shtekn* danced in the Wolozyn *yeshive* in Lodz before World War I: the students performed it during the intermediary days of *Sukes*.[25] Another version of this dance was the *bezem* (Yid.: broom) dance. I was told by Simkhe Bina Wajc from Pionki, Poland that there was a *bezem* dance at his sister's wedding: "The bride would sit in a chair in the middle of the room and different people came up and danced in front of her while holding the broom. Some used the broom to sweep the floor in front of the bride while the *kapelye* played. The sweeping meant that a path for the bride had been cleared of all life's obstacles. And that she should only know from happiness and never sadness."[26]

- The *sirba* was a traditional Romanian genre in circle, line, or couple formation in 2/4 time. It combined brisk running and hopping steps in short phrases emphasized by the triplets in the melody. The dance was also popular among Ukrainians, Hungarians, Ruthenians, and the Polish *gorale* (Pol.: highlanders) of the Tatra Mountains.

- The tango, an intricate dance with long gliding steps and elaborate poses, originated in Argentina and became very popular among Polish youth in the 1930s. Many of the most popular tangos of the day were composed by Jews. "Rebeka," which is still sung today in Polish cabarets, was composed by two Jews, Zygmunt Białostocki (music) and Andrzej Włast (lyrics), and tells the following tale. A young Jewish girl named Rebeka works at a kiosk selling cigarettes and other items. Every day a handsome man buys cigarettes from her, and she begins to imagine that the two of them are slowly falling in love with each other. But one day she is crushed when she sees the man with another woman sitting beside him in a car. The Jews called the song by its Jewish name, "Rivke," as did those Poles who considered the song a Jewish one.

- The *wingerka* (Rus.: Hungarian) was a dance whose melody sounded Hungarian; it was in two parts and in 4/4 time, and was enjoyed by the Russian and Polish upper classes.

---

[25] Rivkind, op. cit., pp. 33–34.

[26] Interview with Simkhe Bina Wajc in Warsaw, November 28, 1984.

- The *Terkisher gebet* (Yid.: Turkish prayer) was a Romanian *klezmer* display piece often played on a violin tuned in the "Turkish" style, with the A-string lowered a fifth to an E, enabling the violinist to play both strings simultaneously and create a unique octave sound. The melodies of this dance sounded Near Eastern due to the Turkish influence on Romania when it was part of the Ottoman empire.[27]

Emancipation and Decline

Ultimately the growing influence of the *haskole* became a threat to both the *misnaged* and *khasidic* rabbis, so they banded together. In 1804, for example, the civil government of Lithuania declared the right of every Jewish community to choose its own rabbis and build its own synagogue. The two factions learned to tolerate each other.

After the *khasidim* and *misnagdim* were able to settle their differences, the former put their energies into spreading *khasidism* throughout Eastern Europe. By the end of the nineteenth century there were *khasidic hoyfn* in Poland, Belarus-Lithuania, Ukraine, Eastern Galicia, Bukovina, Bessarabia, Transylvania, and in the Carpathian Mountains. The *khasidim* left an indelible mark in the *klezmer* world with their impassioned singing, playing (both sometimes improvisational), and dancing. Their tunes helped make up what Walter Zev Feldman calls "the core dance repertoire," which "had three major sources: 1) older Central European dance music, which by the nineteenth century had largely blended with 2) dances based on the Ashkenazic prayer modes and *khasidic nigunim,* and 3) Greco-Turkish dance music."[28]

At the same time as the *maskilim* (Heb: proponents of the *haskole*), *misnagdim,* and *khasidim* were changing in the social fabric of their communities, events outside those worlds were affecting Jewish life in lasting ways. The extensive French military campaigns of the Napoleonic era (1795–1814)

---

[27] Feldman, op. cit., pp. 23–24.
[28] Ibid., p. 5.

changed the political and social map of Europe several times. In the Germanic lands west of Prussia where the *haskole* began, the Holy Roman Empire was gradually eliminated between 1801 and 1806. As the German states were secularized, the Austrian Empire, proclaimed by Francis I (r. 1804–1835), emancipated the Jews and set into motion liberal policies that extended through the eve of World War I. Of the three empires—Russian, Ottoman, and Austro-Hungarian—that ruled the countries between Germany and the Black Sea, Jews were most tolerated under the imperial crown of the Habsburg-Ezterhazy family during the reign of Franz Joseph I (r. 1848–1916), when universal suffrage was granted to all the different nations in the Kaiser's empire. This was the first time Jews of Eastern Europe were able to vote.[29]

The Austro-Hungarian Jews loved Kaiser Franz Joseph and nicknamed him Froyim Yosl. Each year on his birthday, August 18th, the Jews in the cities, *shtetlekh,* and villages celebrated by decorating their homes and synagogues, then singing and dancing in homes and parading in the streets. In synagogues and *shtiblekh* (Yid.: houses; usually small *khasidic* houses of prayer), prayers were said for the well-being of the kaiser not only on his birthday but on every Sabbath and holiday. His liberal policies toward the Jews were still remembered seventy-five years after his death by those old enough to have lived in the Austro-Hungarian Empire. While doing field research in the Carpathian Mountains I met Yudl Schlesinger, who had been a carpenter, in the synagogue in Berhovo; one afternoon I went to his home in Velika Bigan, only ten kilometers away, where he told me, "Even in the twenties and thirties my father still talked about Franz Joseph and how wonderful he was for the Jews. Every August 18th—the Kaiser's birthday—he drank a toast to his health and hummed a melody he called 'Froyim Yosl's *Freylekh.*'" Unfortunately, Yudl remembered only a few bars of the tune.[30]

---

[29] Joachim Schönfeld, *Shtetl Memoirs: Jews in Galicia under Austria and in the Reborn Poland, 1898–1939* (Hoboken, New Jersey: KTAV, 1985), p. xx.

[30] Interview with Yudl Schlesinger (originally from Iršava, Ukraine) in Velika Bigan on July 13, 1992.

The emancipation of the Jews in Bohemia allowed some Jewish musicians to make the transition from *klezmer* to classical. One of the most famous composers with *klezmer yikhes* was Jacques Offenbach, whose father, Issac Juda Eberst, was born in Offenbach in 1779, and had been an itinerant cantor, voice teacher, violinist, and *klezmer.* Eventually Issac settled in Deutz, near Cologne, where he joined a *klezmer kapelye* (flute, *tsimbl,* and violin) in one of the town's taverns. After getting married (despite his father-in-law's displeasure that his daughter was marrying a *klezmer "yingle"*), he moved to Cologne and began calling himself Issac Offenbach, since he was already known among his peers as the "Offenbacher" Jew. He still performed at Jewish festivities, but also taught guitar, flute, violin, and voice, and composed choral music for his local synagogue. The *haskole* was in full force at this time and duly influenced Issac Offenbach's synagogue compositions. "He was satisfied with his modest position as 'Chassan.' In this capacity he belonged to a certain group of 'Chassans' who were responsible for the deterioration of synagogue music as a direct consequence of the emancipation of the Jews in 1800."[31] Years later, several of Issac Offenbach's compositions were given new life in his son's operettas *The Duchess of Gerolstein* and *The Bridge of Sighs.*

After the Congress of Vienna (June 1815), the German *haskole* movement swept through the Germanic Confederation (a mutual defensive alliance of thirty-nine princes of independent states, including twelve of Austria's mostly Germanic provinces and four free cities), forcing many German *klezmorim* to travel outside of the Confederation in search of employment. Leaving Moravia and Bohemia, they sought employment in Silesia (a province of Prussia), in eastern Hungary (part of the Austrian Empire), and in Poland and Galicia (both part of the Russian Empire). In Moravia and Bohemia there was less and less work, as Jewish families were not hiring large *kapelyes,* or were not having *klezmer* music as often at their religious or secular functions. And the *klezmorim* were tired of the various local taxes they had to pay to be allowed to perform. Here is one example of the

---

[31] Paul Nettl, *Forgotten Musicians* (New York: Philosophical Library, 1957), p. 42.

demise of *klezmer* music in the mid-nineteenth century, as told by Ludwig Phillipson, who grew up in Dessau, Germany:

> I remember the community feast that was held when I was a boy. There was so much joy as the *klezmorim,* the Jewish music band, played their happy tunes. They were all fine musicians. There was violin, *bratsche,*[32] bass-violin, flute, and French horn. Even the peasants from the villages came. Every year a few people would not want to come to the meal, so the *klezmorim* would go and play tunes outside of their house and convince them to come. Eventually the event was not held outdoors anymore, as the local Jews did not want to call attention to themselves. Finally the community feast was canceled and the *klezmorim* found other work to do.[33]

Here is an example of a *klezmer* who moved to Breslau, Silesia (Prussia) but could not stay: the local *klezmorim* did not want the competition, so they put pressure on the local non-Jewish authorities to have him expelled.

> Sometimes foreign *klezmorim* did not have permission to perform in Silesia, like Samson Rind, who came there from Mannheim (Confederation of the Rhine) in 1802. After two years in Prussia, he was forced to leave with his wife and two children. In Breslau, he wanted to earn a living playing zither, and with his mouth he would imitate bird calls. Instead of receiving permission to perform he was asked to leave because he was a foreign "beggar Jew." If he did not leave the province immediately he would be fined and deported.[34]

---

[32] *Bratsche* (Ger.): viola. Sometimes *bratsche* meant the second violin (or *sekund* in Yiddish) as well. The one who played *bratsche* or *sekund* in the *kapelye* generally only played rhythmic chords.

[33] Albert von Wolf, *Fahrende Leute bei den Juden* (Berlin: Mitteilungen zur Jüdische Volkskunde, 1909), vols. 24–32, p. 19.

[34] Ibid.

The Austrian *klezmorim* that traveled to Silesia in the beginning of the nineteenth century searching for work often encountered such obstacles, not from Christian musicians or local authorities, but rather from Polish *klezmorim* from the duchy of Warsaw who had also traveled to Silesia for work, and from the local Silesian *klezmorim,* neither of whom welcomed the competition or wanted the privilege of *schutzjuden* (Ger.: protected Jews)[35] extended to other *klezmorim.*

Some of the better-known *kapelyes* that traveled throughout Silesia (Breslau, Falkenberg, Fraustadt, Gleiwitz, Hundsfelt, Kronstadt, Lissa, Schrau, Trebnitz, Wartenberg, and other towns) were the Kempner and Rogoznicer; their Austrian counterparts were the Zulzer and Hotzenplotzer *kapelyes.* These *kapelyes* often passed each other on the roads as they traveled to their respective weddings, usually without incident. But sometimes they stopped to argue about who should be in the area. Occasionally civil discussions would lead to heated arguments and even fistfights, with the instruments bearing the brunt of the damage. At times a *kapelye* would have the audacity to take the time and effort (before his own wedding job) to go to the local Christian authorities, asking them not to let the competition play at a wedding, even if it meant that there would be no music at all—or, at minimum, force his rivals to pay a "performance" tax.

One of the best-known and longest-lived *kapelyes* of that region and time was the Kempner *kapelye* (from Kempen, near Posen) of Prussia. They performed throughout Bohemia, Moravia, Lower Silesia (all part of the Austrian Empire), and Silesia from the mid-nineteenth century through the eve of World War I. They were so famous that they were asked to play for Kaiser Wilhelm I and his son the crown prince on two different occasions. The five musicians in the *kapelye* could all read music, which was usually not the case with *klezmorim.* The instrumentation was flute, clarinet, vio-

---

[35] The local *graf* granted protection to certain Jews, generally the only ones in the vicinity who provided him with a specific service. The skills the *graf* wanted were usually financial, clerical, or linguistic, but sometimes artistic as well.

lin, viola, and *brummbass;*[36] when they performed in Markish-Friedland, Prussia, an old man often played *tsimbl* with them. Their wedding repertoire consisted of the usual Jewish dance melodies, military marches, and patriotic songs; but at festivals and in restaurants they also sang songs not common among *klezmorim* in this region, including political, humorous, and popular theatrical verses.

Many Silesian *klezmorim* also found work in Warsaw at this time (the city was occupied by Prussia from 1796 to 1807). The Prussians wanted Warsovians to have an easier life during the occupation, so they sent for Prague and Silesian *klezmorim* to come and entertain them. The *klezmorim* played for Jews and non-Jews alike at taverns and parties; this was the first time the Jews had heard German melodies. The popularity of the *klezmorim* grew so great that dance halls were built just to accommodate the huge crowds. The *klezmorim* also introduced the *katarynka,* a music box they brought with them from the Tyrol, which eventually became synonymous with Warsovian street life.[37]

The Tsimbl

During my travels I encountered a number of Rom *tsimbalists* who asked me to play with them. Having never seen a *tsimbl* until I had visited Eastern Europe, I became curious about this instrument that was such a vital part of *klezmer kapelyes* in the nineteenth century through World War I. Once as popular as the violin, the *tsimbl* came in several sizes and shapes and was the grandfather of the piano.

The *tsimbl's* origins lie in the ancient psaltery. The idea of the beaten psaltery, or dulcimer, probably came first from China; the instrument

---

[36] The *brummbass* (Ger.: buzz bass) may have been a type of a *tromba marina,* an Italian single-stringed bowed instrument that had a very long and narrow body. It was used sporadically through the eighteenth century. Most likely it was a bass that had a piece of paper set under the strings near the end of the fingerboard, giving it a buzzing percussive sound when bowed.
[37] Geshuri, op. cit., p. 476.

then traveled to India and gradually westward into Iran, where they called it a *santour,* and Greece, where they called it a *santouri.* In the late Middle Ages the instrument was quite popular in Germany, Switzerland, and Bohemia, where it was called a *hackbrett.* It was trapezoidal in shape with many strings tuned chromatically, sloping alternately to left and right, which made it easier for the wooden hammers (beaters) to hit them. These hammers often had wound thread around them to help dampen the shimmering *tremolando* (It.: quavering) sound. The smaller *tsimbl,* the one used by most *klezmorim,* was held by straps hung over the shoulders and could be played while standing and walking, especially during the processional and recessional of a wedding. The most developed *tsimbl* is the one the Rom still play in Hungary, Transylvania, Moldavia (Romania), and Carpathian Ukraine (the *tsimbl* was originally introduced to these regions by Galician Jews in the early eighteenth century). This instrument, called *cimbalom,* is much larger than a *tsimbl* (approximately thirty to thirty-six inches wide and standing twenty-four to thirty inches from the ground), with a damper pedal (like the piano). Those who played a *tsimbl* without a damper pedal used their elbows to dampen the ringing.

The *tsimbalist* could create a haunting drone under the sonorous sounds of the violin or could solo with the accompaniment of the *sekund.* The *doyne, vulekhl,* and *taksim* were three pieces particularly suited to the *tsimbl*-violin combination.

- The *doyne,* or, in Romanian, *doina,* was a rubato, semi-improvised melody that was the cornerstone of Romanian *klezmer* repertoire. In this listening piece, the *klezmer* showed off his virtuosity through improvisation and *fioritura* (It.: musical ornamentation), imitating the coloratura of the *khazn.* This expressive and plaintive melody was often played during the *bazetsn* or for the newlyweds and their parents while they dined. The folk tale behind the plaintive tune told of a shepherd's grief upon finding that he had lost his flock, and how he took out his *nai* (Rom.: panpipe) and played this lament. Gradually, as the sheep responded and returned, the melody segued into a lively, ecstatic *bulgar.* Today the playing of at least one *doyne* in a *klezmer* concert is a must and is often the highlight of the performance. *Klezmorim*, especially clarinetists, love to display their skills and sing the "Jewish blues" this way.

• The *vulekhl* (Yid.: little Wallachian) originated from the Romanian province of Wallachia and was similar to the *doyne,* with the same tetrachordal scale (d-e-f-g#-a-b-c-d). It became a prayer melody sung in several synagogues in Moldavia during the High Holidays after the Ba'al Shem Tov visited the synagogue in Piatra Nemţ on *Yom Kiper* eve. In commemoration of the pogroms the Jews in Wallachia underwent between 1456 and 1462, he sang a *vulekhl* to the *Ya'ale V'yavo* (Heb.: he will rise and he will come) prayer, using the 3/8 triple meter common to the Romanian *hora.*

• The *taksim* was another kind of display piece that utilized improvisation mixed with *fioritura.* It derived from Arabic music, and became popular in Romania through Turkish influence. It was part of the *klezmer's* repertoire during the nineteenth century, but by the twentieth century most *klezmorim* played the *doyne* instead. Beregovski confirms this: "The younger *klezmorim* don't even recognize the concept of *taksim;* they have played *doynes* instead of *taksims* since the beginning of the twentieth century; in addition to the fiddler, the clarinet or flute used to play solos at the table."[38]

After a plaintive *doyne* the *tsimblist* often immediately went into a melodic, rhythmic, and percussive lead in a *freylekh* or *skotshne.* Tsimbalists usually were part of small *klezmer* string ensembles (violin and bass or cello) or performed as soloists. After World War I, the larger *klezmer* ensembles were primarily made up of some combination of woodwinds, brass, percussion, and a few strings, which made the inclusion of *tsimbl* nearly impossible. Despite its size, the *tsimbl* could not compete in volume with the brass instruments, and it was difficult to tune. Today very few *klezmer* bands include a *tsimbalist.*

---

[38] Slobin, op. cit., p. 539.

But the *tsimbl* was once extremely popular among all folk musicians, from Riga to Turkey to the German lands, and especially so among the Jews of Galicia, Bessarabia, and Belarus and among the Rom of Transylvania and Maramureş. Some of these Rom played in *klezmer kapelyes;* others often included *klezmer* music in their regular repertoires; and others played the *tsimbl* accompanying a chained dancing bear. This circuslike act, originally from Rajasthan, India, spread through parts of the Balkans and Northern Europe; written sources tell of *klezmorim* in Riga in May 1694 marching with their *tsimbls* while their bears followed behind.

This custom of having a bear dance while a *klezmer* performed (usually on violin or *tsimbl*) carried into the nineteenth century, but instead of on the streets, the *kapelye* usually performed in front of some Polish landowners or aristocrats, and rather than using a real bear, a Jew would dress up in a bear costume. However, this kind of performance was a means of deliberately humiliating the dancer and the *klezmorim.* One of the most popular tunes played during these performances was a Polish folk melody that the *klezmorim* had incorporated into their repertoire and that had spread throughout Poland, Ukraine, Belarus, and Russia, becoming the nineteenth-century equivalent of "Hava Nagila." The tune had many names but was most often called "Ma Yofis" (Heb.: how beautiful). Eventually playing "Ma Yofis" just meant ridicule and humiliation, so most Jews stopped playing it; those who still performed it, or said or did things just to please the Polish landowners or aristocracy, were called *Mayofisniks*— the nineteenth-century equivalent of "self-hating Jews."

One of the earliest sources to mention the *tsimbalist* was the town chronicle of Lissa (Leszno), Silesia. In 1662 a *tsimbalist* there, the first mentioned in this region, was granted permission to play. From then through the end of the eighteenth century several legal privileges were granted to the *klezmorim* of Lissa, allowing them to perform at all functions without interference from Christian musicians, except at non-Jewish weddings and baptisms. Ludwig Kalish, who was born in 1814 and grew up in Lissa, also remembered a *klezmer kapelye* from his childhood:

There was this band of Jewish musicians, all of whom were talented, but especially the *tsimbalist*. He had a talent like that of the gypsies, a "natural musician" who could read notes. The group performed at happy festivities and were well paid, especially when they played at a wedding party for a rich family. They performed in very strange clothes. They wore very long caftans[39] and tremendously high conical hats made from quilted material. They looked ridiculous and people told all sorts of anecdotes about them.[40]

Of the many different types of *klezmer* instrumentalists, the *tsimbalists* were some of the most colorful characters. Franciszek Syzmala, a tourist from Paris, wrote in 1832: "Many of these musicians were craftsmen and peddlers traveling from village to village by foot or, in the best case, with a broken-down cart pulled by a starving horse. In addition to selling goods and playing music, they sold books and smuggled political booklets across borders. Despite the Czar's threats and border guards, these traveling tradesmen also provided music at inns and at village weddings."[41]

Some of the more famous *tsimbalists* were:

- Yankl the *Tsimbler*, a heroic character in Adam Mickiewicz's (1798–1855) famous Polish national epic poem *Pan Tadeusz*. Yankl is based upon the real-life *tsimbalist* (he also played cittern) Yankl Liebermann, whom Mickiewicz heard play in St. Petersburg. Known among his patrons as Yankl Tsimbalist, he was respected by both Jews and the Polish aristocracy.
- Mortko (Mordecai) Fajerman (1810–1895), one of the most renowned *tsimbalists* in Poland, especially in Warsaw. Fajerman mostly performed as a soloist, but for a period in the 1880s he led a small all-Rom *kapelye* that performed both *klezmer* and Rom music.

---

[39] These caftans were long garments with wide sleeves that were fastened with a sash or belt. Orthodox Jewish men, especially *khasidim*, wore them as everyday outer garments. In Yiddish the caftan was called a *kapote*.

[40] Wolf, op. cit., p. 155.

[41] Marian Fuks, *Muzyka Ocalona* (Warsaw: Wydawnictwa Radia I Telewizji, 1989), p. 36.

- The Lepianski family from Vitebsk, Belarussia (today Belarus), who all played the *tsimbl*. In Vitebsk and its environs the *tsimbl* was common both in *kapelyes* or in a duo with the Russian *husle*.[42] Yosef ben Yitzkhok was the first in the Lepianski family to study the *tsimbl*, and became a soloist playing in synagogues, for weddings, and in concerts like the one he gave at the 1902 St. Petersburg Ethnographic Exhibition. By 1917, his four young sons joined their father and they formed a *tsimbl* orchestra. Eventually only three sons stayed in the *kapelye*: Mikhail played the lead melody, Yehoshua played the second voice, Matitiahu played chords, and the father played the bass line. They became well-known and continued to play into the 1930s in the Soviet Union, with Yehoshua's daughter Helena joining the *kapelye* in the early thirties.[43]

Lastly, there was Mikhl Joseph Guzikow (1809–1837), the most famous and admired *klezmer* in Europe of his day and perhaps of all time. He was born in Shklov, Belarus, to a family of *klezmorim*: his father, a flautist, was the leader of a *kapelye* made up mostly of Mikhl and his other brothers. Taught by his father, Guzikow learned the flute and played some clarinet and oboe; but because of weak lungs and shortness of breath, he learned to play the *hakbreydl* (see the discussion of the *hackbrett* in Part I). Eventually Guzikow formed his own *kapelye* and traveled throughout the province of Mogilev. Once he performed in General-Governor Woroncow's home, where the French poet Alphonse de Lamartine (1790–1869) heard him; the latter later helped Guzikow's career. Gusikow then gave concerts

---

[42] A *husle*, also known as a *gusle* in Ukrainian, was an instrument with two or three strings and a bow. It was played with the fingertips or the flat of the fingernails pressing lightly on the strings without pressing them to the fingerboard. All the notes were thus produced as harmonics, with a softer sound than a violin.

[43] Joachim Stutschevsky, *Ha-Klezmorim: Toldotehem, Orakh-hayahem, v'Yezirotehem* (Jerusalem: Bialik Institute, 1959), p. 70. Russian musicologist Nicolai Findeisen wrote about the *tsimbl* and specifically the Lepianski *kapelye* in an article called "Yevreiskie Tsimbali i Tsimbalisti Lepianski" [Leningrad, 1926].

in Moscow, Odessa, and Kiev; the Polish virtuoso violinist Karol Lipinski, Paganini's primary competitor, said, "Actually, Guzikow, you are a greater artist than I am. I was modern in how I interpreted the music, but you have created a style for yourself."[44]

When Guzikow moved to Warsaw he played in the streets, courtyards, cafés, and restaurants, carrying his bag of straw and wooden bars. His repertoire included *mazurkas,* polonaises, and Russian, Ukrainian, and *klezmer* pieces, along with transcriptions from popular classical compositions by Rossini, Weber, Paganini, Hummel, Mendelssohn, and others. In the 1830s Guzikow's international career began when he played in Berlin, Frankfurt, and Leipzig; in the latter city Mendelssohn was so taken with his virtuosity that he wrote about him in a letter to his mother.[45] Newspapers throughout Europe sang his praise: "The clarity of the tone is incredible. It seemed as if the angels were blowing into the straws."[46]

Franz Liszt saw Guzikow in Paris and wrote to George Sand (who was rumored to be Guzikow's lover), "He was really and truly amazing."[47] After the Paris concert, Guzikow was offered a four-year contract for 32,000 francs to play flute and be oboe concertmaster, health permitting, with the Theatre de Royal de St. Charles in Naples, but he refused because of his lung ailment which eventually turned into tuberculosis. During a trip back to Poland from Germany, where he had spent most of the summer recuperating, he stopped in Aachen, where he was asked to give a concert. On October 21, 1837, Guzikow collapsed on stage. He was buried in Aachen.

After Guzikow died, Yankel Eben of Vilna (who was a friend of and

---

[44] Fuks, op. cit., p. 41.

[45] Felix Mendelssohn, *Mendelssohn's Letters from 1833 to 1847,* translated by Lady Wallace (Philadelphia: Frederick Leypoldt, 2nd ed. 1865), pp. 98–99. "I am curious to learn whether Guzikow pleased you as much as he did me. He is quite a phenomenon; a famous fellow, inferior to no virtuoso in the world, both in execution and facility; he therefore delights me more with his instrument of wood and straw, than many with their pianofortes, just because it is such a thankless kind of instrument."

[46] Fuks, op. cit., p. 44.

[47] Ibid., p. 43.

worked with Eliakum Zunzer) became his musical successor in Poland, composing as well as playing the *hakbreydl* and several other instruments. After he toured Tilsit, Königsberg, Elbing, and Danzig, the critics praised him as an extraordinary talent and humble person. Unfortunately they also always compared Eben to Guzikow, his mentor, and wished he could produce a better tone—one closer to Guzikow's—from his instrument.

Jewish Music in Hungary

Jewish musicians played a vital role in disseminating and interpreting Hungarian and Rom folk music during the eighteenth and beginning of the nineteenth centuries. Jews played in Rom orchestras so often that Franz Lizst called these bands *Jüdische Zigeunerkapellen* (Ger.: Jewish-Gypsy orchestras) and falsely said, "For ninety years Gypsy music did not exist, but thanks to the Jewish musicians, it spread from Vambéry across all of Asia to the Ganges."[48] During the reign of Austrian Empress Maria Theresa (1740–1780), several of the *klezmer* musicians in her official court orchestra came from Hungary and played Hungarian tunes. And Jewish historian Albert Wolf wrote in 1909:

> There are still a few *klezmorim* in Hungary today. One of the best known conductors today is Lajos (Ludwig) Bikszenspann, who leads his own *klezmer kapelye*. And when there is no Jewish work for the *klezmer*, the musicians often will find work in the Gyspy bands. Sometimes they are even the *primas*[49] of the band. Today *klezmer* Poldi Feher (Leopold Weiss) is the *primas* of one of the best known Gypsy orchestras in Hungary.[50]

---

[48] Lehrer L. Von Schlosz, "Jüdisches Zigeunerkapelle in Ungarn," *Mitteilungen zur Jüdische Volkskunde*, Ed. Dr. M. Grunwald (Berlin: Verlag S. Calvary, 1907), Vol. 23, p. 65.
[49] *Primas* (It.): first; the leader (usually the violinist) of the band.
[50] Wolf, op. cit., p. 6.

Wealthy non-Jewish Hungarian landowners often hired *klezmorim* instead of Rom musicians to play Rom and *klezmer* music. This was because the Rom were on the lowest rung of the social ladder and were considered by many *gaje* (Romani: non-Rom) as pariahs. In Romania, Rom had no civil rights, and were slaves until they were emancipated in 1864.

In the eighteenth and nineteenth centuries the European nobility and cultural elite romanticized and created myths about the Rom, and hired Rom musical virtuosi. However, this exalted acceptance and worship was short-lived and practiced by few. Because the Rom steadfastly clung to their independence and itinerant ways, they remained outcasts, the "untouchables" of European society. False stories circulated about roving Rom bands who would steal from their audiences and even sexually violate some women. These stories were hard to dispel and, ironically, helped the *klezmorim* economically. The prevailing perception among non-Jews was that Jews never became publically inebriated and were less likely to approach non-Jewish women. Thus if an employer wanted Rom music and a *klezmer kapelye* was available, the latter were often hired in place of a real Rom band.

While the *klezmorim* helped disseminate Rom melodies across parts of Central and Eastern Europe and the Balkans by including them in their repertoire, the Rom themselves, who had left in various waves between the seventh and twelfth centuries from northwestern India, were the main disseminators of their own folk music—and helped to spread some *klezmer* melodies as well.

The tradition of the Rom in Moldavia/Bessarabia playing in *klezmer kapelyes* continued into the twentieth century. While doing research in Yas (Iaşi), Romania, I met Paul Babici, a Rom who had played the tenor sax in several different Jewish *kapelyes* for forty years. He told me:

> My father played the *tsimbl* with some Jews in the twenties and thirties throughout Moldavia. Once he traveled to Ştefăneşti with this violinist named Avram Bughici. It was for a Jewish festival in the spring [*Legboymer*]. The *tsadek* [Heb.: pious, saintly; the leader of a *khasidic*

sect] was celebrating with all his followers that whole day and night. Just before they were to leave to go home, the *tsadek* asked my father rather than Avram to play a solo piece for him. Avram had been playing all the solos while my father played rhythm and harmony. So my father played his solo and the *tsadek* was so pleased he gave him this small wine cup. My father told him that whenever he would make a toast from the wine cup he would remember the *tsadek* of Ștefănești and the wonderful time he had playing for him.[51]

From the end of the eighteenth through most of the nineteenth century, the Jews of Toponar (today Slovakia) were some of the best-known and popular of the Hungarian *klezmorim.* In Mihaly Vitez Csokonai's 1773 epic poem *Dorottya,* a section describes the *klezmorim* (violinists and *tsimbalists*) of Toponar, led by one Isak, as playing with fire and enthusiasm until the morning, as everyone danced and drank wine.

Several *klezmer* bands also lived in the southwest part of Hungary proper at this time, namely in Kaposvár and Zala. One of the more famous *klezmer* families from this region was the Finalyschen band, who traveled throughout this region, even into Croatia-Slavonia and Styria, and who included Anschel Finaly, a well-known *klezmer* who conducted a court orchestra and is buried in the Jewish cemetery in Obuda.

Another well-known Hungarian *klezmer* musician was Joseph Schlesinger, born in 1794, who was famous for his flute playing and in particular for the *klezmer* nuances he gave to Jewish and Hungarian folk tunes. At an early age he showed a great talent for music, playing both the violin and piano by ear, but was forced to leave home because he did not want to become a businessman like his father. He joined the Hungarian army and served in Serbia, where he became the conductor of his regiment's wind ensemble. After his military duty he decided to go to Bonyhad because they had a Jewish Music Society, the head of which was Mordecai Rosenthal

---

[51] Interview with Paul Babici, in Yas, Romania, March 23, 1988.

(Márkusz Rószavólgyi, 1787–1848).[52] Rosenthal, who had been guest conductor of the Vienna Symphony Orchestra for thirty years, welcomed the young Schlesinger into his own orchestra and had him learn to play the flute, since that chair was vacant. The orchestra traveled around central and southwestern Hungary performing for Jews and Christians.

However popular these *kapelyes* and individual *klezmorim* were, by the late nineteenth and early twentieth centuries the itinerant *klezmer* in Hungary proper had all but vanished due to Jewish assimilation in the western and central parts of the Austro-Hungarian Empire.[53] By 1860, the Jews of Western and Central Europe had consented, as a price of their "emancipation" from discriminitory legislation, to be listed in the censuses of the various countries in which they lived not as a linguistic national group, but only as members of the Mosaic faith. (But in the eastern part of the Empire—specifically in Galicia, Bukowina, and Carpathian Ruthenia—as well as in the Russian Empire, the "national" character of the Jews remained relatively intact due to the strong influence of the orthodox and *khasidim* until the eve of World War I.) As the Jews eliminated many of their religious traditions, there was less music work in the Jewish communities, sometimes forcing Rom musicians and *klezmorim* into bidding wars, which meant lower earnings for everyone. Those *klezmorim* who managed to earn a living did so by staying closer to home (or at home) and supplementing their music incomes with more regular day jobs. Thus, by the beginning of the twentieth century, the *klezmorim* in Hungary proper mostly lived in the Carpathian region: Maramureş, Bereg, and Ung; a few *klezmorim* also remained in Kaposvár, Nagykanizsa, Szeged, Érsekújvár, and Budapest.

---

[52] Mordecai Rosenthal was a famous composer and arranger; one of his arrangements is of the famous Hungarian melody "Rakoczi March," still played at the end of most concerts or dances in Hungary as a signal to the audience/dancers that it is time to go home.

[53] The Austro-Hungarian Empire (1848–1914) included Austria and parts of northeastern Italy (Trieste) to the west; Slovenia, Croatia, and Bosnia to the south; Bohemia and Moravia to the north; Hungary in the center; Galicia to the northeast; and Transylvania and Bukowina to the east.

From the turn of the twentieth century through the 1920s, several Hungarian *klezmorim* tried to make a living playing in the coffeehouses of Budapest. The most famous was Elek Város, who conducted one of the best bands of the time; he was so good that the Austro-Hungarian government sent him to the Paris Exposition, where he performed at the Hungarian hotel everyday. *Klezmorim* who couldn't find work in Budapest often went to the Romanian border during the 1920s and '30s, boarded the trains there, and played for the passengers (particularly for Jews traveling for business or visiting relatives) during the long trip back to Budapest.

In Ocna Mureș, Romania (in Transylvania, south of Cluj-Napoca) I met Herman Blau, a Hungarian Jew who had been a *klezmer* flautist and wheelwright. He told me:

> When I was sixteen I played with my father in a small *kapelye*. My father played violin, a cousin played bass, and I played flute and drums. We played for both Jews and non-Jews—weddings and dances in Ocna Mureș, but the better-paying jobs were in Kolozsvar [the Hungarian name for Cluj-Napoca] with the wealthy Jews. After World War I we had less work. Things changed after the war since we were no longer part of Hungary. Many of the Jews could not afford to pay us to come from Ocna Mureș so they hired some Gypsy musicians in Koloszvár, while others were just not as religious. They said this was a new country and new times.[54]

By the end of World War II, assimilation, changes in cultural tastes, and the murder of some 450,000 Hungarian Jews had virtually put an end to the strains of *klezmer* music. If Jewish music was played, it was most likely by Rom. A typical Rom band's repertoire included Rom and Hungarian folk tunes, classical, popular, and a few Jewish tourist tunes such as "Hava Nagila," "Haveynu Sholom Aleykhem," "Papirosn," "Sheyn Vi Di Levune,"

---

[54] Interview with Herman Blau (originally from Ocna Mureș) in Cluj, Romania, August 23, 1981.

and, from the 1960s on, songs from *Fiddler on the Roof* and Israeli songs such as "Yerushlayim Shel Zahav."[55] This "Jewrist" music, which was never part of the *klezmer* repertoire, is still played today, especially in the restaurants and cafés of Budapest; but now one can also hear real *klezmer* music.

While doing field research in Hungary in the early 1980s, I gave lectures and *klezmer* concerts throughout the country in community centers and private homes. At a concert I gave in Budapest in 1988 I met folklorist and ethnomusicologist Bob Cohen (the son of a Hungarian survivor) who had moved to Budapest from the United States to do *klezmer* research as well. In 1990 Cohen joined Hungary's first *klezmer* band since the Holocaust, the Budapest *Klezmer* Band, led by Ferenc Javori, who was originally from the Carpathian region of the former Austro-Hungarian Empire, Vinogradiv (formerly Nagyszöllös), Ukraine. Rather than draw from his childhood Carpathian environs, though, Javori chose to perform repertoire from Yiddish theatre and American *klezmer* from the 1920s, '30s, and '40s. Cohen, however, was more interested in researching and playing music that came from the region, so in 1993 he left the band to form his own group, Naye Kapelye, which specialized in performing the material Cohen had found in his field and archival research—the *klezmer* music of eastern Hungary and Romania in the *shtetlekh* prior to 1930.

The Shtetlekh *of the Pale*

Much of the traditional *klezmer* music performed today is based on the music of the *klezmorim* of Belarus, Lithuania, Poland, Romania, Russia, and Ukraine from the late nineteenth century to the eve of World War I. The earliest sound recordings (1895), the published and unpublished sheet

---

[55] For example, Janos Nemeth, a Rom *tsimbalist* whom I met, performed, with a bassist and violinist, all kinds of music (including "Jewrist") on a tourist ship that plied the Danube River. His nickname was "Alter Yid" (Yid: old Jew) since he still played the *tsimbl* in the Jewish style, and was the last in all of Hungary, according to him, to play this way.

music, and the oral histories from *klezmorim* who lived at that time all help to give us a more complete picture of the *klezmer* and his increasingly complex world.

The majority of these *klezmorim* at the turn of the century lived in the Pale of Settlement, a territory in Czarist Russia established in 1805, which comprised twenty percent of the total area of European Russia. Most Polish and Russian Jews (with the rare exception of some high school graduates, wealthy merchants, doctors, and ex-cantonists) were forced to live within this crowded (5,500,000 Jews in 1900), economically depressed area of twenty-five provinces from 1835 to 1915. Rural *shtetlekh,* such as Boyan (Bojani, Ukraine), Dawidgrodek (Davyd-Garadok, Belarus), Dorohoi, Hust, Kobrin (Kobryn, Ukraine), Nay Sants (Nowy Sącz, Poland), and Shpole (Spola, Ukraine), in which Jews often outnumbered non-Jews, dotted the landscape of the Pale, parts of the Austro-Hungarian Empire, and Romania.

Unfortunately, because of the power and popularity of such films as *Fiddler on the Roof* and *Yentl,* the *shtetl* image has been distorted beyond recognition. Yes, there were some idyllic, nostalgic times, but they were mixed with a good measure of daily rigors. Poverty was a constant companion, the streets and alleys were often muddy, the outlying areas were swampy, winters were harsh with snow and freezing temperatures, summers were replete with sweltering heat and swarms of mosquitoes, rabbis passed religious laws that other rabbis overruled, and coexistence with the non-Jewish neighbors was an up-and-down affair depending on the level of local anti-Semitism.

Within a *shtetl,* the social strata in the Jewish community were clearly demarcated, and the *klezmer*'s ranking was a fluid one. At most *shtetl simkhes* (Heb.: celebrations) the *klezmer*'s presence was assured, emphatic, and duly honored; and at a wedding it was nearly as important as that of the wedding couple. Several Yiddish sayings give a sense of how important the *klezmer* was in *shtetl* life:

- *Vos far a klezmer, aza khasene.* (The wedding's only as good as the *klezmer.*)

- *A levaye on geveyn iz vi a khasene on klezmer.* (A funeral without tears is like a wedding without a *klezmer.*)[56]
- *Az tsvay kaptsonim gayen tancn raysn zikh bay di klezmorim di strunes.* (When two paupers go dancing, the *klezmorim* play harder.)[57]
- *A khasene on klezmer iz erger fun a kale on a nadn.* (A wedding without a *klezmer* is worse than a bride without a dowry.)
- *Az a yesoyme gayt khasene hobn raysn bay di klezmorim di strunes.* (When an orphan girl got married, the *klezmer* played harder.)
- *A shtile khasene iz oomeglikh vi a shtetl on a betler.* (A quiet wedding is as impossible as a *shtetl* without a beggar.)[58]

The Wedding

Most weddings were not given by wealthy families. At poor weddings the *klezmorim* earned only a small amount of money from the bride's family. Most of the *klezmer's* earnings came from the guests, who "bought" dances to honor the newlyweds by approaching the *kapelmayster*[59] or the *batkhn*[60] and asking to pay for either one dance or several dances in a row, to be played in honor of the newlyweds. The *kapelmayster* or *batkhn* told them

---

[56] In an interview with Leopold Kozlowski (originally from Przemyslany, Poland, today Peremišljani, Ukraine) in Kraków, Poland, December 12, 1984, he gave me the following variant: "*A khasene on klezmer iz erger fun a levaye on trern*" (A wedding without klezmorim is worse than a funeral without tears).

[57] These three sayings are found in Moshe Beregovski, "Yidishe Instrumentale Folks-Muzik," *Kabinet far Derlernen di Yidishe Sovieteshe Literatur, Sprakh un Folklor, Folklor-Sektsye,* Kiev, 1937, p. 21.

[58] These last three are from an interview with Gedalia Mandel (originally from Skierniewice, Poland) in Dżieroniów, Poland, December 11, 1984.

[59] *Kapelmayster* (Yid.): leader of the band. The first violinist was generally the leader; if there was no violin in the group, the *kapelmayster* was often one of the lead melody instruments, such as clarinet, flute, or trumpet.

[60] The *batkhn* sometimes performed the *aroysrufn* (Yid.: calling out): in witty, florid speech, he would announce the names of those who wanted to honor the newlyweds with a dance or two. Then the *klezmorim* were paid and the music began.

the cost of the dance(s) and the money was put into a *pushke*.[61] The *puskhe* often was attached to the belt of the youngest *klezmer*, who was sometimes no more than ten or twelve years old, and was often the drummer.[62] In *kapelyes* with a *tsimbalist*, guests stuck the money in a *pushke* that hung either from the *tsimbl* or from his belt, thus explaining the saying, "*Az du gibst tsu der tsimbl gayt di tancn*" (As one pays the *tsimbl*, the dances continue).[63] After each dance the *klezmorim* stopped and the *kapelmayster* or *batkhn* would call out for another guest to honor the newlyweds or in-laws with a dance or two.

At a poor wedding the newlyweds' parents made sure to keep the *kapelye* happy—if not with money, then at least with generous portions of food and drink. If the wedding lasted a week, all the food and drink helped to make up for the meager earnings. At a rich wedding, the earnings were obviously better, but some hosts tried to save money and did not serve the *kapelye* the same fine food the guests were given. This disrespect often resulted in the *klezmorim* taking matters into their own hands, as this *klezmer* did:

> Once I was playing with my father at a wedding in Boiberik [Bibrka, Ukraine] when we took a short break for some food. It was a fancy rich wedding but all they gave us to eat was some tea and liverwurst sandwiches. So when we took the next break, Dugi Brandwein (bassist) and Shia Tsimbler (*tsimbalist*) went to the kitchen to fool around, drink some *mashke* (Heb.: liquor), and distract the female cooks and servers. As Shia distracted them, Dugi brought in his bass case and filled it with

---

[61] *Pushke* (Yid.): tin can, alms box. The *pushke* usually could only be opened from the bottom with a key and only in the *kapelmayster*'s home.

[62] The youngest was often responsible for holding the money during weddings and other celebrations because if a fight broke out (which often happened at non-Jewish gigs when the hosts became drunk) the youth had a lesser chance of getting beaten up and having the money stolen. During the fights adults fought among themselves and did not usually engage the youths, who were often the quickest runners and could escape the fastest. See the *Yizkor Bikher* chapter for examples of fights *klezmorim* encountered.

[63] Rivkind, op. cit., p. 23.

cooked goose, ducks, chickens, *kreplekh*,[64] and *kugl*.[65] Then Dugi dragged the bass case outside to the cold air, where he left it until after the wedding. After the wedding, which ended early in the morning, Dugi put his bass in the wagon with us as we rode home the twelve kilometers. There was no room to fit him, the bass, and the case in the wagon so he dragged and carried that heavy bass for three hours until he reached his home. Now he had enough food to feed his family for several weeks.[66]

Besides the wedding, the *klezmer* had to busy himself with all the pre- and postwedding customs. Before the engagement was announced, the bride's *nadn* (Heb.: dowry),[67] of which sometimes as much as a tenth was given to the *shtetl*'s poor, was thoroughly discussed and agreed upon between the prospective in-laws. Then, with the help of the *shatkhn* (Heb.: match-maker), the engagement agreement was signed by all and sealed by break-ing in half a ceramic dish with the groom and bride each keeping half. The *klezmorim* were then brought in to play for the *tnoim* (Heb.: engagement party). Each of the four weeks preceding the wedding had a special name: iron, copper, silver, and gold. During the first week the wedding clothes were sewn, special foods (honey cake, wine, chicken made with mead, etc.) were eaten, and the *klezmorim* played lively dances and a special *vivat* for the bride. During the last seven to eight days before the wedding, neither bride nor groom were supposed to leave their homes. To help make the time go by, friends would visit and *klezmorim* would play at the homes of the engaged couple each night, except on the Sabbath.

---

[64] *Kreplekh:* small fried (or sometimes boiled) pockets of dough (similar to Polish *pierogi)* filled with meat, cabbage, mushrooms, onions, or some other food.

[65] *Kugl* (Yid.): pudding. This could be a savory or sweet dish made either from potatoes, onions, garlic, and noodles or from cooked fruit and noodles.

[66] Interview with Leopold Kozlowski, op. cit.

[67] The *nadn* was very important. Some weddings were canceled because the bride's parents did not give as much in the *nadn* as they had agreed upon. Other times the bride's parents canceled the wedding because the future in-laws asked for more than everyone had agreed upon. Sometimes weddings were delayed until the issue of the *nadn* was rectified.

Two days before the *khupe* there was a meal given in honor of the groom, where he received special presents given to him by the bride: a *kitl*, *tales*, and *gartl* [68] with a distinctive silver buckle on it. On the next day the groom sent the bride a *sider* (Heb.: prayer book). [69]

The evening before the wedding, the bride was led to the *mikve* accompanied by the *klezmorim* and close women relatives and friends. "And they would play in the other room while the older women drank and danced, sometimes—and not so seldom—until their heads spun." [70] That same evening the *klezmorim* played at both the bride's and groom's homes.

If the groom did not live in the same town as the bride, then the *klezmorim* helped welcome him and his parents as they entered the *shtetl*:

> The men stopped a few kilometers outside of the *shtetl* while waiting for the arrival of the groom. A herald and the father of the bride harnessed up four horses to a coach and set forth to greet the groom with music. The groom and his family followed with great pride. Without any music the men would not have been able to walk in time. [The *klezmorim* played marches or *horas*.] The *klezmorim*, who had waited a long time for such a wedding, played the whole time proudly and loudly. Their music resounded over the entire *shtetl*. [71]

---

[68] *Kitl* (Yid.): a man's solemn white linen robe. Wearing the *kitl* was a sign of purity. It was worn on certain Jewish holidays, particularly on *Rosheshone* (Rosh Hashana, the Jewish New Year) and *Yom Kiper*. *Tales* (Heb.): a fringed prayer shawl. Wearing a *tales* in the synagogue on the Sabbath, certain holidays, and for being called up to the *Toyre* was mandatory for men thirteen and older who had a *bar mitsve*. Among some *Khasidim* (like the Stoliner) it was the custom to wear a *tales* only when you were married. *Gartl* (Yid.): belt, sash. The *gartl* was worn by orthodox and *Khasidic* men, separating the holy spiritual upper half of the body from the profane bodily functions of the lower half.

[69] J. B. Levy, "Jüdische Hochzeitgebräuche Im Alten Frankfurt," *Ost und West*, Ed. Leo Winz, Vol. 14 (Berlin: Verlag Ost Und Leo Winz, June 1914), p. 428.

[70] S. Weissenberg, "Eine Jüdische Hochzeit in Sudrussland," *Mitteilungen zur Jüdischen Volkskunde 1898–1929*, Vol. 15 (1905), p. 64.

[71] Abraham Barnholtz, "Leybele's Khasene un di Khasene in Shtetl," in *Yiskor-Bukh tsu Vlodave*, Ed. Shimon Kanc (Tel Aviv: Wlodowa Societies in Israel and North and South America, 1974), p. 333.

Sometimes the *klezmorim* received a small fee or a gift of bread called *beknbroyt*[72] for coming to the outskirts of the *shtetl* and welcoming the groom. Occasionally the *kapelye* would then split in two, one part going with the groom, playing at his *tish,* and accompanying him to the *khupe,* the other entertaining the bride as she prepared for the wedding ceremony, then accompanying her to the *khupe.* At the *khupe* the two halves once again joined together for the recessional and wedding feast activities.

Occasionally, however, rather than one *kapelye* splitting into two, the reverse happened, as Aron Gluck related to me:

> My oldest sister Khaya told me I should go to Czortkow and hire the *kapelye* there since our *shtetl,* Budzanów, didn't have a *kapelye.* The Czortkow *kapelye* were known in our *shtetl* since they had played for other celebrations there. I went and gave a deposit of some money to the leader of the *kapelye,* the cellist. In return he gave me a gold ring which guaranteed that they would be there on the day of the wedding ready to play for the arriving groom. Then my sister, for no apparent reason, changed her mind and decided she wanted the *kapelye* from Skalat, near Tarnopol [Ternopil, Ukraine], instead. I sent a telegram to the Czortkow [Čortkiv, Ukraine] *kapelye* saying they shouldn't come, but they replied that they had turned down another wedding engagement for my sister's and were coming to play. When both *kapelyes* arrived to welcome the groom they realized they knew each other. Altogether there were twelve *klezmorim* in the two *kapelyes,* both of which we had to pay for. It was a big deal for our small *shtetl* to have so many *klezmorim* at a wedding. It was also very expensive.[73]

---

[72] *Beknbroyt* (Yid.): baked bread. The groom's side of the family gave a special *beknbroyt,* sometimes with money in it, to the *klezmer kapelye* as a gesture of good will, laying the groundwork for a problem-free wedding celebration. See Rivkind, op. cit., p. 21.

[73] Interview with Aron Gluck (originally from Budzanów, Poland) in New York City, February 2, 1984.

Weddings could be any day of the week except on the Sabbath. In Germany, weddings were often on Friday afternoon, just before the Sabbath, because that was the day that man was created. When this was the case, non-Jewish musicians were sometimes hired to play during the Sabbath, as *klezmorim* were forbidden by Jewish law. But some weddings that began on the Sabbath eve had music only for the processional and recessional; the evening wedding meal was accompanied with singing, and the next day the newlyweds came to the synagogue and celebrated with a big *kidesh*[74] after services. Only that evening, after *havdole*,[75] did the real celebrating begin, with the *kapelye* playing until daybreak, as well as during the *sheva brukhes* for the next six days. The celebrating ended in the synagogue the following Friday evening, just as the Sabbath was to begin. Some couples got married on a Tuesday because it was said that on the third day of creation (Tuesday) God was especially pleased: the phrase "It was good" appears twice (Genesis 1:10–12).

On the wedding day itself the *klezmorim* were extremely busy. First there was the groom's *tish* and then the bride's *bazetzn, baveynen,* and *badekn,* all before the processional to the *khupe* began. Sometimes no music was played for the bride and groom as they marched (often with their heads bowed) toward the *khupe.* Other times the music was rather solemn, reflecting the religious significance of the wedding ceremony, the seriousness of the choices the bride and groom had made about embarking on a new life together, and the stress and fatigue the couple experienced from the wedding fast that had begun the night before. In Frankfurt, it was still the

---

[74] *Kidesh* (Heb.): benediction over the wine. The *kidesh* was a meal that immediately followed the synagogue service: wine, whiskey, *khale,* chickpeas, and honey cake were the common dishes in the synagogue, but most Jews had a *kidesh* in their homes, where these foods along with *tsholnt* (a traditional Sabbath dish consisting of meat, potatoes, beans, barley, and onions, cooked on a low fire for twenty-four hours beginning on Friday) were served. In America some synagogues began the tradition of serving a larger *kidesh.* For very poor Jews in Eastern Europe, the *kidesh* provided a free small meal.

[75] *Havdole* (Heb.): separation, distinction. The *havdole* ceremony performed at the close of the Sabbath distinguished the Sabbath's holiness from the profaneness of the regular work week. The ceremony used a special twisted candle and a blessing over wine and spices.

custom in the 1910s and 1920s to play *Kol Nidre* as the groom walked towards the *khupe*. One informant told me that at her wedding in 1925 the *klezmer* violinist, accompanied by alto horn, played a *zogekhts* based upon the *Unesane-Tokef* (Heb.: let us declare), a prayer sung on *Rosheshana*.[76]

Before World War I in parts of eastern Germany, Moravia, and Bohemia, the *klezmorim* often played the *Ma'an* (from the Hebrew *may-on*, refusal) *nign* at weddings. This gave the bride and groom the opportunity to change their minds about getting married while standing under the *khupe*. This custom arose because many marriages had been arranged by the parents with the help of a *shatkhn* (Heb.: matchmaker, marriage broker), and the parents may have coerced the bride and groom to go through with the marriage ceremony. Though one could afterwards get a Jewish divorce, it was not easy, especially for the wife. So when the *Ma'an nign* was played and sung it expressed the couple's true love and happiness for each other. Neither left each other to stand alone under the *khupe*. After the singing, Psalm 147 verse 14[77] was recited because the numerical value of the last three words in the verse, 519, was the same as the words *khosn v'kale*.[78]

After the groom smashed the glass with his foot, everyone shouted "*Mazltov!*" Immediately the *klezmorim* broke into a lively dance leading the guests to either the local inn, the bride's, a wealthy relative's, or a family friend's home. As the wedding couple left, wheat or corn kernels were sometimes thrown at them as a symbol of fruitfulness. Other times, money was thrown for *tsdoke* (Heb.: charity, alms) to be later picked up by the poor

---

[76] Interview with Motl Zogot (originally from Zaporižžja, Ukraine), in Dnipropetrovs'k, Ukraine, July 10, 2000.

[77] Psalm 147, verse 14: "He Who makes your borders peaceful, and with the cream of the wheat He sates you." Levy, op. cit., p. 431.

[78] *Khosn v'kale* (Heb.:) groom and bride. The numerical value of *khosn* is 55 and *v'kale* is 464; the last three words in Psalm 147, verse 14, and their numerical values are: *khelev* (40), *khitim* (67), *yasbyakh* (412). Both add up to 519. (All Hebrew letters have a numerical value, and when you add the letters of a word this value has meaning. Assigning special *aggadic* (homiletic expositions of Bible, stories, legends, folklore, anecdotes, and maxims) meaning to words because of their numerical value is called *Gematria*.

in the town. And if the wedding took place in winter and there was snow, children would throw snowballs at the newlyweds just for the fun of it.

> The music was also heard in the alleys. Men danced in the snow. The youngsters made snowballs, preparing for the moment when the bride and groom were led to the synagogue's courtyard. In the street you could hear *Khasidic nigunim* being played. Reb Shlomo Klezmer's fiddle cried, while the *kapelye,* with his son Berl on bass, Abramtche on clarinet, Shepsl Klezmer on *sekund,* and Pesekh on fiddle, let loose so everyone could hear.[79]

Before the newlyweds presented themselves as husband and wife, they were escorted to a private chamber for *yikhed* (Heb.: privacy). This custom dates from ancient times, when the couple consummated the marriage there. However, in Eastern Europe the newlyweds simply had some private time together before celebrating with their family and friends. The next day, after the couple had slept together for the first time, the groom's mother came to the home to check the sheets for blood: stains proved that the bride had been a virgin, and to marry a nonvirgin could bring great shame on the groom and his family, especially if his father was a rabbi.

One informant from Dombrovitsa (Dubrovicja, Ukraine) told me a story told to him by his uncle, a bassist in a *kapelye,* revealing that some *klez-morim* enjoyed a good humorous *bobe-mayse* (Yid: grandmother story; tall tale), especially a sexual one, just as much as musicians today. Once a bride's mother asked the violinist of the *kapelye* that had accompanied the couple home in the early hours of the morning to stand outside their bedroom window and play something that indicated to her how things were between the couple, sexually speaking. "*A posheter tish-nign iz gevayn beser vi a get-satskete skotshne*" (A simple table melody is better than a fancy *skotshne*).[80]

---

[79] "Klezmorim," *Sefer Ha-Zikaron Le-kihilat Ostrov-Mazovyetsk,* ed. A. Margalit (Tel Aviv: Association of Former Residents of Ostrow-Mazowieck, 1960), p. 373.

[80] Interview with Sol Tishler (originally from Dubrovicja, Ukraine) in Lviv, Ukraine, Nov. 1, 1981.

After the newlyweds came to sit with the rest of the guests, one of the first dances offered in their honor was the *koyletsh tants,* after which the blessing over the *khale* was said and everyone tasted the *koyletsh.* Then came out the *gildene yoyikh* (Yid.: golden broth; chicken soup), the first substantial food the newlyweds had eaten in twenty-four hours.

During the party, family and friends gave speeches and toasts while swigging wine and whiskey and eating delicious dishes. If the wedding was given by a rich family, it was the custom to invite the poor and set a lavish table for them. Again, this custom originates in the *mitsve* of giving *tsdoke.* Some wealthy families gave to various charities throughout the year, but since the wedding celebration was one of the most important events in a lifetime, it was the best opportunity to exhibit one's generosity to the *shtetl.* A rich family in a *shtetl* did not want to have its daughter begin her new life under a cloud of shame, and if the poor were not invited or the food was not sumptuous, guests might disrupt the celebration, yell rude things at their hosts, and leave.

While the people were feasting, the *klezmorim* (often just the violinist with bass or *tsimbl* accompaniment) played slow *tish-nigunim* or *gaguyim-nigunim.*[81] Afterwards the *batkhn* who was supervising the wedding celebration got up on a table and conducted the *droshe geshank* in a loud voice with the help of one or two of the *klezmorim.* It was the *batkhn's* responsibility to keep things moving; if one wasn't present, the responsibility rested upon the shoulders of the *kapelmayster.* A wedding could function well without a *batkhn,* but not to have at least one *klezmer* was a great *shande* (Yid.: shame), as the following reminiscence makes clear:

> Once in our village there was a wedding between an orphan boy and girl. But there were no *klezmers* in our village and the closest *khevrisa*

---

[81] *Gaguyim-nigunim* (Heb.): longing/yearning songs. These were *Khasidic* spiritual vocal songs that used improvisation and rubato. When the klezmer played a *gaguyim-nigun,* he used the same techniques. It was also known as a *dveykele,* which came from the Hebrew word *dveykes:* adhering to God through ecstatic prayer.

[*kapelye*] to us was a days ride away in Teytch (Tjačiv, Ukraine). And besides, who was going to pay for the *khevrisa*? But to marry off [without music] a couple who already had such an unfortunate life would have been a great shame. A *shtile khasene* [Yid.: quiet wedding] was unacceptable. So we had Bishke the butcher come and play some tunes on his violin. He was truly a *grimpler,*[82] but the music made the atmosphere happy and we sang louder than his playing."[83]

During a wedding the *klezmorim* might perform over fifteen styles of dances, not all of which cost the same or had the same honorific value. The *sever tants* (Yid.: server or waiter dance), in which the waiters danced in front of the bride and groom with a special plate of food, such as *tsimes* (a sweet casserole made from either cooked carrots or plums mixed with potatoes and beef) or the first piece of roasted goose, cost less than the *mekheteneste tants* (Yid.: in-laws' dance), danced by the new mothers-in-law. (In the latter dance the bride's mother acted as if the groom was not good enough for her daughter, and the groom's mother vice versa. The music would be slow and deliberate as the two ladies, often with their noses in the air, circled each other. The dance is sometimes called the *broyges tants* (Yid.: angry dance) because of the arrogance the women pretended to display toward each other. Eventually the music became a *freylekh* as the two mother-in-laws danced happily hand-in-hand at the end.) Because there were so many dances (some so new the guests were unfamiliar with the steps), some weddings had a special dance instructor. In the following reminiscence one of the *klezmers* was also a dance instructor.

---

[82] *Grimpler:* from the Yiddish word *grimpl,* which means to strum tunelessly. A *grimpler* was a person who walked down the street either whistling, singing, or humming to himself some nondescript melody that was usually out of tune. To call a *klezmer* a *grimpler* was a great insult.

[83] Interview with Meyer Blecher (originally from Strij, Ukraine) in Hust, Ukraine, September 1, 1993.

There were two *kapelyes* in Lublin, one led by Shpilfogel who played the violin, and the other led by Rakhmiel, whose *kapelye* was the better of the two. Rakhmiel played the flute; the other instruments in the *kapelye* were violin, trumpet, drum, and bass. The trumpet player was also a good dancer, and sometimes in the middle of a piece he put his trumpet down and led a dance if the guests were having trouble remembering the steps. And even though mixed dancing was not allowed, he stood in front of the tables and taught the women how to dance a *sher* or a *mazurka*. The trumpet player loved to dance, so he knew all of the latest, most popular dances, as well as the traditional ones. Once, after the older guests went home, he showed the young people how to dance the *shimmy* [a popular jazz dance of the 1920s originating in the United States, in which the whole body shook rapidly]. I can only imagine what a hilarious scene it would have been if the grandmothers would have tried dancing the *shimmy*.[84]

Social Standing

Despite the *klezmer*'s importance at a Jewish wedding, his social standing in the *shtetl* was rather fluid, and sometimes his *yikhes* was just a rung or two higher than the local *treygers* (Yid.: porters). Playing music generally paid poorly, thus making it difficult for the *klezmer* to provide for his family. *Klezmorim* were looked upon as not being close followers of or learned in the *Toyre* and *Talmud*. And to compound things, even though *klezmorim* traveled less at the turn of the twentieth century than they had in the early nineteenth, the impression of them being usually away from home still stuck, leading to suspicions and rumors that they fraternized with all kinds of drunks, thieves, smugglers, gamblers, *proste goyim* (Yid:

---

[84] Interview with Simkhe Bina Wajc (originally from Pionki, Poland) in Warsaw, November 28, 1984.

vulgar or lowly gentiles), Rom, and loose women whom they met at the inns they slept in or the taverns they stopped at. Finally, to make the *shtetl* public even more apprehensive and wary, the *klezmorim* even had their own argot—*klezmer loshn* (Yid.: language)—which they used both at Jewish and non-Jewish festivities, and which only they and a few other professionals could understand. The *klezmorim* used this argot specifically so they could speak in secret about the people they met traveling and the people they played for in converations about the host, guests, food, and pay, filled with sarcasm, disdain, humor, and sexual innuendo.

To many *shtetl* inhabitants, the *klezmer* was a kid who just never grew up. To play music as a youth, for an avocation or even occasionally for a paying job, was all right. But, as many parents still say even today to their musician children, "When are you going to get a real job?" This idea of perpetual immaturity was conveyed to me by an informant who said:

> When I was twelve I had a good friend, Nosn, who played the violin. When I used to tell my mother I was going to see my friend she would say, "*Oi dos klezmer yungt*" (Oy, this *klezmer* youth). Several years later I went and saw Toscanini conducting the NBC Radio Philharmonic, and who did I see sitting in the first violin section but my old friend Nosn, now known as Nathan Arkoti. When I got home and told my mother she replied, "A klezmer yungt nokh" (still a *klezmer* youth).[85]

Here are some sayings about the *klezmorim* that indicate their low *yikhes* and the difficulties of the profession.

- *A batkhn makht di gantse shtub freylekh un aleyn hot er in der heym tsures.* (A *batkhn* makes the whole house merry and has trouble in his own.)
- *Dray mentchn oyf der velt zingn far tsures: a khazn, a betler, un a marshalik.* (Three people in the world sing out of need: a cantor, a beggar, and a *marshalik*.)

---

[85] Interview with Hannah Friedman in New York City, October 28, 1983.

- *Az men tsaylt sfire, kumt oyf di klezmer a pegire.* (When they count *sfire*,[86] the *klezmer* can drop dead.)[87]
- *Er hakt mir vi a tsimbler.* (He bothers me like a *tsimbler*.)[88]
- *Khasene gehat mit a klezmer iz gevayn a khusn mit knap yikhes.* (Marrying a *klezmer* is like a groom with hardly any *yikhes*.)[89]
- *Klezmer musik, dos iz gevayn a niderike madreyge.* (*Klezmer* music, that's on a low level.)[90]
- *Er zingt vi myn zeyg.* (He sang like my saw [his playing sounded like sawing].)[91]
- *Er hat a ton vi azoy men pisht oyf blekh.* (He has a tone which sounds like a man pissing on tin.)[92]

---

[86] *Sfire* was the seven weeks between the second day of *Peseykh* and *Shvues* (Shavuot: the holiday celebrating the first fruits of the summer and the Jews, receipt of the *Toyre* from God), when one counted the *omer,* a barley offering that was brought to the Temple for the entire seven weeks. Not until this was done could a single Jew eat bread made of the new harvest. Later on, this period became a time of semi-mourning commemorating the great difficulties Rabbi Akiva and his students had in studying *Toyre* under the Romans, who forbade it, while at the same time trying to survive a plague that was killing many of the students. To emphasize these difficulties, rabbis introduced prohibitions against people getting married, cutting or trimming hair, putting on new clothes, listening to religious and nonreligious music, and making merry. Thus the *klezmorim,* whose job was never very stable to begin with, now had no work for seven weeks in the Jewish community. Many *klezmorim* left their families during this time, looking to play weddings and parties for the non-Jews. The one day that the rabbis' restrictions were lifted was on *Lagboymer* (the 33rd day of the *omer*), when the ancient epidemic ceased, and in Eastern Europe *Lagboymer* became known as "the students' festival." To celebrate there were weddings, parades, outings into the forests, and other festivities, at all of which the *klezmer* could earn a living.

[87] These last three sayings are from Beregovski, op. cit., p. 21.

[88] Stutschevsky, op. cit., p. 60.

[89] Interview with Moishe Kolodny (originally from Pinsk, Belarus) in Bronx, New York, September 19, 1982.

[90] Interview with David Kagan (originally from Bedzin, Poland) in Wrocław, Poland, December 7, 1984.

[91] Interview with Felix Groveman (originally from Bronx, New York) in Los Angeles, California, October 15, 1984.

[92] Interview with Marty Levitt in Brooklyn, New York, January 25, 2002.

Conscription

Gentile attitude toward the Jews in the nineteenth century in Eastern Europe, particularly in the Pale, vacillated from grudging acceptance to progroms. Czar Nicholas I (1825–1855) was consumed by hatred for the Jews and wished to convert them all. During his reign he abolished the local autonomy of the *shtetl kahal* (Heb.: Jewish community organization), expelled Jews arbitrarily, taxed them exorbitantly, and introduced twenty-five years of mandatory service in the Czarist army. But before male Jewish children served they were often kidnapped, between the ages of twelve and eighteen, and forced into indentured servitude on Russian or Ukrainian farms. The living conditions there were shocking, and many of these *cantonists* did not survive to their eighteenth birthday, when they had to begin their twenty-five years of military duty. At twenty-one, most boys were married, so army service became another method to break up Jewish families. Jewish communities had to supply an annual quota, which caused some wealthy Jewish families to pay a ransom to have their sons replaced by Jewish boys from poor families. Nearly half of the fourteen thousand cantonists were forcibly baptized. This horrendous system began in 1827 and ended in 1856 during the reign of Nicholas I. As one descendant of a Russian *klezmer* related,

> My grandfather was only eight years old when the *khapers*[93] took him away. His parents never saw him again. The *khapers* took him to some town where he worked as a field hand at a Ukrainian farm. When he was eighteen they put him into the Czarist army. Because he was nice-looking, stood erect, and had a nice beard, they taught him the clarinet so he could play at the officer parties. Being able to play music spared my grandfather the worst of all those military years. One day

---

[93] *Khapers:* from the Yiddish *khap:* catch, grab, seize, capture. Thus the *khapers* were those forced to do the dirty work of the Czar's military: to hunt for stray young Jewish boys who were of the proper age and to *khap* them to fill the Czar's quota.

he was in a town where no Jews were allowed to live but only to pass through. So this Jew met my grandfather and asked him how much longer he had to serve. Then the man said that he had a little daughter and that by the time my grandfather was released from the army his daughter would be marriageable. He told him to go to Konotop. Since my grandfather had no family, when he was honorably discharged from the army he went to Konotop. And he married that young woman, my grandmother.[94]

In the army, Jews were not only introduced to wind instruments, but many also learned to read and arrange music. There was not much room in a czarist military band for string players, so many *klezmer* violinists became trumpeters to avoid combat. After their release, some of these Jewish musicians were able to parlay their new musical talents into higher social standing and better-paying jobs, such as playing in the *požharne komande*[95] bands and/or semi-professional orchestras, or teaching children whose parents (Jewish and non-Jewish) could afford private lessons. Their years of playing military music also changed the makeup of the *kapelyes* in Europe in the late nineteenth century, whose woodwind-and-brass sound (sometimes led by a violinist) crossed the Atlantic and in turn influenced the repertoire and makeup of the *klezmer* bands in America. The ensembles could be as large as fifteen musicians, and played a combination of violin, bass, clarinet, flute, piccolo, cornet, trumpet, trombone, alto saxophone, tuba, snare and bass drums, cymbals, and woodblock.

One hundred years later, the opportunity to fulfill one's military obligation by playing in the military band rather than serving in a combat unit remains viable. As one *klezmer* told me, "When I was nine I could already play the piano and read music, but my mother wanted me to be a woodwind player so that when I had to serve my mandatory military service in

---

[94] Interview with Kia Williams, New York City, December 11, 1983.
[95] *Pozharne komande* (Yid.): fire brigade.

the Red Army, I would be in the military band instead of being sent to fight in the Afghanistan war."[96]

After Nicholas I's death, Alexander II (1856–1881) decided to follow a more liberal policy concerning the Jews and issued amnesties and suspensions of taxes and fines. He also ended the conscription of Jewish children and liberalized educational policies for Jews. Those who had obtained a higher education were allowed to live outside the Pale. Consequently the number of Jews enrolled in the universities increased, including some *klezmorim*, who could now formally study music at the new and prestigious music conservatories in St. Petersburg and Odessa. These and other liberal reforms helped the *haskole* to penetrate even the most remote and religiously controlled *shtetlekh* in the Pale's hinterlands; they also encouraged many Jews to adopt Russian culture and practice less of their own.

Jewish Music in Turkey and Romania

While the *klezmorim* in the Czarist army performed marches, waltzes, and pieces in other musical genres, with this repertoire influencing the *kapelyes* of Poland, Belarus, and the northern Ukraine, the repertoire of the *klezmorim* in Romania and in the Ottoman Empire represented more of a Near Eastern sound. In Constantinople, many members of the significant Ashkenazic minority living among the much larger Sephardic community were ancestors of those who came from Ukraine and Poland seeking refuge during the Chmielnicki pogroms (1648–49) and Great Deluge. Others came at the end of the eighteenth century searching for better economic opportunities, while still others had been traveling to Palestine, stopped on the way, and stayed.

Constantinople was the nexus of several major trade routes—going north to Odessa via the Black Sea; west to Vienna via the Danube River through Galați, Belgrade, and Budapest; and south to Jerusalem. For the

---

[96] Interview with Leo Chelyapov (originally from Moscow), June 22, 2000.

Jewish musicians living in Constantinople between the mid-nineteenth century and the beginning of World War I, these trade routes gave them easy
access to a variety of places, and traveling these routes enabled them to
pick up new tunes (particularly from Rom musicians traveling the same
routes) and teach their own to others.

As I stated earlier, one of the three major sources that created the *klezmer's* core dance repertoire was Greco-Turkish dance music. The Middle
Eastern modes were already familiar to the *klezmer* (from synagogue
prayers), as were the improvisational melismatic singing and playing exhibited in many of the tunes. But by the beginning of the nineteenth century
the repertoire of the Rom *lautari* (Rom: folk musician) was involved. The
repository for this mixing, exchanging, and borrowing of Greco-Turkish
tunes was the region of Moldavia/Bessarabia. Dance tunes such as the
honga, sirba, zhok, and *bulgarish* and display tunes such as the *Terkishe freylekhs, Terkishe gebet, vulekhl, doyne,* and *taksim* now formed the core of the
Romanian-Turkish *klezmer* sound.

Traditional *klezmer* music performed today can be put into two broad
musical styles. One is the Polish-Ukrainian (with some Belorussian, Slovakian, and Russian influences) sound and the other is the Romanian-Turkish
(with some Hungarian, Galician, and Carpathian Ukrainian influences).
The capital of the Polish-Ukrainian sound was Barditshev (Berdičiv,
Ukraine), where, near the end of the nineteenth century, there were over
fifty *klezmorim,* among them several *klezmer* virtuosi who led *kapelyes* that
became legendary throughout the Ukraine, parts of Poland, and Russia. The
capital of the Romanian-Turkish sound was Yas, Romania, which from the
turn of the twentieth century through the eve of World War II was the
home of several virtuosi and their *kapelyes* famous throughout Moldavia
and Bessarabia.

To learn more about the history of *klezmer* in Yas and its environs, I
traveled there many times, met with many retired *klezmorim,* including
several Rom who played in *klezmer kapelyes,* and spoke to the world's leading authority on Moldavian/Bessarabia Jewish culture, Itsik "Kara" Svart
(1906–2001). His account exhibits the richness of Jewish culture in Moldavia

and Bessarabia before World War II, and how vital it was to the development of Romanian *klezmer*.

> I was born in Podu Iloaiei, just outside of Yas. In my *shtetl* there were no Jewish *klezmers* [he said *klezmers* instead of *klezmorim*], but in Yas there were many *kapelyes*. So when there was a wedding we brought them from Yas by train. When we did not, we hired the Gypsies. These Gypsy *klezmers* knew Jewish music very well and played at our local balls and for the Jewish festivals. On *Purim* they went from house to house accompanying the *Purimshpilers*. The Jews were not ignorant *klezmers*: they all knew how to read notes. And by the 1920s most *klezmers* in this region read music because they had gone to the conservatory.
>
> Several *kapelyes*, particularly the famous Sigally and Bughici families, made a good living only from music. This was rare for most of the *klezmers*, but in Yas with the Yiddish theatre, outdoor garden cafés, restaurants, weddings, parties, and the movie theatre in the 1930s, there were many opportunities for the *klezmers* to find work. The Yiddish theatre where I worked as a translator and dramaturge had an orchestra made up only of *klezmers*.
>
> The reputation of most *klezmers* prior the 1920s was not a good one. The *klezmer* was looked upon like an actor or circus entertainer who lived a Bohemian life, so the public expressed a great deal of uneasiness about him.
>
> In the 1800s the Jewish *klezmers* of Moldavia played in the court of Prince Linye. He said: "The Jews of Moldavia are the best musicians, businessmen, and brokers." In the mid-1800s some *klezmers* from Galicia traveled throughout Moldavia introducing the local Jews and non-Jews to Jewish and non-Jewish music from Poland and the Ukraine. But the greatest influence, one that can still be heard today from the few who play *klezmer*, was that of Balkan music. Throughout the 1800s Jewish, Gypsy, and Romanian musicians traveled often to Constantinople. There they played Jewish and Romanian music and brought back new Turkish tunes which they introduced to the public. The

klezmers played the Turkish music the best because they already knew the scales from many of their synagogue prayers.

Before World War II in Yas we had several well-known *kapelyes* that either originally came from Yas or from the Moldavia-Bessarabia region. They were the Lemeși, Bughici, and Sigally *kapelyes*. The Lemeși *kapelye* originally came from Bălți, Bessarabia. They played Romanian *klezmer* music during the reign of Czar Alexander II, who was very harsh against the Jews and Romanians. The Lemeși *kapelye* had a wide reputation, and when the Italian Opera Company came to Bucharest to play in the Romanian National Theatre they asked that the Lemeși *kapelye* be part of the orchestra.

The violinists in Lemeși, Sigally, and Bughici were great talents, but the most famous of all the *klezmer* violinists in Romania was Jacob Psanter [1828–1896]. He was the oldest child in his family and had to support them after his father died when he was very young. He played by ear and performed for the Jews, non-Jews, poor, and rich. Though he knew his work was considered a low profession, he never regretted having become a *klezmer*. He wrote in a book he published in 1875 that had he been a religious Jew he would have been very learned in *Toyre* and as famous for his rabbinical skills as he was for his violin playing.

After World War I most *klezmers* in Yas were not religious but you could still find some with long beards and *payes*[97] in a few towns and villages like Buhuși. The Buhusher *Rebe* had his own *kapelye* that played at all the religious affairs in the town. Finally the introduction of the gramophone in the late '20s hurt the small *kapelyes*. Instead of hiring a *kapelye* for a dance or to play in a restaurant or café, people played the gramophone. Of course the rich always could afford the

---

[97] *Payes* (Heb.): earlocks. Many of the orthodox and all of the *khasidim* obeyed the *Toyre* rule that said one should not have hardened steel touch and cut the hair on the face. The five areas not to be cut were the two temples, two cheeks, and the chin. Thus many orthodox and all *khasidic* men never shaved and grew beards.

best and they kept the Sigally and Bughici *kapelyes* busy until the war began.[98]

And here is an intimate look at the *klezmer* scene in Yas before World War II through the eyes of a *klezmer* who was a member of the Bughici *kapelye.*

My name is Dumitru Bughici, and my whole family were musicians. My great-grandfather was a contrabassist, my grandfather was a cellist, and my father was a violinist. I used to be a violinist, and now my son Pavel is the fourth-generation violinist.

Unfortunately I don't remember my great-grandfather since he died before I was born, but I remember my grandfather. He had four sons who all played in his *kapelye.* The oldest was Fayvl—he played the violin and was the best. Then came my father Avram, who played violin and some flute. After him came Moyshe, who played the violin, and then the youngest, Yossel, who played violin and some clarinet. My Uncle Yankl, my grandfather's brother, also played in the *kapelye,* but he immigrated to America just after World War I. I never saw him but I heard he was a good violinist. We lost all contact when the [Second World] War came.[99] None of them really were composers but my grandfather did compose this piece that became well known among Jews in Moldavia called "A Alt Yidishe Lid" (An Old Jewish Song). My grandfather's *kapelye* played throughout Moldavia and made a good living. When I was ten I began the violin, then at twelve the

---

[98] Interview with Itsik "Kara" Svarţ (originally from Podu Iloaiei, Romania) in Yas, Romania, February 25, 1985. (Itsik wrote under his pen name, Kara, which means *black* in Turkish, because his last name, Svarţ, means *black* in Yiddish.)

[99] When Yankl Bughici immigrated to America he was still involved with *klezmer* music for a few years. He composed two tunes, "Bulgar No. 19" and "Serba La Booga No. 31," both of which are well-known among current *klezmer* musicians, since they were published in the *Kammen International Dance and Concert Folio No. 9* in 1934. Yankl anglicized his name to Jack Boogich.

accordion, and by age thirteen I was in my father's *kapelye* playing the accordion.

The weddings in Yas were beautiful and full of traditions. You had to know the exact repertoire for each dance that was performed before and immediately after the *khupe*. In the summertime a wedding might start as late as nine P.M. At a typical wedding my father played only as a soloist, so only a bassist, a *bratsche* [Ger.: viola], and I would accompany him while he played for the *khupe* and the *tish*. Through the *tish* there was only Yiddish music. After the *tish* my father didn't play as much. We played some Jewish dances like a *mitsve tants, sirba,* and *khusidl,* but as the evening continued we played more and more modern dance tunes like tangos, fox-trots, etc. Our repertoire was large and there was only singing if the guests sang while we played. We did not ever work with a *batkhn*. It was hard work because we usually played until four or five in the morning. Yas had a reputation of having good musicians and the Sigally and Bughici families were known as the best. By the time I was fourteen I only played in Yas with my father since I had begun studying at the conservatory. This is when I began studying the piano.

My father was sought after by Jews and non-Jews, religious and nonreligious. Once my father was asked to play for the *Tsadik,* the *Stefaneshter Rebe,*[100] on *Lagboymer.* Since there were several weddings on *Lagboymer* because of *sfire* my father could have chosen any one to play for, but he chose only to play for the *rebe*. It was an honor to be asked by the *rebe,* so the rest of us played at the wedding. My father was good friends with this Gypsy *tsimbalist,* so he went too and accompanied my father. They played *khasidishe* music, which everyone loved.

---

[100] The Stefaneshter Rebe, Rabbi Abraham Matathias Friedman (1848–1933), lived in Shtefaneshti (Ştefăneşti), Romania. His grandfather was Rabbi Israel of Ruzhin (Ružin, Ukraine), who had established a magnificent court in Sadagora (outside Chernovits) in Bukowina, where he led an opulent life. The Stefuneshter Rebe maintained the splendor into which he had been born, but outwardly was known to all his followers as a modest, sincere, and wise *rebe.*

Before my father left to return to Yas the *Stefuneshter Rebe* gave him a special gold coin. Then the *rebe* made a blessing and drank a *l'khayim* [Heb.: to life; a toast] with some *tzuica* [a strong Romanian liquor usually made from plums or pears]. My father carried that gold coin in his pocket his whole life because he believed it kept away the evil eye. Another time I went with my father to the *Stefuneshter Rebe* because he was asked to write a special *nign* for them. We played it in the synagogue while everyone danced, including the *rebe*.

When my father wasn't playing at a wedding or a dance he, two of his brothers, and two of the Segal [or Sigally, the Romanianized version of their Jewish last name] brothers played in the Yiddish theatre called *Pomul Verde,* the first Yiddish theatre in Romania.[101] I enjoyed watching the plays and listening to the music. I saw Chaim Prizant, Sidy Thal, Molly Picon, and many other great Yiddish actors. Sometimes he played the music for the silent films as well, but I only saw him do this twice.

My father's *kapelye* was an elite group. We never played in the street with the *Purimshpilers.* We had a certain kind of dignity and only played certain weddings and dances. The *klezmers* who played in the streets played at the lesser weddings. My father earned a good living, so that when he married, my mother stopped her work as a tailor and only worked at home. My father wasn't a religious Jew but he never

---

[101] The first formal Yiddish theatre in the world was established by the father of Yiddish theatre, Abraham Goldfadn (1840–1908), in 1876 in Yas, Romania at the wine garden called *Pomul Verde* (Rom.: green tree). Goldfadn, along with Shimen Mark, the owner of the wine garden, put on touching, stirring plays that spoke to the Jewish audience of their great and trying history. The first actors were known as *broder singers,* Yiddish balladists, sometimes *batkhonim* who were also professional singers. The first was Berl (Margolis) Broder (c. 1815–1860), from the town of Brody in Galicia. The Yiddish theatre put on plays until World War II began, then reopened in 1949 and didn't close until 1961, when the Jewish population in Yas became too small to support it. Many of those who worked at the theatre went to the Yiddish State Theatre in Bucharest (established in 1958), which is still in existence today as one of only two Yiddish theatres in all of Eastern Europe (the other is the Yiddish State Theatre in Warsaw).

played on the *Shabes* unless it was for non-Jews. After *Shabes* there was usually a dance or a wedding.

In Yas, unlike any other city that I know of, we had a *klezmer* syndicate.[102] Every Monday evening we met in our synagogue, *Di Klezmers Shil*,[103] on Pantilimon Street, number eleven. There we got together to talk about business and to relax, playing cards and chess. During the business part of our meetings we discussed many matters, like who was in need of some financial help. There were *klezmers* not as good and successful as we were, but deserved our help. Since everyone who belonged to the syndicate paid a small monthly due according to their earnings we were able to give some money to certain *klezmer* families who were poor and had difficulties paying rent and buying food. We also helped those *klezmers* who had a contract for a wedding or a restaurant job and were not paid their full amount. If the people still refused to pay even after the syndicate interceded on behalf of the *klezmer* or *kapelye*, then word was given throughout the city not to play for them or any of their relatives for the next two years. Believe me, even though there were a lot of *klezmers* in Yas, most belonged to

---

[102] *Klezmorim* formed guilds to help each other and to have more strength as a unified group, especially when they had to fight the various edicts and restrictions that the non-Jewish authorities constantly placed upon them. The earliest *klezmer* guild we know of was started in Prague in 1558, and another in Lublin in 1654.

[103] *Di Klezmers Shil* (Romanian Yiddish): the *klezmer* synagogue. It was destroyed during World War II. Today the street that it was on is near the Jewish community center and the main synagogue, the *Mare* (Rom.: great). In other towns and *shtetlekh* in Eastern Europe Jews got together by trades to build their own synagogues, which were firstly places of worship for any Jew in the community, and secondly substitutes for a union hall, where tradesmen could talk shop and other matters that concerned them all, even if the men who built the synagogue actually did not have a formal union. In Bucharest the *Shnayders' Shil* (Yid.: tailors' synagogue) still stands, with a small *besmeydresh* (Heb.: house of study) known as the *Shnayders' Vaybers, Shil* (Yid.: tailors' wives' synagogue), where the wives went to pray and socialize by themselves. In Dorohoi, until it was torn down in 1988 for apartments, stood the *Dorfishe Shil* (Yid.: rural synagogue), which was built by farmers living outside town and who wanted a place to pray on the Sabbath. They traveled by horse and cart on Friday afternoon, stayed overnight at a local inn, and went home Saturday evening.

the syndicate or sympathized with us, so it was extremely difficult if not impossible to get any *klezmers* to play for someone who basically had a *kheyrem* (Heb.: ban, excommunication) put upon them.

This beautiful life I cherished as a child all came to a tragic end when the Nazis came. Yas unfortunately became the capital of the Romanian fascists, the Iron Guard. When they seized power from King Carol II on September 4, 1940, mass arrests, tortures, extortions, confiscation of property, and the murder of Jews began. In Yas this culminated with the pogrom the Iron Guard and Nazis conducted on June 28–29, 1941. The Germans rounded up twelve thousand Jews, including my Uncle Moyshe and his two sons. Half were shot in the town square, the other half were shipped to concentration camps, with only a few surviving the suffocating train ride. Many *klezmers* were murdered—many so talented they could play Paganini as well as "Vu Zaynen Mayne Zibn Gute Yor" ["Where Are My Seven Good Years," a Yiddish song written by American David Meyerowitz (1867–1943) in 1925].[104]

Many *kapelyes* took care of each other in times of need, even if they did not have a union or guild to support them. If a *klezmer* was sick and not able to perform at a job he was still paid his full portion. "His life was our life. His problem our problem. His fate our fate."[105] The *klezmer* who stopped working because he was too old or he had an injury and was not able to find another job was still paid a percentage of his former *kapelye* share. If the *klezmer* died and his widow was old and did not have any children, she received her husband's full salary if the *kapelye* could afford it. If they could not, then she received a percentage of his former salary. If the widow had children and they were too young for work, then she received half her husband's salary, or some other percentage. From all the

[104] Interview with Dumitru Bughici (originally from Yas, Romania) in Bucharest, Romania, March 13, 1985.
[105] Stutschevsky, op. cit., p. 60.

interviews I did among former *klezmorim* in Eastern Europe and all of the first-person narratives I read from them, fraternity was a strong virtue among them. The following account exemplifies this *klezmer* kinship:

> I had left Rahov [Rahiv, Ukraine] early in the morning on my way to visit my brother who lived in Kassau [Košice, Slovakia]. The train stopped in Mukács [Mukačeve, Ukraine] because it was having some engine problems. It wasn't going to be until the next morning that the engine would be repaired. It was summertime—very hot and humid. I didn't want to stay in my seat inside the train the whole night. It was like a furnace. So I went for a walk when I heard music coming from this restaurant. I went inside where I saw three *klezmorim* playing. I knew they were *klezmorim* because I heard them speaking Yiddish mixed with a little *klezmer-loshn*. There was an accordionist, violinist, and saxophonist. The violinist came up to me after having seen my violin on the floor next to me. I told him what happened and why I was in Munkács for the night. Immediately he invited me to stay that night at his home. He had an extra bed and he lived only a few blocks away from the station. He and his wife were very nice and I slept very well. I meant to keep in contact with him but I never did. After the war I was visiting Munkács on business and asked about the violinist. He died in Auschwitz [Ošwiecim, Poland].[106]

Cross-Pollination

One did not have to travel to Constantinople (Istanbul, Turkey) to find *klezmorim* and non-Jewish musicians exchanging tunes and adapting them to their own musical genres. In the regions of Bessarabia, Transylvania, and the Carpathian mountains, *klezmorim* and non-Jewish musicians (mostly

---

[106] Interview with Shaiya Shindelman (originally from Rahiv, Ukraine) in Hust, Ukraine, August 17, 1997.

Rom) often exchanged dance melodies. While conducting my field research in the Carpathian village of Vylok, Ukraine, I met several Rom bands that played *klezmer* and Yiddish folksongs at non-Jewish dances, weddings, and other celebrations. Some of them even remembered the Yiddish lyrics and knew what they meant. But though they still played some of the Jewish repertoire, to a man they all lamented the fact that there were no Jews left to really appreciate and play this music for. One told me:

> I had a band with two Jews and three Rom, including myself. During the 1970s through the mid-'80s we traveled throughout the Carpathian region, even sometimes playing in Bukowina. I played the accordion, my brother the violin, my cousin the violin, and the two Jews drums and bass. Both Jewish guys had graduated from the conservatory of music. When we played for Jewish weddings and other parties the drummer was the leader. First, he could speak and sing in Yiddish. Second, the clients felt more comfortable if a Jew was leading the band since he knew their ways. When we played for the *gaje* [107] like Ukrainians or Hungarians, it was good to let them know that several of our musicians were Jewish and conservatory graduates. For them, having Jewish musicians play at their wedding meant they got the best for their money and they could be trusted more than us Rom. We played a lot and we were all close. When the bassist and drummer immigrated to Israel I went with them to the airport in Budapest to say goodbye. We were good friends. We lost many talented musicians to Israel. [108]

There are also several examples of cross-pollination between *klezmer* and Ukrainian folk music. Since the Jews in the *shtetlekh* had regular contact

---

[107] *Gaje* (Rom.): non-Rom (pl.). Though technically I was an outsider, a non-Rom, whenever I told my Rom informants that I was Jewish, they emphasized that I was not a *gajo*. As fellow minorities and outsiders, the Rom, particularly the musicians, felt a special kinship with the *klezmorim*.
[108] Interview with Shani Virag in Vilok, Ukraine, June 23, 1992.

with their Ukrainian neighbors for work and commerce, it was natural that *klezmorim* and Ukrainian instrumentalists would borrow from each other. Those Jews who lived in Ukrainian villages had an even closer relationship with their neighbors, and often spoke fluent Ukrainian. As Beregovski wrote:

> Jewish musicians used to play frequently at non-Jewish weddings and festivities, where they undoubtedly played Jewish tunes in addition to the Ukrainian dance repertoire. In the same way they brought their Ukrainian repertoire to Jewish weddings (e.g. *kozachoks, skochnes,* [*kolomeykes*]). Non-Jews often played in Jewish bands. . . . A *klezmer* (G. Rizitski, 57, clarinet) told me that in the 1890s he played in a band in Brusilov (Kiev area), which used to play for Ukrainian artisans (at that time there was a great number of shoemakers in Brusilov who made boots they sold in Brusilov and other towns) at their weddings and celebrations, to which they invited Jewish musicians. The Ukrainian youth there danced the *sher* as well.[109]

The advent of recorded *klezmer* music in the late nineteenth century in America and early twentieth in Europe, along with the publishing of Yiddish folksongs and *klezmer* tunes, helped to codify the melodies and lyrics of the *klezmer's* varied repertoire, which had been mostly an oral tradition. These recordings and sheet music made it easier, for example, for the *klezmorim* of Kovno (Kavnas, Lithuania) to know what their colleagues hundreds of miles to the south in Arad were playing, and encouraged the borrowing of musical styles. These hard copies of *klezmer* tunes also created a standard by which the *klezmorim* could compare themselves. As more and more Jews had access to these recordings (and radio in the 1920s), they expected and sometimes asked that the repertoire be performed as they had heard it recorded.

---

[109] Slobin, op. cit., p. 526.

The *kapelmayster,* who was often the violinist, now had the responsibility of making sure his fellow *klezmorim* kept learning new music so their repertoire could remain current. Learning music by ear from other musicians had been his main resource. But learning by ear left room for interpretation and the vagaries of memory. If the *kapelmayster* wrote music, he could transcribe exactly what he heard from a record, radio, or live performance. He could then teach it to the rest of the *kapelye* note for note, whether they read music or not. Sometimes it was another *klezmer* in the *kapelye* who could read and write music, so he did the transcribing. However, in the following account the *kapelmayster* kept the *kapelye* current.

In my town of Drohobycz (Drogobič, Ukraine), the *klezmorim* played Yiddish folksongs as well as swing, fox-trots, rhumba, cha-cha, waltzes, Russian songs, and so on. Many learned how to read music so they could play the tune exactly as it had been recorded. There were *klezmorim* who had great ears and could write down exactly what they heard on the radio after listening to the tune only once. They not only wrote the melody line but the harmony and rhythm parts for all the instruments. I played in one *kapelye* where a lot of the music was from the radio, which came to Drohobycz in the 1930s. The leader was Dr. Staszek Vilder. He was very clever, with great ears. He wrote the parts for saxophone, trumpet, piano, bass, and two violins. I played in this ensemble for weddings, restaurants, and even for the silent films. We use to play "Bar Kokhba"[110] under Tom Mix and Valentino films. We had to play note for note what Vilder wrote down in our parts to help the film along. There was no room for improvisation. The audience was not pleased when we played the wrong music under a scene. Once my music fell on the floor and it got all mixed up. I quickly picked it up and began playing this fast and loud trumpet solo while Tom Mix was kissing a woman. Everyone in the audience started to yell: "Quiet! Stop playing,

---

[110] Bar Kokhba (Heb.: son of star), whose real name was Bar Koseva, led the Jewish revolt against Rome under Hadrian (132–135 C.E.); he died in the battle of Betar.

you idiot!" From then on I memorized all my parts and occasionally looked down at my music while keeping one eye always on Vilder.[111]

The Klezmer *Violin*

The violinist was also affected by the liberal reforms that allowed Jews to study in the universities of Czarist Russia. Since the mid-sixteenth century, when the violin as we know it today was invented, it had become the leader and symbol of *klezmer* music through the nineteenth century. On my ethnographic treks I found violins as decorative art carved into the *Toyre* Arks in several synagogues in Poland; carved into Jewish tombstones in Dorohoi, Romania and Şiroki (Soroca), Moldova; and painted on the ceiling of a synagogue with zodiac motifs in Vaslui, Romania.

As stated earlier, up until the nineteenth century and the introduction of woodwinds and brass, most *klezmer kapelyes* consisted of strings (violin, cello, bass, *tsimbl*), percussion (Turkish drum, cymbals, woodblock), and some plectrum instruments (mandolin, *bandura*[112] in southwestern Ukraine, and *cobza*[113] in Bessarabia). Even as the clarinet began to grow in popularity

---

[111] Interview with Mikhl Lepert (originally from Drohobycz, Poland) in Wrocław, Poland, March 12, 1984.

[112] *Bandura:* one version of this Ukrainian/Russian plectrum instrument looked like a mandolin with either a bulbous or flat back, and had six to eight strings. The other kind (sometimes called *bandora* or *pandora*) was a zither-like instrument with some seventy to eighty strings. There were no felt pads and some even had frets. It was a difficult instrument to play.

[113] *Cobza:* this Romanian plectrum instrument is related to the Arabic-Persian *oud* and was introduced to Romania by the Turks. It had four strings which were arranged in double courses, mainly in octaves (as d' d, a' a, d' d, g' g, though each player had his own tuning preference), and was picked by quill robustly and rhythmically. It often provided percussive and chordal accompaniment to other instruments, usually the violin. In the Ukraine in the nineteenth century blind minstrels were often called *cobzars* because the most common instrument among them was the *cobza*. Both the *bandura* and *cobza* are rarely seen in *klezmer kapelyes* in America or Europe. I have seen the *bandura* played by Ukrainian peasants in Žmerinka (near Vinnicja), and I have seen a Rom *cobza* player in a band in Chişinău (Kishinev), Moldova.

in the last decades of the nineteenth century, the violin remained the favorite of the Jews. The violin's sonority was closely identified with the human voice. In Tomashov (Tomaszów Lubelski), Poland, they said:

> When the wedding guests had gathered around the *rebe,* in walked Shulik, who immediately stretched his right hand out to the *rebe* while the left one held the violin. The *rebe* shook Shulik's hand and said, "Sing to our God with the violin." With his beating oblong fingers, which so deftly and tremulously dashed back and forth upon the fiddle, Shulik proceeded from the depths of his soul to touch upon the precious strings of his heart. His music caused a river of tears to flow from the women, who sat still and quiet in the room. Shulik's fiddle was able to take you from the greatest feeling of sadness one moment and throw you into a joyous mood the next moment. In such an estactic atmosphere one could not help but allow one's feet to dance.[114]

The *klezmer* violinist was an extension of the *khazn*'s voice. "The *khazn* made a *krekht* (Yid.: groan, moan) from the neck up and a *klezmer* made a *krekht* from the neck down."[115] His ability to imitate the crying, ululating, moaning, and laughing cantorial techniques he had heard since he was an infant was shaped into specific *klezmer* ornamentations. The *klezmer*'s conservatory was the synagogue, his lessons the daily prayers, and his concerts the Jewish holidays. According to the *khazn* Abraham-Moshe Bernshteyn (born in Vilna, 1866–1932), the *krekht* was the cornerstone of Jewish music. "It was an outbreak of ecstatic joy. It was the source of exaltation and spirited pleasure for the masses of Eastern European Jews."[116]

---

[114] "Shulik Klezmer," *Sefer Zikaron Le-Kehilat Tomaszow Mazowiecki,* ed. M. Wajsberg (Tel Aviv: Tomashov Organization in Israel, 1969), pp. 333–34.

[115] Interview with Felix Groveman (originally from Bronx, New York) in Los Angeles, October 15, 1984.

[116] Issacher Fater, *Yidishe Musik in Poyln Tsvishn beyde Welt-Milkhomes* (Tel Aviv: Velt Federatsia fun Poylishe Yidn, 1970), p. 61.

Out of the many fine *klezmer* violinists in the nineteenth and beginning of the twentieth centuries, only a few reached such renown that legends were created around them. To have any one of these violinists at a wedding or some other affair said to the Jewish community that this was not an ordinary celebration. Here are a few of them:

- Pedutser (1828–1902) was born in Radomsyl (Radomišl, Ukraine), near Kiev. (His name means the Rock redeemed in Hebrew; Gamliel ben Pedutser—Pedahzur in the *Toyre*—was a member of the Tribe of Menasseh and was one of those chosen by Moses to bring an offering for the new Tabernacle [Numbers 1:10, 23].) He grew up in a family that followed the teachings of the *Kartshever Khasidim*. When he left home he settled in Barditshev, where he gained a reputation as the "lord" of the *klezmers*. At a wedding, after the *kapelye* had played a few tunes and had warmed up the guests, Pedutser would come out holding his violin and walking like a king, surrounded by complete silence. He was also famous among the rich Russians and Ukrainians. "When I play for the poor I am the most important dish, and when I play for the rich my violin sounds like jewelry, but all they want to do is eat."[117] Pedutser loved to show off his talent, imitating birdcalls on his violin or juggling the violin and bow. But he was foremost an artist. His *kapelye,* with thirteen musicians, was famous throughout Barditshev and its environs. To play with Pedutser was a great honor. Natan Sapir played violin and was the *kapelmayster* when Pedutser was not there, Raphael played clarinet, Shakhne played trombone, and Pedutser's brother-in-law Pedutser Brodsky played trumpet—he led the *kapelye* after Pedutser died. Pedutser was also known for his beautiful compositions. The guests shouted "Pedutser Kholodenko music" when they wanted one of his tunes. In and around Barditshev his music was the "meat and potatoes" of most of the *kapelyes* for fifty years. Unfortunately only a few of his tunes survive.

---

[117] Stutschevsky, op. cit., p. 111.

- A competitor of Pedutser's was Alter Tchudnover (1846–1912), who was born in Tchudnov, Volyn (Čudniv, Ukraine). Instead of birdcalls Tcudnover became famous for the train sounds he made on his violin. One of the most famous *klezmers* in Eastern Europe, he wrote music that made people laugh and cry. He owned two violins—one a cheap one he played with his *kapelye,* the other his Amati,[118] which he played as a soloist. One wealthy Russian merchant was so impressed by Tchudnover's Amati that he offered to buy it. At first Tchudnover refused, but eventually he gave in, and in exchange the Russian merchant built him a huge home with a large stone wall surrounding it.

- Tchudnover's *klezmer yikhes* was carried on by his nephew, student, and *kapelye* member Louis Grupp (1888–1983), who immigrated to America. "Sure we read music; he taught us," Grupp said. "We practiced Kreutzer, Screidek [popular music method books of the day]. My uncle used to get sheet music like this with a melody and he used to orchestrate it. He had a brother in America who used to send him big music, overture selections. My cousin that went to the Conservatory in Warsaw used to send me books."[119]

- Then there was Stempenyu (1822–1879), who was immortalized by the great Yiddish writer Sholom Aleichem (1859–1916) in his novella *Stempenyu.* The book, written in 1888, made him more famous than he already was. Stempenyu was born with *klezmer* in his blood: he came from ten generations of *klezmorim.* His father Berl Bass played the bass, his grandfather Shmulik Trompeyt played the trumpet, his great-grandfather Fayvish played the *tsimbl,* and his great-great-grandfather Efrayim played the flute. Berl did not read music, but his son was sent

---

[118] The best violins in the world were made in Cremona, Italy; all violins since the seventeenth century have been judged against these incredible pieces of art. Of the various luthiers in Cremona in the late sixteenth and seventeenth centuries, these names stand above any others: Nicolo Amati (1596–1684), Guarneri del Gesu (1698–1744), and Amati's greatest and most famous pupil, Antonio Stradivari (c. 1644–1737).

[119] Henry Sapoznik, *Klezmer! Jewish Music from Old World to Our World* (New York: Schirmer, 1999), p. 10.

to a private teacher; at fifteen he left his father's house and toured the country as a kind of freelance *klezmer*, joining whatever *kapelye* needed a violinist. By eighteen he had his own *kapelye* in Odessa and was known for his virtuosity as well as his composing skills. Eventually he settled down in Barditshev and continued to polish his reputation. As one listener commented, "Every place Stempenyu went, everyone waited to see him open his case. When he put the violin under his chin the rest of the violin players felt like burying themselves alive. He was envied by the men and eyed by the women."[120] Sholom Aleichem wrote:

> The public sits with great respect as the *klezmer* plays a cheer-less *maralne* [Yid.: moral; a display piece played rubato with a great deal of improvisation], a tearful one. This violin cries while the fat strings are worshiped...and every *krekht* from the violin—*tiokh-tiokh-tiokh*—called out to the wedding guests and continued to echo in their hearts. In every heart, but espe-cially in the Jewish heart. Such a violin. He squeezed the dif-ferent strings and mostly sad and tearful songs came out.... For such a mood one only needed the right musician, a skill-ful one, a *klezmer*; such a skillful one as Stempenyu was.[121]

• The Barditshever tradition of producing excellent *klezmorim* contin-ued with Wolf Tcherniowski (1841–1930), who was Stempenyu's brother-in-law. He inherited the leadership of Stempenyu's *kapelye* and was a very successful *klezmer* even though he could not read music. He used his financial success to start a brick factory, which became one of the largest in Barditshev. His son Duvid became *kapelmayster* after his father died.

---

[120] Stutschevsky, op. cit., p. 115.
[121] Sholom Aleichem, *Stempenynu,* in *Ale Verk fun Sholom-Aleykhem* (New York: Sholom-Aleykhem Folksfond, 1919), pp. 128–29.

Some *klezmorim* chose the profession, but for most, the profession chose them. The *klezmer* was part of a chain leading from one generation to the next, from father to son to grandson. If a man was not born into a *klezmer* family and wanted to become one, it was certainly possible but was more difficult. He had to learn an instrument on his own or from another *klezmer,* and he had to learn about the *klezmer's* world from the outside. Most *klezmorim* could not pay for private lessons; consequently a father would not only teach his son about the traditions and music, but how to play his own instrument. If the son mastered everything the father could teach him on the violin, and even passed his father in technique, then, in some instances, the father got him private lessons or sent him away to learn from a master teacher. The father knew that his oldest would be the one who would take over as *kapelmayster* of the *kapelye* one day. And the only way to assure that the stature of the *kapelye* grew—which meant more work, better pay, and a greater reputation—was to increase the level of musicianship of all the *kapelye* members, and especially that of his oldest son. Those boys sent off for more lessons—or sent because they did not come from a *klezmer* family—often served a kind of apprenticeship. Sending a young boy of ten or eleven away from home was always hard for the mother and sometimes horrendous for the boy. The following account, which illustrates this, is taken from a letter Beregovski received from the *klezmer* Abraham-Yehoshua Makonovetski, who was born in 1872. He was the most fecund informant that Beregovski worked with. The original letter, a response to Beregovski's questionnaire inquiring about the lives and professions of *klezmorim,* was more than fifty pages long.

> My father was a violinist and had studied in Bebryhen, Lithuania. After he got married he and my mother moved to Khabno where he established the Khabensker *kapelye.* He was known as Yisroel Fidler. He wasn't only a *klezmer,* but also a watchmaker, barber, and glazier. But above all he was a beggar.
>
> I began playing the violin when I was seven and learned from my father. But before I really could contribute to the *kapelye* with my violin

I played only the tambourine and earned thirty to forty kopeks per wedding. By the time I was ten I was playing *sekund* in my father's *kapelye* and earned sixty kopeks per wedding.

Then my father sent me away to this old *klezmer,* Aron-Moshe Sirotovich, in Malin, near Kiev. Sirotovich gave me lessons, room, and board; in return I cleaned up his glazier workshop and played *sekund* in his *kapelye,* where I learned the dances by ear. After two years of apprenticeship I would receive fifty rubles [c. twenty-five dollars]. Unfortunately, Sirotovich didn't teach me any notes or scales, didn't let me play in the house, and rarely fed me. Weddings are where I ate most of my meals. I used to get sheet music from another *klezmer* in the *kapelye* and take it to the attic and study it by a little light that came through a hole I made in the wall.

After seventeen months I couldn't take the suffering, so I ran away to Radomsyl. I joined a very fine *kapelye* whose *kapelmayster* was Khunya "Nakhum" Vaynshteyn. He was an amazing violinist and taught me everything. In 1893, I left his *kapelye* and returned to Khabno where I formed my own *kapelye.* We had two violins, two clarinets, two trumpets, one trombone, one cello, one flute, and one drummer who also played cymbals. We played in Khabno and in the surrounding towns for the Jews, peasants, and Polish gentry.[122]

Like Makonovetski's father, many Jewish barbers were part-time *klezmorim,* and many part-time *klezmorim* worked as barbers for their main source of income. The following poem by the batkhn Alexander Fidelman tells of the different jobs a *klezmer* had to do to earn a living:

> *Lebn fun eyne klezmeray iz epes oykh nit keyn plan,*
> *Varem nit alemol iz khasene faren.*
> *Der tsimbler iz aft bay kahal a meshoret,*

---

[122] Stutschevsky, op. cit., p. 91.

Der paykler iz a shames afn bes-kvures.
Haynt past nokh tsu zayn shpitsik berdl,
Az er zol hobn on eygenem ferdl.
Der fidler, fun ven on ikh gedenk,
Halt alemol a shenk...[123]

The life of a *klezmer* is just not a plan,
Because weddings are not always available.
The *tsimbler* often works in the *kahal* as a servant,
The drummer is a beadle in the cemetery.
Today it is right to match his pointed little beard,
Just as he should have his own horse.
The fiddler, from what I remember,
Always stops at the tavern...

Whether a young boy learned from his father or was sent away to another teacher, the core techniques of *klezmer* music could not be learned from a methodology or manuscript book, but only through listening, watching, and mimicking. To execute the playing of any *klezmer* tune or make an adopted melody (Ukrainian, Polish, Ruthenian, Romanian, etc.) more *klezmer*-like, the *klezmer* had to have the knowledge and ability to incorporate the *dreydlekh* (Yid.: twists, turns; ornaments) into the tune. Here are the core *dreydlekh,* the vertebrae of all *klezmer* music:

- The *glitshn* (Yid.: slippery, sliding areas) were glissandos. The violinist would slide, usually rapidly, his finger from the lowest note to the highest.
- The *krekhtsn* (Yid.: groans, moans) were the moaning, achy long notes that gave *klezmer* music its distinctive sound, used usually by the violinist and clarinetist to evoke a lament.

---

[123] Ibid.

- The *kneytshn* (Yid.: fold, wrinkle, crease, crumple) were short notes with the achiness of the *krekhtsn,* but they were swallowed sharply as if squeezing the tip of the sound.
- The *tshoks* (Yid.: lavishness, splendor, bluff, swagger) were "bent" notes (purposefully not in concert pitch but just slightly under or over the actual note) with a laugh-like sound that was more cackle than giggle.
- Finally the *flageoletts* (It.: small flute) were harmonics, generally produced on the violin. Their use allowed the *klezmer* to create rapid whistling sounds evoking the heavens.

Incorporated into any tune, but especially in display pieces like the *doyne, vulekhl,* or *zogekhts,* these *dreydlekh* gave *klezmer* its unique Jewish feel. The respect the *klezmer* violinist who used these *dreydlekh* received from audiences everywhere he traveled cannot be overstated. His music was a form of therapy before music therapy ever became an academic subject, as this statement attests: "Many Jews found solace from studying the *Toyre;* the *klezmer* violinist gave solace by singing the *Toyre.*"[124]

Two of the leading Jewish musicologists of the twentieth century, Arno Nadel[125] and Abraham Z. Idelsohn, had their own criteria that defined the components of a Jewish melody. Nadel said there were seven criteria found in the Jewish repertoire, though not all tunes met all seven:

- There was a recitative and melismatic quality to the melody.
- The melody was based upon a diatonic scale.
- The rhythm was strong and often anapestic (the first two notes accented and short, followed by a long note).
- The melodies incorporated fifths and octaves.

---

[124] Interview with Izu Gott (originally from Dorohoi, Romania) in Yas, Romania, August 25, 1981. Gott's original Yiddish was: "A sakh yidn hobn gefinen nekhome in Toyre limood, un di klezmer hobn aza nekhome geshafn zingendik di toyre."

[125] Arno Nadel was a poet and liturgical musicologist born in Vilna. He moved to Berlin in 1895, where he amassed a huge collection of religious and Jewish folk music. He was murdered in Auschwitz; most of his collection was lost.

- The melody was meditative.
- The melody mixed different voices.
- The melody incorporated improvisation.[126]

As for Idelsohn, he said, "We see that just as the Jew, being of Semitic stock, is part of the Oriental world, so Jewish music—coming to life in the Near East—is, generally speaking, of one piece with the music of the Orient."[127] *Shteygers* (Yid.: manners, ways, kinds, modes) formed the basis of most of the *klezmer* repertoire. Their main musical property was the use of variant scales based on the dorian (d e f g a b c d) and phrygian (e f g a b c d e) tetrachordal modes. The following four *shteygers* gave *klezmer* music its distinct Semitic sound, and Idelsohn identified them by the name of the Sabbath prayer the melody was sung to:

- The *Ahava-Raba* (Heb.: a great love) is known as *freygish* among *klezmorim* today. It is similar to the phrygian, but with a permanent raised third; the occasional raising of the penultimate note in the musical phrase creates another augmented second (e f g# a b c d# e). This scale has a distinct Arabic feel; sometimes known as the Gypsy or *Hedjaz-Kar* mode, it is also often used by the *muezzin* when he calls his fellow Moslems to prayer.
- The *Magen-Avos* (Heb.: guardian of our fathers) mode was based on the dorian scale but with a flatted sixth.
- When the *Ahava-Raba* and *Magen-Avos* modes were combined, the scale was known as *Mishebeyrakh* (Heb.: he who blesses) or sometimes *Ov-Horakhamim* (Heb.: father of mercy) (d e f g# a b-flat c# d). Much of the southern Ukrainian and Romanian *klezmer* repertoire utilized this mode; it was thus sometimes refered to as the "Jewish" scale by both *klezmorim* and non-Jewish musicians.

---

[126] Stutschevsky, op. cit., p. 103.
[127] Abraham Z. Idelsohn, *Jewish Music: Its Historical Development* (New York: Henry Holt, 1929), p. 24.

• The *Adonoy Molokh* (Heb.: the Lord is king) mode was based on the lydian mode with a flatted seventh (c d e f# g a b-flat c). Many *khasidic* melodies from sects in Galicia (e.g. Belz, Bobov, Boyan, Dinov, Grodjisk) used this mode.

Thus the root of *klezmer* music—what made it sound "Jewish"—was not to be found in the folk music of Central or Eastern Europe but in the meditative chants and prayers of our Middle Eastern ancestors and neighbors.

By the end of the nineteenth century, many young *klezmer*—and other—violinists had obtained permission from the Czar to study in the music conservatories of St. Petersburg under Leopold Auer (1845–1930, born in Veszprém, Hungary) and Odessa under Pjotr Solomonovich Stolyarsky (1871–1944, who started off as a *klezmer*). The "Russian school" led by Auer grew out of the Franco-Belgian school led by two of the greatest classical violinists of the nineteenth century, Belgian Henri Vieuxtemps (1820–1881) and Belgian Eugéne Ysaÿe (1858–1931). Auer created a unique "Russian sound" by combining some of the violin techniques the *klezmer* violinists had been using for years with classical techniques. *Klezmer* violinists used a lot of vibrato and portamento with their left hand; they also held the violin securely under the chin (unlike most folk fiddlers), using various kinds of shoulder pads. This relieved their left hand of any responsibility for holding the instrument, which allowed them to concentrate freely upon fingering, ornamentation, and vibrato. They also held the bow closer to the nut and more firmly (also uncommon among folk fiddlers), with their bow arm held freely away from the body, giving them a more natural and powerful stroke. Thus the Russian classically trained violinists became famous for their broad, sumptuous tone.

Some of these young *klezmer* violinists went on to become classical musicians in orchestras, never to return to *klezmer* again. Others kept their feet in both the classical and *klezmer* worlds (affecting the *klezmer*'s style of playing and the band's repertoire); a few became world-famous virtuosi. Some of the most famous child prodigies weaned on *klezmer* include:

- Bronisław Huberman (1882–1947) of Czestochowa, Poland. His first teacher was Isidor Rosen Lotto (1840–1937), who taught Huberman, at age six, *klezmer* melodies Lotto had learned from his father, who had been a *klezmer*. Seeing that Huberman was a "wunderkind," at age seven he sent him to Berlin to one of the world's most famous violin teachers of his day, Joseph Joachim (1831–1907; he taught Auer, among others). Eventually Huberman finished his studies under Stolyarsky. In 1936 Huberman founded the Israeli Philharmonic Orchestra; he got the idea when he saw how many great Jewish instrumentalists had been persecuted and forced from their jobs by the Nazis.
- Efrem Zimbalist (1889–1985), born in Rostov-on-Don, Russia. He heard *klezmer* music from his grandfather, a *tsimbalist,* and studied under Auer.
- Mischa Elman (1891–1967) born in Talnoye (Tal'ne, Ukraine). His grandfather was a *klezmer* violinist from Uman. Alter Goyzman heard the six-year-old Elman and helped him get into St. Petersburg, where he studied under Auer.
- David Fyodorovich Oistrakh (1908–1977) of Odessa. He studied with his father, a *klezmer,* and eventually studied under Stolyarsky. In June 1981, I met David Kamhi, a classical violinist and a pupil of Oistrakh's, in Sarajevo, Bosnia. Oistrakh had kept up the tradition of first teaching *klezmer* tunes to his pupils: he taught Kamhi a *doyne* because it had a lot of ornamented and repeated sixteenth- and thirty-second-note runs.
- Jascha Heifetz (1901–87), born in Vilna (Vilnius, Lithuania), and Nathan Milstein (1904–1992), born in Odessa. While there is no direct *klezmer* connection to either of them, it makes logical sense that Heifetz, who studied under Auer, and Milstein, who studied under Stolyarsky, most likely heard and digested plenty of *klezmer.*

These and other Jewish violinists became household names in many Jewish homes. As a result, by the turn of the twentieth century, the violin had become known as the Jewish instrument, so much so that if a family could afford it, violin lessons were given to all the boys in the family. "My son the violinist" were the words many Jewish parents proudly declared to their family, friends, and acquaintances—only to be transformed to "my son the doctor" two generations later.

Into the Twentieth Century

After Alexander II's assassination in 1881, the Jews found themselves in a cauldron of anti-Semitism and political agitation. Every movement from anarchism to Zionism was sweeping the Pale. The proletarianization of the Jewish masses, accompanied by the *haskole,* changed forever the traditionally insular *shtetl* life. Even the *khasidic rabeim* could not hold back these radical alterations.

More and more *klezmorim* worked as artisans or day laborers and only played *klezmer* music part-time. If *kapelyes* traveled it was usually no more than a half-day's ride by horse and wagon. One can see from the following accounts that *klezmorim* now had other professions in the *shtetl:*

- "There were in Skierniewice three handsome Jews, all three dear *klezmorim.* The first was named Nison the Baker, the second was Lipman the Tinsmith, and the third was Berl the Cotton Weaver."[128]
- "The leader of the *klezmorim* in Semiatich [Semiatycze, Poland] was Shepsl the Hairdresser. He was a tall, handsome, manly person with a black twisted mustache like a Polish lord. He had two professions but was entirely poor. All the *klezmorim* from his band had two professions, and they were still poor."[129]

---

[128] Ahuvah Sidkuni Bernstein, "Dray Sheyne Balabatim," in *Sefer skierniewice,* ed. J. Perlow (Tel Aviv: Former Residents of Skierniewice in Israel), 1955, p. 356.

[129] Yasha Halpern, "Semiaticher Klezmorim," in *Kehilat Semiatycze,* ed. E. Tash (Tel Aviv: Association of Former Residents of Semiatich, 1965), p. 142.

• "In Ryki, Moshe Britzman played the bass in the *klezmer kapelye,* but this was not his profession. He owned a coach in which he would drive people to and from the train."[130]

At the beginning of the twentieth century oppressive poverty and unrelenting anti-Semitism were still part of the East European Jewish experience. However, the masses were renewing their interest in Judaism. Having been enticed by acculturation and assimilation under the Russian and Austro-Hungarian empires, the Jewish community began to reaffirm its Jewish identity. This did not mean that those progressive Jews who were Zionists, Labor Zionists, Yiddishists, or Bundists abandoned their political ideals; rather, they incorporated them into expressions of Hebrew and Yiddish culture. For many, Yiddish became the vehicle to express one's Jewish identity.

As in the revival of Ashkenazic culture in America over the last thirty years, the Jewish artists of a hundred years ago were at the forefront of this passionate return. One outgrowth from all of this Yiddish creativity was the Chernovits (Černivič, Ukraine) Yiddish Language Conference held in Chernovits, Bukovina, August 30–September 4, 1908, in which Jewish writers from Europe and the United States gathered to discuss the role of Yiddish in Jewish life. One issue was the relationship between Yiddish and modern Hebrew, which was undergoing its own renaissance in conjunction with Zionism. At the end of the conference, Yiddish was proclaimed a national language, which heightened its prestige considerably. The conference also made it painfully clear to many of its participants that many aspects of Yiddish culture were disappearing with the *shtetl.* The *haskole* had spread its tentacles into the hinterlands of Jewish Eastern Europe, proclaiming the twentieth century as the dawn of a new era. Progress meant ridding oneself of old Jewish traditions and customs in Eastern Europe that had developed over nearly a thousand years. Thus a number of Yiddishists decided

---

[130] Moses Tatebaum, "Khasones," in *Yizkor-bukh Tsum Fareybikn Dem Ondenk Fun Der Khorev Gevorener Yidishe Kehile Ryki,* ed. Shimon Kanc (Tel Aviv: Ryki Societies in Israel, Canada, Los Angeles, France and Brazil, 1973), p. 323.

to conduct ethnographic expeditions collecting all kinds of Jewish folklore: sayings, poems, songs, music, stories, photographs, clothes, religious and secular objects. Some of these artists significantly contributed to the body of *klezmer* culture:

- Sh. An-ski (Solomon Zainwil Rapaport, 1863–1920), a folklorist and ethnographer best known as the author of the Yiddish play *The Dybbuk* (*Dibek*),[131] collected Yiddish folksongs, *klezmer* melodies, oral histories, photographs, handicrafts, and instruments during his momentous ethnographic expedition (1911–14) in southern Ukraine.
- Menahem Kipnis (1878–1942), a singer, writer, and folklore collector, published 140 Yiddish folksongs with music in two volumes in Warsaw in 1918 and 1925.
- Yehuda Leyb Cahan (1881–1937), a collector of Yiddish folksongs and music and one of the founders of YIVO,[132] published his collection of over five hundred Yiddish folksongs (many with the music) in New York in 1912.
- Sholom Aleichem (1859–1916), a Yiddish writer and humorist, wrote his novella *Stempenyu* in 1888, in which he intimately portrayed the *klezmers'* world, including their personalities, work, music, travel, dalliances, and their use of *klezmer-loshn*.
- Yitskhok Leyb Perets (1852–1915), a Hebrew and Yiddish writer, wrote a short story called *The Klezmer's Death* in 1892, which relates how the

---

[131] *Dibek* (Heb.): evil spirit. *The Dybbuk,* the most famous of all Yiddish plays, was based on a compilation of many legends Anski had collected. In it, a young couple is betrothed at birth by their respective fathers. As they grow older the families lose contact with each other, and when the girl is ready to marry, her father decides to find a rich suitor. The young man, who is a poor Yeshive student, finds out, and out of hurt and anger, invokes dangerous forces through *kabule* (Heb.: mysticism) and dies. He then inhabits the body of the bride as a *dibek* and possesses her. She dies before her wedding and joins her intended in death.
[132] YIVO (Yidisher Visenshaftlikher Institut [Yid.: Institute for Jewish Research]) was founded in Vilna, Lithuania in 1925 to research, catalogue, and document all aspects of East European Jewish life. During World War II some of its archives were destroyed by the Nazis, but most were saved and brought to New York City, where YIVO reopened.

haskole movement caused pain and conflict to a typical *klezmer* family. While the father, the old *kapelmayster,* lies in his bed dying, the sons show their indifference; his hysterical wife admonishes them for their nonreligious ways and her husband for being unfaithful.

• Marc Chagall (1887–1985), an artist, worked in paint, stained glass, and fabric, portraying *shtetl* life with a keen sense of whimsy and fantasy. *Klezmer* violinists, wedding couples, and chickens floating above the *shtetl* can be seen in much of his work, and became some of his most identifiable icons, influencing many artists who portrayed *shtetl* life.

• Then there was Joel Engel (1868–1927), who composed the music for An-ski's Yiddish play *The Dybbuk.* He helped to establish the Society for Jewish Folk Music in St. Petersburg in 1908 with encouragement and help from Rimsky-Korsakov, who said: "Why should you Jewish students imitate European and Russian composers? The Jew possesses tremendous folk treasures.... Jewish music awaits its Glinka."[133] Engel, along with several others, many of whom became famous in their own right (Joseph Achron, Samuel Feinberg, Mikhail Fabianovich Gnesin, Alexander Krein, Moses Milner, Salomo Razovsky, Lazare Saminsky, and Ephraim Shklyar) collected, composed, concertized (as far as Kaliningrad, Leipzig, and Budapest), and published Jewish folk and classical music until the Russian Revolution of 1917.

The peace treaties that ended World War I proved cataclysmic for the Jews of Eastern Europe, for they brought about the demise of the Austro-Hungarian, Ottoman, and Russian empires. After the war, four new countries were established in Central and Eastern Europe: Czechoslovakia, Lithuania, Poland, and Yugoslavia. However, Italy, Romania, Albania, and Greece expanded their boundaries; Germany, Bulgaria, and Turkey lost land; and Serbia and Montenegro ceased to exist (having been absorbed by Yugoslavia). During this political maelstrom the Jewish community was

---

[133] J. Braun, *Jews in Soviet Music* (Jerusalem: Hebrew University, Research Paper No. 22, June 1977), p. 6.

transformed by political, social, and economic changes. Politics was seen by many Jews as an instrument for strengthening Jewish identity and increasing Jewish self-reliance. Since parliamentary government did not provide a public forum for the Jewish masses to express themselves, they took their grievances to the streets, seeking solidarity with equally poverty-stricken non-Jews. Strikes, protests, boycotts, and demonstrations against violent pogroms and the exclusion of Jews from civil rights were common. Some *klezmorim* became active in various political movements, playing anthems and labor songs while accompanying rallies and protest marches. These movements included:

- The *Bund* (Yid.: abbreviation for General Jewish Workers' Union). Founded in 1897 in Russia, the *Bund* was a Marxist socialist party specifically for Jewish workers in Lithuania, Poland, and Russia. Most socialist activity among Jews up until this time was conducted in Polish or Russian; but with the *Bund,* the Jewish socialists had a party that championed Yiddish as the language for the Jewish masses. *Bund*ists were committed to Yiddish autonomy and secular Jewish nationalism, and were avidly opposed to Zionism.
- *Po'ale Tsion* (Heb.: workers of Zion). Founded in 1907 in Russia, *Po'ale Tsion* was a Marxist socialist Zionist movement.
- *Tsair Zion* (Heb.: youth of Zion). Founded in 1903 in Russia, *Tzair Zion* was a radical movement, but more moderate than the socialist-Zionists.
- *Hashomer Ha-Tsair* (Heb.: the young guardians). Founded before World War I in Poland, *Hashomer Ha-Tsair* was a socialist-Zionist pioneering youth movement. It merged with *Tsair Zion* in 1916 and became a movement to prepare Jewish youth for kibbutz life in Israel.
- *Agudas Yisroel* (Heb.: association of Israel). Founded in Kattowitz (Katowice, Poland) in 1912, *Agudas Yisroel* was a world organization of orthodox Jews. They were passionately opposed to Zionism, socialism, and Yiddish secularism, and often supported non-Jewish candidates so they could help defeat Jewish socialist or Zionist candidates.

Here is one account of this new, political *klezmer* music:

> When it was the first of May the Jewish Worker's party made prepa-
> rations for the demonstration. The entire *kapelye* came with their wind
> instruments to help celebrate the worker's holiday and march around
> the marketplace and through the wide street to the professional union
> headquarters. Then they performed the Marseillaise and the Interna-
> tional, in that order. Next to the union headquarters was the house
> of Moses Meller of the *Bund.* From the balcony he gave a speech, at the
> end of which he called out: "Long live the First of May!" Then Arish
> took his clarinet and gave a signal that they should play.... Meyer
> Wolf stood with his violin, holding it next to his neck, while the peak
> of his cap was off to one side; his eyes were closed as he took a nap.
> When he heard the second exclamation—"Death to the bourgeoisie!"
> and the immediate loud response from the entire demonstration, Meyer
> Wolf began to play.[134]

Economic and ethnic diversity also influenced the *klezmorim* during
the interwar years (1920–1939). In regions—Bohemia, Moravia—and
cities—Posnan, Berlin, Bratislava, Budapest, Riga—with healthy economies, the Jewish communities modeled themselves after their Western European brethren. Assimilation generally led to the abandonment of Yiddish
and orthodoxy, especially *khasidism.* These assimilated Jews did not need
or want the *klezmorim*—*klezmer* music was *shtetl* music and not admired.
But this was not the case in the regions of sub-Carpathian Ruthenia, Transylvania, Bukowina, and Galicia, Poland, which were mostly agrarian and
nonindustrialized, and where non-Jewish peasantry made up the majority
of the population. These much more depressed local economies fed the
nationalism of the right wing and its insatiable appetite for anti-Semitism; the traditional safety valve of immigration to the United States was

---

[134] Mordecai Greenstein, "Klezmer," in *Opatow: Sefer Zikaron Le-ir Va-em Be-Yisrael,* ed. Z.
Yasheev (Tel Aviv: The Apt Organization in Israel, USA, Canada and Brazil, 1966), pp. 138–39.

no longer viable as new restrictions against immigration from Central and Eastern Europe were implemented in 1924. Despite the various progressive Jewish political parties and youth movements in nonindustrialized Eastern Europe, the Jewish communities there in the 1920s and '30s remained basically Yiddish speaking, lower middle class, proletarian, and strongly influenced by the orthodoxy. Consequently there was still work for the *klezmorim*.

The *klezmer's* repertoire during the interwar years still consisted of many of the traditional wedding melodies, dances, military marches, and light classical overtures. But it was significantly changed, too. The popularity of Yiddish theatre, from both the theatrical troupes based in Eastern Europe and those from America, was on the rise. Sheet music and recordings were increasingly available. More people had access to radios and listened to popular European and American tunes. Yiddish films from America and Eastern Europe were screened. And some Jews now had the means to travel back and forth from the new world to the old world. All of these factors created a flood of new Yiddish music.

Yiddish songs like "Roumania Roumania," "Mayn Shtelle," "Papirosn," and "Vu Zaynen Mayne Zibn Gute Yor" were all written in the United States, yet became very popular among Jews in Central and Eastern Europe during the 1920s and '30s—so popular that many Jews and Rom I met in Eastern Europe who sang or played these tunes thought they were originally from their countries.

• "Roumania Roumania" was written by Aaron Lebedeff (1873–1960), who was born in Gomel, Belarus. He initially studied to be a *khazn;* after he immigrated to America via Shanghai, he became a very successful singer, actor, and comedian in the Yiddish theatre. In 1925 he recorded "Roumania Roumania," and instantly it became a hit among Jewish audiences. It started slow and rubato, like a *doyne,* and eventually segued into a fast *freylekhs.* The song was a nostalgic (like many Yiddish theatre songs) look at the pleasures of Rumania: its food, wine, women, and camaraderie. Today it is the most requested Yiddish song of *klezmer kapelyes* and a common vehicle for Yiddish vocalists to show off their talents.

- "Mayn Shtetle" was written by the Yiddish vaudevillian and theatre star Jacob Jacobs, with music by Alexander Olshanetsky (1892–1946). Olshanetsky was born in Odessa and trained as a classical violinist, then immigrated to America (via China), where he became a very successful Yiddish songwriter. In 1932 he composed "Mayn Shtetle Belz," another nostalgic song about the old country. The song concerned the *shtetl* Belz in Bessarabia, and became so popular among the Jews in Eastern Europe that some substituted their town's name for Belz so they could sing about their idyllic lives when they were children in the *shtetl.* Thus in Yas, the Jews sang "Mayn Shtetle Yas," while in Poland the song was translated into Polish ("Mia Steczko Belz") and sung by Jews and non-Jews.

- "Papirosn" (Yid.: cigarettes), written in 1932 by the Yiddish actor, songwriter, and playwright Herman Yablokoff, was originally song in a play called *Der Payets* (Yid.: the clown). This plaintive ballad about a poor orphan cigarette peddler was eventually made into a Yiddish 35-mm silent film with the same title, in which the orphan ragamuffin was played by Sidney Lumet, the eleven-year-old son of Yiddish actor Baruch Lumet. During World War II many Yiddish songs that were sung in the ghettos and camps used this melody with different lyrics. Although the melody was attributed to Yablokoff, who said he composed the song in the mid-1920s, I found several different versions (different from Yablokoff's) played by the Rom, Ruthenians, and Ukrainians. So I suspect that rather than composing the original music, he arranged his version from a beautiful, haunting folk melody known to many musicians (including *klezmorim*) that eventually found its way to America, and it became the version everyone learned to sing.

- "Vu Zaynen Mayne Zibn Gute Yor" (Yid.: where are my seven good years) is a tune I learned from Eli Mermelshteyn, who was both a bookkeeper and amateur violinist in Košice, Slovakia. He told me this poignant story:

I was born in the village of Batfa. We didn't have a *shil* [Yid.: synagogue (Carpathian pronunciation)] so we walked about ten kilometers to Velki Kapušany every *Shabes*. My father was the *bal-tfile* [Heb.: master of prayer] and loved to sing. So while we walked to *shil* he practiced singing his prayers and made me repeat them so I knew them too. He said it wouldn't look good if the *bal-tfile*'s son couldn't *daven* [Yid.: pray]. He also liked to sing the new Yiddish songs he learned when he visited Užhorod for business. Traveling Yiddish theatre troupes occasionally came through Užhorod on their way to Košice, then to Budapest. "Vu Zaynen Mayne Zibn Gute Yor" was one of his favorite songs, because he said a Jew always should accept what God had given him, but you still had the right to ask and even argue with Him for something better. When the war began we were all deported to Auschwitz: my parents, sister, and younger brother. Only my sister and I survived. The last time I saw my father was when he was led into the gas chambers.[135]

Though the advent of Yiddish theatre, film, and wine-cellar cafés did provide more performance venues for the *klezmer* in larger towns and cities, the majority of *klezmorim* lived impoverished lives until the final death knell of the Holocaust. One result of these more difficult economic times during the late 1920s through the mid-'30s was the formation of a stratum of *klezmorim* who were forced to become beggars. Jews rarely write or speak about this subject because of the great shame communities felt about not being able to take care of their own. I became much more aware of these beggars of the interwar years (especially during the Depression) after reading Lucjan Dobroszycki and Barbara Kirshenblatt-Gimblett's *Image Before My Eyes: A Photographic History of Jewish Life in Poland Before the Holocaust*,[136]

---

[135] Interview with Eli Mermelshteyn (originally from Batfa, Ukraine) in Košice, Slovakia, Nov. 9, 1984.
[136] New York: Schocken Books, 1977.

which includes the now quite famous photograph of "Yankel the *klezmer*" playing in the streets of Warsaw in the 1920s.

Here is a *klezmer* bemoaning his fate: "A few years ago it was difficult for me to play the clarinet. I had no air, no strength to breathe, and because of this I lost my profession. Then, when I became healthy, I hardly earned anything. The poor celebrations paid very little and the rich weddings happened very seldom. So this is how it is: because I cannot earn anything for my family and I am forced to go from courtyard to courtyard, I am a 'broken tool,' unsuccessful."[137]

In some big cities in the 1920s and '30s—such as Warsaw, Łodž, Kraków, and Wilno (Poland); Mukačevo and Užhorod (Czechoslovakia); and Chișinău (Kishinev), Cluj-Napoca, and Černăuti (Czernowitz) (Romania)—apartment buildings often had either a window or a small balcony opening onto a central courtyard, with usually just one dark narrow passageway leading out to the street. Sometimes paved with stone, or with patches of grass and a lone tree growing in one corner, these courtyards were oases for the poor who inhabited these crowded dwellings. They provided a place for the children and adults to relax, recreate, and get some glimpses of nature in a dirty urban environment. The tenants of these buildings were generally Jewish, and that often meant there was a *shtibl*[138] or *kheyder*[139] adjacent to the courtyard, with a steady stream of boys and men coming in and out. The courtyards teemed with Jewish life: the voices lifted in prayer or study, the children playing, the adults conversing or reading on benches, women beating their carpets clean, dogs and cats roaming freely, and *klezmorim* playing and singing for their captive audiences.

---

[137] Ruven Branin, "Der Yidisher Musikant," in *Pinkes Zaglembye: Memorial Book,* Ed. J. Rapoport (Melbourne: Zaglembie Society and Zaglembie Committee in Melbourne, Tel Aviv Hamenorah Society, 1972), p. 242.

[138] A *shtibl* (Yid.: small house) was a small *khasidic* house of prayer.

[139] A *kheyder* (Heb.: class) was a Jewish elementary religious school. Most orthodox boys and girls in Poland during the 1920s and '30s went to *kheyder.*

The level of these performances ranged from amateurish to professional. Depending on their audience, they played current popular tunes, Jewish folksongs, *klezmer* tunes, Polish, Ukrainian, Russian, and Rom folksongs, melodies from operas, and classical pieces. Sometimes the *klezmer* played alone; if he brought a *kapelye,* the instrumentation could be as varied as violin, mandolin, trumpet, accordion, small drums, and cymbals. In the Jewish courtyards in Poland the *klezmorim* often played sections of the opera *La Juive* by Halévy, while in the Polish courtyards they played themes from Moniuszko's *Halka.* Conversely, the *klezmorim* who wandered from courtyard to courtyard in Cernauti would play themes from Enescu's *Romanian Rhapsody.* After each performance the people in the courtyard put money in a can or in an instrument case, while those who leaned out of their windows and balconies threw money down. Some listeners, though, were not so happy to have these itinerant musicians ply their trade in their courtyard, and instead of throwing money they threw garbage or water out of their windows.

An eighty-two-year-old Jew I met while doing field research in Michalovce, Slovakia in 1984 told me this anecdote:

> I remember when Yoel Simkhe the *klezmer,* who played alto in his uncle's band, lost his right hand. He was in an accident at the lumber mill. Now he couldn't work at the mill or play alto. After several years, during which I hadn't seen Yoel, he appeared one day in our courtyard on Ulica Żydowski (Jew Street). He was pushing a dilapidated carriage, and in it was a big gramophone with a big copper tube coming out of it. He had a few records he would play. Two that I remember were "Tango Milongo" [composed by the Jewish jazz composer and pianist Jerzy Petersburski (Jerzy Melodysta, 1897–1979)] and "A Khazn—A Shikur" (A Cantor—A Drunk). After he played a couple of records, the people who were listening from their windows would throw Yoel a few *kroner* [coins], which he would stuff in a little purse that hung from his belt. He would come to our courtyard once a week. I looked forward to his visits even if he played the same

tunes over and over again. I never thought of Yoel Simkhe as a beggar. When he appeared my mother used to say, "God respects all Jews, especially those who bring joy to others."[140]

Here is another account of a *klezmer* who was a regular in the Jewish courtyards in Muranów, a neighborhood in Warsaw that was ninety percent Jewish before World War II:

There was a *klezmer* musician called by the children "one-man orchestra." He walked from courtyard to courtyard with a bass drum on his back that had two copper cymbals attached on springs, each one with a piece of twine connected to his right shoe. With his shoe the *klezmer* tapped very energetically. With one hand he played the snare and with the other he played the trumpet. On the trumpet he played a *skotshne* while he danced. It was said that he played very well. Along with the drums and cymbals, he would sometimes shout as well. These shouts were like a coda to the piece he was playing, letting the audience know he was about to end. Accompanying him was a little girl who he introduced as his daughter. She held a small tambourine in her hand, occasionally playing with her father, but mostly using it to collect money that had been thrown from the windows or given by passersby. With a high-pitched voice she sang popular songs, like one by Gold called "Don't Leave Me, Don't Go Away from Me," and Petersburski's song "I Am Afraid to Sleep Alone." This song in particular sounded very funny in her high-pitched voice. All the ladies were disgusted that a young girl sang such songs. Other songs she sang that were extremely popular with the people were "Rebeka" and "Mia Steczko Belz." These songs made them cry and softened their hearts. After each of these songs it would rain change that fell from the windows in tightly wrapped papers.[141]

---

[140] Interview with Yiska Eisikowicz (originally from Velki Kapušany, Slovakia) in Michalovce, Slovakia, Nov. 11, 1984.

[141] Fuks, op. cit., p. 31.

The Holocaust and Its Aftermath

During World War II, *klezmorim* performed in various ghetto ensembles, playing popular and Jewish music. They played for Yiddish theatres, choirs, classes, and for public and private celebrations. But in the ghetto the *klezmer* was also relegated to begging in the streets with his instrument, if he was lucky enough to still have one. Instrumental and vocal music was a source of entertainment, therapy, and hope for all the Jews until the ghettos were liquidated.

Those *klezmorim* that managed to survive the ghetto and deportation to one of the hundreds of concentration camps often found themselves playing in the camp orchestra. They still had to do their slave labor every day, but in addition some had to perform for the Nazis at their dinner parties and other social events. If they were lucky, they received a little more food. Good musicians were not a plentiful commodity in the concentration camps, so the Nazis sometimes prolonged their lives a bit longer than those of the other prisoners.

Leopold Kozlowski was one such *klezmer*. He played in the labor camp orchestras of Jaktorów and Kurowica (near Lvov) in occupied Poland. Leopold was born in a *klezmer* family in Przemyslany, Poland; his grandfather, Peysekh Brandwein, who played the violin, had ten sons and four daughters from four different wives, all of whom played in his *kapelye*. They performed throughout the county of Volyn in Galicia, and were hired to play for many of the rich Polish landowners. They even played for the Kaiser Franz Joseph when he got married and for the Premishlaner Khasidic *rebe* Rabbi Meir ben Aaron Leyb (?1780–1850) during the intermediary days of *Sukes* and *Peysekh*. Just before and after World War I all the sons immigrated to America, except the youngest, Tsvi-Hirsh (Leopold's father), and the oldest, Eli. Among the immigrants were Leopold's uncles Naftuli and Azriel Brandwein; Azriel played the cornet and Naftuli played the clarinet. Many *klezmer* aficionados consider Naftuli one of the best *klezmer* clarinetists ever recorded. Tsvi-Hirsh Kleinman, who took his mother's maiden name as his own so that he could perform without always being compared to his father, formed his own large *kapelye,* consisting of three violins and two *sekunds,* cello, B-flat clarinet, C clarinet, E-flat clarinet, two flutes, two *tsimbalists,* contrabass, and drum. They performed in Galicia as well as Lvov, Tarnopol, Stanisaw (L'viv, Ternopil, Ivano Frankivs'k, all in the Ukraine), and other towns in eastern Poland. When the Depression came, Tsvi-Hirsh's *kapelye* disbanded and he formed a *kapelye* with his sons Leopold on accordion and Dulko on violin, along with Shia Tsimbler on *tsimbl,* Dugi Brandwein on *sekund,* and Hirshele Dudlezack on drums. In 1933 he went to Tres Arroyos, Argentina, where he was concertmaster in the philharmonic. He returned in 1937. Four years later, on November 5, 1941, he was led into a forest with 360 other Jews from the Przemyslany ghetto and shot by the SS.

Leopold Kozlowski recalled:

I was in the ghetto with my mother and brother when we found out my father was murdered. Eventually they liquidated the ghetto, but before the Germans came we helped our mother to escape. She was caught in a peasant's barn and shot. Dulko and I were taken to several labor camps.

In the first one, in Kurowica, I was taken to the SS commandant Unterscharführer Karl Kempka. He knew I was a musician and said he had a proposal for me. If I could teach him to play Strauss's "Blue Danube" in seven days so he could play it at this SS party I would not have to work as hard as the other prisoners. If he didn't learn in the week, I would be shot. He had this Hohner accordion that I was supposed to use to teach him. Unfortunately, he knew nothing about music and was tone deaf. I was in complete despair, but every evening, after working many hours in the swampy fields, I gave him a lesson. He would call me "Herr Professor." At the end of the week at the party, Kempka managed to squeeze out the waltz to great applause. They then threw me out of the door, breaking my leg. That night they gave me a double portion of our usual shit dinner.

In Jaktorów I played music on either a piano or accordion. It was much harder for Dulko because he didn't have a violin and it wasn't easy to find one. Finally I got a violin for him and we were able to occasionally see each other when we played together for some event. But once there was this big ball for all the SS in the camp, and they only brought me to play. In this room was this table set with all this food and drink. It was excruciating to be in the room, smelling all this food, while playing and feeling such starvation. Half way through the party they ordered me to take off all my clothes, get up on the table, and play the accordion. I did this for a few minutes when they ordered me to bend over. As I bent over they put a lit candle in my anus. Everyone then took turns lighting their cigarettes and cigars as I continued to play while they laughed.

In Jaktorów, in the beginning, there was a small orchestra. We were gradually getting smaller and smaller as the SS shot the musicians. One day SS Shaul ordered me to compose a tango. He then forced me and a few others to play this Death Tango, even when we had no more physical or emotional strength. We played the Death Tango as the prisoners were led to execution. We played as they took their last steps.[142]

The following passage describes the deepest despair a *klezmer* could feel.

Itsik Klezmer and his sons had a good reputation in town. He was the leader and first violinist in the *kapelye*. Nearly everyone in his *kapelye* was a family member or relative. There was Shmerl on bass, Meyer-Shakhnes on flute, Yisroel the Tall with the long trumpet, and Khamyia on violin. The drummer was Yisroel's son Elal. They played at Jewish and gentile landowners' weddings and celebrations in towns and villages. They were the only *kapelye* in the Kozieniecer district. Itsik played with great strength and was an immense artist.

---

[142] Interview with Leopold Kozlowski, op. cit. The author directed a documentary film about Kozlowski called *The Last Klezmer: Leopold Kozlowski: His Life and Music* (1994).

During the Holocaust Itsik's son Shloyme worked in the gas chambers in Treblinka. He stood by the entrance of the gas chambers and played with the orchestra as the bodies were gassed. While he stood there he saw his nine-year-old son being led in. He grabbed his son by the hand and pulled him out of the line. An SS officer saw and laughed and kicked the little boy in his stomach. At that very moment Shloyme smashed his violin over the SS officer's head and marched with his only child into the gas chamber.[143]

Most of those lucky enough to find a short reprieve by playing in the camp orchestra were eventually murdered anyway. We do not have the exact numbers of how many *klezmorim* were murdered during the Holocaust, but of the approximately four to five thousand *klezmorim* living in Eastern Europe before the war,[144] some ninety percent perished.

Yes, a significant number of *klezmorim* had immigrated to America and contributed to the rich *klezmer* and Yiddish popular-music scene from 1890 to the late 1940s. But the cradle of Yiddish culture, which had nurtured Ashkenazic instrumental and vocal music for nearly one thousand years, was all but wiped out. Those few *klezmorim* who survived and returned to their homes after the war found the Soviet Union's hegemony over the rest of Eastern Europe total and, for the most part, there was little interest in reviving any kind of Jewish life. They also found that professing

---

[143] "Itsik Klezmer (Nodelman)," in *Sefer Zikaron Le-Kehihat Kozieniec,* Ed. B. Kaplinski (Tel Aviv: Former Residents of Kozieniec in Israel, 1969), p. 253.

[144] Beregovski estimated that in the second half of the nineteenth century there were some two thousand *klezmorim,* and by the turn of the twentieth century three thousand in Ukraine and Russia. In his ethnographic research he found that in every region in the Ukraine there were fifty to sixty *kapelyes* with three to five players. Stutschevsky figured that since some cites like Barditshev had fifty *klezmorim* and Radomsyl with approximately five thousand Jews had two large *kapelyes,* if you averaged at least four to five *klezmorim* per *shtetl,* by World War I there were four to five thousand *klezmorim* in Poland, Galicia, Lithuania, and Ukraine. This did not take into account Romania, which had several hundred *klezmorim* at the same time. Beregovski, "Yidishe Instrumentale Folks-Muzik," op. cit., p. 15; Stutschevsky, "Klezmorim," op. cit., p. 78.

one's Jewishness in any way was not advantageous and led to harassment by authorities.

Occasionally one heard *klezmer* music and Yiddish folksongs live or on a record at the Jewish clubs established by the local governments with financial aid from the American Joint Distribution Committee, beginning in 1946. The music was also heard at private gatherings in Jewish homes; at *Khanike* and *Purim* celebrations in the synagogue; in the Yiddish theatres of Yas and Lodz, then Bucharest and Warsaw; at occasional Rom celebrations; at cabarets; and even at some Jewish weddings. But those *klezmorim* who came of age before the Holocaust found very few young Jews who were interested in learning how to play and sing Yiddish music.

It would take fifty years after the Holocaust began for politicians and the Jewish communities to accept and promote the revival of Yiddish culture in Eastern Europe and the former Soviet Union. Is it too little, too late? Would the creative directions Yiddish culture (i.e., *klezmer* music) has taken have been the same whether or not the Holocaust had happened? Is the revival of *klezmer* music in Eastern Europe aesthetically anchored or directionless? On the surface the resurgence mixes irony with incongruity. It took only two generations for Jewish culture (often with few Jews participating) to resurface in the very countries where six million Jews were murdered. To be able to hear the occasional strains of *klezmer* music as I walk the streets of Eastern Europe where my ancestors once walked is both hauntingly beautiful and bittersweet.

> Without the music the public didn't make a move. The *klezmer,* who had long looked forward to the wedding, played throughout with great pride and fanfare. His music rang throughout the *shtetl....* The *klezmorim* demonstrated once again their magic by making the public sad and happy, as they had done in the past, while filling the heart and soul with bliss.[145]

---

[145] Abraham Barnholtz, "Di Khasene in Shtetl," *Yizker-bukh Tsu Vlodave,* ed. Shimon Kamc (Tel Aviv: Wlodowa Societies in Israel and North and South America, 1974), p. 532.

The Drutt family *kapelye* in Tomaszów Lubelski, Poland, in the mid-1920s. On the right, holding the violin, is the *kapelmayster* Chaim Yitzchak Drutt. COURTESY OF HELEN GRZESH

The Lerman family *kapelye* in Plotsk, Poland, before World War I. Far right, with trumpet, is Mendel Lerman; far left, with bass, is *kapelmayster* Abraham Lerman; Aaron Lerman is holding the violin upright on his lap. COURTESY OF MICHAEL BRENNER

The Oszmiana *kapelye* accompanying the production of the Yiddish play *Shulamis*.

The Saratchikis's wedding being led by the *klezmorim* past Kheykl Milner's house in Drohiczyn Poleski, Poland (1917).

The Tyszowcer *klezmorim.* PINKAS TISHOVITS

Bughici family *kapelye* in 1915 in Iaşi, Romania. From right to left: Feivel, Moyshe, the father [Dumitru Bughici's grandfather], Yossel, and Avram. COURTESY OF YALE STROM ARCHIVES

The Eldelberg brothers, who performed
klezmer in and around Lvova, Russia, and
occasionally as far as Kherson before World
War I. COURTESY OF SARAH L. M. CHRISTIANSEN

Shlomo Klezmer (Vilenberg) in
Luniniec, Poland. *YISKOR KEHILOT*
LUNINIEC/KOZHANHORODOK

Klezmorim playing at a Jewish wedding in Belarus (Soviet
Union) in the 1920s. COURTESY OF YEFIM GERIBOW

Mikhl the Klezmer (Solomovitch) and his students in Baranowicze, Poland (1920s).
BARANOVITZ SEFER ZIKARON

A *kapelye* in Kleck, Poland, in 1928. From right to left: Asher Vaynberg, Efrayim Shpilberg, Yosef-Leyb Vaynger, Yuzik Martsinkovsky [a Christian]. *PINKAS KLECK*

Zogot *kapelye* in Zaporozhye, Soviet Union (Zaporižžja, Ukraine), in 1935. Top row, right to left: Sheyl Zogot on bass baritone, Zalman Althoys on tenor, Yidl Belinky on alto, and Motl Zogot on alto. Bottom row, from right to left: Yudl Olechov on cornet, Meyer Lefkovitch on cornet, *kapelmayster* Leybl Rotshteyn (played cornet), Berl Solos on cornet, Tevel Yezeriets on cornet, Semekh Khodus on baritone, and Vevel Olechov on bass drum and cymbal. COURTESY OF YALE STROM ARCHIVES

David Kagan playing the piano in his home in Wrocław, Poland (1984). BRIAN BLUE

Leopold Kozlowski *kapelye* in Przemyslany, Soviet Union (Peremišljani, Ukraine), in 1941. Leopold Kozlowski holds the accordion; to the right, his younger brother Dulko holds the violin. COURTESY OF LEOPOLD KOZLOWSKI

Hirsh Kleinman (right), Leopold Kleinman (Kozlowski) on piano, and Dulko Kleinman on violin in Przemyslany, Poland (Peremišljani, Ukraine), in 1930.
COURTESY OF LEOPOLD KOZLOWSKI

The cast for the production of *The Dybbuk* in Buczacz, Poland (Bučač), in 1933. The main characters, Chonon and Leah, are seated in the center of the third row from the top; Barry "Bishka" Melnick is in the top row, third person from right. COURTESY OF BARRY MELNICK

The Yiddish State Theatre, built in 1958, in Bucharest, Romania, in the Jewish neighborhood, today a predominantly Rom neighborhood (1985). YALE STROM

An actor prepares to perform *A Goldfadn Khulem* at the Yiddish State Theatre, built in 1955, in Warsaw, Poland (1984). BRIAN BLUE

Borya "Ben" Bazyler at age fourteen in his school uniform playing the drums in Warsaw, Poland (1936). COURTESY OF MANYA WEBER

Izu Gott, playing the accordion, leads his *kapelye* in a rehearsal in the kosher kitchen in Iaşi, Romania (1985). BRIAN BLUE

Berko Gott (right) during morning prayers in the *Dorfishe* synagogue in Dorohoi, Romania (1985). YALE STROM

Duvid Gott in his home in Dorohoi, Romania (1985). BRIAN BLUE

A Jewish wedding in the synagogue in Roman, Romania, with Rom musicians, led by an Albanian violinist, performing *klezmer* music. YALE STROM

Shani Virag (accordion) playing with his fellow Rom in his home in Vylok, Ukraine (1993). YALE STROM

Dumitru Bughici in the Yiddish theatre in Bucharest, Romania (1985). BRIAN BLUE

The gravestone in Iaşi, Romania, of Dumitru Bughici's uncle (Moyshe) and cousins, who were killed in the pogrom of July 29, 1941. YALE STROM

Jewish concentration camp musicians leading a fellow prisoner to be shot in a French concentration camp. COURTESY OF THE SIMON WIESENTHAL CENTER

Tzvi Segula playing a *klezmer* tune in his home in Kraków, Poland (1988). YALE STROM

Nikolai Radu, a Rom who played *klezmer* music throughout Bessarabia before and after World War II, playing at a Jewish friend's home in Kishinev, Soviet Union, (Chişinău, Moldova) in 1984. BRIAN BLUE

Paul Babici, a Rom who played *klezmer* music with many different *kapelye*s throughout Moldavia, including the Gott *kapelye,* playing in the kosher kitchen with the author in Iaşi, Romania (1985). BRIAN BLUE

The Mare synagogue in Iaşi, Romania, built in the seventeenth century down the street from the *klezmer* synagogue on Pantelimon Street (1985). YALE STROM

A *klezmer* playing on *Purim* in the Mare synagogue in Iaşi,.Romania (1988). YALE STROM

Cili and Itsik Svarţ in their home in Iaşi, Romania (1996). YALE STROM

The *Dorfishe* synagogue in Dorohoi, Romania, where many local *klezmorim* played at Jewish weddings; it was torn down in 1990 for an apartment building (1985). YALE STROM

The synagogue *hoyf* in Košice, Czechoslovakia, (Slovakia) where *shames* Benyomin Rozenberg lived and worked (1984). YALE STROM

The synagogue *hoyf* in Miskolc, Hungary, where Rabbi Yidl Weiss, a Satmar *khasid,* also served the Jewish community as the *shoykhet* (1988). YALE STROM

Eli Mermelshteyn in the Jewish community offices in Košice, Czechoslovakia (Slovakia) (1987). YALE STROM

János Németh, a Rom, tuning his *tsimbl* on a tourist boat on the Danube in Budapest, Hungary (1993). YALE STROM

A *klezmer* whom the author met while having lunch at the kosher kitchen in Miskolc, Hungary (1988). YALE STROM

Grave of the Kalever *Rebe* Rabbi Eizik (Isaac) Taub (1751–1821), the founder of *khasidism* in Hungary and composer of the famous song "*Szol A Kakas Mar*" (Hung.: The Rooster Crows Already), in Nagykálló, Hungary (1985). BRIAN BLUE

A Rom musician playing some *klezmer* tunes on the street in Budapest, Hungary (1988).
YALE STROM

Max Levitt (1863–1936) in 1898: he was born in a *shtetl* outside of Kiev, Russia (Kÿiv, Ukraine), and was the leader of a *kapelye;* he immigrated to New York City in 1909. COURTESY OF MARTY LEVITT

Marty Levitt (1931–), Max Levitt's grandson, in a publicity photo in 1961. COURTESY OF MARTY LEVITT

Jack "Yankl" Levitt (1901–1974), who was born in a *shtetl* outside of Kiev, learned to play the violin from his father Max, and also played trombone, piano, and accordion (c. 1914–15). COURTESY OF MARTY LEVITT

Klezmer in der Naye Velt: 1880–1960

•

(*KLEZMER* IN THE NEW WORLD: 1880–1960)

The Great Immigration

Between 1880 and 1914, nearly one-third of East European Jewry, most from Czarist Russia and Poland, emigrated from their homelands, the majority to America, in the largest movement of Jews since the Spanish Inquisition. Wretched poverty, pervasive anti-Semitism, and violent pogroms gave the Jews ample reason to seek a better life in the *Goldene Midine*.[1] A small minority undertook the journey for ideological reasons, but most simply went to better their chances of a life unfettered by the daily grind of *shtetl* existence. During the first twenty years of this immigration, many orthodox and *khasidic* Jews, feeling that America was a "*treyf*" (Yid.: not kosher) land and would corrupt the Jews, did not leave Eastern Europe. For example, Rabbi Khayim Eliezer Spira (1868–1937), the Munkatsher Rebe, was

---

[1] *Goldene Midine* (Yid.): golden country. Immigrants often received letters from family members who had immigrated to America, exaggerating the success their families were having in their new home (often to cover up the reality of their failings in America). The *goldene midine* with its streets of gold was a common metaphor used by the East European Jews to describe America.

virulently against Zionism and Jews immigrating to America: "It is my duty to proclaim that, according to our Holy Law, it is forbidden to offer the slightest assistance to the Zionist heretics and free thinkers.... The Jews in America don't keep *Shabes,* eat non-kosher food, and sleep with gentile women. America is a *treyfe* land."[2]

The majority of East European Jews settled on the Eastern seaboard, primarily in the New York area. By 1910, there were nearly two million Jews in New York City; between 1880 and 1924, approximately two-and-a-half million arrived from Eastern Europe. They set out to establish many of the same social organizations as they were used to in their homelands: burial societies, synagogues, Jewish schools, aid organizations, Jewish shops (butcher, book, and bakery), and *landsmanshaftn* (Yid.: organizations of expatriate Jews from the same East European town). As they built infrastructures that assisted the Jews in education, economics, and religion, they also transplanted and reconstructed Yiddish culture; based on the language, this manifested itself in literature, theatre, and music.

While speaking Yiddish for business, everyday life, and pleasure was the norm for the vast majority of Jews in Eastern Europe, the Yiddish world in America during these years was destined to be a transitional one. In the beginning there were enough enthusiastic first-generation Yiddish speakers who wanted and needed Yiddish-language newspapers, books, theatre, and music. But as American culture (particularly the English language) seeped into and influenced East European Jewish culture, the immigrants' perceptions of themselves and what it meant to be a Jew in America changed. Just having to work on the *Shabes* became a problem and threatened the hegemony of the rabbis and religion. *Shtetl* life might have been confining to many Jews, but life in America, particularly in the urban centers, was chaotic. Until 1924, when the United States government halted legal immigration, a renewable source of Yiddish-speaking Jews kept coming to America. But after the doors to Ellis Island were slammed shut and

---

[2] Menachem Daum and Oren Rudavsky, *A Life Apart: Hasidism in America* (film), distributed by First Run Features, prod. in 1997.

assimilation for many Jews became a means to an end, Yiddish culture in America began to recede rapidly, evolving from a necessity of Jewish life to a nostalgic memory for the immigrant and finally to a piece of clothing that no longer fit.

In this chaotic urban cauldron, the immigrant tried to make a living. Though most *klezmorim* had struggled with poverty and their fluctuating social status in Eastern Europe, they nevertheless had a specific and important role to perform in the Jewish community. In America, though, immigrants were immediately thrust into a bewildering industrial society, one that either gave them the opportunity to succeed economically if they had the willpower, physical strength, and luck, or one that swallowed them whole with all its vices of graft, gambling, prostitution, and alcoholism. The immigrant also had to contend with the abundance of material goods available for all who had the money. Such items as fresh produce were available every day, not just on *shtetl* market days; new clothes were more abundant and cheaper because of mass production; there were new kinds of appliances they'd never even heard of back home; and, especially for the *klezmer*, there was an array of used and new instruments. Sometimes the Old World mentality took longer to catch up:

> I played the violin for a little while. My parents could only afford a used one that had been scratched and nicked quite a bit. I saw a brand-new one in the music store window not far from where my grandparents lived on Norfolk St. [in the Lower East Side]. I *hakt* (Yid.: chopped, hewed, minced; fig. bothered) my father day and night to buy me that new violin. All he ever said was, "No, be happy you have a fiddle. In Europe, my first fiddle was made from a wooden cigar box." Needless to say I didn't get the violin. But it didn't matter: I became a *khazn*.[3]

---

[3] Interview with Felix Groveman (originally from New York City) in Los Angeles, California, October 15, 1984.

Obtaining more material goods made everyday life easier and more interesting, but consumerism was a false messiah. Socioeconomic divisions between Jews were becoming more defined and difficult to surmount. Working harder and longer hours held out the false promise to many that they too could one day become part of the leisure class and no longer just "greenhorns." Many immigrant Jews saw assimilation, which had been the means for German Jews to achieve a certain social and economic success in America, as a way to be socially acceptable, to become part of the rising middle class, and, maybe, even one of the Jewish millionaires like the Loebs, Lehmans, Schiffs, and Seligmans. And the *klezmer* had to contend not only with material consumption, but with overwhelming cultural consumption as well.

> The deluge of new popular, urban, commercial entertainments (theatre, vaudeville, amusement parks, dance halls, restaurants), all but previously unknown to Eastern Europe, were soon the focus of the enormous collective Jewish "thirst for entertainment almost as strong as the hunger for upward mobility." Jewish immigrants flocked to forms of urban leisure that combined elements of the Eastern European culture (Yiddish language, sub-ethnic nationality groupings, literary and political movements) with the commercial, social and physical realities of New York life.[4]

The intense concentration of Jews in New York City meant overcrowded and filthy tenement houses, unemployed sweatshop workers, peddlers, and beggars. The streets and courtyards provided plenty of easy-access venues and earning possibilites for the new immigrant *klezmer* who did not yet have any business contacts. Just as he had in urban centers like Warsaw, Lemberg (L'viv), Kiev, and Chernovits, the *klezmer* played in the tene-

---

[4] James Benjamin Loeffler, *A Gilgul Fun a Nigun: Jewish Musicians in New York, 1881–1945*, Harvard Judaica Collection Student Research Papers, No. 3, Harvard College Library, Cambridge, 1997, p. 17.

ment courtyards as the neighborhood itinerant minstrel. As one witness told me:

> I remember when I was eight we lived on Ludlow St. This *klezmer* fiddler would come around to our yard around seven A.M., just after most of the men had gone to work. He didn't carry a case for the violin. He carried it just under his arm with the bow. As he played a slow waltz, suddenly the wives would lean out of their apartment windows with a smile, enjoying the music. Then, after maybe two or three minutes, these women went back inside their homes and returned with some money. After the tune was finished, they clapped and threw some coins down. It was usually a few pennies, a nickel, or, if he was really lucky, a dime. But what I remember most was that some of the women also threw down small pieces of rolled-up paper. The *klezmer* gathered these as well, stuffed them into his pocket, and left. When I told a friend of mine what I had seen he said it was probably the women giving him the different times of the day when their husbands came home from work. But later I found out that on these pieces of paper were numbers which corresponded with certain racehorses. He was running these numbers over to a bookie who then placed small bets for the women.[5]

Another witness told me:

> *Klezmorim* never played actually in the streets for money—this was demeaning. However, those who were poor and needed to feed their families went from courtyard to courtyard of these three-to-six-story apartment buildings, sometimes with a singer, to perform. They did this especially during summer when the women were hanging their wash to dry. They wrapped a penny or two, maybe even a nickel, in

---

[5] Interview with Aaron Penner (originally from New York City) in San Diego, California, May 1, 1981.

some paper and threw it down to the *klezmer*. Occasionally the women yelled out a request which of course always got the *klezmer* more money if he could play the tune. Remember these weren't all Jewish women. There were Italians, Slovaks, Croatians, Ukrainians; and the *klezmer* who went from courtyard to courtyard knew who lived there so he had to have a diverse repertoire.[6]

Coming to America did not completely change the attitude of all Jewish immigrants: many still looked askance upon *klezmorim*. Dealing with a new land and new language was hard enough for many *klezmorim* in America, let alone trying to rise above their poverty and social caste; but there were exceptions to this rule:

> My uncle played the clarinet in the Czar's army. But the *klezmer* was the lowest of the low in Konotop [near Kiev], so when he immigrated to Baltimore he refused to play any *klezmer*. But of course he was forced to play his violin and flute at weddings and other *simkhes* when he came to America because he hadn't learned how to read music. He had to know how to read music if he was going to audition for an orchestra. My aunt didn't want him to play but rather get a job in some garment sweatshop. When she was angry with him she called him "*a navenadnike yid*" (Yid.: a wandering Jew). He never learned to read music, but all of his six sons became successful musicians. The oldest, a violinist, played in the Baltimore Symphony Orchestra and wrote parts out for the other sections.[7]

For most *klezmorim* in Eastern Europe, the wedding had been the "bread and butter" gig, with celebrations generally held in a home or synagogue courtyard and lasting seven days. Weddings were equally important for the

---

[6] Interview with Felix Groveman, op. cit.

[7] Interview with Kia Williams (originally from Baltimore) in New York City, December 11, 1983.

immigrant *klezmer*, but were smaller, usually just for one day (except when they observed the *Sheve-Brukhes*), and held in social and catering halls. Some catering halls had house bands; those *klezmorim* lucky enough to be employed by one had a certain amount of economic security. However, this made it quite difficult for the "greenhorn" *klezmer* who had just come off the boat to find employment. Most of the wedding rituals for which the *klezmorim* had played in Eastern Europe (*bazetzn, bazingen, baveynen, badekn, droshe-geshank*) were cast off, except among certain orthodox and *khasidic* Jews. With the *batkhn* no longer needed, the maitre-d' or head of the catering hall was the one who kept the wedding moving. The custom of paying for each particular dance during the party was transformed into tipping the *klezmorim*. Sometimes the tips were larger than the agreed-upon fee (at rich weddings). But most weddings were of modest or even poor means, not held in catering halls but in apartments or synagogues.

I was once hired as a sideman to play at an orthodox wedding in a catering hall in Brooklyn (Boro Park). The maitre-d' promptly cued the band to play at 1 P.M., as the guests arrived for the party. Every detail and every ceremonial ritual was carefully orchestrated and scheduled, from the blessing over the *khale* to the *mitsve-tants* between the rabbi and the bride. At 7 P.M. the wedding celebration was over, the guests were encouraged to exit the building promptly, and the maitre-d' was now the foreman of a cleaning crew who were furiously preparing the same room for a wedding party to begin at 8 P.M. Just as I was about to leave, he asked me if I would stay and play for the next wedding party with the band that was just arriving. They did not have a violinist and the maitre-d' said the groom especially loved the violin and wanted some strolling music for the individual tables. I negotiated my fee and played until 2 A.M. This would not be my last gig in a catering hall, which was fondly called *Simkhe Central* by the drummer.

According to J. B. Loeffler, catering halls

formed the site for a range of large-scale entertainments and public events, including weddings, *bar mitsves,* charity balls, social dances, and political meetings. They held hundreds of people at full capacity, and the Lower East Side teemed with them. *Klezmorim* found themselves in catering halls for a variety of events, and performed for several different immigrant ethnic groups. But it was the Jewish wedding which continued to define much of the character of their work, and the Jewish wedding in America was profoundly determined by the catering hall.[8]

Just as, back in Eastern Europe, the *klezmer* had to be versed in several folk genres (Bessarabian, Hungarian, Polish, Rom, Romanian, Russian, Ruthenian, Slovakian, and Ukrainian), in America he had to be equally well-versed, or even better. On the Lower East Side many different ethnic groups lived and worked side by side. And though the core audience for the *klezmorim* were Jews, they had to know other genres of music, as non-Jews often hired them for weddings and parties.

In 1916 Nat and Wolf Kostakowsky published their *klezmer* anthology, *Hebrew International Wedding Music,* which contained three hundred tunes. Then, in 1924, Joseph and Jack Kammen (twins) published the first of several music books that became the "fake books" for all *klezmer* musicians. If a non-Jew was hired for a Jewish gig and did not know any Jewish music, he would more than likely be given one of the Kammen books to play from. If a Jewish musician came to a gig with the Kammen books, his fellow *klezmorim* knew he did not grow up hearing and playing the music. The first one was called *International Dance and Concert, New Folio No. 9* and collected fifty-six *klezmer* and other European melodies. On the cover it stated that it contained American, Bessarabian, Bulgarian, Greek, Gypsy, Hungarian, Italian, Jewish, Polish, Romanian, Russian, Serbian, and Ukrainian tunes. Some of the tunes were actual folk melodies and songs from these countries and regions, but many of them were Yiddish folksongs and *klezmer* tunes that were performed with nuances as if they were, for example, of Greek or Serbian origin. Today, if a *klezmer kapelye* shows

---

[8] Loeffler, op. cit., p. 19.

up at a concert with the Kammen books it is still an indication that they have not been playing the music long or have a very limited repertoire.[9]

Another significant change from Eastern Europe to America was the instrumentation of the *klezmer* bands, which was reflected in the arrangements for these music books. Instead of *tsimbl* they had piano and, eventually, accordion parts. Instead of *bandura* or *cobza,* the music was written for mandolin and, eventually, guitar and tenor banjo. And instead of just clarinet, there were now parts arranged for E-flat alto and B-flat tenor saxophones. *Klezmer* violin gave way to the ever-increasing popularity of the clarinet, which became the dominant melodic voice in the *klezmer* band. And *tsimbl* players in America became scarcer to find, since they could not compete against the louder and more readily available accordionists or pianists.

In the *shtetl,* parades that celebrated famous persons, holidays, or political causes had been quite common. In America, the *klezmer* found some work performing in parades, particularly in marches championing political or labor causes. As working conditions worsened, particularly in the needle trades, where so many Jewish immigrants were employed for extremely low wages, more Jews became politicized, finding a new religion called socialism.

The largest and most important Jewish union was the International Ladies Garment Workers Union, established in 1900. Their 1910 strike (July 7–September 3) captured the hearts and minds of thousands of Jewish workers in New York City. During the strike, Yiddish was the language of solidarity among the Jewish workers: Yiddish placards were carried, Yiddish slogans were chanted, and Yiddish songs were sung, often accompanied by *klezmorim.*

Since Jews in Eastern Europe traditionally did not go to taverns to drink and cavort with their non-Jewish neighbors, in America they did not frequent the local bars. Instead they created Jewish social clubs and cafés.

---

[9] Henry Sapoznik, *Klezmer! Jewish Music from Old World to Our World* (New York: Schirmer Books, 1999), p. 101.

Here workers, professionals, and artists met to relax, *shmues* (Yid.: converse, chat), discuss union business, and argue about politics. Sometimes the *klezmer* was hired to complement the "European" atmosphere; other times he took part in the discussions and contributed to them with his music. When a café was too expensive. the social gatherings were often held in private homes.

Charles Zimmerman, who in the twenties became the leader of the communist bloc in the needle-trade unions, recalled one such informal gathering at his home in 1914: "Our whole young crowd, we hadn't much to eat, so we used to gather at my house. My mother would cook a big pot of potatoes, we used to buy a couple of herrings, and we would sing [David] Edelstadt's [Yiddish] poems. Also those of [Joseph] Bovshover, but mainly Edelstadt, his proletarian songs. Such was the spirit of the East Side at that time."[10]

Dance halls, which had created the need for *klezmer* music back in the twelfth through fourteenth centuries, again provided work opportunities at the turn of the twentieth century. They were popular among early immigrants because they provided a place to socialize with the opposite sex, to learn English, and to acculturate more easily into American society. Some dance halls played predominantly music from Europe: the *mazurka, lancer,* polka, quadrille, *sher,* and *tarantella.* But most of the dance halls and dance schools (portrayed so well in the film *Hester Street*) played and taught ragtime, society dances, and, in the 1920s and '30s, big band swing and tango. *Hester Street's* director Joan Micklin Silver explained why the dance hall was an important location in her film:

> I made *Hester Street* as honest a portrait of immigrant life as I could. I used Yiddish in the film because this was part of the everyday experience of the immigrant. At the same time, the two main characters met at a dance hall that played American music. Both really wanted to get away from their East European Jewishness. But assimilating was not so easy for all immigrants. The mother tried to learn English

[10] Irving Howe, *World of Our Fathers* (New York: Schocken, 1990), p. 309.

but did so poorly and was quite frustrated when she saw how easy it was for her child.[11]

Some *klezmer* musicians were not able to play American popular music as well as their old repertoire. For some it was because they could not read music and the genre was foreign to their ears. Others felt that since there were plenty of other musicians who had played this new music longer and better, why would someone hire a *klezmer* who played it only so-so? And some just did not feel the need or interest, for, in addition to the dance halls and vaudeville, the Yiddish theatre provided other venues for the *klezmer* who wanted to use his East European repertoire. But those who did learn this new repertoire got more work and fairly decent pay.

The Catskills

Another European tradition that was transplanted to America was that of getting out of the hectic, crowded, and all-too-often foul-aired city for the fresh air and serenity of the country. In Bohemia, Jews (even those of modest means) who lived as far as eastern Galicia had frequented the resorts of Mariensbad and Karlsbad, rejuvenating themselves with the fresh air and mineral baths. In Srodborów, Poland (outside of Warsaw), just before World War I, a wealthy Jew built a Jewish resort with a hotel, restaurant, sport facilities, and a synagogue, which also offered farm-fresh food and clean forest air. *Klezmorim* knew that the vacationers needed a diversion from all their exercising and eating, so they played in the resorts—some playing as street musicians, passing the hat after impromptu concerts, and others being formally hired to play in the restaurants, on the lawns, and even near the open-air mineral baths.

As early as 1890, a few East European and German Jews began going up

---

[11] Interview with film director Joan Micklin Silver (originally from Omaha, Nebraska) in New York City, September 25, 2000.

to the Catskill Mountains to escape the humid confines of summers in New York City. (There were some existing resorts in the area, but they generally prohibited Jews, so the Jews built their own). By 1902, the Yiddish press began advertising Catskill resorts catering specifically to the East European Jewish immigrant. In the beginning, most were just plain boardinghouses grouped together around a lake and a small patch of forest. Eventually most of these gave way to fancier hotels, although some vacationers preferred the solitude of nature and lived in plain but cheaper *kokhaleyns* (Yid.: cooking alone; a small bungalow with a kitchen). The hotels dotting the Catskills landscape hired *klezmorim* to play, mostly for dances and background music during dinner. The ensembles often consisted, in various combinations, of violin, piano, accordion, clarinet, trumpet, saxophone, and drums. The repertoire included *klezmer,* light European classical, American popular dance music, and, beginning in the 1920s, a strain of music that mixed American popular song arrangements with nostalgic Yiddish lyrics and some *klezmer* nuances. Some of the more popular tunes were "Yosl Yosl" by Nellie Casman and Samuel Steinberg (1922), "Shabbes Tzu Nakht" by Sholom Secunda (1923), and "Hoo-Tza-Tza" by Fischel Kanapoff (1924).

By the 1930s the entertainment at the various Catskill resorts included comedy, comedic skits, Yiddish/English one-act plays, and musical revues. The *batkhonim* of Eastern Europe had ceased to exist for the most part in the United States (except among the *khasidim*), and were now replaced by "Borsht Belt *toomlers.*"[12] Combining jokes, music, song, and dance, such performers as Joey Adams, Milton Berle, Georgie Jessel, Jan Murray, and, later, Fyvush Finkel, Buddy Hackett, Danny Kaye, and Jerry Lewis became modern-day *batkhonim.*

Besides comedians, other entertainers—musicians and singers—also

---

[12] The phrase *Borsht Belt* was supposedly coined by *Variety* editor Abel Green; it comprised all the Jewish hotel and bungalow resorts in the Catskill Mountains just north of New York City. The *Yinglish* word *toomler* comes from the Yiddish *tuml,* which means noise, din, racket. See Richard Shepard and Vicki Gould Levi, *Live and Be Well: A Celebration of Yiddish Culture in America From the First Immigrants to the Second World War* (New York: Ballantine Books, 1982), p. 26.

got their start performing in the Catskills. As *klezmer* clarinetist Marty Levitt recalled, "My father Jack[13] was a trombonist who played at the Presidents Hotel when it first opened in Swan Lake, New York, in 1932. The leader of the band was Jan Peerce, who played the violin. On certain tunes Peerce would put down the violin and sing; but the people in the audience yelled at him to play the violin instead. Of course he made it as an opera singer, not as a violinist."[14]

Some *klezmorim* found work in the Catskills, but this did not always mean a steady gig. First, there were more *klezmorim* than there were band positions. The same "house" band of seven to ten musicians usually accompanied all the acts in the hotel during the entire summer season. Secondly, there was competition from non-Jewish musicians, who were often hired regardless of their religious affiliation.

Klezmer *Recordings and* Klezmer *Stars*

Some of these same *klezmorim,* when not playing in the Catskills during summer, were part of a developing recording industry. *Klezmer* music in Eastern Europe had been recorded since the late 1890s, so it only made sense that the burgeoning Jewish immigrant population in America would want to listen to recordings that filled them with nostalgia for their former homelands.

Abe Elenkrig (1878–1965), with his *klezmer* ensemble the Hebrew Bulgarian Orchestra, was one of the earliest to record *klezmer* tunes. The band's style was a brassy, very rhythmic sound with a strong connection to the Romanian folk music of Moldavia and the brass-band sound of southwestern Ukraine. These brassy sounds so common to early *klezmer* recordings

---

[13] Jack Levitt (Levinsky) was born in Kiev, Ukraine and came to New York City at the age of eight. He played trombone and violin with many of the great *klezmer* musicians, including Brandwein and Tarras.

[14] Interview with Marty Levitt (originally from Brooklyn, New York), October 25, 2001.

reflected a musical phenomenon that had begun in Eastern Europe some twenty-five years earlier. For Harry Kandel (1885–1943), who studied clarinet at the conservatory in Odessa, the military marching-band sound is what he tried to re-create with his *klezmer* ensemble. After a short stint in New York City, Kandel moved to Philadelphia, first playing under John Phillip Sousa, and then becoming the pit conductor for the Yiddish plays and vaudeville shows at the Arch Street Theatre. From 1917 to 1927 Kandel recorded a slew of records, many of which became the standards of their day. His large-wind-ensemble recordings, along with those that attempted to fuse *klezmer* with jazz elements, became seminal recordings for revival *klezmer* bands in the late 1970s and early '80s; some of his more noted *klezmer* recordings include "Di Mama Iz Gegangen In Mark Arayn"(The Mother Has Gone to the Market), "Der Shtiler Bulgar" (The Quiet Bulgar), and "Mamaliga." For his foray into jazz, Kandel changed the instrumentation of his band, adding three saxophones and a tenor banjo. His most famous *"jazzmer"* tune was "Jakie, Jazz'em Up," recorded under the heading Kandel's Jazz Orchestra.[15]

The Jakie in the aforementioned title was Jacob "Jakie" Hoffman (1899–1874), who played percussion in Kandel's band and also helped to create the Philadelphia *klezmer* sound. Hoffman transposed the sound and method of playing the *tsimbl* to the louder American xylophone and can be heard on several recordings, including "Firn Di Mekhutonim Aheym" (Leading the In-Laws Home) and "Der Gas Nign" (The Street Tune). A xylophone virtuoso, Hoffman played with several symphony orchestras, including the Philadelphia Orchestra and the Boston Pops. His daughter Elaine Hoffman Watts followed in her father's footsteps and became a percussionist playing classical and *klezmer* music.

Other *klezmer* ensemble leaders during the golden age of Yiddish popular music who made recordings included Joseph Rumshinsky (1879–1956), I. J. Hochman, Lt. Joseph Frankel (1885–1953; he served in both the Czarist

[15] *Jakie Jazz'em Up: Old Time Klezmer Music 1912–1926*, CD produced by Global Village Music, New York, 1984 (liner notes), p. 6.

and United States armies), and Abe Schwartz (1881–1963). Schwartz may have been the most successful of these. Born in a small town outside of Bucharest, he came to the United States in 1899 and soon thereafter became a leader in the *klezmer* scene. A violinist, pianist, arranger, composer, and bandleader, he performed on several of his own recordings, including a few on which he played solo violin accompanied only by his daughter Sylvia on piano. Some of the most famous tunes he composed and recorded were "Shwer un Shweeger Tantz" (In-Law's Dance, 1921), "Di Grine Kuzine" (The Greenhorn Cousin, 1922), and "Romanian Volach" (1921). In the background of many of Schwartz's recordings one can hear the virtuoso Naftuli Brandwein playing on the "screamer" (the E-flat clarinet).

One of the last recordings Schwartz produced on which Brandwein played was Brandwein's own composition "Firn Di Mekhutonim Aheym." This *gas nign*, with its continuous sostenuto and legato clarinet solo, displays all of Brandwein's incredible skills. His improvisation, his fingerings, his lightning-fast scales, his breath control, his glissandos, and his *knaytches* made this one of the most listened-to and played recordings of the *klezmer* revival years, especially among revival bands who were playing the repertoire and style of the smaller ensembles of the 1920s and '30s rather than that of the large brass ensembles.

Naftuli Brandwein (1889–1963) was born in the small town of Przemyslany, Galicia (Peremišljani, Ukraine), just outside of Lemberg (Lviv). His father, Pesekh Brandwein, was a *batkhn*, violinist, and leader of his family *kapelye*, which traveled throughout eastern Galicia. Naftuli was one of fourteen children from four different wives. Around the end of World War I, he, along with his brothers, immigrated to America, with the exception of two brothers, both of whom were subsequently killed by the Nazis.

Brandwein was known not only for his clarinet virtuosity but also for his wild, sometimes impetuous actions. He played hard and lived hard: he was a womanizer and drinker, and some said that if you hired Naftuli for your party, all you had to do to keep him satisfied and playing all night was to provide him with plenty of liquor and a woman. He was known to be the favorite *klezmer* among the Jewish gang Murder, Inc. He loved to spice up his stage act while performing by pulling his pants down, or wearing an electric neon sign on his chest that read "The Naftuli Brandwein Orchestra." His on- and offstage actions made it difficult for him to stay with only one band, as his fellow players grew tired of his histrionics. As Mickey Katz related:

> I remember once visiting New York in the late 1920s. I was taking a drive down Essex Street when I saw this huge crowd spilling over into the street surrounding this guy who was playing the clarinet. Next to him sat at large dog with a sign around his neck that said: "Naftuli: he is the greatest." It was Naftuli Brandwein. They were throwing dimes, nickels, even quarters into his basket. They were even petting the dog and giving him some treats. This was my first encounter with the great clarinetist.[16]

Besides the Abe Schwartz Orchestra, Brandwein was also a member of the Joseph Cherniavsky (1895–1959) Yiddish-American Jazz Band. Between 1922 and 1927 he recorded dozens of records; but then he stopped. His lifestyle took a toll on his health and on his fellow musicians, but he kept busy playing gigs at parties, weddings, and hotels. Finally, in 1941, Brandwein returned to the recording studio for the last time. As Henry Sapoznik tells it,

> Made under the modernized moniker of "Nifty" Brandwein, the recordings—"Klayne Princesin," "Naftuli's Freylakh," "Freylekher Yontef," and "Nifty's Eygene"—trace Brandwein's development over his fourteen-year absence from the studio. His tone is edgier than before and his wind is cut down; nonetheless, he still is a powerful presence. Though no longer playing with the same fire, he demonstrates strong introspection and maturation. Gone are the rapier swoops and tears, replaced by gentler, no less impressive extended phrases. Most telling, however, are the rich lower-register passages, a popular hallmark of

---

[16] Interview with Mickey Katz (originally from Cleveland) in Los Angeles, July 7, 1984.

Tarras's style, now part of Brandwein's playing, in honor of his ascended rival.[17]

Dovid Tarraschuk (1897–1989), better known as David Tarras, came from the small town of Ternovka (Ternivka), near the Ukrainian city of Uman. He was exposed to *klezmer* music early in his childhood because his father was a *klezmer* trombonist and *batkhn*. Tarras played balalaika, *cobza,* guitar, mandolin, and flute for a while in his father's family *kape-lye*. But in 1915, Tarras (already playing clarinet) was conscripted into the Czar's army. Like many *klezmorim* before him, his music skills gave him the opportunity to serve as a musician in the military ensemble instead of in the trenches. Eventually the Russian Revolution, pogroms, and an unstable economic environment forced Tarras to immigrate to New York City in 1921. There he first worked in a garment factory as a janitor because he did not think he was good enough to be a musician. "I thought that in America to be a musician one has to have—he must *be* something; I didn't think I'm good enough to be a musician," Tarras said.[18]

Soon, however, Tarras found out he was good enough (and better than most), and earned a lot more money for something he really loved to do: playing the clarinet. Tarras's ability to transpose and sight-read music (something Brandwein could not do) with a completely placid disposition got him Brandwein's chair in Cherniavsky's ensemble. Soon he was recording with Abe Schwartz, who had fired Brandwein. As Tarras's reputation grew, so did his list of employers: Joseph Rumshinsky, the Abe Ellstein Orchestra, the Alexander Olshanetsky Orchestra, Al Glaser's Bucovina Kapelle, Moishe Oysher, Sholom Secunda, Molly Picon, Seymour Rechtzeit, Maurice Schwartz, Aaron Lebedeff, the Barry Sisters, and many others. Along with his Jewish records, Tarras also recorded Greek, Polish, and Russian tunes.

Klezmer aficionados, particularly clarinetists, often like to argue who was better, Brandwein or Tarras, and who was truer to the music. Tarras's

---

[17] Sapoznik, op. cit., p. 152.
[18] Ibid., p. 114.

style of playing was smoother, more dignified, with a slow vibrato, while his phrasing was deliberate and rhythmical. His playing was not like that of Brandwein's, which was influenced by the traditional *klezmer* violin-playing in Galicia. Tarras already played less traditionally when he lived in Ternovka, perhaps because he had played in a military band, which emphasized ensemble playing rather than individual soloists. Zev Feldman, an ethnomusicologist whose father was born in Yedinitz, Bukowina (Romania), not far from where Tarras was born, and who knew the style, repertoire, and dances of the local *klezmorim* very well, explains,

> Though Andy [Statman] was Tarras's student and I was Shloimke Beckerman's student, we were always looking at what came before Tarras. Andy was studying the recordings of Brandwein's and Beckerman's[19] music quite intensively, while I was well aware from my father that the style Tarras was playing was not quite what they played back in Bessarabia. In fact, his style and repertoire was quite different and wasn't that Jewish. Tarras had a mostly Bessarabian repertoire. When you compare Tarras to Brandwein and Beckerman, he is the least Jewish of the three. Beckerman and Brandwein were different from each other as well, but we don't have that many recordings of the former to compare with. Brandwein's repertoire was closer to what the *klezmorim* actually played in Eastern Europe. He certainly played a few American *bulgars,* but most of his repertoire already existed in Galicia, according to Hescheles.[20] Many of the pieces Brandwein played were display pieces he had learned in Europe and not here in New

---

[19] Shloimke Beckerman (1883–1974) was born in Rizish, Ukraine to a family of *klezmorim.* He played the clarinet and was one of the first of the well-known early *klezmer* musicians to easily cross over to jazz and back to *klezmer.* His son Sid continued the family *klezmer* tradition, playing his father's tunes along with others from the late 1940s through today.

[20] Jeremiah Hescheles (1910–) was the former *kapelmayster* from Glinyany, Poland. According to Leopold Kozlowski (son of Tzvi-Hirsh Brandwein-Kleinman), Hescheles's *kapelye* and his father's were friendly competitors as they plied their trade around L'vov and its environs.

York. And when he played dance pieces they were for solo clarinet, because there were *klezmorim* in Galicia and even Bukowina who were primarily professional soloists. Also in Brandwein's father's band in Przemyslany they had a professional dancer, so some of Naftuli's repertoire comes from when he played for the solo dancer and not for the common dancers. Tarras really didn't perform display pieces; they were almost always dance pieces. Tarras was a great composer and musician but his ambition was to "Bessarabianize" Jewish dance music as much as possible. And sometimes this fusion worked beautifully, like his classic "Ternovker Sher." It has elements of Bessarabian, Gypsy, and Jewish dance music. Brandwein hadn't gone so far—he still responded to the Jewish *melos* and modality.[21]

Tarras was the most popular *klezmer* clarinetist from the mid-1930s to the end of the 1950s, heard on recordings and radio; in the Catskills; and at the Yiddish theatre, weddings, and other social events. His style of playing has influenced a generation of *klezmer* revival clarinetists, most notably his protégé Andy Statman. As Seth Rogovoy writes,

Tarras is widely credited with the growth of the *bulgar* as a popular style of Jewish dance tune. A minor genre in the Old World *klezmer* rooted in Bessarabia, the *bulgar* came to be synonymous with American *klezmer* by the 1940s, to the point that the music as a whole was often merely referred to as the *bulgars*. Tarras composed and recorded dozens of these tunes, which he favored over the Old World core repertoire, most of which he viewed as too "simple" and audiences viewed as too "religious."[22]

---

[21] Interview with Walter Zev Feldman (originally from the Bronx) in New York City, October 16, 2000.

[22] Rogovoy, Seth. *The Essential Klezmer: A Music Lover's Guide to Jewish Roots and Soul Music, from the Old World to Jazz Age to the Downtown Avant-Garde* (Algonquin Books: Chapel Hill, NC, 2000), p. 67.

Jewish radio programs on such stations as WHN, WBBC, WBNX, and the leader, WEVD (subsidized and eventually owned by the *Forverts* newspaper), were great venues for the most popular Yiddish singers and *klezmorim*: Dave Tarras, Abe Ellstein, Aaron Lebedeff, Molly Picon, Max Epstein, Sammy Muziker, and others. The exposure broadened their reputations, sold their records, and secured more theatre and "casual"[23] gigs. But for the majority of the more *proste klezmorim*, without the means or connections to be heard on the radio, the increased exposure for the stars made it much more difficult to find work.[24]

Some *klezmorim* attempted the crossover to American popular music by arranging, composing, and performing *klezmer* music in a jazz style. One of the simpler novelty tunes was "Lena From Palesteena," written in 1920 by Con Conrad and J. Russell Robinson, and made popular in the 1930s by singer Eddie Cantor: the tune had been a popular *bulgar* known as "Nokh A Bisl" (Yid.: A Little More). Another celebrated tune, still quite popular today, is Joseph Rumshinsky and Chaim Tauber's "Sheyn Vi Di Levune" (Yid.: Beautiful as the Moon), which was arranged and recorded in 1939 by Abe Ellstein with solos by Dave Tarras. One of my favorite swing songs with Jewish flavoring, performed in the film *Hellzapoppin* (by Slim Gaillard and Slam Stewart), was "Matzo Balls,"[25] which Gaillard wrote in 1938. The two biggest *jazzmer* (jazz and *klezmer*) hits to make the music charts were "Bay Mir Bistu Sheyn" and "Frailach in Swing." Written in 1932 by Sholom Secunda (music) and Jacob Jacobs (lyrics), who sold the rights for thirty dollars, *Bay Mir Bistu Sheyn* became an international hit when the Andrews

---

[23] *Casual:* a West Coast slang term for a private, one-night gig. These were weddings, *bar mitzves*, and other kinds of parties featuring live music. Most *casuals* paid a lot better than hotel, club, and theatre gigs.

[24] Sapoznik, op. cit., pp. 155–56.

[25] The whole album, and particularly "Matzo Balls," inspired me to begin composing "new" Jewish music that incorporated jazz, blues, and other ethnic genres. In addition, the wordless singing of bassist Slam Stewart encouraged me to sing in a *khasidishe* style while playing the violin. Lastly, the first recording I made with my *klezmer* band Hot Pstromi, *With a Little Horseradish on the Side*, took its title from this very song: "Matzo balls, gefilte fish, what a really, really nice dish, with a little horseradish on the side."

Sisters recorded it in 1937. With this taste of success the Andrews Sisters recorded "Joseph Joseph" in 1938, their version of the popular Yiddish theatre song "Yosl Yosl," which had been recorded by singer Nellie Casman in 1923. "Frailach in Swing" was the only crossover tune to have been originally performed as a *freylekh* performed in Eastern Europe by *klezmorim*; it had been published by the Kammen brothers as "Frailach No. 15." Jazz trumpeter Ziggy Elman (Harry Finkelman) had played *klezmer* music before joining Benny Goodman's band; he took the tune Abe Schwartz recorded in 1917 called "Der Shtiler Bulgar" and re-recorded it on the Bluebird label as "Frailach in Swing." In 1939 lyrics by Johnny Mercer were added to the tune, and a new arrangement by fellow band member Ernani Bernardi (tenor saxophone) was written for Goodman's band. With Elman blowing his *bulgar klezmer* licks during the solo parts and with Martha Tilton singing the vocals, the song became number one on the hit parade for five consecutive weeks under the new title "And the Angels Sing."

Probably the most successful of the *klezmorim* who performed both in the *klezmer* and jazz worlds was Sammy Muziker (1916–64). Descended from a family of *klezmorim*, Muziker played both clarinet and saxophone in Gene Krupa's band in the late 1930s and early '40s. When he married Dave Tarras's daughter, his father-in-law welcomed his new son-in-law to the family and his *klezmer* world; eventually they would collaborate on the 1956 album *Tants!*, which used Musiker's arrangements to merge *klezmer* and big band swing. As Dick Hyman, one of America's finest jazz pianists, confirmed, "Sammy Muziker was a fine clarinetist and saxophonist. He is probably the best example of how a *klezmer* musician could evolve to such a high level of versatility. It seemed so natural for him and other guys like him to go back and forth from jazz to *klezmer*."[26]

Though Jewish jazz really did not find its niche among the American public and record companies, a few Jewish tunes (i.e., "Bei Mir Bistu Sheyn," "And the Angels Sing," "Tzena Tzena") became international hits.

---

[26] Interview with jazz pianist and film composer Dick Hyman (originally from Mt. Vernon, New York) on October 28, 2000.

But only one ever made it to the top forty in American rock and roll: "Ikh Hub Dikh Tsufil Lib" (I Love You Much Too Much). Originally written by Alexander Olshanetsky (1892–1946),[27] with lyrics by Chaim Tauber, for the Yiddish actress Luba Kadison (1907–)[28] (who performed it on stage in the Yiddish play *Di Katerinchik*), the song was recorded by many internationally known singers—including Seymour Rechtzeit, who sang it in Yiddish, and Connie Francis, Dean Martin, and Ella Fitzgerald, who sang it in English. But the rock and roll version was recorded as an instrumental ballad by Carlos Santana in 1981 on the top-ten album *Zebop!*

Making a Living

Of all the various venues (resorts, social clubs, vaudeville, movie theatres) available to the *klezmer* between the turn of the twentieth century and the early 1940s, the Yiddish theatre provided him with the most steady work and pay. Yiddish theatre in New York City attracted thousands of theatregoers. To be able to be hired by one, the *klezmer* had to belong to the Progressive Musicians Union (formed around 1890), which was folded into

[27] Alexander Olshanetsky was born in Odessa. He studied the violin, as well as other instruments, beginning at age six; by age fifteen he was playing in the Odessa Opera Orchestra and traveling all over the country. After he enlisted in the army he was stationed in Kharbin (in present-day China), where he became involved with a Yiddish theatre company and began writing operettas for the group. There was no money to be made in the Yiddish theatre, so he joined a Russian opera company and traveled with it to Japan, China, and India. Eventually he made it to America, where his uncle Hymen Meyzel (a Yiddish actor) introduced him to the New York Yiddish theatre scene. Olshanetsky wrote the music to many successful Yiddish plays, including *Di Freylekhe Kapsonim*, *Der Litvisher Yenki*, and *Bar Kokhba*.
[28] Luba Kadison was born in Kaunas (Kovno), Lithuania and was a founding member of the renowned Yiddish theatre *Vilna Troupe* and daughter of its cofounder Leib Kadison. She performed in the original production of *The Dybbuk* and played the lead role of Leah. With her husband, famed Yiddish actor Joseph Buloff, she moved to America in 1927 and joined Maurice Schwartz's Yiddish Art Theatre. She and her husband toured throughout North and South America, Europe, and Israel, starring in such plays as *The Brothers Ashkenazi* and *God of Vengeance*.

the American Federation of Musicians in 1923. As working-class Jews became more and more politicized because of their daily economic struggles, unions became an important place for artists to seek redress for work-related problems. The unions also provided a place where they could meet, discuss common problems, and hold their own events. Composers and conductors belonged to the *Idishn Muzik Farband* (Yid.: Jewish Music Union), while other employees of the Yiddish theatres belonged to the United Hebrew Trades.[29]

In the Yiddish theatres the *klezmorim* encountered an artistic world with one foot in Eastern Europe and the other in nascent Jewish America. Secular American culture induced them to look at their art form not only in terms of providing a musical service and pleasing the public (weddings, parties, etc.) but exploring their own musical aesthetic. The Yiddish theatre also created some divisions among *klezmorim:* those who could read music (Dave Tarras) and those who could not (Naftuli Brandwein); those willing to deal with the various artistic whims of the actors, conductors, and directors, and those who did not have the patience; those willing to deal with unscrupulous theatre owners and those who were not; and finally, those who were willing to participate in the Americanization and commercialization of their folk culture and those who found this anathema.

Some *klezmorim* were able to adapt to the ever-increasing assimilation of the Jewish world in New York City and play music full-time. But most *klezmorim* held down day jobs while playing music at night and on the weekends. One of the better day jobs was giving music lessons, which became the craze among Jewish and non-Jewish immigrants in the 1920s. Many Jews thought that one's *yikhes* increased in the Jewish community, and even in the gentile community, if the children took private music lessons. This idea, originating in the European *haskole,* was brought to America with the Jewish immigrant, as Sy Zaks's account illustrates:

---

[29] For a more comprehensive look into the various Jewish Music unions, read Loeffler, op. cit., pp. 25–27.

I was eight when my mother said I had to take violin lessons. She said it would give me something better to do after school than just playing ball with my friends, and maybe I would earn a little spending money for myself playing at the *shul*'s *Khanike* and *Purim* parties. My teacher was this old *muzikant,* a friend of my mother's from Tuczyn. He was nice but it was hard to stand next to him as he gave me a lesson. His breath always smelled from onions and garlic and he was a heavy sweater. My first recital, which I wasn't all that enthused about, was for some women's organization that my mother belonged to that met in the basement in our *shul.* I played a short piece by Moszkowski and a *sher* that my teacher taught me. In the middle of the *sher* my E string broke, poked me in the eye, and caused it to bleed. I never picked up the violin again. I told my mother if I was going to get hurt doing something I wanted to get hurt playing baseball and not the violin.[30]

It is interesting that Zaks did not use the word *klezmer* to describe his music teacher. In fact, he had been a *klezmer* in Eastern Europe and played *klezmer* music in America; but by World War I, one rarely heard the term *klezmer* used to designate one who performed Jewish music. The term *klezmer* still carried a great deal of negative baggage for many immigrant Jews. In fact, many second generation American-born Jews rarely heard the term *klezmer* while growing up. Jewish musicians consciously replaced it with other, more American and more professional-sounding names. When I asked several American-born children of immigrants if they had heard *klezmer* music in their home while growing up or if their parents ever spoke to them about the Jewish wedding music of Eastern Europe, the replies were typically like these:

- My father or any of the other musicians never called it *klezmer* music. It was just Jewish music. In fact the term *klezmer* was pejorative. The ranking of the musicians was as follows: the lowest was the *yardnik* who

---

[30] Interview with Sy Zaks (originally from Tuczyn, Poland) in San Diego on May 3, 1981.

played on the streets and in the courtyards for donations. Then there was the *klezmer* who could play, but never got a job playing in a theatre or a society gig because he couldn't read music. Then there was the *muzikant* who not only could read music but played several kinds of music. I was a *muzikant,* a studied musician.[31]

- My uncle and his sons played Jewish dance music at all our family *simkhes* but I never heard him use the word *klezmer* to describe himself or his sons. In fact my uncle always said quite proudly he was a *kunstler,* an artist that played Jewish *freylekhs,* Jewish dance music.[32]

- We never called this music *klezmer* in our home. To us it was just Jewish wedding music, *freylekhs.* My mother once told me a story about this *muziker* from her *shtetl* who played the violin with his band at all the Jewish weddings; he was blind and played by ear and none of the other *muzikers* read music either. To me a *klezmer* was a kind of amateur musician, one who did not have any formal training, a *grimpler* of sorts, who if you asked him to play some Bach would just give you a blank look as if you were *meshugene.* One did not study in the conservatory to play Jewish wedding music.[33]

- The music we had for the Yiddish theatre in Edmonton while I was growing up was just called Jewish music. If there was dancing involved with the music we called it Yiddish wedding music. Some of it was obviously *klezmer,* but I really wasn't aware of calling this music anything but Yiddish wedding music until I went to a concert here in Los Angeles where they called the music they performed *klezmer.*[34]

Having said this, there were those, such as Leonard Nimoy, who grew

[31] Interview with Marty Levitt, op. cit.

[32] Interview with Nosson Zilberzweig (originally from Bibrka, Ukraine) in Brooklyn, New York, on November 29, 1982.

[33] Interview with Yoel Braun (originally from Stary Sącz, Poland) in San Diego, on May 18, 1981.

[34] Interview with film director Arthur Hiller (originally from Edmonton, Saskatchewan) in Los Angeles, California, on October 30, 2000.

up calling it *klezmer,* and had no negative memories of the music or of the musicians:

> My father had a barbershop about a block away from our apartment in the neighborhood called West End in Boston. At home there was some Jewish music but not a lot. We had some old Yiddish recordings by people like Seymour Rechtzeit and Moishe Oysher. However, there was a group of *klezmer* musicians who lived in our neighborhood. These were people who did not necessarily make a living from it, but played it well. One of the musicians was a clarinetist named Bass, who owned Bass Beauty Parlor. My first memory of *klezmer* music was of Bass playing for this fundraiser at our *shul.* There was this party where women raised their hands as they gave donations of one or two dollars for the *shul.* The master of ceremonies would say, "Oh, here comes Mrs. Rosenberg, play, *klezmers,* something for Mrs. Rosenberg." So while they played she marched up with great dignity and dropped her dollar in the bowl. When she turned around to walk back to her table the *klezmer* musicians played another little piece for her. The music was timed perfectly so that when she got to her seat it ended with a *bum...bum...bum...buuum!*
>
> I also heard *klezmer* music at family affairs. My father's uncle was a terrific musician and he had four sons who all played instruments. One son was Buzzy Drootin, who went on to play with some pretty good jazz bands.[35] They played at all the family weddings, *bar mitsves,* etc. All I can remember was they had clarinet, piano, and drums in the band. The music was great, like home music to me, and never carried any kind of negative connotations for me. In fact I enjoyed it

[35] Benjamin Buzzy Drootin (1920–2001) was born in Russia and came to Boston in 1925. His father, Leonard Nimoy's great-uncle, had been a *klezmer* clarinetist in Russia. Drootin began playing the drums as a teenager; from 1947 to 1951 he was the house drummer at Eddie Condon's in New York. Eventually he performed with many famous jazz musicians, including Wingy Manone, Jack Teagarden, Jimmy McPartland, and Tommy Dorsey. The last band he played with was his and his younger brother Al's, the Drootin Brothers Jazz Band.

so much I took up the clarinet for a short period of time. However it was pretty clear I didn't have a natural talent or certainly wasn't obsessed about it, so I quickly gave it up.[36]

The Decline

The presence of the piano rather than the violin in American immigrant homes also affected the American *klezmer*. For many immigrants, renting or buying a piano meant having an item in the house that brought them just a little closer to the American middle-class world. The piano was not only a musical instrument: it was also a large distinguished piece of furniture that made a statement to everyone who visited. Many immigrant families could afford such a beautiful instrument, one that should be used not to play just the mundane Yiddish folk music of the *grimpler* in the *shtetl*, but rather to play the popular music of the day. Playing and singing classical and American pop tunes in English with a gathering of friends around the piano was a way of exhibiting that an immigrant family had become a "Yankee Doodle Dandy."

The popularity of the piano, clarinet, saxophone, and trumpet, all synonymous with swing and big band music, pushed the more traditional *klezmer* violin, which already was on the wane, even more into the background. The art of *klezmer* violin began to disappear in the 1920s when the clarinet became the popular and preferred leader of *klezmer kapleyes*. The few known *klezmer* musicians (Sam and Ray Muziker, Sid, Sammy, and Shloimke Beckerman, Max Epstein, Paul Pincus, Mickey Katz, Howie Leess, Marty Levitt) who kept playing Jewish music through the 1950s and '60s were almost invariably woodwind and brass players. These ensembles could be more easily transformed into a "pop" or jazz ensemble that played contemporary tunes for the Jewish hotels and club dates. It would not be

---

[36] Interview with actor-director Leonard Nimoy (originally from Boston) in Los Angeles on November 1, 2000.

until the mid-1980s that young *klezmer* revivalists (particularly the violinists) sought out the very few *klezmer* violinists who had learned and practiced their craft in Eastern Europe and still played a little in America, violinists such as Leon Schwartz and Joshua Hescheles.

By the 1930s the first-generation American-born Jews were growing up in a transitional American Jewish culture. The *klezmer* in the *shtetl* had belonged to a community that was much more insulated against the encroachment of the gentile world. The *haskole* had changed attitudes, but for every young Jewish man who had divested himself of his religious and folkloric trappings, there were plenty who had chosen to live in these uniforms. The outside world had not been a true democracy, and Jews would never fully be a part of society. They had been thought of as Jewish first, then Polish, Ukrainian, Russian, etc. Incidences of continued anti-Semitism had ranged from slander in the local newspaper to the murderous pogroms. And Yiddish had still been the lingua franca for most East European Jews.

In the United States things could be different. The Jewish immigrant had never experienced a real democracy, where the more you assimilated into American culture, the better were your chances to be accepted. And the use of Yiddish helped to clearly define the Jewish experience for the early immigrants. For the religious orthodox, exclusively using Yiddish in all aspects of daily life helped insulate themselves from the *treyf* world. For the secular Yiddishists, it helped define them politically, socially, and culturally. But for the majority of the modestly religious and cultural immigrants, knowing only Yiddish was a major stumbling block in the process of becoming American. Consequently, thousands of Jewish immigrants went to day and night schools to learn English. With less Yiddish being spoken (and fewer new Yiddish-speaking immigrants arriving), there was less need for that nostalgic connection to the "old country." This in turn reduced the number of Jewish cafés, restaurants, social clubs, Yiddish theatres, traditional Jewish weddings, and other celebrations that wanted *klezmer* entertainment. Then the Great Depression began in 1929, and there was less money to hire *klezmorim*, buy *klezmer* recordings, and produce *klezmer* on the radio.

The final death knell for *klezmer* music for most Jews in America came after World War II. The Yiddish world was in turmoil. With the destruction of nearly ninety percent of East European Jewry, the spigot that had supplied American Yiddish-speaking communities with fond memories, opportunities to exchange cultural ideas in the arts, and letters and visits from families and friends was all but shut off. Many survivors felt guilty, as did a good portion of American Jewry for not being able to do much for their brethren during the war. Yiddish culture reminded these immigrants and their children of a world that they wanted to forget because it hurt too much to remember. They now needed to identify not with a ghetto culture perceived as weak and victimized, but with a fresh, vibrant Hebrew culture. After the War of Independence (1948), in which Israel defeated the surrounding Arab countries, Jews throughout the world were proud to be Jewish again, and felt they had an independent homeland of their own— a homeland where the Israeli Jew could be religious, secular, or everything in between without being pressured to assimilate into the gentile world.

American Jewry looked to Zionism, the *halutzim* (Heb.: pioneers), and the fledgling Israeli culture to create a new Jewish consciousness, one that emphasized hope, physical strength, and the future. *Klezmer* music was thus no longer the attractive, inspiring music it had once been. The *klezmer's* repertoire at Jewish events in the 1950s now included mostly popular American tunes, with some Israeli material and even less *klezmer.* Tunes such as "Mayim," "Harmonika," "Zum Gali Gali," "Havenu Shalom Alecheim," "Hinei Matov," "Hava Nagila,"[37] "Zemer Atik," and "Tzena Tzena"[38] were now taking the place of *freylekhs* and *bulgars.* When *klezmer*

---

[37] *Hava Nagila* (Heb.): come let us be joyful. *Hava Nagila* is easily the world's most famous Jewish melody. It was originally a Sadgora (a shtetl in the Ukraine near Chernovits) *khasidic nign,* some say composed by the Sadgorer *Rebe* Abraham Jacob Friedmann (1820–1883). The words were written by Moshe Nathanson, who was a music student of A. Z. Idelsohn's and eventually became the *khazn* of America's first Reconstructionist synagogue, the Society for the Advancement of Judaism in New York City.

[38] Tony Schwartz, sound and folklore collector, introduced "Tzena, Tzena" to Pete Seeger of the Weavers. Having sent out queries around the world for folksongs, he received about

was performed at weddings or *bar mitzves* (and eventually *bas mitzves*), the repertoire often consisted of three to five of the standard *klezmer* dance tunes like "Lustig Zayn" (also known as "Ma Yofis"), Kammen's "Freylekh No. 1" (also known as "The Silver Wedding"), "Freylekh No. 15" (also known as the "Shtiler Bulgar" or "And the Angels Sing"), "Khusn Kale Mazltov," and Russian *shers* numbers 1, 2, and 3.

Though the heyday of *klezmer* had already passed by the 1950s, a significant core of immigrant Jews (mostly in the New York region) still enjoyed listening to the Yiddish repertoire. Those *klezmer* musicians who kept playing into the 1950s found plenty of work because there were so much fewer of them and they had already established a following in the 1920s, '30s, and '40s. The most noted *klezmer* artist who was still revered, still recorded, and still heard on the radio was Dave Tarras. The youngest member of Tarras's hotel and club ensembles was Sheldon "Shelly" Hendler, who played with him from 1952 to 1959. His recollections give a poignant, down-to-earth perspective on *klezmer* during that era.

When I was either a sophomore or a junior in high school, I got my first steady music job during the summer playing up in the Catskills at a place called the Vegetarian Hotel in South Fallsberg. The music I played there was more like club date music. The crowd was rather young and they wanted to hear what was more hip in those days. Then in my senior year, while going to Boy's High School in Brooklyn, I again wanted to play in the Catskills because it was good money. I joined the union in 1952. Through the union I met this bass player who came to audition me in his car down in Sheepshead Bay [Brooklyn], where I lived. He represented the bandleader, who was Dave Tarras. He asked me to play any song, so I chose to play the tune that inspired me to take up the trumpet, and that was "Tenderly." When

46,000 in reply. In addition to "Tzena, Tzena," Schwartz introduced American audiences to "The Lion Sleeps Tonight" from Western Africa, "Everybody Loves Saturday Night" from South Africa, and "The Banana Boat Song" from Jamaica.

I was ten or eleven years old my parents used to take me to the Apollo Theatre and that is where I saw Tab Jordan playing "Tenderly." So I played the piece and he hired me. The gig was at the Majestic Hotel in South Fallsberg, New York. The reason they were so desperate was they had had a trumpet player who was heavy into drugs and couldn't make the gig. A trumpet player by the name Red Rodney [Robert Chudnick].[39] He was probably one of the most important trumpet players to have played with Charlie Parker. Red didn't play long with Tarras, maybe a week to two weeks. Red, by the way, was a tremendous *klezmer* player and played at a number of *bar mitsves* and weddings, where he showed off his *klezmer* chops. Red got his trumpet when he was *bar mitsved*. He was just a natural and by seventeen he was playing with Charlie Parker. Red actually replaced Miles Davis when he joined Charlie Parker. And just think, I replaced Red Rodney when I joined Dave Tarras's band.

I had played club dates before in New York so I was familiar with the Kammen books. So I knew the *freylekhs* and the *shers;* but playing with Dave was a whole new world. So that summer I transcribed for trumpet all of his tunes he was playing and really practiced them. Dave would do the non-Yiddish music too, but he was actually God-awful. He never had a sense of the ABA form. I would be playing the A section and then he was supposed to take the B section, and instead he called another tune entirely. Now you have to realize that I saw Dave Tarras in an entirely different light than these *klezmer* revivalists today see him. I was just a kid when I started playing with Dave, maybe sixteen or seventeen years old, and I didn't have too much respect for older people in general, and I certainly did not have that

---

[39] Red Rodney was hired on the recommendation of his good friend Sammy Musiker, who was Tarras's son-in-law. Marty Levitt saw Rodney playing with Tarras at the Delano Hotel in Monticello, New York in 1952. "Red was fired after only two weeks with Tarras because when he would take a solo in the middle of a *bulgar* he started doing his bebop stuff, which drove Tarras crazy. Tarras would yell, 'Vas shpilt ir? Vas tut ir?' [Yid.: What is he playing? What is he doing?]" Interview with Marty Levitt, op. cit.

much respect for Dave either. I even talked back to him, telling him when he wasn't playing something right. After several years of having played with Dave I then came to realize he was really good with the Yiddish stuff, the *klezmer* stuff. When it came time to play what he called "the American stuff" he just didn't get it. And the other thing that drove me up the wall was every time he made a mistake on his clarinet he turned around and pointed to me so to direct the audience's attention to me as if I had made the mistake. So for the first couple of years I really didn't have any great love for him. And every time I had a girlfriend he got very nosey. "Make sure her father's rich, don't marry anyone but a rich girl." He was constantly interfering in my affairs like a parent that I wanted to stay away from. It must be funny for you to hear me say this about a man who has become so revered by many musicians today.

Another hotel I played at was the Loch Sheldrake Inn in Loch Sheldrake. Dave's band did a few weeks at this hotel, which was owned by Alan Eager's mother. Alan Eager was one of the great jazz tenor saxophone players of that era. He would invite all his friends to come up for a week or weekend and hang out, enjoy the fresh country air, eat, swim, do drugs—which a lot were doing at that time, unfortunately—and listen to Dave Tarras. The fact that these guys came up to hear Dave Tarras got me more interested in what he was doing. Some of the people I am talking about included Charlie Parker and Miles Davis. According to some of the people I talked with, including Red Rodney, whom I became very good friends with, Charlie Parker said Dave was an incredible musician and had tremendous improvisational skills. They weren't interested in any of the American stuff we played— they were interested in only the modal stuff Dave was playing.

Dave rarely played the clarinet on the American stuff but instead played the tenor saxophone. For the *klezmer* music we basically would start together and then he would start his improvisations, which could last sometimes an hour, particularly when he played a *doyne*. Then I really realized what a giant he was on the clarinet. The band consisted of a bassist, drummer, pianist, trumpet, and Dave. Sometimes the bassist did vocals as well.

I actually played with them from '52 to '59, not just in the Catskills, but gigs in the city like weddings and *bar mitsves*. While with Dave I got to meet and play for many of the great Yiddish actors like Picon, Lebedeff, and Fyvush Finkel. Even though it was the '50s and the first-generation immigrants were getting rather old, Dave still kept busy with club dates, even playing some radio shows. There was a lot of work actually, playing weddings, *bar mitzves*, and recording. I played a lot of these gigs with Dave, including Herbie Mann's wedding, where he actually wanted more *klezmer* than jazz.

I picked up the *klezmer* style by listening to Dave, but I actually learned how to *kvetch* probably from listening to Harry James. He was a *kvetcher*, along with his buddy Ziggy Elman. Occasionally Dave gave me a note here and there about doing something at the end of the piece a bit differently, etc., but never an actual lesson. With Dave I never played the Kammen repertoire except for the first week or two because he knew I knew his stuff. Most of his tunes didn't have names but just numbers. He would just call out "play number 3," "number 5." He also loved playing "The Second Avenue Square Dance," but his favorite piece was "Ikh Hob Dikh Tsufil Lib," or "I Love You Too Much." Dave would get off the bandstand and go and play standing right in front of his wife. He played right in her face as if making love to her.

The other big *klezmer* clarinetist at that time was of course Naftuli Brandwein, who Dave thought was crude. All of Naftuli's *shtik* bothered Dave. He felt he didn't take the music seriously and acted like a clown. Dave was very serious about the music and how we appeared on stage. With Dave there was always a dress code. A white shirt, tie, dark slacks, and a jacket. With Dave it wasn't just the music, it was the image of being a clean-cut American.

When I look back on it now I have many fond memories of playing with Dave. I was probably the youngest guy to play with Dave. He was a very proud guy and enjoyed being called the "Jewish Benny

Goodman," which I and Paul Lanken (one of the sons of the owner of the Majestic) coined. Paul had a great sense of humor, and at least once a week he would get on the loudspeaker and say: "There is a call for the 'Jewish Benny Goodman,' Dave Tarras," which of course pleased Dave no end.[40]

From 1948 to 1990, Marty Levitt played *klezmer* clarinet with many of the great *klezmorim* of his day, including Abe Schwartz, one of the biggest *klezmer* icons of the 1920s and '30s. Schwartz was still able to find work in the Catskills after World War II, as Levitt relates:

My first union job and second hotel gig was in 1949, playing with Abe Schwartz at the Brookside Hotel in Loch Sheldrake. I went from making only fifteen dollars a week the summer before, when I wasn't in the union, to making fifty dollars a week after I joined the union. I was the youngest guy in the band—only eighteen years old. Everybody else was in their fifties, while Schwartz was nearly seventy. All the guys picked on me in the beginning, but once they saw I knew the repertoire as well as, if not better than, they did, I was fully accepted. Schwartz was like an icon, a cult figure to many in the audience who had been following his career since the early twenties. To me he was just a miserable bandleader, but a good Jewish violinist. Once I started to play a *bulgar* when he was not on the bandstand. He really got angry at me. I found out that you never started any of the Jewish tunes without Schwartz leading the band. He wanted to show the audience he knew the Jewish repertoire better than anyone else.[41]

Some *klezmorim* did change along with their constituents' tastes and learned to play swing, Broadway, Latin, classical, and other American pop

---

[40] Interview with Shelly Hendler (originally from Brooklyn) in La Jolla, California, on October 29, 2000.
[41] Interview with Marty Levitt, op. cit.

styles; but just being proficient was not good enough, as there was plenty of competition from non-Jewish musicians. Those *klezmorim* who had played classical music in Eastern Europe as part of their wedding repertoire found the same or similar tunes when they played in a symphony orchestra in America. And though some jazz melodies had made it to Eastern Europe by way of recordings or sheet music, most *klezmorim* were not as familiar with this genre as they were with classical and thus could not get work in jazz and swing bands as easily. A few first- and second-generation *klezmorim* kept up their "chops" by playing Jewish club dates in the Catskill resorts and in the Yiddish theatre, which, by the early 1950s, would cease to exist but for a few venues. Those who played the Jewish club dates found themselves playing mostly American music and a little *klezmer* at weddings and *bar mitzves*—except when employed by the *khasidim,* who only had Jewish music at their celebrations.

The following anecdote from Leonard Nimoy describes Yiddish theatre in the early 1950s in Los Angeles:

A lot of people think there wasn't much Yiddish theatre in Los Angeles, but there was a nice Yiddish theatre scene here from about 1950 to 1954. But before I went to Los Angeles I did some Yiddish theatre under a director named Boris Sagal. This was Katie Sagal's father. She played for years in the TV sitcom *Married With Children.* Then I moved out to L.A., where I worked with several famous Yiddish directors such as Mikhel Mikhalesco and Chaim Tauber. With Tauber I acted in *Di Freylekhe Kaptsonim* (Yid.: The Happy Paupers) and with Mikhalesco I was in *Dos Leben iz a Khulm* (Yid.: This Life Is a Dream). I also worked with [Maurice] Schwartz, but he mainly did Yiddish plays in English. He was trying to develop an English-speaking audience. The most successful play I did with him was *Shver tsu Zayn A Yid* (Yid.: Hard to Be a Jew), which ran for sixteen weeks at the Pacific Playhouse, which is now defunct. The Yiddish stuff I did was when Tauber and these other guys came out for a couple of weeks. Some of the plays had little to no music, while others, like *Freylekhe Kaptsonim,* were all singing and dancing. The music was live and definitely Jewish. It was a *klezmer* band that played Yiddish tunes and *freylekhs* that accompanied the entire show.[42]

Mickey Katz

There was another Jewish clarinetist, who lived not in New York but in Los Angeles and who became as well, if not better, known to Jews and non-Jews than Brandwein, Tarras, and Beckerman. This was Mickey Katz (1909–1985). His Jewish recordings sold more than any other at that time and were listened to by many of the *klezmer* revivalists and their parents in the 1950s and '60s, thus helping to maintain a link (however thin) between those who came of age with *klezmer* prior to the Holocaust and the post-Holocaust generation. Mickey Katz was able to play his style of Jewish music into the mid-1960s, even though most *klezmer* musicians had retired a decade earlier. Many said disparagingly that Mickey Katz "only" played Jewish novelty music, and it was never really *klezmer;* but nothing could be further from the truth. His two instrumental albums, *The Family Danced* and *Mickey Katz Plays Music for Weddings, Bar Mitsvehs, and Brisses* show, according to Rogovoy, his true "genius as a bandleader, composer, and musician. His band's arrangements by Nat Farber are also works of subversive vision prefiguring Radical Jewish Culture."[43] In truth, his arrangements were innovative and his lyrics jocular and acerbic. However some *klezmer* purists called Katz's art *shund*[44] because he dared to make people laugh—and, in particular, laugh at their Jewish identity

---

[42] Interview with Leonard Nimoy, op. cit.

[43] Rogovy, op. cit., p. 189.

[44] *Shund* (Yid.): literary trash. Most Yiddish plays from the 1880s to the present were labelled *shund*—popular rather than high culture. The term is considered an insult, and defining it is difficult. Yiddish theatre that was truly *shund* was concerned only with box-office receipts rather than with enlightening the audience in some way.

through his parodies of American popular songs in English, Yiddish, and Yinglish.[45]

Jazz clarinetist Don Byron, who played *klezmer* for the Klezmer Conservatory Band for several years, was so moved by some of Katz's recordings that he recorded *Don Byron Plays the Music of Mickey Katz*. "Comparing Katz to the late jazz composer and saxophonist Rahsaan Roland Kirk, Byron defends Katz by remarking, 'They figure if you're funny you're not serious.' "[46]

I was lucky enough to be able to conduct one of the last interviews with Mickey Katz before his death. Here he discusses his introduction to and experiences with *klezmer:*

> I was born in Cleveland to immigrant parents. My father was from Lithuania and my mother was from Latvia. Before I even played a note on the clarinet I used to go to the Yiddish theatre with my parents, which later on influenced my playing and perception of what Jewish music was and what the audience wanted to hear. I began playing the clarinet when I was eleven in grade school on an old beat-up instrument that was used during World War I. In order to have lessons I went to an uncle's tailor shop on Saturday afternoons and played for all his customers and earned $1.50. I was aware of Yiddish songs as a youngster because my sister sang professionally at lodges and other Jewish organizations. And *klezmer* music I knew because I played it at weddings and other Jewish events. Then in high school I formed a band and that's when I began my legitimate career as a musician. I was playing clarinet and sax—a lot of jazz and concert music. In fact I was the second clarinet player in the world to play *Rhapsody in Blue*.
>
> I played with this all-male orchestra in Cleveland when I was seventeen years old. I was hired because I was the only guy who could play

---

[45] Yinglish is the combination of Yiddish and English words, e.g. *boychik, alrightnik, nogoodnik, yardnik.*

[46] Josh Kun, *The Most Mishige: The Music and Comedy of Mickey Katz,* unpublished manuscript, p. 6.

it with all the shmears and glissandos and everything. There was really no call for legitimate Jewish music in those days. None at all. You learned how to play "Khusn Kale Mazltov," a *kozatshka,* and a *sher,* and that would be it. They weren't interested in hearing a musician play note for note what was recorded in 1911, and if they were they listened to the record and not the live music. In my opinion some of the songs of the old *klezmers* were not so great. Some were just not good musicians. Just because a player could blow a *krekht* didn't mean the music wasn't *drek* [Yid.: dirt, filth, excrement]. There were legitimate *klezmers* and homemade *klezmers* who learned how to play just enough to be hired for weddings, *bar mitsves,* funerals, and things like that.[47]

Katz loved Yiddish theatre but perceived that it was vanishing as the Yiddish-speaking immigrant audiences were aging and dying, and their offspring were busy forgetting Yiddish and assimilating. So Katz decided to combine the art of scholarly rhyme and the timing of the *batkhn* with lively *klezmer* music.

I came to L.A. in 1943, originally with Spike Jones. With Spike Jones I recorded a few novelty records and toured with him for a couple of years. I quit because I saw no future in it for me and I had a wife and children. So I left him in 1947. Encouraged by trumpeter Manny Klein, I went to RCA Victor and recorded "Haim Afyn Range" and "Yiddish Square Dance," which sold 150,000 copies in less than six months. To sell an ethnic record 150,000 to 200,000 was terrific. Broadway was on fire selling my records.

Then in 1948, with Hal Zeiger and my band Mickey Katz and His Kosher Jammers, I organized a beautiful Yiddish musical revue show called the *Borscht Capades.* It ran for six months in L.A. My son Joel Grey toured with us in the show when he was sixteen. In my heart I knew that those in my generation needed a new kind of Yiddish the-

---

[47] Interview with Mickey Katz, op. cit.

ater. A theater in Yiddish and English with some talented young Catskills performers doing the comedy mostly in English while our vocalists sang the nostalgic and familiar folksongs of the people. We got a
lot of complaints from the Yiddish theatre. "It's not nice what you are
doing..." All I know was we were bringing in more people to our
shows than the Yiddish theatre was doing. We played all over the
county and drew big crowds. We played in Carnegie Hall twice. In fact
Joseph Rumshinsky[48] even wrote for our New York shows.

Then my records were becoming very big overseas so I went to
England on two different trips, one trip to play theatres and the other
to play concerts. When I went to Australia and South Africa, no other
klezmer was going abroad to play Yiddish and *klezmer* concerts. I
couldn't hire a *klezmer* who only scratched or *phummphed*. I had to
have musicians like Si Zenter on trombone and Sammy Weiss on
drums. These guys played the *freylekhs* like nobody else. Then I had
the great Manny Klein on trumpet, Ziggy Elman in the early '50s on
trumpet, Benny Gill on fiddle, and Larry Breen on bass. We also had
a fantastic arranger and pianist named Nat Farber who helped us with
all the orchestration. He arranged for Carol Burnett too. All these guys
enjoyed playing the music because it reminded them of the songs they
heard as kids from their parents. We were reliving our *bar mitsves* every
time we played this music.[49]

In all of Katz's parodies, his band followed the tune's original form and
then would insert a *klezmer* break, an up-tempo *freylekh* led by Katz on the
clarinet. This happened several times in a tune. These "*Yidishe*" jive instrumental breaks exhibited the great facility with which Katz and the rest of

[48] Joseph Rumshinsky (1879–1956) was born in Vilnius (Vilna), Lithuania, and came to
New York City in 1903. A composer of Yiddish songs and operettas, he worked with
most of the great Yiddish actors and writers during the heyday of Yiddish theatre (the
1900s through the mid-1930s).
[49] Interview with Mickey Katz, op. cit.

his band could go from novelty to swing to *klezmer* in one tune. And anyone who thinks Katz could not play straight *klezmer* just has to listen to his two purely instrumental albums with all his own compositions.

> We even made an instrumental album that sold 50,000 copies, which no *klezmer* ever sold before us and probably not after us. Each tune on the record was an original I wrote. I made eleven albums. What is remarkable to me is everyone has forgotten what I did. I came too early. I was ahead of everybody. A lot of the revivalists today just have style and not a good sound. They are just imitating what they heard on these old 78 LPs. I never tried to imitate anybody. I just wanted to be myself. Naftuli Brandwein and Dave Tarras were superb players but I didn't copy them. For twenty years we had no competition, because there was no one else who knew how to play it. I would mix the playing in our shows. To hear only *klezmer* or *khasidic* for a whole concert was too monotonous. Whenever I went down to Florida I played with the Epstein Brothers: Max, Willie, and Julie. Willie would play trumpet so well it knocked you on your ass.[50]

From 1947 to 1957 (when most of Katz's recordings were released), Katz's music became some of the most popular Jewish music available in stores and on radio. (Katz was a DJ at KABC in Los Angeles from 1951 to 1956 and played all kinds of Jewish music on air.) At the same time there were Jews who did not find Katz's kind of Yiddish humor funny. It was strutting his Jewishness for everyone to see, in all its finery and warts. American Jews in the 1940s and '50s rarely proudly announced their Jewishness in public. Even a few radio shows refused to play his music. Katz was well aware he was causing many in the Jewish mainstream to squirm. As he told me, "It took television's *All in the Family* to kick the hell out of the frightened ones, and it took the Six-Day War in 1967, when a few thousand brave Jews in Israel proved to be more than a match for a hundred million Arabs,

---

[50] Ibid.

for "Jewish" finally to become popular and acceptable. But 1967 wasn't any help to me in 1947."[51]

Tarras, Musiker, the Epstein Brothers, Marty Levitt, and Brandwein played in the 1950s on the East Coast, primarily at casuals, hotel resorts, and rarely, if ever, a concert. However, Katz toured the country and played primarily concerts to packed Jewish venues in big and small cities. Immigrants, their children, and Holocaust survivors came to be injected with a little *Yiddishkayt* and to experience a *shtikl* (Yid.: bit, piece) of the Yiddish theatre and a *klezmer* world that had all but vanished. It was Katz's own special brand of American-*klezmer* music. "In my band we were all studio musicians, all Jews. We could only be what we were, a fresh flavor. The American sequel to the *klezmers* of Eastern Europe."[52]

The End of the Line

For the *khasidim* in America, *Yiddishkayt* was part of everyday life. After the Holocaust those *khasidim* who had survived in Europe found refuge and rebuilt new *khasidic* dynasties, primarily in Brooklyn. The three most important items the *khasidim* brought with them on the ships to America were Yiddish, their religious practices, and folk culture. The *shtetl* wedding with all its rituals of preparation and celebration—which of course included the *klezmer* and *batkhn*—was transplanted to the synagogues and catering halls of Brooklyn, and gave much-needed employment to a few *klezmorim*, of whom some of the better known were the Epstein Brothers, Marty Levitt, Howie Leess, and Pete Sokolow. But even the strict orthodoxy of the *khasidim* could not stop their traditional *klezmer* dances and *nigunim* from being influenced by American and Israeli culture. By the mid-1960s, the acoustic bass was replaced by the electric bass, the violin was replaced by the clarinet and saxophone, and the accordion was eventu-

---

[51] Mickey Katz, *Papa, Play for Me* (New York: Simon & Schuster, 1977), p. 133.
[52] Interview with Mickey Katz, op. cit.

ally replaced by electric keyboards and electric guitar. The repertoire—with Hebrew text (rarely did they sing in Yiddish) from their daily prayers— also became more Israeli and Middle Eastern-sounding. The dance tunes were repeated over and over with no improvisation, generally loud and fast, with a driving rock-oriented back beat. As Howie Leess, one of the mainstays of the *khasidic* music scene, commented,

> The *hasidic* music was written primarily by *yeshive* boys, who would fit songs to the text of the bible, and they had no musical talent. They would sing it to a tape recorder and then have somebody copy down the tunes for them. They had less musical value than the *klezmer* musicians, who were pretty schooled in their own field and knew music and the number of measures per song. The *hasidim* knew nothing about that. And it would sound like that, too. So I thought it was a lower grade than *bulgars*.[53]

Marty Levitt recalls, "I played the *khasidic* jobs for a while, but I quit because they were boring and [the audience] didn't seem to appreciate any of our musicianship. All they wanted was the melody to be loud, repeated ad nauseam, with the percussion on autopilot. Ironically, my best selling record was my *50 Hasidic Hits*, which I recorded in 1973."[54]

By the 1960s *klezmer* music had been all but relegated to the *khasidic* enclaves of Brooklyn and to Florida's "condominium circuit." Most first-generation American-born *klezmorim* had left the world of *klezmer* to pursue steadier work (some opened music stores), or had retired. Unlike the tradition in Eastern Europe, where the son or nephew had followed his father's or uncle's footsteps and become the leader of the family *kapelye*, the immigrant *klezmer* in America discouraged his children from pursuing a career in any kind of music, especially *klezmer*. He wanted his children to be more financially successful than he, and to pursue a career that was not

[53] Sapoznik, op. cit., p. 163.
[54] Interview with Marty Levitt, op. cit.

burdened with financial uncertainty and negative social stigmas.

As the urban American Jewish community steadily climbed the ladder of economic success, and as they began to move from the inner cities to the quieter climes of suburbia, they encouraged their children to become doctors, lawyers, professors, and CPAs. Some children and grandchildren of immigrant parents did pursue the arts—but not *klezmer*. Many of the young Jews who went into music followed the path of such Jewish classical musicians as Leonard Bernstein and Isaac Stern. Others followed the popular music and theatre routes of composers like Sammy Cahn, Betty Comden, and Adolf Green; still others, like Dave Brubeck, Stan Getz, and Red Rodney, went into jazz. Other Jewish musicians went out west and found work in the pit orchestras in Las Vegas or Hollywood. These studio musicians and composers found a lot of work in the burgeoning film industry. So while many Jews went into music, a scant few went into Jewish music of any kind.

If some kind of nostalgic mood swept over you in the 1960s or early '70s and you wanted to hear some *klezmer* music, you pulled your 78-rpm records out of the closet. You dusted them off, paid nothing to sit in the comfort of your home, and listened to them on your phonograph. But this need to remember and reconnect with Jewish life in the vanished *alte haym* (Yid.: old home; birthplace)—or even with the kind of Jewish life that had once existed on the Lower East Side of Manhattan in the teens and 1920s—was generally limited to immigrants. Their children and grandchildren were now active participants in the 1950s beat generation and eventually the 1960s counterculture movement, replete with "sex, drugs, and rock 'n' roll."

Fun Zev biz Zorn: Di Bale-Kulturniks

•

(FROM ZEV TO ZORN: THE MASTERS OF CULTURE)

When I played *klezmer* music, whether it was for Jews, Moldavians, or Bessarabians, it did not matter to them that I was a Gypsy. They only cared if the music was good and being played with *neshome* (Heb.: soul). You see, one could go to engineering school and become an engineer, but one could not go to the conservatory and become a *klezmer.* You had to have grown up with some knowledge of the culture. Without knowing—and I mean really knowing—the culture of the *klezmer,* it didn't matter how long you studied in the conservatory. That person's playing of *klezmer* never went deep. The music never touched the *kishkes* (Yid.: guts). *Klezmers* were not just great technicians but carriers of a great culture.[1]

---

[1] Interview with Nikolai Radu (originally from Orgeyev, Moldova) in Chișinău, Moldova, November 10, 1984. Radu's influence reached the United States: many Jewish musicians now playing *klezmer,* particularly accordionists, played with or were taught by Radu, including Zinovy Goro, David Kasap, and Isaac Sadigursky.

The Klezmer *"Revival"* and the Bale-Kulturniks

As I traveled throughout Eastern Europe in the early 1980s—collecting field recordings, oral histories, and sheet music, and giving concerts in homes, Jewish clubs, and synagogues—I saw myself not as a reviviscent artist, but rather as a transmitter of Yiddish culture. There had been, of course, a major rupture in Yiddish culture in Eastern Europe, but the culture had never been completely extinguished. Among the some 200,000 Ashkenazic Jews (those who officially declared themselves as Jews) living in the former Eastern Bloc countries (Czechoslovakia, East Germany, Hungary, Poland, Romania, Yugoslavia) and the approximately 2.5 million Jews in the former Soviet Union (the majority of them Ashkenazim living in Russia, Ukraine, and Belarus, with significant minorities in the Baltic republics, Moldova, and Uzbekistan) some Yiddish culture remained alive. One subset of this culture was Jewish music.

Where was this music performed? For starters, wherever there was an active synagogue or *shtibl,* I heard beautiful Jewish melodies. I heard these melodies in synagogues that had prayers three times a day, seven days a week; in synagogues that were open only on the days the *Toyre* was read (Monday, Thursday, and *Shabes* mornings); in synagogues open for worship just on *Shabes;* in others open only on the High Holidays. I heard Jewish music at Jewish clubs, at private *simkhes* (weddings, *bar mitsves*), funerals, and at peoples' workplaces and homes. Whether it was actual *klezmer* music, Yiddish folk or theatre songs, or prayers (the DNA of all Ashkenazic music), these Jews had maintained a vital link with Jewish culture.

Though most of the Jewish music in the former Eastern Bloc countries was sung and played in the synagogues, there were other opportunities after World War II for Jewish musicians to ply their trade. The Yiddish State Theatre of Lodz closed in 1948 and that of Iași in 1961, but the Yiddish theatres in Warsaw and Bucharest and semi-professional ones in Vilnius and Chișinău never stopped performances. In the Soviet Union, bands made up of primarily Jewish musicians did not advertise that they played *klezmer.* They were hired to play jazz and pop music, but at a Jewish wedding they knew without being asked to add some *klezmer* and Yiddish tunes to the repertoire. It was much more difficult for Jewish musicians living in Russia than for those living in Lithuania, Moldova, Poland, Romania, and Ukraine because local communist authorities there could be a bit more lenient, more inclined to turn a blind eye to the customs of the Jewish community—and less likely to be carefully scrutinized by Moscow.

One way of saying the word "revival" in Yiddish is *emune-shtarkung,* which is a conjunction of the words *emune* (Heb.: faith, creed) and *shtark* (Yid.: strong). The Jews I met during my ethnographic travels were each in their own ways "faith strengtheners," each doing something to continue the thousand-year-old Ashkenazic culture of Eastern Europe. Some Jews affirmed their identities through daily involvement with both religious and cultural aspects of Judaism; at the other extreme were those whose sense of their own Jewishness was limited to blood and Jewish surnames. But most fell somewhere in between. It was not a matter of revival but of continuance, which is in itself an accomplishment after the Holocaust. Thus, when I traveled in the Eastern Bloc countries and in the former Soviet Union, I never considered myself a "revivalist," but rather a *bal-kulturnik* (Yid.: owner or master of culture), one who returns to his culture and transmits it to others. To use the word *revival* when we speak about *klezmer* music in America—today, ten, or even twenty-five years ago—is to misuse the word. As Bob Norman puts it, "Revivals never spring up full-blown. There are always antecedents, lines of continuity, and those quietly heroic individuals who keep important things alive when they are no longer popular, sowing seeds others will reap."[2]

The orthodox and *khasidic* communities in the United States never stopped having Jewish music played at their *simkhes* (especially at weddings). Some would argue that the *khasidic* music played from the mid-1960s through today is not *klezmer,* because it does not sound anything

---

[2] Bob Norman, "Echoes from the Shtetl: Reviving Jewish Klezmer Music," *Sing Out! The Folk Song Magazine,* Vol. 28, Number 4, July/August 1980, p. 3.

like the 78 rpms that were recorded prior to World War II. In answer to that I would say that the *klezmer* music of the late nineteenth century played in Eastern Europe, with its particular instrumentation and dances, was quite different from the *klezmer* music played at Jewish weddings in Bohemia in the late sixteenth century. Was this not Ashkenazic instrumental music too?

What these *klezmer* musics from two different eras had in common with the *khasidic* music of today is the music of *davenen* (Yid.: prayer). As *klezmer* clarinetist and mandolinist Andy Statman told me, "The *klezmer* tunes never died; they were and still are kept alive through *davenen*. I live in a community where the *klezmer* tunes live on a daily basis in the synagogue. The *khazn* will use elements of the *doyne* and other aspects of *klezmer* ornamentation to help express and evoke the deep spirituality of the prayer. The music used in prayers brought Jews closer to God. *Klezmer* music is just the child of *khasidic* vocal music."[3]

I take this a step further. Even though *klezmer* music—in the form we often narrowly define as Ashkenazic instrumental and dance music—became less popular in the United States in the years between the end of World War II and the 1960s, it had maintained itself in another form: in the *davenen*, the liturgy sung and chanted in most synagogues across America. After all, playing *klezmer* melodies on an instrument was just an extension of singing the liturgy. The modes used in Ashkenazic, Sephardic, or Arabic liturgy form the backbone of all *klezmer* music. *Davenen* among a core group of Jews did not die in the former East Bloc, Soviet Union, or America after World War II. As Statman told me:

> There is a purposeful omission among many *klezmer* musicians today. The *klezmer*'s wide emotional and artistic palette comes from *khasidic nigunim*, but you never hear people speaking about Tarras's or Brandwein's *khasidic* roots. The music was used as a spiritual vehicle to make the bride and groom happy at their wedding. This was the *mitsve*: to

---

[3] Interview with Andy Statman, May 31, 2001.

play for the various honored guests meditative *khasidic* tunes and rubato songs. And the dance music was not necessarily light music. It was used to entertain but also could induce the dancers into a trance-like state of mind. *Khasidic* dance, which was so common to Jewish weddings in Eastern Europe before World War II, was all about spirituality. In American Jewish culture *klezmer* music has been defined as party music, the antithesis of what the music was originally all about. There is definitely a conspiracy of silence among many *klezmer* musicians today when it comes to describing the music's real spiritual roots.[4]

For most of the musicians in the mid-1970s to the early 1980s, playing *klezmer* music was not a true revival—a stirring-up of religious faith among those who had been indifferent—but rather a return to a specific kind of cultural milieu, the one in which either their parents or grandparents had grown up. These *bale-kulturniks* re-created a specific kind of *klezmer* music that existed in East European Jewish culture during the mid-nineteenth century through the eve of World War II. They played music that was found in the few *klezmer* manuscripts and on the earliest 78-rpm recordings.

In the twentieth century there have been five different generations—five waves, so to speak—of *klezmer* music in America. The first two were the historical and musical mentors for the three *bal-kulturnik* generations. The first-generation *klezmorim* were those who were born and trained in Eastern Europe before World War II. Some of them immigrated to America, while others never left. These included Naftuli Brandwein, Ben Bazyler[5], Shloimke Beckerman, Avram Bughici, Jeremiah Hescheles, Leo-

---

[4] Ibid.

[5] Ben Bazyler was born in Warsaw in 1922 and came from a family *kapelye*. He learned to sing Yiddish songs and play the drums as a youth. When Poland was invaded by Germany in June 1941, Bazyler fled to Soviet-occupied Poland and was eventually deported to a labor camp in Siberia. Music literally saved his life—the camp guards gave him bigger food rations in exchange for his entertaining them. After the war he made it to Tashkent, Uzbekistan, where he continued to play and sing at Jewish and non-Jewish parties, events, and weddings.

pold Kozlowski, Leon Schwartz, and Dave Tarras. Their studio and field recordings and/or manuscripts formed the core repertoire for all the subsequent *klezmer* generations.

The second generation came to America from Eastern Europe as young children or were American-born. They actively played and recorded *klezmer* music from the 1920s to the early '60s. Their repertoire still included the tunes of the first generation, but they also began to combine elements of swing with their *klezmer* tunes. Some of these musicians were Sid Beckerman, the Epstein Brothers, Mickey Katz, Howie Leess, Marty Levitt, Sammy and Ray Muziker, and Paul Pincus.

The third generation were the first *bale-kulturniks* who began playing *klezmer* in the 1970s. They learned both from recordings and firsthand from those first- and second-generation *klezmorim* who were still alive. This generation includes Michael Alpert, Lauren Brody, Stu Brotman, Marty Confurius, Zev Feldman, Giora Feidman, Barry Fisher, Julian David Gray, Lev Liberman, Ken Maltz, Zalman Mlotek, Hankus Netsky, Henry Sapoznik, Andy Statman, and Josh Waletzky.

The fourth-generation *bale-kulturniks* were those who began playing *klezmer* in the 1980s. They learned equally from the three previous generations, but by the late '80s they began to push the boundaries. *Klezmer* bands began to experiment with elements from jazz, rock 'n' roll, and ethnic genres like Rom, Balkan, and Arabic musics. The establishment of KlezKamp in the Catskills became a kind of one-week seminar of sorts for *bale-kulturniks* and second-generation *klezmorim* to meet, learn, play, and exchange musical ideas with each other. By the late '80s, Western Europe (particularly Germany) was becoming more receptive to the growing interest in Yiddish culture, and brought several *klezmer* bands from

---

In 1957 he moved with his family to Lodz, Poland, where he continued to perform with other Holocaust survivors. He immigrated to America in 1964. Eventually he moved to Los Angeles, continuing to play Jewish music until his death in 1991. Before his death, Bazyler had become well-known to the early *bale-kulturniks* and was sought after by many of them, as they wanted to learn from a *klezmer* who had grown up in Eastern Europe. One such *bal-kulturnik* was Michael Alpert, who became very close to Bazyler.

America to tour. The overwhelmingly positive reception these musicians received from critics, audiences, and record companies in Europe convinced some to either base much of their performing in Europe or to completely relocate there. Some of these musicians are David Buchbinder, Don Byron, Ismail Butera, Kurt Bjorling, Adrienne Cooper, Jack Falk, David Krakauer, Margo Leverett, Lori Lippitz, Frank London, Wendy Marcus, Lee Musiker, Jeff Pekarek, Joel Rubin, Lorin Sklamberg, Deborah Strauss, Yale Strom, Alicia Svigals, Gerry Tenny, and Jeff Warschauer.

Finally, the fifth-generation *bale-kuturniks* are those musicians who began playing *klezmer* in the 1990s and continue to forge ahead into the twenty-first century. Many of these musicians came of age musically during the 1970s and '80s and learned the repertoire not necessarily only from the old recordings by the first- and second-generation *klezmorim,* but from the cassettes and compact discs of the third- and fourth-generation *bale-kulturniks.* Another resource, outside of recordings and *klezmer* music books, which was barely available for the previous *bale-kulturniks,* was the various Yiddish and *klezmer* festivals that began in America, Europe, and the former Soviet Union. In addition to this, several documentary films[6] had become important for many musicians. The venues for playing the music had expanded. Two important downtown clubs in the New York City alternative music scene became a mecca for many of the *bale-kulturniks:* the Knitting Factory, established in 1987, and Tonic, established in 1998 (Makor, on the Upper West Side, joined them in 1999). In particular, the Knitting Factory has been a club in which audiences have been exposed to everything from traditional ensembles with violin, bass, and *tsimbl* to the avant-garde music of John Zorn. At the same time, not only Western Europe but Eastern Europe, with the advent of the fall of the Berlin Wall, became the place for many American *klezmer* musicians to concertize. The

---

[6] *A Jumpin' Night in the Garden of Eden* (directed by Michal Goldman, 1988), *Fiddlers on the Hoof* (directed by Simon Broughton, 1989), *The Last Klezmer: Leopold Kozlowski: His Life and Music* (directed by Yale Strom, 1994), *A Tickle in the Heart* (directed by Stefan Schwietert, 1996).

bale-kulturnik klezmer movement really became ensconced there (there are several *klezmer* bands in Oceania too), with many new bands and recordings. This fifth generation includes Steven Bernstein, the Budapest Klezmer Band, Leo Chelyapov, Jordan Chernovsky, Bob Cohen, Anthony Coleman, Matt Darriau, Kaila Flexer, Ben Goldberg, Misha Heitzler, Daniel Hoffman, the Jascha Lieberman Trio (Poland), Joshua Horowitz, Klezmokum (Holland), Kroke (Poland), Eve Sicular, Psamim (Germany), Sabbath Hela Veckan (Sweden), Merlin Shepherd (England), Karsten Troyke (Germany), and John Zorn.

The Beginnings of the Movement—Bikel, Carlebach, Rosenbaum, Feidman

It is difficult to say precisely when the *klezmer bal-kulturnik* movement began. And though The Klezmorim (from Berkeley, California) are considered the first of the *bal-kulturnik* bands (having formed in 1976), a number of individuals and ensembles played some form of Ashkenazic Jewish folk music before them. For some Jewish musicians, there was no rupture of Yiddish culture between the mid-1950s and the mid-1970s. Whether it was through speaking Yiddish, listening to Yiddish records and radio, or playing the music, East European Jewish culture was very much alive for popular figures of the 1960s and early '70s such as Theodore Bikel, Rabbi Shlomo Carlebach, Giora Feidman, and Avraham Rosenblum.

Theodore Bikel began singing Hebrew and Yiddish songs while studying at the Royal Academy of Dramatic Arts in London in the early 1950s. Many a Jewish baby-boomer in America (including myself) listened to Bikel records in his or her childhood. As Bikel told me,

> I did a lot of singing outside of school. I sang at parties, at home, and on my days off. People would come to the apartment and stay until all hours and we'd sing. It was never meant to be a profession. It wasn't until I got to America that it became a profession. Eventually I signed

a recording contract with Elektra Records, which was a fledgling company at that time. I think the songs I sang were successful because of a certain sensibility they had. Obviously *Mittel Europa* gave me a sense of culture, a sense of appreciation, and a sense of being, if you will, as an intellectual human being. Even though I didn't come from the *shtetl,* I knew the songs and the language.[7]

Rabbi Shlomo Carlebach, who was born in Berlin, came from an illustrious rabbinical family. In America, Carlebach is credited with having started and making extremely popular the neo-*khasidic* folksong genre. Some called him the "hippie" rabbi because of his long, curly locks, beard, casual attire, "hip" youthful speech and large following of young Jews, many of whom were part of the 1960s hippie-flower-power anti-establishment movement. He even ran, for a short time, a synagogue in the Haight-Ashbury section of San Francisco called "The House of Love and Peace." Carlebach's simple melodic tunes, which he sang while accompanying himself on guitar, were based on one of the building blocks of nineteenth-century *klezmer* music, the *nign.* Years before the *balkulturnik klezmer* clarinetist Giora Feidman approached *klezmer* with the same *kabbalist* and spiritual philosophy, Carlebach had already introduced tens of thousands through his music and *khasidic* homilies. Rabbi Shlomo Carlebach told me, "The guitar and my singing, Yitskhok, are all parts of the *kley-koydesh*[8] that *Hashem*[9] gave me to use to spread his holy word. The understanding and love for the *Toyre*."[10]

These *nigunim*—some wordless, most with Hebrew text—are still sung by many thousands of Jews around the world today. In fact, before any *balkulturnik* band played in Eastern Europe, Carlebach had toured the Eastern

---

[7] Interview with Theodore Bikel on October 4, 2000.

[8] *Kleykoydesh* (Heb. and Yid.): clergy, holy vessels. Carlebach in this instance referred to the holy vessels that the priests used in the ancient Temple for various religious duties.

[9] *Hashem* (Heb.): the name. When speaking about God outside the context of actual praying you could not say his name; thus one would say "hashem" to indicate God.

[10] Interview with Shlomo Carlebach in Kraków, Poland, December 11, 1988.

Bloc, the former Soviet Union, and Poland, and played to sold-out audiences in 1988. The concerts attracted all kinds of Jews, particularly those who were just beginning to feel comfortable publicly acknowledging their Jewishness. However, the majority of the audiences were made up of non-Jews who attended for reasons including curiosity, exoticism, and philo-Semitism. Carlebach sowed some of the early seeds of the *klezmer bal-kulturnik* movement that became a regular part of the Jewish cultural renewal.

Avraham Rosenblum came from a secular Yiddish-speaking home before becoming a rock musician. He told me, "I played what I called country-rock/fusion groove, with elements of Buffalo Springfield; Crosby, Stills, Nash and Young; Blues Project; Seatrain; Procol Harem; and the Band. Then, in 1971, I met up with Jewish wedding music and I began to let the *kvetch* (Yid.: squeeze; complaint) into all of my music. We played weddings and *mlave malke*[11] jams in Philly and New York."[12] Feeling spiritually empty, rudderless, Rosenblum moved to Israel. There he studied in a *yeshive,* became a *bal-tchuve,*[13] started the Diaspora Yeshiva Band (1975), and recorded his first album (1976) with other wayward Jews from America. After twelve years he moved back to the States along with his fellow *yeshive* students. The band combined a San Francisco rock 'n' roll sound with Israeli, Middle Eastern, and *khasidic* music, and became very popular on the college circuit through the early and mid-1980s. Rosenblum said, "It was a revolutionary thing happening in Judaism, bringing in contemporary music and using it as a vehicle to promote this new thing happening for all of us. . . . We didn't grow up *frum* [Yid.: pious, devout] and discover religion, rock later, and try to force one . . . into [the] other. . . . It wasn't just giving Jewish music a rock 'n' roll veneer. Our synthesis was much deeper."[14]

---

[11] *Mlave malke* (Heb.): escorting the queen. The last festive meal of *Shabes,* which usually features singing and dancing.

[12] Interview with Avraham Rosenblum, August 20, 2001.

[13] *Bal-tchuve* (Yid.): penitent. When Jews not raised as orthodox become orthodox they are called *bale-tchuves* (pl.), those who return to Judaism.

[14] Alexandra J. Wall, "Rhythm & Jews: Post-Klezmer Music—A Ride to Everywhere," *Moment,* Vol. 24, No. 4, August 1999, p. 45.

Synthesizing religion with music was Giora Feidman's whole approach to playing *klezmer*. His mystical approach and definition of *klezmer* as all music with Yiddish lyrics or with roots in the *shtetl*, not just East European Jewish wedding music, expanded his audience. Some secular *bale-kulturniks* felt he made the music too "religious" sounding, and did not want it to come solely under the rubric of the synagogue. Feidman justified his approach:

> Jewish music doesn't exist except as music with prayer in the synagogue. We all pray from the same book, but everyone must say the prayer in his own way. God says the words are for you to understand. The *nigun*, the melody of it, is for men. Religion is prayer and one can pray only if one sings the prayers. Jews pray three times a day, and music is born naturally of prayer. Go stand in the back of one of those small synagogues and you will hear different singing, what we call today a cacophony. But you will absorb that energy, and you know that that particular music you are listening to will never happen again in exactly the same way.[15]

On another occasion, he said, "The term *klezmer*...combines two Hebrew words, *kli zmer*, which mean *tool of the song*. This does not refer to the instrument, but the musician.... The term *kli* stands for *Cohen* [priest], *Levi* [Levite], and *Yisrael* [Israel], the three classes of Jews. And the term *zemer* can be understood as *remez shel zerem*, a hint of the divine stream that flows to mankind. Anyone who plays *klezmer* is part of the 'Tree of Life.' "[16]

Though Feidman has been playing Jewish music of some kind since 1972, he has never been regarded by many of the *bale-kulturniks* as a mem-

---

[15] Richard F. Shepard, "Whether Klezmer or Classical, It's Music for This Man's Clarinet," *New York Times*, November 14, 1987, section C, pp. 1 & 22.

[16] Hank Bordowitz, "Klezmer Rocks: Yiddish Music is on a Roll," *B'nai Brith Jewish Monthly*, February–March 1993, p. 10.

ber of the *klezmer* community. Some explain this as because of his classical background (for twenty years, he played clarinet and bass clarinet for the Israeli Philharmonic; he left having served as principal clarinetist); the cultured tones seemed almost too refined to lend themselves to the spontaneity of this folk idiom. Perhaps to compensate for this, and for not coming from a musical background that lends itself to improvisation, Feidman ornaments his solos to the point where they become *shmaltzy* (Yid.: greasy; over-the-top) and almost parodic of the *klezmer* style.

Feidman was born in Buenos Aires to a family that had emigrated from Bessarabia. His grandfather and father were both *klezmorim*. At age twenty, when most classical musicians are studying in the conservatory, Feidman was living in Israel and playing in the Israeli Philharmonic. Fifteen years before the violinist virtuoso Itzhak Perlman performed his classical renditions of Yiddish and theatre songs with the Israeli Philharmonic, Feidman performed Yiddish and Hebrew melodies with orchestras throughout the world. Due to his failing eyesight, Feidman left the Israeli Philharmonic to pursue playing *klezmer* full-time. He also played *klezmer* concerts in (West) Germany ten years before any *bal-kulturnik* bands were invited. Some say he laid the groundwork for many of the *bal-kulturnik* bands, as he helped to initiate an interest in Jewish music in general among a German public that was beginning to have enough distance to confront their unfortunate history in World War II and embrace and even nurture what little remained of Ashkenazic Jewish culture.

After Feidman played the role of Heiken, a *klezmer* clarinetist in the Vilna ghetto in Joshua Sobol's critically acclaimed controversial play *Ghetto*, to sold-out audiences for six months in 1984, he became known as the "king of *klezmer*" in Germany and throughout the rest of Europe. The German director Peter Zadek had created the role of Heiken, the only survivor in the drama, expressly for Feidman. Seeing the play was very cathartic for many Germans. And since Heiken was the last character seen on stage, Feidman became his embodiment for much of the audience. He described his impact as follows: "Over 100,000 members of the new generation in Germany saw this play during the run.... I am the voice of the people of

Vilna.... I am the man who brings sound to the inner walls of this society. The people there had no way to express their pain. My clarinet was the only way.... It's my way of telling the Nazis, 'You see? We're still here. You can destroy the man, but you can't kill the spirit.' "[17]

The fifth-generation *bal-kulturnik klezmer* Leo Chelyapov, who recorded his first *klezmer* CD with my band (*The Last Klezmer: Leopold Kozlowski*) and then went on to form and codirect the Los Angeles–based band Hollywood Klezmer, was greatly influenced by Feidman. He told me,

> My first clarinet teachers had me concentrate on only the classical repertoire. When I was twelve I participated in a music competition among all the music schools in Moscow. I took first place and was then accepted into the Moscow College of Musical Arts. There I was exposed to jazz and pop music, but my teacher didn't want me to study jazz improvisation for another two years. Then at fifteen, I saw Giora Feidman give a concert at the Gnesin Music Institute in Moscow. It was a great concert. Then and there I decided *klezmer* would be fun and interesting to study. So I began to play and study *klezmer* on my own. Recently I found out that my grandfather's grandma was one of the younger sisters to Sholom Aleichem. This made the famous Yiddish writer my great-great uncle, so I was destined to become a *klezmer.*[18]

Another *bal-kulturnik* influenced by Feidman is Swiss musician Michael Borzykowski, who told me:

> I got into *klezmer* about six years ago when I formed a band with my neighbor, an accordionist, and another friend who played clarinet. Then once after a concert a woman approached us. She was just beginning to rediscover her Jewish identity, particularly as it related to culture,

[17] Marc Shulgod, "'Ghetto' Sounds: The Song of a Survivor," *Los Angeles Times* (San Diego County Edition), November 29, 1986, pp. 7–8.
[18] Interview with Leo Chelyapov, June 22, 2000.

and more specifically to Yiddish songs. She joined our band and Rozinkes Mit Mandlen was born.

For repertoire and style I listened to a lot of different CDs, but the greatest influence on me to this date has been Giora Feidman. I spent a week at a *klezmer* workshop he gave here in Switzerland. It was extremely helpful—even the *goyim* seemed to have been touched by him and his music. I learned that *klezmer* speaks to the heart of everybody who hears it and expresses not only one human feeling but many feelings simultaneously—which I consider typically Jewish.[19]

Kapelye

The pursuit of *klezmer* was more organic for several of the *bale-kulturniks* (Michael Alpert, Henry Sapoznik, Josh Waletzky) than for others because these grew up speaking Yiddish and were immersed in many other aspects of East European culture. This was particularly true of Michael Alpert, one of the key practitioners of Yiddish folksong and *klezmer* today, and a member of the *klezmer* ensemble *Brave Old World*. He explained:

> My father's side of the family was orthodox, but while I was growing up in Los Angeles, my parents sent me to a left-wing progressive *shule* run by people who came out of the IKUF, the *Yidishe Kultur Farband.* So I grew up with a foot in both worlds, the orthodox and the left-wing.
>
> I grew up hearing four kinds of Jewish music. First, American Jewish wedding music of the 1950s and '60s, which I heard in L.A. and Boston. I moved to Boston when I was twelve, into a large extended family that encouraged my speaking Yiddish.
>
> The second kind of Yiddish music was the old 78 rpms that either my relatives played or I heard on the radio. In Boston there was a great

---

[19] Interview with Michael Borzykowski, June 28, 2000.

Jewish radio show hosted by Ben Galling for years. On this show they would spin the old discs—like Lebedeff, Schwartz, and Kandel. Sometimes they even played some of the European Yiddish and *klezmer* recordings. I really enjoyed listening to this music. It was like looking into a window of an older world that my family and relatives often spoke about.

The third kind of music was *khasones* and *davenen* in *shul*. I loved hearing the old-time *khazn*. To me there was an obvious difference between the older *khazonim* and the newer smoothed-out American style of *khazones*. Usually the *shuls* I attended just had a *bal-tfile* [Yid.: prayer leader] who sang well—with all the *dreydlekh*.

Lastly, the fourth kind of music I grew up with I called "boardwalk" music. This was the music of the mandolin, accordion, Russian seven-string guitar, and balalaika that was played by older Jews in Plummer Park in West Hollywood, or on the boardwalk in Venice, Santa Monica, and in Brighton Beach. These Jews played and sang Yiddish and Russian folk melodies. And I liked this music very much because on my father's side, that was more Russian-*Litvok* [Yid.: Lithuanian]; we heard this kind of repertoire a lot at Jewish celebrations and weddings. Everything was not just this "Romanianized" or what we now call this orientalized repertoire.

Somehow I always had the feeling—I knew—that a *klezmer* meant a professional East European Jewish folk musician. And in my family I was referred to as the *klezmer* because I played the guitar and *bouzouki*. My father use to always say to me, "*Klezmer mayne, nu kumt klezmer mayne, vus makhstu klezmer mayne?*" [Yid.: My klezmer, so, my klezmer, what are you doing, my klezmer?] So Yiddish and *klezmer* music were part of my youth.

I became actively involved in this *klezmer* phenomenon in 1976. My old friend and former roommate Mark Simos, in late '76, went back to Philadelphia, where he attended the meetings of the American Folkore Society. There he met Zev Feldman, Andy Statman, and Barbara Kirshenblatt-Gimblett. When he returned he was very excited and told me about this Jewish music they were playing that was from these 78 rpms. Mark had made a cassette recording of some of the stuff Zev and Andy were playing. The cassette had *Azeri,* Greek, and *klezmer* tunes all played on the clarinet and *tsimbl.* One tune in particular I remember. I think it was Hoffman's *Baym Rebns Sude* [Yid.: At My *Rebe's* Meal]. I immediately recognized this stuff as tunes I heard on my relatives' 78s and on the radio. At this time I had been playing Russian, Romanian, and Balkan music, much of which overlapped each other, and the Yiddish as well. So we decided to add Yiddish to our repertoire and formed the Khutzpe Yiddish Orchestra in 1977.

The group consisted of Mark Simos, Stu Brotman, Maimon Miller, Barry Fisher, Ron Holmes, Alex Shube, and myself. There were a few others who were peripheral to the group or were part of it at one time or another including Stewart Menin, a fine clarinetist who went on to form the New Shtetl Band in Albuquerque. Three of the members of *Khutzpe*—Stu Brotman, Barry Fisher, and Ron Holmes—had been playing Jewish music together since the late '50s. Barry's dad was in the catering business so he helped get them the gigs. So we all had a variety of a Jewish musical *yikhes.* At this same time Lev Liberman and David Julian Gray of the Klezmorim would come down to L.A. occasionally and we'd all jam together. I was aware of what they had been doing when they just began exploring *klezmer* in 1975.

We played all sorts of gigs, including out on the street in the evenings—on Fairfax. But I remember one particular gig that was a sort of seminal experience for me. We got hired to play at an eightieth birthday party at the Sportsmen's Lodge in the Valley. It was a big catering hall and they had to take us through a bunch of rooms to finally get to the room where we were to play. Though the rooms were fairly soundproof you could still hear what the bands were playing. So there was this one room we went past, the Silverman wedding or Brumbard *bar mitsve.* The doors swung open as someone was exiting, and out poured this band playing a cover of "You Are the Sunshine of My Life" by Stevie Wonder. It hit me like a shock. Wow, this is what they are playing at Jewish *simkhes* now, that style of music I would have never associated with *simkhes*. And here we were going to play this old stuff that in many ways was irrelevant to a lot of people there, particularly the young.

The band lasted only for a short while. Some of the other members of *Khutzpe*—Barry Fisher, Stu Brotman, and Maimon Miller—went on to form the Ellis Island Band.[20] I moved to New York City in 1979 and subsequently joined *Kapelye,* which I was in for thirteen years.[21]

Kapelye was founded in 1979; its original members were Josh Waletzky (piano, vocals), Lauren Brody (accordion, vocals), Michael Alpert (violin, vocals), Ken Maltz (clarinet), Dan Conte (tuba; replaced by Eric Berman in 1981), and Henry Sapoznik (banjo, violin, and vocals). They became one of the main early *klezmer bal-kulturnik* bands, and performed both in America and Europe for the next fifteen years. Kapelye's "old-timey" sound was a combination of *klezmer* tunes transcribed from 78 rpms found in the YIVO sound archives, and Yiddish folk, theatre, and novelty songs. What set Kapelye apart from the other *bal-kulturnik* bands of the 1970s was their appreciation and knowledge of Yiddish. Because of their fluency, Kapelye became known as great interpreters and arrangers of Yiddish vocal tunes, rather than virtuoso instrumentalists.

Sapoznik grew up in a home filled with Jewish music. His father was a *khazn* who made his son sing in the synagogue choir, and his mother sang East European folksongs. In the 1950s Sapoznik accompanied his father, who would lead both the *sederim* and the services, to various hotels in the Catskills. Despite growing up hearing various genres of Jewish music, Sapoznik, like other *bale-kulturniks,* did not go into Jewish music when he first began to play professionally. Instead he was attracted to old-time Appalachian string band music. Playing the banjo, Sapoznik went on to

---

[20] The Ellis Island Band still performs in Los Angeles, led by Barry Fisher, one of the leading lawyers for Rom rights.

[21] Interview with Michael Alpert, June 7, 2000.

enjoy success as a member of the Delaware Water Gap String Band, which
toured America and Europe. Eventually Sapoznik found his way back to
Jewish music, specifically *klezmer,* while taking fiddle lessons from Tommy
Jarrell, an Appalachian fiddler who lived in Mt. Airy, North Carolina. Many
musicians who got turned onto various kinds of American folk roots music
in the 1960s trekked down to the south searching for the authentic old-
timers who could teach them the music and the culture. Thus the apocryphal story goes that Sapoznik was taking lessons in the summer of 1977,
and was asked by Jarrell, "Hank, don't your people got none of their own
music?"[22] From that moment on, Sapoznik became immersed in researching Yiddish roots music.

Working as the curator of the sound archives at the YIVO Institute,
Sapoznik went on to form, with assistance from Adrienne Cooper and
Becky Miller, the Yiddish Folk Art Institute—better known as Klez-
Kamp—in 1984.[23] The concept of the one-week Yiddish folk arts camp
was to create an intergenerational environment where young and old
novices could intermingle, play, and create with young and old practitioners of the various Yiddish folk arts (Yiddish folksongs, folk history,
khazones, klezmer, art songs, and poetry) connected with *klezmer* music.
More importantly, besides these various Jewish art forms, KlezKamp provided a week of total immersion in the Yiddish language. One could
listen, learn, and speak the language of the *klezmorim* of Eastern Europe.
Lastly, one of the most important contributions KlezKamp has provided
the *bal-kulturnik* movement for the last eighteen years is teaching new
musicians the art of *klezmer.* Many of these left Klezkamp with such
enthusiasm and passion for the music—and for Yiddish culture in
general—that they became emissaries for it in their hometowns and
helped begin numerous *klezmer* bands across America—and, eventually,
Europe.

---

[22] Rogovoy, op. cit., pp. 92–93.
[23] Today KlezKamp is no longer connected with YIVO and is part of the Living Traditions Organization. Sapoznik, op. cit., pp. 271–72.

One of the most important contributors to the *bal-kulturnik* scene was Josh Waletzky. Though he had been a member of Kapelye only for a few years (full-time for two years, part-time for several more), and only had recently gotten back into performing again, his knowledge of Yiddish text and song helped popularize several Yiddish folksongs. These songs (as well as some instrumental pieces) are now standards of the repertoire. He told me:

> I am literally the product of a secular Yiddish upbringing. My parents came from Yiddish-speaking homes, spoke Yiddish to us in our home, and were always singing in Yiddish. My father, especially, loved to sing. He had a wonderful voice and an amazing repertoire. One of the songs on Kapelye's first album, sung by Yiddish vocalists throughout the world today, is "Vi Azoy Trink Di Keyser Tey" (How Does the Czar Drink His Tea). I learned this tune from my father when I was very young.
>
> My parents were active members of the Sholom Aleichem movement and sent me to Camp Boiberik in upstate New York. We had fantastic music counselors at the camp, including Lazar Weiner, Vladimir Heifetz,[24] and Chana Mlotek. They all had a rich repertoire. For me, Camp Boiberik was my musical hometown, where I learned that singing Yiddish songs was always special and conveyed a tremendous range of experiences in the tunes and the text.
>
> I began writing my own music at an early age. When it was time for my *bar mitsve* we went to a restaurant, celebrated with family, and then I sat at the piano and played a special piece of music I had composed especially for this day.

---

[24] Vladimir Heifetz was born in 1893 in Chasnik, Belarus. His father Khayim was the first violinist at the Imperial Court for twelve years. Vladimir composed over 150 Jewish tunes, including the score for the Yiddish film *Grine Felder* (Green Fields, 1938), starring the child actor Herschel Bernardi. Besides being a composer and arranger, Heifetz left his mark in the Jewish music world as a highly regarded and well-liked music teacher and Yiddish choral conductor at various music camps.

In my early teens I met this great music teacher, Fishl Kolko, who worked at the camp. He had a great collection of Jewish 78s. So one day at his home in the Bronx he brought out this record called "Khusn v'Kale." It had a kind of *klezmerish* accompaniment. Years later this tune also appeared on Kapelye's first album. Working with Kolko I learned a lot about various *klezmer* tunes—and this was twelve years before Kapelye.

In graduate school I studied film. Some people from YIVO had seen my thesis film and hired me to make the documentary film *Image Before My Eyes*. The film was an extension of the wonderful book and photo exhibit by the same title. When I began to build the sound track, I pulled from many different resources, including YIVO's 78 archives. Henry Sapoznik had just begun to investigate what was in these archives and I recruited him to bring me twenty to thirty of the tunes he thought were the best. One of these tunes was Naftuli Brandwein's *Firn Di Mekhutonim Aheym,* which I used in the film. The tune has since become very famous and a signature piece for many clarinetists.

Henry, certainly one of the first *bale-kulturniks,* came to me and asked me if he thought we could form a band that could produce traditional *klezmer* music as it sounded on these archival records rather than the *shtik* sound the Klezmorim were making. For me this was such a given. Of course, we could create a band, it wasn't a question. I had grown up with Yiddish music my whole life. Being a musician was being part of the *kley-koydesh.* Yiddish music in a way was our sacred text. In Kapelye, everyone brought their unique talents to the group. My contribution was being an insider, having internalized the music my whole life. Henry's talents were not so much musical but he was a great patter man. That was important because it made the music sort of hip. The audience was afraid. Can we enjoy this music without it being too retro, being totally nostalgic? Henry gave people a way to enjoy the music in a contemporary way.[25]

---

[25] Interview with Josh Waletzky, October 18, 2000.

The Klezmorim

While Sapoznik found his return to *klezmer*—where he got "religion"—
in the backwoods of North Carolina, Lev Liberman, one of the founders
of the Klezmorim, found *klezmer* closer to home. As Seth Rogovoy writes,
in 1971 he

> realized all the different kinds of music he liked had a common styl-
> istic influence. "Jewish was the common denominator between Rus-
> sia, New York, the radical European stage, early film, and New Orleans
> jazz," he says. Intrigued by this realization, Liberman began searching
> for the missing link, the Jewishness, in Russian and Romanian folk
> music, Depression-era cartoon sound tracks, early jazz, and the com-
> positions of Gershwin, Weill, and Prokofiev.[26]

Having moved to Berkeley upon graduating college, Liberman, who
played alto and soprano saxophone and flute, joined forces with David
Skuse (percussion) to perform a wide variety of ethnic musics in the Bay
Area. Then, in 1975, Liberman and Skuse were shown a box of Yiddish 78s
that were at the Judah Magnes Museum in Oakland. When they listened to
them, they realized these tunes could form the backbone of a Yiddish
repertoire that Liberman had only intellectualized before. They carefully
transcribed many of the records, found four other musicians, including
David Julian Gray (clarinets, mandolin, violin, vocals), and formed the
Klezmorim.

Much of the Klezmorim's early repertoire came from those Yiddish
78s and from the huge record library of Dr. Martin Schwartz. Schwartz, a
professor of Near Eastern Languages at the University of California at
Berkeley, was also a musicologist and audiophile of Greek and Jewish 78s.
Because he was fluent in Yiddish and knowledgeable about the history of
klezmer music and the groups on the 78s, Schwartz became the band's

---

[26] Rogovoy, op. cit., p. 77.

private tutor. His keen ears for the music and sharp insight into the culture enabled the band to get beyond musical transcriptions.

The Klezmorim were the first of the *bal-kulturnik* bands in America to tour nationally and record (*East Side Wedding*, 1977) since Mickey Katz's last tour in the mid-'60s. Their recordings revealed an eclectic array of styles, which they all played well. They played *doynes* and other display *tish nigunim* on the violin, clarinet, or flute, revealing a quieter, more spiritual side to their repertoire. But for the most part they played with a loud brassy sound, mixed with a lot of zany theatrical stage antics.

Street music and theatre, common events in the Bay Area, influenced the Klezmorim, who experimented with mixing different costumes and theatrics with early jazz, Greek, Turkish, and *freylekh* tunes, all incorporated into a concert set. This created a "rollicking vodka-soaked sound of a steam calliope."[27] Liberman recalled, "In the Bay Area, there is a tradition of street music, lots of ferment and experimenting, a receptivity to different music."[28] More recently, he added, "I'd like to think that the current *klezmer* revival had its origins in our early experiments with tight ensemble playing, improvisation, *klezmer*/jazz fusions, neo-*klezmer* composition, street music, world beat, and New Vaudeville."[29]

Over the years critics have disagreed about whether the eclecticism of the Klezmorim's repertoire, particularly their jazz-influenced Jewish melodies and onstage antics, pioneered a path for future *bal-kulturnik* bands or just muddied the waters by not deviating from what some called more traditional *klezmer* music. The latter camp of critics seem to have forgotten that many nineteenth-century East European *klezmer kapelyes* would switch from a gut-wrenching *zogekhts* and jump immediately into a stately Viennese waltz, just as their counterparts in the 1930s would segue from

---

[27] Ibid., p. 81.

[28] Richard F. Shepard, "Klezmer Music Makes Leap to Carnegie Hall," *New York Times*, February 18, 1983, Section C, p. 1 & 20.

[29] Barbara Kirshenblatt-Gimblett, "Sounds of Sensibility," *Judaism*, Issue No. 185, Vol. 47, Number 1, Winter 1998, pp. 49–50.

an emotional *tish-nign* into a seductive tango without dropping a beat. Some critics went as far as to say that the Klezmorim used the word *Jewish* as infrequently as possible on their album covers, liner notes, and onstage patter, and instead hid behind the code words *klezmer* and Yiddish. But if they had been hiding they would not have sung in Yiddish, the language of East European Jewry. And the Klezmorim purposely used the Yiddish term for Jewish musicians as their band's name to denote exactly the genre of music they performed, unlike many of the pre– and post–World War II *klezmorim,* who insisted on being known as musicians who played in orchestras.

One of the watershed moments during the first ten years of the *klezmer bal-kulturnik* movement—a moment that helped to cement it as a permanent and vital part of the renaissance of American Jewish culture and took it out of the Jewish ghetto (Jewish community centers, synagogues)—was the Klezmorim's appearance at Carnegie Hall on February 26, 1983. It was the first (and not the last) *klezmer* concert there. I remember it well. I was singing quietly to myself in *khasidic nign* style to the various tunes while bouncing in my chair and tapping my feet. An older woman turned around and sternly shushed me. I promptly said, "Lady, *klezmer* music ain't *shush* music, it's *dance* music. If you want *shush* music, go to the philharmonic!" At one point the Klezmorim played a beautiful *doyne* and then seamlessly segued into Sidney Bechet's "Song of Medina." The audience loved it. The Klezmorim's music was as varied as the audience and they played to that fact very effectively, not unlike their forbears in 1883.

Feldman and Statman

Klezmer musicians Andy Statman and Zev Feldman were equally important to the nascent *bal-kulturnik* movement in the mid-1970s. Both were considered by their peers to be foremost in their respective areas of *klezmer:* Statman was one of the finest *klezmer* clarinetists and mandolinists and Feldman was one of the leading scholars and practitioners of nine-teenth- and early-twentieth-century *klezmer tsimbl.*

Feldman grew up with *klezmer* in the home. His father was born in the small Bessarabian *shtetl* of Yedinitz and immigrated to the United States in 1922. He told me:

> My father spoke both Yiddish and Romanian, but Yiddish was his first language. He had vivid memories of the *kapelye* and he used to talk to me about them. The *kapelye* was made up of Jews and Gypsies; the leaders were the Jewish violinist and the Gypsy clarinetist. My father was not a musician but he loved to dance. He knew how to dance the Jewish and Bessarabian dances. I have this memory as a child of see-ing my father leading the line and dancing a *sher* or *bulgar.* It was quite a transformation for me because he was a rather dour character most of the time, but when it came to dancing he was very light on his feet.
>
> My father belonged to only two organizations in America: the Yed-nitzer *landsmanshaft* and the *shul.* At the *landsmanshaft* they had dances in which they hired *klezmorim.* Sometimes Dave Tarras used to play there. He had a special relationship with us because he lived in Yed-enitz before he came to America. In fact, a lot of Tarras's music comes from the very same *kapelye* my father grew up listening to. He even wrote a *bulgar* for us, which he recorded on one of his early 78s. So I heard *klezmer* music at the *landsmanshaft* and *khazones* from the *bal-tfile* in our orthodox *shtibl.*
>
> After the *landsmanshaft* stopped having their dances, the music for their *simkhes* became less interesting for me, because it became more American. And since I was only a youth I wasn't going to break my head trying to figure out why this had happened and where was this Jewish music I really like alive and flourishing.
>
> Instead I gravitated to Greek and Armenian music in my early teens. I met many Greeks and Armenians from my Sephardic friends who lived in my neighborhood in the Mosholu Parkway area of the

Bronx. I joined a Greek band, playing percussion. We toured the Greek hotels up in the Catskills, near many of the Jewish hotels. The Greeks loved Jewish clarinet playing. Immediately, as soon as they found out I was Jewish, they started talking about Jewish clarinetists. Some even knew of Tarras.

At that time I was collecting all different kinds of ethnic recordings. I would bring them home for my father to listen to and he really ate them up. Some of the music reminded him of Jewish music. Caucasian and Armenian folk music reminded him of *khasidish* music.

In 1969 I went to Romania for the first time and *shlepped* (Yid.: pulled, yanked) back a *tsimbl.* I began taking *tsimbl* lessons from various teachers, including a Greek cimbalom player who lived in Astoria, Queens. He also played some Jewish music, including some numbers from Kostakowsky's collection. He couldn't understand why I wanted to play the little, more primitive *tsimbl* rather than the large Hungarian *cimbalom,* and I couldn't explain why I felt it was more appropriate.

Then in late '73 or early '74 I met Andy Statman, and together we joined a Greek rebetika band. He played mandolin and I played *santuri* [a Persian *tsimbl*]. Then one day Andy came across some 78s at some flea market in Brooklyn. He learned the tunes, some of which were *freylekhs,* and then taught them to me. Soon thereafter, we had this Greek concert at Columbia where we played a set of Greek and Armenian tunes. Then we tried out some of these Jewish tunes, and the Greek audience went wild, with a standing ovation. So the Greeks we worked with asked us if we knew more Jewish tunes. This spurred us on to learn more Jewish tunes, and yet we were playing for Greeks, not yet Jews.

Then at some point later that year I suggested to Andy he look up Tarras, since he wanted to learn Jewish clarinet playing. So Andy got busy studying with Tarras while I was getting my Ph.D. at Columbia. Then I took a year off to travel in Europe and Turkey. When I returned in the beginning of 1976, Andy and I got together to rehearse some of Tarras's music and other *klezmer* from some 78s. Andy's enthusiasm for the music and his passion from learning with a master like Tarras was stimulating for me. This is where *klezmer* really began for me.

We talked with Ethel Raim, the founder of the Balkan Art Center, now the Center for Traditional Music and Dance, about what we were doing and this idea we had—to apply for an NEA grant to help record and put Tarras back on stage. We had more grandiose ideas as well. We thought there were many other *klezmer* musicians from Tarras's generation whom we planned to record as well. Then we didn't realize it was a bit too late. While Andy continued to study with Tarras, I began to study with Sam Beckerman, Tarras's accordion accompanist in the 1940s. Sam was the nephew of Shloimke Beckerman, the clarinetist. Then in November 1978 we put on this concert at the Balkan Arts Center with Tarras, Beckerman, and Irving Graetz on drums as a trio and Andy and myself as a duo. The concert was sold out and somehow put the music on the map again. We did several other concerts after that and eventually got Tarras to go back into the studio to record his last album, called *Master of Jewish Clarinet*.

After the success of this album and our concerts with Tarras, we felt confident enough to record our own album. With Andy's thorough understanding of Tarras's style and approach to the music and my research into the musicological history we recorded [with Marty Confurius on bass] *Jewish Klezmer Music* in 1979, one of the best recordings of traditional *klezmer* from before World War I.[30]

Statman came to the *bal-kulturnik* scene already established as one of the best bluegrass and country music mandolinists in the country. A few of the internationally known musicians with whom Statman played were David Bromberg, Vasser Clements, Bob Dylan, and Tony Trishka. Here is his story:

As a youth in Jackson Heights [Queens, New York], I grew up hearing old Jewish 78s. Some of the records were like the semi-Yiddish tune

---

[30] Interview with Walter Zev Feldman, October 16, 2000.

"Yosl Yosl" and others were *klezmer*. On my father's side there were some cousins who played *klezmer*, but they just called it Jewish music. We played these records and everyone would sing and dance. I remember seeing my relatives dance the *sher*. On my mom's side they were *khazonim* going all the way back to the Vilna Gaon. Besides this Jewish repertoire, my parents listened to the typical Broadway and Tin-Pan Alley music. I had a cousin, Sammy Fain, whom the family was quite proud of. He went to Hollywood and wrote some tunes in the 1930s that became big hits like "Love Is a Many-Splendored Thing," "April Love," and others. And my mom's father lived with us until he died, and for a while he was a *Gerer Khasid*. I also went to a *Talmud Toyre* when I was six and seven years old. The rabbi taught the students to sing *nigunim*. I remember that it was a tremendous experience when he sang. What elation it gave me.

I also was exposed to rock 'n' roll and bluegrass music from my brother, who was seven years older than me. When I was eleven I really became enamored of bluegrass. I had a shortwave radio and I would tune into this Grand Ole Opry–like show every evening. It was on WWVA out of Wheeling, West Virginia. They had a lot of the lesser-known musicians playing, rather than the real famous ones in Nashville. When I was thirteen I started playing the banjo. Then when I met David Grisman, I switched to the mandolin.

After a few years of just playing bluegrass I began to feel limited and I began to get into jazz, particularly Albert Ayler. His music really spoke to me. It was incredibly emotional and sounded real folksy, with wonderful freestyle improvisational passages. So I began to learn first the alto, then tenor, sax. For me, playing wind instruments was a very emotional experience. My teacher was Richard Grando, who played with Art Blakey's band. He introduced me to other artists who were combining their spirituality with their music; guys like Shankar, Coltrane, Sonny Rollins, and Pharoah Sanders, and different ethnic music from around the world. Eventually this led me to study Carl Jung and the *I Ching*.

Then it hit me. Here I was studying all of these other spiritual paths and one of the oldest in the world was one I was born into, Judaism. So I began to study Judaism and my family's genealogy, and listening to these old Jewish records in 1967–68. I continued to play bluegrass for money and funk and blues with the sax. Then I met Zev Feldman in 1972–73 and we hit it off immediately. We totally immersed ourselves into world music, playing Irish, Jewish, Greek, *Azeri* [Azerbaijzhani], *Kavkazi* [Caucasian], while I was studying with these various great practitioners of these various musics.

Then in 1975 I decided that I wanted to know more about Jewish music, and since I was playing a few of Tarras's tunes I had learned from the 78s, I decided to see if I could take some lessons from him. When I met him he was amazed I had learned his repertoire. The first lesson I had with him went like this. He would show me a tune on the clarinet and then want me to copy him on my clarinet. When I took out the tape recorder to tape him playing so I could listen and learn while at home he said: "You came here for a lesson, I played for you; now you want me to make a record too?" Eventually the lessons consisted of us slowing down the 78s and listening very carefully to his solos, Dave playing for ten to fifteen minutes, us eating, and he taking his medicine. I learned most by watching Dave play. His body gestures evoked a deep spiritual quality to his playing. We became very close and our relationship became like grandfather to grandson rather than teacher to student. Today I play on his clarinet.[31]

The Klezmer *Conservatory Band*

While some of the *bale-kulturniks* in the 1970s searched out first-generation *klezmorim* and others searched through old *klezmer* 78s, Hankus Netsky only had to look as far as his family. Netsky's grandfather and several

---

[31] Interview with Andy Statman, May 31, 2001.

uncles—including Sam Netsky, who played cornet in clarinetist Itzikl Kramtweiss's *klezmer* band—were active in the Philadelphia *klezmer* scene before World War II. Netsky told me:

> In my early youth, I gravitated to synagogue music. Then, from ages fourteen to seventeen, I was a member of our synagogue's adult choir. I remember fondly the leader of the choir and cantorial teacher Joe Levine. He gave us an impressive repertoire to sing. Every now and then my family would go down the shore (Atlantic City) and hear one of my uncles play at a Jewish hotel. But my grandfather and uncles did not try to teach me this music. They were convinced that *klezmer* was on its last legs. Then, when I was nineteen (1974), I went to my Uncle Sam's house and started asking him about *klezmer*. He had a lot of old 78s, some tapes, and sheet music. I transcribed several of the tunes and began to play the music on the oboe with a pianist whose father was a wedding musician named Barry Shapiro. Then in 1978 I attended a Celtic jam session in Philadelphia. I had a great time and it inspired me to teach our ethnic music (*klezmer*) to others. Eventually those I was teaching, mostly students from the New England Conservatory, came to form my band, the Klezmer Conservatory Band. We rehearsed during the fall and early winter of 1979 and gave our first performance in February 1980.[32]

Today the Klezmer Conservatory Band is the only American *bal-kulturnik* band that began in the 1970s still performing under its original founder. One of the major contributions that Netsky has given to the *bal-kulturnik* movement over the last twenty-two years is his great ability to attract good musicians, teach them the history and how to play *klezmer*, encourage their input and creativity, and inspire the same passion he has for the music in them. Several musicians who have passed through the band have gone ahead to create their own *klezmer* ensembles, playing

---

[32] Interview with Hankus Netsky, May 26, 2000.

various kinds of Jewish music, including Frank London (Klezmatics, Hasidic New Wave), David Harris (Shirim, Naftule's Dream), Ilene Stahl (Klezperanto), Jeff Warschauer and Deborah Strauss (Warschauer and Strauss), and Don Byron, who was the band's first clarinetist.

Byron, an African American, was fluent in the classical and jazz repertoire when he was asked to join Netsky's band. He told Peter Watrous,

> The first year or two was terrifying. This is a community not used to having deep cultural stuff examined by outsiders, and most of our performances were in temples. The clarinet is the main instrument; I was one of two persons who fronted the band, and the reception I got wasn't always pleasant.... For me, this is world music. It's hard, though, because I'm expected, because I'm black, to only play jazz. It's not very easy for me, as a black person, to exercise a world music option. A white musician can just say he's a blues musician, and nobody will challenge him and deny an ethnic connection. But it's not so easy the other way around—you don't see a lot of black musicians saying they play Bulgarian music.[33]

After leaving the Klezmer Conservatory Band in 1986, Byron went on to form a wedding band playing all kinds of music, including *klezmer.* Attracted to outsiders who liked to stretch the boundaries, Byron recorded *Don Byron Plays the Music of Mickey Katz* in 1993. The recording resurrected Mickey Katz, who had been long regarded solely as a comedic musical parodist; now he became, as Rogovoy says, "a forerunner of Radical Jewish Culture, one who drew upon the deep well of *yidishkayt* to comment, sometimes acerbically, on American culture and Jewish American culture in particular."[34] Today Byron is one of the leading avant-garde jazz clarinetists in the world, and still occasionally plays *klezmer* music.

---

[33] Peter Watrous, "Remember Mickey Katz? No? Well, Just Listen to This," *New York Times,* January 19, 1990, Section C, pp. 1 and 24.

[34] Rogovoy, op. cit., p. 172.

The San Diego Scene

As for myself, I grew up in a home (first in Detroit, then, at age eleven, in San Diego) where various kinds of Jewish music were sung and heard on the stereo: Yiddish, Hebrew, and Israeli folksongs, *zmires, khazones,* and *khasidic nigunim.* Getting involved in *klezmer* was a natural progression in my growing interest in playing different kinds of music on the violin (besides classical, which I had been studying for thirteen years). In the 1970s, the largest folk festival west of the Mississippi River was held in San Diego every year. I heard *klezmer* live for the first time there, when the string swing band Stones Throw played a couple of numbers from the Kammen books in swing fashion. I became even more aware of the music when my father brought home the Klezmorim's first album *East Side Wedding* after hearing them live in 1976 at the Old Time Café in San Diego.

A few more years went by, during which I studied in Sweden for a year, returned to finish my B.A. and started another in furniture design, formed my first band, called Second Wind (1920s–'50s swing and pop music), and decided to go to law school. In March of 1981, I went to an alternative-music dance space called Sushi's to see a few friends who were playing in San Diego's first *klezmer bal-kulturnik* band, the Big Jewish Band. Until this time, most of the *bal-kulturnik* bands played primarily at concert venues, where people sat and listened passively to the music (occasionally singing) instead of dancing, which was, after all, one of the original purposes of the music. At Sushi's that night there were no chairs; everyone danced. After the first set, my endorphins were raging, and I was thoroughly enthused with the spirit and sound of the music. The second set was just as good, and I was one of the last off the dance floor. That very night, in the wee hours, I had an epiphany: forget about law school. I would start my own *klezmer* band. San Diego was big enough for two *klezmer* bands, but I was going to make mine unique.

The Big Jewish Band (like many others) was using transcribed tunes from 78s and the Kammen books for its repertoire. I decided that my band's repertoire would be based upon tunes that had never been recorded, tunes that might be found in forgotten archives and in the recesses of the memories of older Jews and Rom. I bought a one-way ticket to Eastern Europe and trekked for ten months, collecting music, oral histories, records, photos, and other pre–World War II Jewish memorabilia. I returned and formed my *klezmer* band Zmiros (now called Klazzj). Impressed with my research, Ron Robboy asked me to play in the Big Jewish Band, which I did for a while. Eventually I left to concentrate on my band's music and continue my research of *klezmer.*

Though the Big Jewish Band never recorded and was basically a phenomenon that stayed local to San Diego, its influence on the *bal-kulturnik* scene was felt nationally and internationally. Besides myself, internationally known jazz bassist Mark Dresser played in the band for a while, and occasionally plays *klezmer* in my New York City band Hot Pstromi. Internationally known bassist and teacher Bert Turetzky played in the band in the early years and is a member of the *bal-kulturnik* band 2nd Avenue Klezmer (San Diego). Trumpeter Phil Tauber, one of the last students of Ziggy Elman, also played in the band and occasionally performs concerts of Elman's *klezmer* arrangements. And finally there is Robboy, who founded the band, and is currently the senior researcher for the Boris Thomashefsky Project.[35]

Robboy became interested in *klezmer* as a conceptual art form before any of the previously mentioned *bal-kulturnik* bands began playing. He told me:

> I heard a lot of Jewish music in the home while growing up and was
> exposed to the work of some important figures, such as Max Helfman
> and Alfred Sendrey, both of whom my mother knew and worked with

---

[35] Boris Thomashefsky (1868–1939) was a star of the Yiddish theatre in America for over fifty years, both as an actor and director. His grandson, who began the Thomashefsky Project, is world-renowned conductor Michael Tilson Thomas.

in Los Angeles in the 1950s and early '60s. My mother served as music director, accompanist, teacher, and choir leader in synagogues and in Yiddish, Zionist, and Jewish community organizations. I got into *klezmer* for the first time in 1971 as a "translation" project for a class I was taking from poet Jerome Rothenberg at the University of California at San Diego. The band consisted of Pauline Oliveros (accordion), Peter Gordon (clarinet), Jeff Raskin (harmonium), and me on string bass and percussion. We used sheet music my mother lent us, and I transcribed one tune from a Paleolithic-sounding dub Rothenberg provided of a European *klezmer* brass and reed band from perhaps the 1910s.

My percussion setup was a bass drum with a cymbal mounted on top. In one hand I held the drumbeater and, inspired by Mahler's instruction in the slow movement of his First Symphony, in the other hand I held a second cymbal. I was realizing the conceptual art text Mahler had embedded in his score, which I knew from my symphony and opera orchestra playing experiences. The famous representations of *klezmer* traditions I was hearing in Mahler, Enesco, and others profoundly moved me, and I was interested in finding my own representation. I organized a series of bands through the 1970s as my ideas gelled. Then, in the late 1970s, we were touched by the *klezmer* revivals, and the Big Jewish Band finally began performing regularly in 1980. Its eclectic membership included experimental composers, folkies, symphony musicians, and many members of the Partch Ensemble. This eclecticism played a huge part in how our *klezmer* sound evolved. Varied as the constituency was, a couple of constants remained. One was my resistance to learning "authentic riffs" from old recordings. The other was that we used music stands, all playing the tunes in unison from a notated version. Though some arrangements did emerge, though there was a rhythm section, and though there was certainly a lot of improvising, the band's signature sound was not based on virtuoso solos. It was anchored in a goofy, fruity heterophony. Even as experienced *klezmers* later joined, their

brave competence was always tempered by a nucleus of equally coura-
geous conceptualists.[36]

Reasons for Returning

It is not a coincidence that various *bale-kulturniks* across the country, many
quite separate from each other, returned to the music of their grandparents
all at the same time in the 1970s and '80s. All had come from a positive
Jewish upbringing, whether religious, secular, or a combination of both.
Some of these musicians' parents were part of the American folk music
movement that began in the late '50s. The liberal wing of this movement
helped galvanize many people, including progressive Jews, to take control
of their lives and fight for economic, social, and political justice after the
searing McCarthy years. The growing diversity of the country and the rise
of the African American and Chicano movements shattered assimilationist
theories and encouraged other ethnic groups to slowly begin to research
and extol their own unique cultures. Some sociologists say that this examination and proclaiming of our own heritages went into high gear with
the tremendous popular success of the book and television series *Roots* by
Alex Haley.

Consequently many young Ashkenazic Jews (second- and third-generation Americans) began to examine and rediscover their East European
roots. Some felt disillusioned about the political situation in Israel, and
turned to these roots as an alternative. Others were tired of the focus of
East European Jewish history and culture on migration, pogroms, and the
Holocaust, and sought more positive aspects. Still others were completely
assimilated; for them, returning to Judaism down the prescribed religious
paths was not an option. Finally, many Jews who were brought up in homes
that were devoid of any Jewish spirituality, or whose Hebrew school/syna-
gogue experience (particularly Reform) left them apathetic, found religious

---

[36] Interview with Ron Robboy, June 28, 2000.

consolation in a return to their roots. Although many of these same disillusioned Jews wandered off searching for some kind of spiritual fulfillment
in other religions and cults instead, others returned to Judaism through
klezmer. Learning to play *klezmer* was often less intimidating than learning Hebrew or studying *Toyre;* and going to *klezmer* concerts was often
easier than going to the synagogue.

A number of artists discussed with me some of the reasons for the *bal-
kulturnik* movement. One of these, a seminal practitioner of *klezmer* violin, is Alicia Svigals. Having started off studying ethnomusicology and
playing Italian and Greek folk music, in 1985 Svigals answered an ad in the
Village Voice about starting up a new *klezmer* band called the Klezmatics.
She explained:

> I feel that many young American Jews today want to be Jewish. There
> was a period of time when everyone wanted to assimilate, myself
> included. Secular Jews who don't have the synagogue and all its reli
> gious rituals to cloak and express themselves still need to feel con
> nected to their tribe. They need to feel their ethnicity and culture and
> not just be passive consumers of the mass-market generic "Madison
> Avenue" culture out there. So secular Jews seized on *klezmer* music as a
> secular way to really be and feel ethnically Jewish. The music is a lot
> of instrumental tunes and the folksongs that deal with religious mate
> rial are thought of in an almost anthropological way by the secular
> Jews, like, "Isn't this interesting—our cousins the *khasidim,* not us,
> sang these tunes." Then there are those Jews trying to rediscover their
> religion. Many came from the suburban Reform synagogue move
> ment that was bereft of almost all *Yiddishkayt.* So for these people,
> *klezmer* is a new way to be religious. It helps fill a psychological, emo
> tional, spiritual need for many Jews who want to connect with their
> roots but felt alienated because of the way they grew up with Judaism
> in the 1950s and '60s. For many Jews there is an inherent tension
> that will never be resolved—"How far do I go into this?" There are the
> fanatics who delve deeply into East European Jewish culture and there

are those who can't pretend we are in the *shtetl* or can even replicate the *shtetl*. There is this tension—created by this huge gap in a lost world—that will never really be resolved.[37]

The actor and singer Joel Grey views the return to roots in a more positive light:

In today's society one can portray a Jewish character or express oneself in the Jewish arts without only having to refer to the Holocaust. During the past twenty years, people have been reaching for their beginnings and their differences. We live in a society that celebrates difference now. For example, the Hell's Angels are involved in having their *vente latte cappuccino* as much as they are in expressing individualism. There has been a big surge in people being different rather than finding different difficult. And Jews are somewhat able to wear *klezmer* as a badge of honor, certainly more so now than twenty years ago. They feel more comfortable in their own skin. When society has literally or figuratively denied you for many years then all of a sudden it becomes very precious when you reclaim and celebrate it.[38]

The actor and folk singer Theodore Bikel's concept of roots takes into account the difference between America and the old world:

America is a great country, but it has antecedents, which is different from having roots. In Europe there was a kind of rootedness. Here nothing seems to be rooted in the soil unless you are from Appalachia or a descendant of Black slaves. Roots betoken a community. America appreciates music a lot but it is always one step removed from being your own. However there is a hankering, a feeling of nostalgia toward music that is your own. That probably accounts for the

[37] Interview with Alicia Svigals, May 26, 2000.
[38] Interview with Joel Grey, November 14, 2000.

immense success of *klezmer* music. Therefore you have young Jews who are looking to link up with their own roots and yet found it possible to do that without learning Hebrew or Yiddish. They suddenly found a way of connecting to their roots through music, a way that does not necessitate the learning of a language. I don't necessarily condone it, because I think languages are vital to the cultural goods that people have. There are, of course, Jews who are completely estranged and have no feeling of nostalgia or any sense that this music is theirs any more than when they listen to rock music. But there are those Jews who connect to it both musically and intimately—perhaps a little viscerally—somehow evoking a world that was never theirs but was either their grandparents' or certainly their great-grandparents'. So in their mind's eye this creates a vision, a *geshtalt* for their antecedents.[39]

David Buchbinder, the *klezmer* trumpeter/composer and leader of the Flying Bulgar Klezmer Band, discussed *klezmer*'s complex relationship with the Holocaust:

Within the Jewish community right now there is this potential kind of healing in our relationship to the Holocaust. Until recently the situation was pretty analogous to being stunned. If you hit your leg really hard the blood leaves that spot for a minute. You don't feel anything for that minute until the flow starts again. It is not as if the pain hasn't been felt from the Holocaust. Pain has been felt. There was this kind of suspended animation of Jewish culture that went into being stunned by the Holocaust. It busied itself with Israel and with assimilating into North American culture. This isn't only the fault of the Holocaust but it certainly was one of the pervasive reasons. Some people felt the culture was totally destroyed and turned away from this culture. On some level in terms of a growing developing cohesive culture the destruction was total. But with distance, through time and memory,

[39] Interview with Theodore Bikel, October 4, 2000.

I think we are coming out of this shock period. And now people are proclaiming their Jewishness in many different ways. In our Jewish festival Ashkenaz, people come out to the streets and proclaim themselves proudly, extravagantly, foolishly Jewish. The people are hungry and *klezmer* music happens to be just one thing these people are feasting on. Quite simply *klezmer* is good music.[40]

Lastly, Michael Alpert told me:

This phenomenon of *klezmer* music is a revival or revitalization or rediscovery or continued discovery or renaissance or whatever you want to call it. Whatever one calls it, for Jews—particularly in North America—it is a rediscovery and reconnection to our ethnic heritage. In the postwar decades—the 1950s, '60s, into the '70s—the focus of the Jewish community was on Israel. Looking backward or to Eastern Europe was too painful. People tried to identify with Israelis and Israeli culture. However, as I say, my parents and certainly my *zaydes* and *bobes* (Yid.: grandfathers and grandmothers) on either side never ate falafel. They don't come from Haifa or Bat Yam and certainly weren't born under palm trees. Of course for me this was a bit blurred, having grown up in Los Angeles. So there is the fact that American Jewry, which is ninety percent Asheknazic, already had a natural inclination to reexamine their European roots. *Klezmer* for many of us was a counterculture phenomenon. It was counter to the mainstream Jewish culture in North America. I didn't grow up Zionist or focused on Israel. I was aware of it but I wasn't a "Federation" Jew. I was always proud of speaking Yiddish and having grown up in this old-time *heymish* (Yid.: homey, familiar, intimate) East European kind of background. That's what I loved and had real substance for me.

The *klezmer* revival is part of the whole revival in Jewish identification. Back in the beginning in the 1970s and early '80s I didn't like

---

[40] Interview with David Buchbinder, July 21, 2000.

calling the music *klezmer*. I argued a lot for calling it Yiddish music. For me calling it *klezmer* was a euphemism. You would go to a folk festival and they would have Irish, French-Canadian, Mexican, Scottish, and *klezmer*. I often used the phrase: "Funny, you don't look *klezmer*." It was a way of not saying Jewish or Yiddish because those things weren't hip yet. There was this belief that if you were to do anything that said Yiddish, it brought out primarily an older crowd. *Klezmer* was a memory device used by the immigrant and first-generation Jews to trigger nostalgic memories. I think people in their teens, twenties, and thirties didn't identify with *klezmer* until it had a hip edge to it, and this came with the interest in the music in Europe.[41]

Diasporism and the Growth of Klezmer

By the mid-1980s, after almost ten years of being played in America, *klezmer* had planted strong roots in American Jewish culture, having helped create a setting of "nostalgic diasporism" (a phrase coined by Mark Slobin).[42] Many of the baby boomers of the 1950s and '60s had been reared in either assimilated or acculturated homes where Judaism was expressed by going to the synagogue on the High Holidays, going to Jewish Sunday school, having a *bar* or *bas mitsve*, eating *matse* during *Peysekh*, buying a tree for Israel, or contributing money to their local United Jewish Federation. But in the last twenty-five years, nostalgic diasporism has often taken the place of these activities. Signs of this include the creation of Jewish film festivals that screened, among others, films about *shtetl* life before its destruction; the airing of *klezmer* music on Jewish radio programs; the screening of Yiddish-language films made between 1910 and the eve of World War II; the publication of new Jewish magazines like *Der Pakn Treyger* (Yid.:

---

[41] Interview with Michael Alpert, July 7, 2000.
[42] Mark Slobin, *Fiddler on the Move: Exploring the Klezmer World* (New York: Oxford University Press, 2000), p. 29.

The Package Porter) that focused on Yiddish culture; the proliferation of East European Jewish studies courses and Yiddish graduate programs offered at Bar Ilan University, Columbia, McGill, Oxford, UCLA, and other schools; the celebration of East European Jewish culture at Yiddish art festivals throughout the United States, Canada, and Europe; the multitude of *klezmer* recordings; the increase in students taking Yiddish language courses; and the huge interest in Jewish genealogy and the subsequent growth of travel to former and current Jewish communities in Central and Eastern Europe.

The Jewish festivals in America, Canada, Europe, and Russia played an important role in nurturing and disseminating the *klezmer bal-kulturnik* movement. Both audience members and musicians made these festivals into annual pilgrimages where they renewed friendships, exchanged ideas, and tried out new material. Some of these festivals initially focused mainly on *klezmer*. Since the establishment of KlezKamp in 1984, several other notable festivals have used *klezmer* as their focal activity. Festival directors invite nationally and internationally known *bale-kulturniks* to participate in giving workshops, lectures, and concerts, which in turn generally attract large, spirited audiences. Other Jewish festivals did not concentrate exclusively on *klezmer,* but also on other Yiddish arts and aspects of Askenazic culture. Some of the more notable festivals include Ashkenaz in Toronto; the Jewish Culture Festival in Kraków; KlezKanada in Lantier, Quebec; the Leeds (England) *Klezmer* Festival; the London Jewish Music Festival; the St. Petersburg *Klezmer* Festival[43]; the San Diego Jewish Arts Festival; the Strasbourg Jewish Culture Festival; the Tsfat *Klezmer* Festival; and the *Yiddishkayt* Festival in Los Angeles.

---

[43] The leading Russian *klezmer* performing at the St. Petersburg festival was Leonid Sonts (1945–2001). Sonts was born in Kazan, the capital of the Russian republic of Tatarstan. I met Sonts when I was in Kiev in 1984. He was doing research at the Ethnographic Museum. I remember how excited he was at meeting another Jewish musician doing *klezmer* research. He studied classical music and performed in the local orchestra in Kazan, but *klezmer* music, which he learned from his father, was his love. Sonts formed Simcha, the first *bal-kulturnik klezmer* band in Russia, in 1989, performing throughout Russia, Western Europe, and in New York City.

Along with festivals and concertizing, recordings garnered the widest audience for the *bale-kulturniks*. Since Giora Feidman recorded *Jewish Soul Music* in 1973, over 450 *klezmer* albums have been released. These range from reissues of early immigrant recordings (e.g. *Masters of Klezmer Music, Vol. 1: The First Recordings* [Global Village Music, 1987] focuses on the earliest recording sessions [1917] of Abe Schwartz's orchestra) to rather non-traditional *klezmer* recordings (e.g. John Zorn's *Masada: Live in Middleheim 1999* [Tzadik, 1999]). Once, if a record store carried Jewish music it was most likely found under the category headings of either "Jewish" or "Israel"; today most stores have separate *klezmer* bin headings under the category "World Music." Some of the *bale-kulturniks* told me that they felt there were too many *klezmer* recordings being issued, some of them quite bad, and that unless you did some concertizing and/or got some radio airplay it was difficult to sell them and keep the retail outlets stocking them. So, of course, if the *bale-kulturniks* wanted to sell their wares, they needed distributors.

One of the first record labels to begin distributing the *bale-kulturniks'* *klezmer* music was Global Village Music, begun by Michael Schlesinger in 1985. To his credit, Schlesinger began to record and distribute all kinds of interesting (often quite obscure) folk music from around the world. Global Village Music in some ways was the philosophical and recording successor or grandchild to the eclectic label Folkways, begun by the venerable Moe Asch[44] in 1948. Schlesinger believed it was necessary to record and reissue folk music so it would not disappear, because it was an integral part of history. As he explains:

---

[44] Moe Asch (the son of the Yiddish writer Sholem Asch) founded Folkways, a label mainly dedicated to recording folk music, in 1948. Asch was famous for recording many musicians ignored by the mainstream, such as Leadbelly, Mississsippi John Hurt, and Blind Lemon Jefferson. Many of the artists Asch recorded went on to become internationally known, e.g. Pete Seeger. Artists did not get paid much, but they knew their records would remain available. For decades he kept 1,500 to 2,000 records in print. Asch died in 1986; Folkways was then taken over by the Smithsonian Institution.

In 1983 I bought a stack of old 78s of Jewish East European instrumental music. We didn't call it *klezmer* then. And I thought, "These are very interesting, why can't these records be reissued? They represent a part of Yiddish culture that is lost and unless this music is reintroduced to the public it is lost forever." But what I found out is that what an old tune meant to the revivalist meant something else to their parents. The people who grew up in the 1930s, '40s, and '50s weren't interested in these reissues of Schwartz or Kandel. Their Jewish music was the music of Tarras and the Barry Sisters.

My criteria for recording new CDs is finding something else no one has ever recorded before or finding a record that hasn't been heard in fifty years. I am kind of a throwback to the time of the early field researchers. I want to enjoy and capture the moment when this particular guy is on his back porch playing his guitar and telling a story or this fiddler is in his kitchen playing something. This music wasn't for the stage. These people were folk artists and the music wasn't a business to them.

Frankly I think the *klezmer* market is saturated with too many recordings. Does every band that has been around for only six months need a recording? Most think so, so they can sell them after a concert. Are we in the souvenir business?[45]

Klezmer *in Europe*

As a result of the establishment of this nostalgic diasporism, some of the *bale-kulturniks* now felt that they needed to explore and expose new audiences to *klezmer*. Europe seemed the next logical destination. The home-

---

[45] Interview with Michael Schlesinger, November 16, 2000. Some of the other record labels that distribute *klezmer* recordings are Angel (Itzhak Perlman), Knitting Factory Works, Naxos World, Nonesuch/Elektra (Don Byron), Rounder, Shanachie, Sony Classical (Andy Statman), and Traditional Crossroads.

land for nearly one thousand years for the exiled wandering Jews, Europe represented a challenge for the *bale-kulturniks*. First, they wanted to reintroduce *klezmer* to the continent where it had been born. Second, for many of the *bale-kultuniks*, by playing *klezmer* in the very continent where six million Jews were murdered, they were making a statement: that Hitler did not fully succeed in eradicating all of Ashkenazic culture.

For the Klezmatics, Kapelye, and eventually Brave Old World, playing in Europe had a strong influence on the bands' aesthetics, playing style, and repertoire. Alicia Svigals relates one example:

> In 1988 we went to Germany for our first European gig. It was at the time when the music industry was becoming hip to world music. We met this guy who had founded this European record label and he suggested that a lot of groups were now taking traditional music and adding some contemporary stuff to it and thought we should try it. Up until then we had been playing a lot of Tarras, 1940s and '50s *klezmer*, sort of a cool sound with a slick saxophone, clarinet, and accordion sound. So when we heard this guy's idea, we thought, "Yeah, why not?" We then started experimenting with a more contemporary sound and we really found our voice in our second album, *Rhythm and Jews*. We started using electric and synthesizer sounds and different beats and rhythms. Then, after four to five years of taking traditional tunes and making new arrangements, we started writing original music. We made new tunes sound old and old tunes sound new. So in a way, the Klezmatics sound is this German guy's idea.[46]

Michael Alpert tells a similar story:

> In 1984, Kapelye went to Europe for the first time. It was really the first year American *klezmer* performers toured Europe. Statman and Feidman both toured Europe that year. This was a crucial year, for it

---

[46] Interview with Alicia Svigals, op. cit.

began the process where American *klezmer* bands toured Europe, particularly in Germany.

Germany really had an effect on us as performers. The German
music industry, with all of its press, presenters, recording studios, and
audiences, pushed *klezmer* to have a more innovative aesthetic and
edge. Up to that point the focus of the music in America had been
re-creation. We were still trying to discover the music, especially the
instrumental music. And suddenly here was Europe with its demands
of wanting something new. The world music phenomenon had already
taken hold of Europe and in America we were slow to grasp this. Then
in 1989, with the Berlin Wall coming down, *klezmer* music became
part of the counterculture.[47]

In the mid-1970s, when the *bal-kulturnik klezmer* scene was just beginning to take back its Yiddish birthright, no one would have guessed that
in less than a generation the dismantling of the Eastern Bloc communist
governments would help create an environment conducive to the rebuilding of Jewish life in Central and Eastern Europe.

Many of those at the forefront of the clandestine revolutionary movements that helped inaugurate this tranformation were Jews. Jews had
been participants in progressive movements since the prophets of biblical
times, so being part or even leading these clandestine cells (Charter 77 in
Czechoslovakia, Solidarnósc in Poland, etc.) seemed natural to their non-
Jewish members.

As I traveled throughout Central and Eastern Europe in 1981, I came
in contact with many of those who were working clandestinely against
the establishment. Meetings took place in different locations all the time
so that the government authorities would have a harder time keeping tabs
on, harassing, or arresting the participants. One such group I met with in
Poland many times was called Żuk (Pol.: insect) or, in English, Flying Circus. In Żuk, the activities and discussions were not only focused on poli-

---

[47] Interview with Michael Alpert, op. cit.

tics but on education. Sometimes people came to the meetings just to learn and discuss subjects that were forbidden and censored by the government. Many of the lecturers were Jews who had been dismissed from their jobs (many from the universities) during the years 1968–69, when the Polish government's anti-Semitic purges caused some 20,000 Jews to leave the country.[48] Consequently, Jewish subjects were often discussed. Studying Jewish culture was an act of defiance against the government and the hegemony and political policy of the Soviet Union.

These subjects were as varied as the lecturers (some of whom were non-Jewish). I heard lectures on Polish Jews during the years of the Council of the Four Lands,[49] Jewish resistance during World War II, Jewish synagogue architecture, Jewish gravestone iconography, Yiddish theatre and literature, the *Toyre,* the *Kabole* (Kabbalah). Even Hebrew was taught.

When I went to the meetings of the Flying Circus, I was usually the only foreigner. After having attended several times, I was asked if I would give a lecture on *klezmer,* since they all knew my research in the subject

---

[48] In 1967, the Jewish members of the Polish United Workers Party were pleased when Israel defeated its Arab adversaries in the Six-Day War. But the Soviet Union supported the Arabs, and the Soviet leaders instructed Polish president Gomulka to dampen Jewish enthusiasm in his party. Gomulka declared that Jewish communists could not have two homelands. He used anti-Zionist rhetoric, promulgated by Soviet leaders, against Polish Jews. With Gomulka's control of the country weakening, Minister of Internal Affairs Mieczyaw Moczar, encouraged by the Soviet government, challenged Gomulka. Without seeking Gomulka's approval, Moczar ordered the secret police to shut the Warsaw State Theatre's production of Adam Mickiewicz's popular play *Forefather's Eve.* The anti-Czarist sentiment of the play was thinly veiled anti-Soviet feeling. The closure of the play brought immediate demonstrations over censorship. Soon after, Moczar ordered mass arrests of students and professors, and then waged a campaign against Jews in Polish cultural life, the sciences and education, and especially state and party bureaucracies. Eventually 20,000 Jews were forced to leave Poland, while those who stayed had to deal with rebuilding their lives in the midst of arbitrary anti-Semitic reprisals.

[49] The era of the Council of the Four Lands (Great Poland, Little Poland, Volynia, and Lithuania), which lasted from the mid-sixteenth century to 1764, was the first time the Jews in the diaspora lived in a semi-autonomous Jewish self-governmented region. The councils were very powerful; they dealt with taxation, settled disputes between provinces, controlled economic life, supervised schools and charities, and directed religious life.

was the main thing that brought me to Poland. My lectures included speaking about the history of *klezmer* in Poland, the contribution of the *khasidim,* playing some of the field recordings, and playing music myself. Throughout the 1980s—until the Berlin Wall came down—I lectured and concertized in homes, Jewish clubs, and kitchens. My lectures were highly anticipated, standing room only. Often they turned into big parties and jam sessions with singing and all kinds of folk music—Hebrew and Israeli along with the Yiddish.

At one of these lecture/concert gatherings in a beautiful apartment in the former old city of Warsaw, the police came because there had been a complaint of too much noise in the early hours of the morning. They asked for identification from everybody. When they looked at my passport they became a bit more suspicious. After a few minutes they told me I had to come down to the police station. Rather perturbed, I went to the station in their police vehicle and waited several hours while they figured out what to accuse me of. In the meantime I took out my violin and played *klezmer* for those police and clerks who wanted listen. Finally I was allowed to leave. Apparently, since I was staying in a private home (which the authorities frowned upon), I had to register my passport (get a stamp) with the neighborhood precinct and tell them with whom I lived and for how long, so they could keep tabs on me. I had not done this.

Many of those Jews and non-Jews who were and are still active participants and leaders in the renewal of Jewish culture in Central and Eastern Europe that began in 1990 came of age, in terms of their Jewish identity and interest, in those clandestine gatherings. And though the *klezmer balkulturnik* bands that toured Central and Eastern Europe helped galvanize this renewal, the seeds had been planted and nurtured for over a decade before any of them toured these countries.

So for the *bal-kulturnik* bands that came from America to perform in the fledgling democracies of Czechoslovakia, Hungary, Poland, and the reunited Germany in 1990, there was already a small but significant audience of countercultural, progressive Jews and non-Jews who had been exploring various aspects of Jewish culture. But if the audiences had consisted only of these, most of the *klezmer* concerts in the various clubs, auditoriums, Jewish community centers, and synagogues would have been more than half empty. Who were all the others? Why were the majority of these enthusiastic concertgoers non-Jews? And who were all these Jews in cities, towns, and neighborhoods we had thought they no longer inhabited? Where did they come from?

For the Jews (some of whom found out they were Jewish late in their lives) and the many others who proclaimed their Jewishness through blood by pointing out they had a Jewish relative (sometimes quite distant), their interest and even sometimes infatuation with *klezmer* was based upon a feeling of being comfortable and proud in one's own skin. During the nearly half-century of communist rule, many Jews hid the fact they were Jewish from their neighbors, friends, work colleagues, and even their own children. Though the volume of anti-Semitic rhetoric was kept generally low—with only occasional vandalism and physical abuse—governments subtly, and not so subtly, used their few Jewish inhabitants as pawns. Whether pressured by the Soviet government or on their own, the Eastern Bloc countries used anti-Semitism to help quell political domestic problems and diffuse accusations against the government. Basically the Jews, the "rootless cosmopolitans" as they were euphemistically called in the press, were to blame for the country's economic and social ills. And after the Six-Day War, many Jews were considered unpatriotic and untrustworthy if they had any connection with Israel or professed any Zionist sentiments.

Going to a Jewish concert, buying Jewish music, or performing it were acts of defiance against the former communist regime, its cronies (many of whom had become overnight some of the biggest capitalists—e.g. Jerzy Urban of Poland, the communist government's spokesperson), and the many non-Jews who, whether passively or forthrightly, took advantage of the government's sanctioned anti-Semitism.

To give the reader a picture of the strength of this sentiment, here are three statements made by young Jews who proudly professed their Jewishness just before their countries became democratic in 1988 and 1989. The first is from Sylvia, who attended the Anna Frank Gymnasium (at that time the only Jewish day school) in Budapest and was in the eleventh grade. She was seventeen years old. The second statement is from another seventeen-year-old, Dariusż, who lived in Wrocław, Poland. The last statement is by Agnes, who was fourteen at the time, and lived in Budapest. She later went to Hebrew University in Jerusalem and returned to Budapest to work as a teacher in the Jewish community.

We moved from Szolnok, which is a small town, to Budapest last year. I wanted to be with Jews my own age and that was very difficult in Szolnok. There are only about seventy Jews in my hometown and many of them do not even know they are Jewish. When I was in primary school, some kids bothered me because I was Jewish, but my mother said "be proud of your Judaism." From that moment on I have had a strong Jewish identity.[50]

I live with my mother, who is Catholic, but four years ago I learned that my father was Jewish. After one year of intense soul searching, I decided that I was a Jew too. I have been called a "dirty old Jew" and a "red-haired Jew," but it is meaningless. This offends me, but only made me want to learn more about my culture and present it to others. Recently, I began to study Yiddish after I went to a concert of Yiddish music at the Jewish club here in Wrocław. I bought a cassette at the concert and play the music loudly so my non-Jewish neighbors can hear the music.[51]

Jewish life here in Budapest is growing because it is less dangerous to be openly religious. Today being Jewish doesn't necessarily mean only going to the synagogue. There are Jewish dance groups, music groups, and even sport groups, so Jewish cultural life is becoming stronger. In fact I have some non-Jewish friends who come with me to these various Jewish events and sometimes even to the syna-

---

[50] Yale Strom, *A Tree Still Stands: Jewish Youth in Eastern Europe Today* (New York: Philomel Books, 1990), p. 94.
[51] Ibid., p. 37.

gogue. Judaism has become a curiosity, even a bit exotic, for many Hungarians.[52]

Many of the non-Jews who began attending *klezmer* concerts and/or began playing *klezmer* since the late 1980s are driven by exoticism, guilt, capitalism, or any combination of the three.

Exoticism worked on two levels in the former Eastern Bloc countries—the faraway and the local. For example, when Andean musicians began crisscrossing Eastern Europe in the mid-'80s, they instilled a strong interest in Andean culture among many young people. This European exoticism was expressed in Andean music festivals, clothing, cuisine, etc. Learning to play the Peruvian panflute became a popular hobby. When Jews in these same countries began to rediscover, write about, and publicly display their religion and culture, many non-Jews, young and old, became fascinated with these local exotics. Forty-five years after the Holocaust, the grandchildren in Central and Eastern Europe of those non-Jews who lived during the war were far enough removed by time to be able to understand the consequences of the large cultural hole that was created in their lands when most of the Jews were killed. They did not have to look across the ocean for some exotic group to admire and study—they just had to look in their backyards, and here were the Jews. The prevailing attitude was: let's study these exotic people and help them be more Jewish since there are so few of them. This paternalistic, ignorant point of view was no different from that taken by many Americans toward the Native Americans since the 1960s. Instead of studying and hanging with *The Last of the Mohicans,* many Poles decided to study *klezmer,* Hebrew, Yiddish, Jewish literature, history, humor, etc., and hang with the last of the Cohens.[53]

For other non-Jews, guilt was the driving force behind their enthusiastic support for *klezmer* and other things Jewish. This was their way of not only asking forgiveness, but bearing a collective responsibility for the

---

[52] Ibid., p. 96.
[53] See Slobin, op. cit., pp. 15–16.

sins committed not by them but by their parents and/or grandparents. The generation that actively or passively supported the German Third Reich will never be forgiven. Consequently, going to Jewish events—even participating and taking the time to learn some aspect of the culture—was the equivalent of saying, "Jewish culture did not and cannot completely vanish from our land." Jewish culture had been so indelibly part of Central and Eastern Europe's development and history for nearly one thousand years that it was almost inevitable that two generations after the Holocaust, non-Jews discovered the great loss they suffered when some fifty percent of Europe's Jewry was murdered. The Germans have felt and accepted these pangs of guilt probably better than any other group of people in Europe. After the end of World War II, some Germans even felt that the only way they could be ever forgiven as a country was to spend the rest of their lives helping to build the new State of Israel.

I found that, for most philo-Semites, their interest in Jews and Jewish culture was based neither on exoticism nor guilt but rather a combination of the two. A good example of this is in the following statement from Mariola Spiewak, a *klezmer* clarinetist in the Kraków-based band Di Galitzianer Klezmorim, whom I met at the Jewish Culture Festival in Kraków.

I grew up here in Kazimiercz, which as you know was the Jewish quarter of Kraków. The Jewish culture was so rich here prior to World War II. What a tragedy it was to lose part of our own Polish heritage. The Poles were victims as well, but anti-Semitism did not start on September 1, 1939, but several hundred years before Germany invaded Poland. We Poles must share some of the guilt of the destruction of Polish Jewish culture. I am sure that my feeling of guilt was one reason why I have always been fascinated by Jewish culture and how it had a tremendous influence on Polish culture. I began to read books on Jewish history and religion, and then went to a *klezmer* concert six years ago. I fell in love with the music and chose to learn to play *klezmer* clarinet. I do not have the patience to learn Hebrew, so I cannot read the bible in its original language. But by learning to play *klezmer* dances and Yiddish folksongs I feel I am able to better understand the Jewish people and their centuries of suffering in the diaspora. By playing *klezmer* music throughout Poland, I am doing my own small part of keeping alive Jewish culture and the memory of the Jewish people in towns and villages where there are no Jews.[54]

The prospect of earning money from Jewish and non-Jewish tourists has been another driving force behind the renewed interest in Jewish culture in Central and Eastern Europe since 1990. For large numbers of tour groups from North America, Israel, and Western Europe, driven by nostalgia and intellectual curiosity, have descended upon the former Soviet Union and the Eastern Bloc countries. Jews had been a vital part of this region of the world for nearly a millennium, numbering some eleven million on the eve of the Holocaust. And though the vast majority were gone (except in Russia and Ukraine), they left synagogues, cemeteries, schools, hospitals, homes, books, poetry, songs, music, paintings, photographs, ritual art, and more. With travel restrictions lifted, many tourists either born in this region or descended from Jews who had been born there wanted to see what and who was left. Though few Jews remained, many of their artifacts still existed. And if the actual artifact could not be found, it was re-created, often without any regard to historical accuracy. Kitsch sometimes bordering on the offensive took the place of reality, while fetishism of the victim (Jew and Rom) became a kind of secular religion for the non-Jews. For example, one could take a tour of the former concentration camp in Auschwitz during the day and relax in the evening at a Jewish café, eating Jewish-style food while entertained by pseudo-*klezmer* musicians dressed in pseudo-*khasidic* garb; one could stay at a hotel in Kazimiercz that was a recreation of a nineteenth-century Jewish inn; one could attend a *klezmer* festival that had local and international groups performing; one could buy paintings and wooden figurines that depicted the itinerant *klezmorim;* and one could eat at a restaurant (in Budapest) that had a *klezmer* concert

---

[54] Interview with Mariola Spiewak, July 4, 2000.

every Sunday brunch. Jewish tourism was driven by the same forces that cause tourists to visit Native American reservations in Arizona and New Mexico, or Aborigines in the outback of Australia—people are interested in cultures that were nearly annihilated.

I've talked with a number of the more successful *bale-kulturniks* about their experiences playing *klezmer* in Central and Eastern Europe. Bob Cohen, for example, is the leader and founder of the Budapest-based *klezmer* band Di Naye Kapelye; I have known him since 1988, when we met at a lecture/concert I was giving in a Jewish center in Budapest. Cohen is the American son of a Hungarian Holocaust survivor, and had traveled several times to Hungary to visit relatives. Hungarian Jewish culture and the "new" Hungary attracted Cohen to such a degree he relocated from New York City to Budapest. After playing with the Budapest Klezmer Band for a few years, Cohen became dissatisfied with the direction the band was taking, and formed his own *kapelye*. He also became extremely interested in Rom culture, especially their relationship and connection with *klezmorim* in Romania. Having done extensive field research in Romania, Cohen is one of the world's leading experts on Romanian *klezmer* music and its connection with the Rom. He told me:

> The popularity of *klezmer* definitely helped to ignite the revival of Yiddish culture in Germany, England, Holland, and Italy. *Klezmer* concerts are a safe and open meeting ground for non-Jews to experience a feeling of co-community with Jews. I think in some ways, however, Jewish culture is being "folklorized," made safe and entertaining in order to distance Europeans from the horrors that occurred sixty years ago. In Poland, the Czech Republic, and Germany I have met enthusiasts of *klezmer* that remind me of Eagle Scouts who like to dress up as Indians and feel close to the noble savages. On the other hand, the majority of *klezmer* fans really do feel the lack of Jewish culture in Europe and educate themselves to fill this void.[55]

---

[55] Interview with Bob Cohen, June 6, 2000.

Zalman Mlotek, who grew up in a Yiddish-speaking home filled with Yiddish vocal music, has been a leading figure of Yiddish theatre music for over thirty years, currently serving as the artistic director of the New York Yiddish theatre *Folksbine*. His father, Yosl, was an instrumental figure for many years at the Workmen's Circle, while his mother Chana, a researcher at YIVO, is a world-renowned Jewish musicologist. He told me,

> When I performed in Berlin for the first time, every emotion came through me. OK, who are these people? Who are these sixty- and seventy-year-old upstanding German individuals who are listening to my music? What's their interest and where were they and their parents during the Holocaust? Is this a freak show? Is this a guilt thing? But playing in Poland is much harder for me than playing in Berlin. This is because in Poland you see the streets and the towns where Jews lived in greater numbers than in any other country in Europe. You really feel it and can't get away from it. But there are no signs of Jewish life— only the artifacts like the streets, former neighborhoods, and the architecture. It can only be found in Yiddish literature and in the Yiddish songs I sing.[56]

Adrienne Cooper grew up in the Bay Area and is a third-generation musician in her family. Her first music teacher was her mother, a classically trained singer whose repertoire included many Hebrew and Yiddish art and folksongs. Eventually Cooper went to graduate school, then to YIVO, where she met Lazar Wiener, the world-renowned Jewish art song composer. She studied with him at the 92nd Street Y in New York. Eventually, Cooper began to focus on researching and singing Yiddish folksongs and joined Kapelye. Today she sings with many different groups, but particularly with Zalman Mlotek and the all-woman *klezmer* ensemble Mikve. She told me:

---

[56] Interview with Zalman Mlotek, October 16, 2000.

When we [Kapelye] performed in Germany, it was both creepy and moving. We represented the *Ost Juden,* who had a moment in Germany but were surgically removed. We provided some kind of spiritual balm for a culture that had a very complex and violent relationship with its Jews. And as artists we were in a position to take advantage of the audience's neediness and guilt they brought with them to our concerts. At the same time we acted like we were offering some kind of spiritual healing from the music and gladly took their money. This was equally corrupting. At least in Germany there has been some renegotiation vis-à-vis their Jews, but in Poland I found it quite different. There you had cities where the majority of the people were Jews. The buildings were still there, the grass was the same, the horse-drawn carts were still being driven, but the Jews were removed. I felt like I was in a landscape that was hit by a neutron bomb. And when we drove through the countryside it felt distressing for me. What did we actually represent for the Poles today?[57]

The playwright/director Tony Kushner was born in Manhattan but grew up in Lake Charles, Louisiana, where both his parents were professional classical musicians. Growing up in the south in a town with only one hundred Jewish families and only one synagogue (a reform temple) left a strong impression on Kushner. He told me:

Klezmer is very hot music and a kind of ecstatic form of Judaism that I have discovered. I have since gone to orthodox *shuls* in various places around the world and seen people dancing, singing, and wailing. Being in temple in Lake Charles was sort of like being in a high church service. You came in and folded your hands in your lap and a bad organist would sort of honk his way through a bunch of songs that always sounded less good than the Christian versions, which were really beautiful. I would be great fan of the Anglican hymn book that

---

[57] Interview with Adrienne Cooper, January 24, 2001.

I think is a collection of unbelievably beautiful melodies. Our pale imitations don't really cut it. So who knew this whole world of *klezmer* existed. I think there is a kind of *klezmer*/East European influence in American popular song that came in through the Jewish community. So *klezmer*'s sexiness, transgressiveness, and ecstatic nature had me hooked. And the sound of *klezmer* clarinet is unbelievable. My father's a clarinetist, so I am sure there is some sort of interesting Freudian reading one could make.

However, *klezmer* in Europe—that is really something. I have a brother who is a musician and lives in Vienna. When I visit him and see posters for *klezmer* concerts, I think, wow! These are incredibly powerful, grand, exhilarating gestures by the people who created the Holocaust. The repressed have returned. A comeback is always in the wings. It must be an incredibly complicated cultural experience for young Germans and Austrians, especially non-Jewish ones, to be listening to this music. I have no idea what they are hearing. I am always so deeply suspicious of them, especially when there is this tendency to embrace the exotic. It is really not an embrace at all but sort of a part of German culture that I think still exists—of celebrating *Ausländers* [Ger.: foreigners, aliens] as freaks. When "Angels in America" was performed all over Germany, I was always worried exactly what the character of Roy Cohn would mean to an audience not necessarily favorably disposed to Jews.[58]

Elizabeth Schwartz, a filmmaker and Yiddish vocalist in Klazzj and Hot Pstromi, grew up in a secular Jewish home in a small town in upstate New York that had very few Jews. She has focused on obscure unknown Yiddish songs as well as originals. She told me:

As a Jew, I find the popularity of *klezmer* music and Yiddish culture among the gentile populations of Germany, Poland, and other parts of

---

[58] Interview with Tony Kushner, January 18, 2001.

Central and Eastern Europe unsettling. These are areas with significantly reduced populations of actual Jews, due to the direct anti-Semitic actions of these people's forebears. It makes me uncomfortable in the same way philo-Semitism from non-Jews makes me uncomfortable. Is Jewish culture exotic to some people because they did everything they could to eradicate the human beings who created it? So I look at Jewish music festivals in Europe with a prejudiced eye, because there is always the stench of racism (or reverse racism) underlying the enthusiasm for *klezmer;* they love the culture, but not the people who created it. I am rarely at a loss for words, but only two came to me: Jew Zoo.[59]

Klezmer *in Israel*

Klezmer music in Israel today, unlike in Europe and America, is primarily associated with, and played only among, the *khasidim* and *haredim*.[60] The *khasidim* have been in Israel since the Baal Shem Tov's death, when several of his followers made *alie* (Heb.: rising; returning to the Holy Land). Some of the Baal Shem Tov's more famous followers were Rabbi Nakhman of Horodenka (?–1786), who settled in Jerusalem; the Premishlaner *Rebe,* Menakhem Mendl (1728–72), who lived in Tiberias between in 1764–5; and Rabbi Menakhem Mendl of Vitebsk who, with several hundred followers, settled in Tsfat in 1777.[61] Through the ensuing years these small,

---

[59] Interview with Elizabeth Schwartz, June 23, 2001.

[60] *Haredim* (Heb.): ultra-orthodox Jews who live in Israel. The root word, *haredi,* means the religious fear of God.

[61] Joel Rubin, "*Rumenishe Shtiklekh: Klezmer* Music Among the *Hasidim* in Contemporary Israel," *Judaism,* Vol. 47, Number 185, Winter 1998, pp. 15 and 20 (footnote 19). Joel Rubin is an expatriate ethnomusicologist who lives in Berlin with his wife and fellow *klezmer* music researcher/writer Ritta Ottens. Rubin plays *klezmer* clarinet in his own ensemble (Joel Rubin Music Ensemble) and has played with several groups in the past, including Brave Old World, which he helped to start. Rubin has recorded several significant compact discs, including *Beregovski's Khasene,* based upon Beregovski's seminal *klezmer* field research during the interwar years.

generally poor *khasidic* communities kept a close relationship with their brethren back in Eastern Europe. *Khasidim* traveled back and forth, carrying all sorts of provisions—in particular *tsdoke*. Since there were many *klezmorim* among the *khasidim* in Eastern Europe by the mid-nineteenth century, it stands to reason that there were some *klezmorim* among the *khasidim* who made *alie* to Israel in the nineteenth and early twentieth centuries.[62] They performed *khasidic nigunim* as well as what present-day Israeli *khasidim* and *haredim* refer to as *Rumenishe shtiklekh* (Yid.: Romanian pieces)[63]— the tunes that the *khasidic* and non-*khasidic klezmorim* brought with them from Belarus, Bessarabia, Hungary, Poland, Romania, and Ukraine.

Within the walls of Jerusalem, instrumental music (except drums) was banned at weddings by Rabbi Meir Auerbach and his tribunal during the 1860s, for the same rabbinical reasons that restrictions were imposed on the *klezmorim* of the Middle Ages. Nonetheless, a few *klezmorim* (and Sephardim) performed in and outside Jerusalem prior to and during the ban. Those who were caught playing a melodic instrument were threatened with excommunication.

One of the best-known *klezmers* in Palestine in the beginning of the twentieth century was drummer Moyshe Poyker. Because of the ban on music in Jerusalem, Poyker was extremely important at weddings. When people heard his drumming they knew that a big wedding was to take place in a week. Sometimes at a wedding he had a female assistant who played the drums for the women in a separate room from the men.[64]

And, according to Joel Rubin, despite Rabbi Auerbach's edict,

> there is now an entire second, third, and even fourth generation of musicians performing *haredi* weddings in Israel who display a tremendous

---

[62] *Klezmer* violinist Asher Wainshteyn told me that a *klezmer* who had played in the *kapelye* he played with in Stolin left for then Palestine just before World War I, but he lost all contact with him.

[63] Rubin, op. cit., p. 12.

[64] J. Stutschevsky, *Ha-Klezmorim: Toldotehem, Orakh-Hayehem, v'Yezirotehem* (Jerusalem: Bialik Institute, 1959), pp. 52–55.

interest in the music currently known as *klezmer* and include it in their repertoire in various ways. . . . A sort of substitute for the *klezmer* band developed, in the form of a single musician singing and accompanying himself on percussion instruments (snare drum, bass drum, and a single cymbal), which were not affected by the ban. . . . Another recent tendency aimed at circumventing the ban consists of celebrating the wedding outside Jerusalem, sometimes barely off the outskirts of the city.[65]

This is, of course, the same solution the Maharil implemented some five hundred years earlier in Central Europe.

As in Eastern Europe, the *klezmorim* in Palestine/Israel played at weddings and other family *simkhes*. However, they also played at specific folk festivals—celebratory days that, although they were in the Jewish calendar, were not singled out as special celebrations requiring *klezmer* in Eastern Europe. There were three of these.

- *Simkhes Bes Hashoyve* (Heb.: The Ceremony of Water Drawing) took place during *Sukes*. During the days of the Temple in Jerusalem, from the second to the seventh days of *Sukes* the priests and their assistants (*Leviim*) performed a ceremony in the Temple courtyard: around an illuminated candelabra with four golden bowls of oil, the priests danced and the *Leviim* played on musical instruments. On the day after *Sukes*, the priests brought back water, which was poured on the altar, along with a libation of wine. This ceremony was done as a prayer to God for a good rainy season. Some *khasidim* and *haredim* in Israel still celebrate *Simkhes Bes Hashoyve* with music and dance.
- *Zibn Fun Adar* (Yid.: The Seventh of Adar, the twelfth month in the Jewish calendar) is celebrated by *khasidim* and *haredim* in Israel as the date Moses died. They commemorate this with a pilgrimage to Mt. Meron (near Tsfat) where they sing, dance, and play music.

---

[65] Rubin, op. cit., p. 14.

The *khasidim* in America celebrate as well but to a much lesser degree.

- On *Lagboymer,* since the second half of the nineteenth century, the orthodox, particularly the *khasidim,* visit Mt. Meron and celebrate all night. Though some have called the music performed by the *klezmorim* on Mt. Meron the Meron style, no matter where it was played, Rubin disagrees:

> According to my informants, this Meron repertoire was actually not unique to the *Lag ba-Omer* pilgrimage, but rather derived from the general wedding and *simkhe* repertoire of the northern Galilee.... It seems clear from an examination of the individual pieces, that the melodies utilized in Meron as well as in other parts of Israel stem from the entire spectrum of the *klezmer* repertoire as it is known from the period circa 1885–1960, and are not restricted exclusively to the *bulgar* dance.[66]

The *klezmer* who probably helped spread the Meron tunes more than anybody in Israel was the clarinetist Avrum Segal (c. 1911–1995), who was born in Tsfat. He trekked to Mt. Meron on *Lagboymer* for many, many years, listening, learning, and playing the *khasidic nigunim.* These tunes, along with the *rumenishe shtiklekh,* Mediterranean, and Arabic ones, kept him busy playing for *khasidic* weddings and other *simkhes* for over forty years. Hundreds of bootleg tapes made of his performances at Mt. Meron, weddings, etc. influenced several generations of *klezmer* musicians even after he stopped performing professionally in the early 1970s. "His dominance was already doomed through the introduction in the 1960s of the tape recorder at Meron. Where previously young musicians would hear tunes only once per year, now they could tape them and study them on their own, thus spreading the Meron style [particularly Segal's style] throughout Israel."[67]

---

[66] Rubin, op. cit., p. 15.
[67] Ibid., p. 14.

The second most influential musician on the Israeli *klezmer* scene was and still is *klezmer* clarinetist Moshe "Moussa" Berlin, born in Tel Aviv in 1938, and living today in Elkana. He told me:

> I was born into a family whose musical virtues were hidden. Nobody played an instrument, but my father, who was from Poland, was a *bal-tfile* and *bal-koyre* (Yid.: reader of the *Toyre*) and prayed on Shabbat and the Jewish holidays in a *khasidic* style with a lot of *nigunim*. He rehearsed at home, so the music entered my bones. Sometimes he also sang Jewish [Yiddish] folk and theatre songs too.
>
> At six my parents made me study the violin, but I didn't like it, so all I did for six years was *grimple* on the instrument. Then, when I went to the *yeshive,* I was exposed to the traditional *klezmer* music of Israel, as it was performed by Avrum Segal in Meron. I was so touched by the repertoire and the Meron celebrations that at age seventeen I began to teach myself the clarinet. At twenty-one I began to play with Avrum at the Meron festivities. He was my mentor, so naturally my repertoire became the Israeli *klezmer* as well as the East European one.
>
> Along with Segal's music, I learned many Brandwein and Tarras tunes off of some old records. I was playing these tunes in Israel more than ten years before the revival began in America. In fact the people of Israel were not influenced at all by this revival. The religious Israelis have had their own *klezmer* tradition that includes mostly an oriental *klezmer* repertoire with some of the East European repertoire for nearly two hundred years uninterrupted.
>
> For the Israelis who came from a Yiddish cultural background and then transformed themselves into Hebrew-speaking Israelis, plus the Sephardic and oriental [Arabic] Jews, *klezmer* music is perceived only as nostalgia and not as a living tradition. In Israel, *klezmer* music is looked upon as the music of the diaspora that was created and performed by a people that had and have no land. This is why much of the music has a melancholic feel. Therefore, *klezmer* music is rarely played in concert halls and at festivals in Israel as it is in the United

States, because in Israel it is the music of everyday life, of holidays and life-cycle celebrations. Unlike the American Jews, we are surrounded by Jewish culture in every step through our main language Hebrew, through speaking, reading, and writing Hebrew, without translation. Therefore we have a deeper understanding of Judaism and are not as connected to Yiddish and Yiddish culture.[68]

American and European *bale-kulturniks* had very little if any contact with their Israeli counterparts until 1990. And still today, besides the occasional visit of a *bal-kulturnik* ensemble performing at a cultural festival like the International *Klezmer* Festival held in July every year in Tsfat, there is very little connection and cross-pollination between the *klezmer* scene in Israel and in the diaspora. And it will be some time before there is a symbiotic relationship between these two *klezmer* worlds. The reasons are political, religious, and cultural.

Many *bale-kulturniks* returned to Judaism through *klezmer* because it was not part of Israeli culture. If anything, their political beliefs, particularly during the past and current *intifada* years, had been either skeptical of Israel's position vis-à-vis the Palestinians or outright opposed to it. Consequently, they chose to ignore Israel and focus on developing their own sense of Jewishness through an Ashkenazic, diasporic point of view, concentrating their artistic energies in a musical genre that developed in Europe. Most of all, the *bale-kulturniks* are Ashkenazim and it was in Europe, the cradle of Ashkenazic culture, where the "... spiritual patrimony of European Jewry had its greatest flowering before it was wiped out."[69] As David Buchbinder puts it,

Playing *klezmer* music gave me a place to experience a kind of Jewish pride that I had lost, that Israel had taken out of me. This is because of what I saw Israel becoming and doing. As a teenager I was in a socialist

---

[68] Interview with Moshe "Moussa" Berlin, August 7, 2000.
[69] Boris Sandler, "The Paradox of Yiddish," *Forward*, December 1, 2000.

Zionist movement called *Hashomer Ha-Tsair*. My parents sent me where
I almost made *alie*. But after seeing what politically and religiously
Israel was becoming I knew I wasn't going to move there—plus it took
a lot of my Jewish feeling out of me. But being involved with *klezmer*
and other aspects of Yiddish culture gave me a way to be proud again.
My activities in this world felt more relevant to me. Israel exists now
and is a real thing but I don't have any real connection to the country.
Yes, we have been talking and telling stories about Israel while being
in the diaspora for over two thousand years, but I have a much stronger
feeling in my body for Eastern Europe. I never thought of that before
but I think it was the music that woke me up to this conclusion.[70]

As one who appreciated Yiddish culture and especially *klezmer*, Tony
Kushner pointedly makes the argument that it is not only the current
politics of Israel that stand between "us and them" but actually the notion
of diasporism verses Zionism:

What is interesting to me, as somebody who really loves the sound of
Yiddish and the music of the Yiddish-speaking world, is the struggle
that this immediately places you in, in terms of Zionism. I did a
panel with Cynthia Ozick [an American writer and essayist who focuses
on Jewish culture] when she said to me: "Isn't the commitment for
young Jews to Yiddish really dressed as sort of an abrogation of a
mature commitment to the State of Israel and Hebrew?" Here Cynthia is saying this and at the same time she wrote this incredible short
story called *Envy*. I read it just around the same time I first started listening to *klezmer* music. The story is about Yiddish poets who can't
get anybody to translate their poetry because Isaac Bashevis Singer
won the Nobel Prize and has all the translators. These other writers
hate him. The story is also this lament that Yiddish is a language that
has no country except the tongues of very old men. The story moved

---

[70] Interview with David Buchbinder, op. cit.

me very deeply and actually made me feel a moral imperative to do what one can do to preserve it. It is such an expressive language of so many things. One of the things that it is expressive of is homelessness, of statelessness. It is really a language that does not absolutely belong anywhere. It is not German and it is not a patois of German. Everyone from Ozick to Ruth Wisse [a historian and writer on Yiddish culture] and all of those people wag their fingers at you and say to embrace the diaspora is to embrace the destruction of the Jewish people. I absolutely disagree with this. To embrace Zionism is to embrace the destruction of the Jewish people. It is just not as clear.

I used to be very much against assimilation, but I really feel that all sorts of Jews, from the Jews who petitioned Thomas Jefferson to pass religious toleration laws, have had a profound impact on American democracy and consequently have created in America, in a certain sense, the Promised Land. This is interesting because it isn't Jerusalem. It isn't the actual Holy Land that we speak about at our *seders* when we chant "next year in Jerusalem." This means that you are not home yet. And I think there is something that is profoundly useful and morally elevating about the position of recognizing oneself as not being an inheritor on sight. By this I mean in some degree eternally disinherited and struggling for something rather than working to defend what you already have. I think that position, that terrible yearning for what was lost, the desire for the future that is expressed in the *Toyre* and in the holy scriptures, is what has given Judaism and the Jewish people its moral genius. It is what has produced Marx, Abraham Joshua Hescheles, Freud, and various other great Jewish thinkers. I think what I love of the culture of *klezmer* and the culture of Yiddish is its disloyalty to an idea of Jewish power as expressed in the State of Israel. I feel *klezmer* positions this. And as far as I know there aren't very many conservative *klezmorim. Klezmer* is a part of diaspora culture as opposed to a Zionist culture.[71]

---

[71] Interview with Tony Kushner, January 18, 2001.

There is a religious schism between the *bale-kulturniks* and the religious *klezmorim* of Israel. *Klezmer* music was the catalyst and means for many secular *bale-kulturniks* to embrace aspects of spiritual and religious Judaism on their own terms. However, for most of them, *klezmer* still served an aesthetic function, not a religious one. But this is quite the opposite of what *klezmer* was all about in Central and Eastern Europe. There, Jews practiced religion as it was written in the *Toyre* and Talmud. For them (including the *klezmorim*), orthodox Judaism was a natural part of everyday life. Even when the *haskole* movement seeped into Ashkenazic life, the religious *klezmorim* still played for the less religious and secular Jews, while the less religious *klezmorim* still played for the orthodox and *khasidim*. And most of the *simkhes* the *klezmorim* played for—until the eve of World War II—were still religious in context. However, they also played for gentile audiences, and for national (meaning non-Jewish) celebrations, like May Day. They performed a necessary communal and/or religious function, whether secular or orthodox, Jewish or gentile. However, the *khasidim* and other orthodox Jews who came to Palestine/Israel from Central and Eastern Europe found themselves in a different situation. *Klezmer* was only played to fulfill a religious function and never for concertizing. In addition to this, the *khasidim* and orthodox in Israel are generally extremely conservative politically in their viewpoints on the Israeli/Palestinian issue and on secular, reform, and conservative Judaism. For those secular *bale-kulturniks* who define and reaffirm their commitment to Judaism publicly by playing *klezmer*, the philosophy of the *khasidim* and orthodox is antithetical to everything they believe in.

Some *bal-kulturnik* bands in Central and Eastern Europe found that after the Berlin Wall came down the support they'd received from the official Jewish community was no longer there. Since 1990, when all the former East Bloc countries reestablished diplomatic relationships with Israel, the official Jewish communities there began to focus on Israel and Israeli culture. This new policy was solidified even more when Israel sent cultural attachés to help create cultural and educational programs emphasizing Israeli culture (Hebrew, music, dance, etc.) in the Jewish commu-

nities. Bob Cohen of Di Naye Kapelye was directly affected by this new
policy:

> There is a Yiddish club at the Balint Jewish House, but it only attracts
> older people. While Yiddish was popular around 1990, it hardly attracts
> a following anymore, and is looked down upon by the official Jewish
> community, who receive most of their funding from Israel. I have
> been told by the Israeli Cultural Attaché that he is a big fan of our band
> but for official reasons could not support it or invite us to play at func-
> tions unless we added Israeli-oriented material to our repertoire. I
> answered that the band was dedicated to playing old *klezmer* music
> dating from before the establishment of Israel.
>
>   Today in Hungary there is a distinct attempt to divorce *klezmer*
> from Yiddish culture and make it something "Hungarian." *Klezmer* is
> distinctly in the realm of a newly created "fakelore" designed to appro-
> priate a popular expression of culture (*klezmer*) and make it Hungar-
> ian instead of Yiddish. This is done mostly by Hungarian Jews
> themselves. So my band plays maybe three to four times a year in Hun-
> gary. All of our other work comes from other countries in Europe.[72]

Lastly, many *bale-kulturniks* had a hard time relating culturally to
Israel. Though the *bale-kulturniks* have basically the same DNA as their
brethren in Israel, for many it is difficult to relate to Israeli culture—particularly Israeli music. They are part of the greater diaspora community
that has existed nearly half as long (according to the Jewish calendar) outside of Israel than the religion and culture have been on earth. Thus the
diaspora community, out of self-preservation, developed into a subspecies
of Jew, if you will, with different foods, tastes, languages, literature, art,
music, political ideas, tolerance to hot weather, etc., that are not easily trans-
ferable to Israel. The diaspora Jew evolved into another social animal over
these two thousand-plus years of living in the diaspora. The American

---

[72] Interview with Bob Cohen, op. cit.

bale-kulturniks are members of the largest, most influential Ashkenazic community in the diaspora. Most are only two or three and at most four generations removed from Europe, where their ancestors lived for some one thousand years. Consequently, for most of them, their Jewish cultural sensibilities and nostalgic memory devices are European, not Middle Eastern.

Obviously, hundreds of thousands of Jews in the diaspora have been able to return to Israel and successfully make it their homeland, and many more will do so in the future. But there aren't the same enthusiastic audiences in Israel clamoring to listen and dance to a *klezmer* concert as there are in Europe and America. *Bale-Kulturniks* who have or would perform in Israel are not seen as exotic, original, or even unique. Though many *bale-kulturniks* feel some kind of uneasiness when they perform concerts in Europe—especially in Germany, Hungary, Poland, and Ukraine—large enthusiastic audiences (most of whom are not Jews, and those who are generally secular) encourage the clubs, festivals, cultural centers, and synagogues to keep bringing them back. In addition, all of these musicians have egos that need to be, from time to time, satisfied.

Jews playing Jewish music in the Jewish homeland are not exotic, and it is not a unique musical experience. Often the response from the secular Jews in Israel, when I posed the question about the *bale-kulturnik* scene in America, was: "So what, been there, done that. What do you have for me that speaks to my daily life in the Middle East and not to something that is part of a pre–World War II, nineteenth- or eighteenth-century Eastern Europe? I can't relate."

Consumed with their struggles against the Palestinians, the widening schism between the extreme orthodox and all the other Jews, the impact of the Holocaust and the death ethos, Israel continues to pull farther and farther away from the diaspora community. The metamorphosis of the diaspora Jew to the "new Jew" has been a major objective of Zionism ever since its inception. It was claimed that the "new Jew" would supersede the diaspora Jew of Central and Eastern Europe. Ironically, the more the diaspora *bale-kulturniks* immersed themselves in Yiddish culture, the more their relationship to their Israeli audience, especially those under forty years old, became strained.

The Future of Klezmer

Since the *bal-kulturnik* movement began nearly thirty years ago, *klezmer* has gone from being only *simkhe* music to being the rubric for any kind of Jewish music. Trying to explain and define what *klezmer* is to someone who never heard of it is as difficult as explaining and defining what is jazz today. Just as jazz is rooted in southern blues, spirituals, and African rhythms, so is *klezmer* rooted in the prayer modalities of the Jews of ancient Israel. Both *klezmer* and jazz are genres born of a diaspora population. Yes, Jews have lived longer in Europe than African Americans have lived in America. But the folk music of both peoples has been used to express a longing for their spiritual and cultural homeland.

Today one can go to a *klezmer* concert and hear Zev Feldman perform traditional nineteenth-century Bessarabian Jewish music on the *tsimbl* and the next day return to the same venue and hear John Zorn perform his own brand of *klezmer*-jazz on the tenor saxophone. Both are playing display and dance pieces. Their styles are completely different from each other, but still take the listener on a spiritual journey rooted in the Jewish experience. Traditionalists will say that what Zorn plays has no connection to the *klezmer* Feldman plays. If this statement is true, then what Feldman plays bears little to no relationship to the music played by the itinerant Jewish musician who lived in the Alsace-Lorraine region in the fifteenth century. And musicians who are playing "post-*klezmer*" music would say that Zorn's "new Jewish" music has nothing to do with *klezmer*. Of course, all these statements are false. Both Feldman and Zorn are Ashkenazic Jews and their antecedents grew up in a European Ashkenazic culture where Yiddish was the *mama-loshn*. Thus their music reflects not only its Semitic Middle Eastern roots (I call it the essence of Ur, or Ur-connection, as in the city in Iraq where Abraham was born), but also its development in Central and Eastern Europe over nearly one thousand years.

Where will the next millennium take *klezmer,* and what are some of the agreements, disagreements, and concerns among many of the *bale-kulturniks?* Here are a few views.

Hankus Netsky:

> I feel *klezmer* today is a point of departure for most musicians. They take what they already play and add a little *klezmer* flavor. This interests me only if they're amazing at what they do. *Klezmer* as a gimmick doesn't get me. I still think the best fusion of Jewish music with jazz is Cannonball Adderly's recording of "Fiddler" from 1967. Second is *Terry Gibbs: Jewish Melodies in Jazztime* (Alice Coltrane's first recording) from 1959. Today musicians like Marty Ehrlich, Roy Nathanson, Anthony Coleman, Burton Greene, John Zorn, Andy Statman, Frank London, and others are all great musicians who have their own unique styles to combine with Jewish elements. On the other hand it's still possible to learn from experts, American and Moldavian alike. Most of us have very little experience compared to the average seventy-year-old wedding musician. My inspiration to do *klezmer* was Brandwein, so I probably put on one of his recordings before I listened to some reggae thing.[73]

Bob Cohen:

> Almost everywhere we [Di Naye Kapelye] perform, people come to me and say they like our music because we don't mix it with jazz. If that's true, why do so many musicians mix *klezmer* with jazz? The Klezmatics and a few other bands have a good reason to do so, but most do it because they really don't do the cultural homework that you need if you want to call your music "Jewish music." They want

---

[73] Interview with Hankus Netsky, op. cit.

the audience to listen to *them*. I want my audience to listen to the music of *my people*. This is one of the reasons I prefer to play and sing Yiddish drinking, mobster, and labor songs rather than nostalgic songs that are well-known. I want to present the culture my grandfather knew and sang about.[74]

Zev Feldman:

In the future I am a little bit concerned that the more established ways of looking at Jewish culture may co-opt the term *klezmer* and some of the cachet of *klezmer* for other more established forms of music. I wouldn't underestimate the desire of the American Jewish establishment to delegitimize Yiddish. By this I mean delegitimizing every aspect of the way of life that went along with the language, including Yiddish song, *klezmer* music, and Yiddish dance. It seems for a long time it was an important priority. So when I see groups being applauded in newer venues for playing Jewish music or *klezmer* I am immediately suspicious because it is an easy way out to reestablish something that is already established and rename it *klezmer*. You see, in that way, the majority of the people would be happy. They will have affirmed already what they know to have been true and they won't have to try to understand something that they actually don't understand.[75]

Klezmer trumpeter Frank London was one of the original founding members of the Klezmatics, and one of the key *bal-kulturnik* innovators. Not just satisfied in recreating the past, something he calls "the hyper-traditional folky thing," London went on to form several other *klezmer* ensembles that explore the *khasidic, khazones,* and *zmires*[76] genres

---

[74] Interview with Bob Cohen, op. cit.

[75] Interview with Zev Feldman, op. cit.

[76] *Zmires* (Yid.): Sabbath songs, specifically sung on Friday night after evening services and on Saturday afternoon after morning services.

of Ashkenazic music. On the topic of the future of *klezmer,* he had this
to say:

> The level of the quality of *klezmer* is so high compared to twenty years
> ago. Twenty years ago you got jobs just because you had a job. It is
> going in every direction and this thrills me. Just when we think we
> hit a wall a new door opens. About four to five years ago the hyper-
> traditional folky thing started taking ascendance with musicians like
> Alicia Svigals, Steve Greenman, and Zev Feldman. Then just recently I
> have seen a number of people who are descended from *klezmer* families
> becoming serious about the music. So you have Susan Sandler playing
> trumpet, Rachel Lemish playing trombone, Elaine Watts, David Levitt,[77]
> and several others not playing the same old tunes everyone has been
> playing for the last twenty years but playing their families' repertoires.
> And then there are the regional styles like the New York style verses
> the Philadelphia style, and jazzy *klezmer,* experimental *klezmer,* and
> the don't-call-me *klezmer* styles. All of it is really great but none of us
> should forget it came from instrumental and vocal Ashkenazic music.[78]

Jazz saxophonist and clarinetist Marty Ehrlich is known internationally as an avant-garde musician and composer; but it is only in the last
dozen years that Ehrlich has become involved with the *klezmer* scene. He
learned the repertoire when he began playing weddings and *bar mitsves*
with my band, Hot Pstromi. He comments:

> I am never comfortable just re-creating the past. But I also feel you
> can't know what is of the moment without constantly filtering your-

---

[77] Rachel Lemish's *yikhes* comes from the famous Lemeş kapelye (see Part II) that played
throughout Moldavia and Bessarabia in the 19th century. Elaine Watts is the daughter of
famed *klezmer* clarinetist Jacob Hoffman (see Part III). David Levitt is the son of *klezmer*
clarinetist Marty Levitt.

[78] Interview with Frank London, October 27, 2000.

self through things that have historical meaning. I always ask myself, if I do this Dylan tune, is this tune overly sentimental? Is this Modzitzer *nign* going to sound like chicken soup or a little bit more immediate? I don't want to *do* chicken soup, I want to *eat* chicken soup. And artistically, I am looking for something of a different nature. Not to comfort necessarily, as it's only emotion. And that is what I am trying to do with *klezmer*. More and more I am drawn to vocal-oriented music and how to approximate that on the instrument.[79]

Always one to push the envelope (and, ultimately, many people's buttons), jazz saxophonist and composer John Zorn's raison d'être the last dozen years has been to purposely straddle the two worlds of the New York downtown avant-garde jazz scene and the New York downtown "new" Jewish music scene. Zorn grew up in Flushing, New York, in a home that was devoid of almost any Jewish culture but where the philosophy of internationalism was stressed. He went to the United Nations International School in Manhattan and eventually went on to study jazz in college. For Zorn, his Jewishness was never an issue until he went, as he told me, "to Germany one too many times." As he became more aware that there were still problems of anti-Semitism abroad and in America, he decided to explore his Jewishness through Jewish music. He coined the term for this "new" Jewish music movement: Radical Jewish Culture. Much of the music that has come out of this Radical Jewish Culture movement has been recorded by Zorn's own label, Tzadik, which he began in 1995. He told me:

There is a renaissance happening, and it feels that people want to take this music and take it somewhere else. They don't want to just do the Wynton Marsalis thing and dig it up out of the grave and prop it up as a skeleton. There are some bands who are doing this and I champion that. Tradition is great. I am glad the *khasidim* living in Brooklyn are

---

[79] Interview with Marty Ehrlich, December 15, 2000.

wearing their black hats and white socks, but it is not for me. But we shouldn't degenerate the people who aren't keeping this tradition but instead are moving it forward. That is just as important. But I know there is tension between these two obvious extremes. For example, jazz musicians who play a concert and say this is Jewish music, because they are Jewish. That is not enough for me. I wouldn't put that on a music series I curate. I don't think it is just a matter of bloodline, tribalism, or even a flat two and sharp four. Is there something else going on aside from a certain way of putting rhythms together? I think there are other sensibilities at work that give the music a Jewish feel. And what is a Jewish feel, anyway? Is it sadness? We don't have a monopoly on angst or guilt. But whatever this new Jewish sound is, just the fact that new stuff is happening is good. However, how long their impact will be felt is another story. I look at a record like *Knitting on the Roof* [a compilation of downtown New York musicians covering songs from *Fiddler on the Roof*] and say to myself, "what a pile of junk." But it is another direction and it may touch somebody somewhere who then might want to explore this music a little deeper. What is interesting to me is that people should keep exploring *klezmer* and other Jewish music in an honest, personal way.[80]

One of the leading practitioners of *klezmer* violin is *bal-kulturnik* Deborah Strauss. She grew up in Buffalo, New York, with a conservative Jewish upbringing, studied classical violin, and eventually came under the spell of *klezmer* in 1985. Today she is a member of several *klezmer* bands, including the duo Strauss and Warschauer. She told me:

I can't generalize about all bands, but there is a lot of bad *klezmer* out there being taught as *klezmer* music. I know I am viewed as a traditionalist, but what does that mean? Pete Sokolow is a traditionalist of his genre of *klezmer*, but we play two completely different styles of

---

[80] Interview with John Zorn, January 8, 2001.

klezmer. If I hear really out music that they are calling *klezmer* and it is honest, deep, and well-grounded, then that is great, but if it is just noodling in a *freygish* mode, they are doing a disservice to the music. Since when is *klezmer* just noodling in a *freygish* mode? It is wonderful that we have all these people playing *klezmer* and performing concerts but we haven't come far enough in terms of really taking it seriously. I think what killed *klezmer* to begin with was it just became something that evoked a feeling, mode, or dance step. *Klezmer* has to be more than just music that evokes a feeling. I think there is still a dearth of deep understanding and focus on the music, language, and criticism. Every time I read a review of recent *klezmer* recordings, the critics like everything. And this is a doing a disservice to the music. When are there going to be some critics who understand that the music was not and is not one monolithic movement, understand its historical context, and write some intelligent criticism?[81]

Finally, David Krakauer came to *klezmer* as a classically trained clarinetist with knowledge of jazz. He was originally asked to audition for the clarinet position for the Klezmer Conservatory Band after Don Byron left, but because he wanted to stay in New York City and not move to Boston, he did not try out. Eventually he joined the Klezmatics and, after seven years, left in 1996 to form his own group, David Krakauer's Klezmer Madness. He told me:

Whatever happens to *klezmer* in the future, it has to stay Yiddish-drenched—just as jazz, if it is worth its salt, is blues-drenched. *Klezmer* has to be drenched with the sounds of the cantor, with the sounds of spoken Yiddish and the feeling of the *doyne*. An analogy would be New Orleans Jazz versus the Art Ensemble of Chicago. You can recognize both of them as jazz. There is a stylistic continuity you can trace. And this is what is interesting about *klezmer* at this point in time.

---

[81] Interview with Deborah Strauss, March 16, 2001.

You can take something and do a reconstruction of the old stuff or you can move ahead. There are bands playing the classic *klezmer* of the 1930s and '40s and lovingly tipping their hat to that style. And that for me has a wonderful place in the current *klezmer* scene. That is not what I want to do, but I appreciate it. So we have many different styles of *klezmer* right now that are coexisting, which is really great. But there are some who are diluting the music so much with all kinds of gimmicks, like adding Balkan rhythms, that I am not sure they are carrying the *klezmer* art form forward. This is fine, but they should call themselves something other than a *klezmer* band. Too often the *klezmer* aspects are lost in the musical translation.[82]

Yiddish and the Essence of Klezmer

Klezmer, the musical language of the Jews, and Yiddish, the spoken language of the Jews, have traveled together down the same roads for nearly the same length of time. As the Jews traveled eastward and eventually settled in the Poland/Ukraine region, Yiddish, rooted in Middle High German and Hebrew, incorporated new vocabularies from Romance and Slavic languages, just as *klezmer* incorporated new musical vocabularies from Germanic, Slavic, Romanian, and Balkan sources. Yiddish has not stayed static and neither has *klezmer.*

Yiddish speakers today have incorporated new vocabularies based upon new cultural trends and technologies. Whether they are discussing Hip-Hop culture, eco-pharmacology, or the poetry of Itzik Fefer, they are still speaking a European-based Yiddish, only one that has been infused with English. The same can be said of the many different *klezmer bale-kulturnik* bands that have infused musical genres like free jazz, rock 'n' roll, Latin, Cajun, and reggae, into a nineteenth- and early-twentieth-century

---

[82] Interview with David Krakauer, January 24, 2001.

East European *klezmer* sound. Thus *klezmer* music was and will always be a reflection of the evolving Ashkenazim, their culture, and their host's culture. But it also must always stay grounded in Yiddish, as *klezmer* is the musical abstraction of the Yiddish language.

From Strasbourg in the west, to Kharkov in the east, to Riga in the north, to Bucharest in the south: these were the furthest borders of where Ashkenazim lived and spoke Yiddish. Then, toward the end of the Middle Ages, Yiddish-speaking Jews of German origin moved toward Central Europe. Finally, by 1825, the largest concentration of Yiddish speaking Jews (4,900,000) lived in the Pale of Settlement. This region became the heart and soul of "Yiddishland." The Jews' daily spiritual sustenance was expressed in Hebrew (although many women learned the *Toyre* and other religious matters in Yiddish when they studied or were read to from the *Tsene Rene*),[83] while their daily lives were expressed in Yiddish. All this was almost completely erased during the Holocaust.

Today where is Yiddishland? Where can a Jew fully immerse him or herself in a Yiddish culture that is vibrant, growing, religious, secular, and everything in between? It is certainly not in Latvia, Lithuania, Moldova, Poland, Romania, Russia, or even Ukraine today. And Yiddishland was not transplanted to B'nai Brak, Jerusalem, Chicago, Miami Beach, Brooklyn, New Square (New York), or even Los Angeles. Yes, there are pockets of Yiddish culture trying to grow and sustain themselves in Central and Eastern Europe through various Jewish festivals, conferences and seminars, but where are the schools and other Yiddish-speaking institutions?

For Yiddishland to ever return, even in the tiniest version of its former self, it needs Jews, more and more Jews (not just philo-Semites), to

---

[83] *Tsene-Rene* (Heb.): go forth and see. The *Tsene-Rene* was the late-sixteenth-century book that contained the Torah, Prophets, Lamentations, the Song of Songs, Ecclesiastes, and the books of Esther and Ruth all translated into Yiddish. Isaac Yanover adapted and compiled the book specifically for Jewish women. In Central and Eastern Europe, Jewish women were denied a general Jewish education, which meant most could not read and understand Hebrew. The *Tsene-Rene* filled a great void in the devotional and cultural life of Jewish women, who were hungry for any kind of knowledge.

nourish it. However, immigration due to poor economies and anti-Semitism, assimilation due to intermarriage, apathy, and very low birthrates are the pivotal reasons why Yiddishland will never return to its former self.

Unlike those musicians who want to study and play, for example, flamenco, Irish, Polish, Russian, *Azeri,* Moroccan, reggae, or even Cajun and can return to the places where these musics came from, the *bale-kulturniks* cannot go back to live in Yiddishland and immerse themselves in the Yiddish culture that gave birth to and nourished *klezmer.* The Holocaust eradicated this region permanently. Ironically, it is the other way around: European, Russian, and Ukrainian Jews and non-Jews travel to the west to the Oxford Yiddish Studies Program, YIVO, the Yiddish Book Center in Amherst, Massachusetts, Ashkenaz, KlezKamp, and other Yiddish-based institutions to seek out teachers and mentors who can instruct them. Consequently English, not Yiddish, has become the *mama-loshn* of the *klezmer bal-kulturnik* crusade. Yiddish has been transformed from a daily language into a language of festivals and celebrations.

Today many *bale-kulturniks* have been attracted to the religious and spiritual side of *klezmer* and have returned to Judaism in some fashion. There were those who were not Jewish and converted, others who partook in some religious traditions (becoming fascinated with *khasidic nigunim* and *khazones*), some who became completely *bale-tchuves,* and still others who were not observant but wore *yarmulkes*[84] or *tsitses*[85] as part of their everyday attire (or only as concert dress) to make it very clear to themselves and everyone else that they were Jewish. Finally there were those *bale-kulturniks* who were completely disinterested in the religious side of *klezmer* but were attracted to the secular expressions of *klezmer.* One way they demonstrated this was by learning to speak and sing in Yiddish.

---

[84] *Yarmulkes* (Yid.): skullcaps. Though there is no Biblical law or directive, to cover one's head with a turban or a skullcap as a sign of humility, respect, or reverence has been a widespread custom among many peoples of the Middle East and parts of Asia, especially among the Jews, Arabs, Hindus, and Persians. Orthodox Jewish men wear some kind of head covering all the time, while Orthodox women wear a scarf, hat, or wig (known as a *sheytl* in Yiddish).
[85] *Tsitses* (Heb.): tassels. Orthodox Jewish men wear four tassels on their undergarments.

One of these was Jeff Warschauer. He came to *klezmer* from playing, as he says, "everyone else's music"—bluegrass, rhythm and blues, and country-western—before he discovered *klezmer* at the New England Conservatory of Music. Eventually he joined the Klezmer Conservatory Band and then formed a duo with Deborah Strauss. Today Warschauer is one of the primary *klezmer* plectrum (mostly mandolin, guitar) musicians in the *bal-kulturnik* scene. He explained:

> I didn't grow up hearing a lot of Yiddish in the home. But I got interested in the language around the same time I began playing *klezmer*. I started studying Yiddish in 1985 when I was working at a Jewish assisted-living facility in Boston. I went and sang Yiddish and played for their dances. I am interested in the connection and interplay between the vocal repertoire and the instrumental. By singing in Yiddish you can connect with the listener through storytelling. Playing purely instrumental *klezmer* wouldn't be as fulfilling.[86]

And, as other *bale-kulturniks* did before and after him, John Zorn became more aware of his Jewish identity at the same time as he explored the burgeoning *klezmer* scene. He explains:

> It wasn't until I was in my thirties when I began thinking about who I was, what my identity had been, is, and will be. Then I went to Japan for ten years, where I tried to belong to that society. No matter how hard I tried, I was never accepted. It was really like hitting a brick wall after ten years of continuous effort. It made me come to grips with my own identity. I came back to being a Jew through the process of being rejected again and again by one scene after another. Then I began to actually look at the people around me and wondered why so many of my close colleagues were Jewish. What is going on here? Is this something to explore and talk about?

---

[86] Interview with Jeff Warschauer, March 16, 2001.

Now not only have I been exploring my own Jewish identity for the last ten years through my music, record label, and the festivals I curate, but now I wear *tsitses*. For me it's a matter of identity and making me feel good. It's a matter of making me think about doing the right thing. I don't get into this sad game of who is the better Jew and how many commandments have you kept today. Wearing these connects me with the past and points me toward the present. For me it is less connected with the religious implications of what this garment is known for and more about a spiritual place that is very personal and relates to pride in our *Toyre* and Talmud. People see me onstage wearing these and this creates a question just like my music does. They have listened to my music in the past and then they see me up on stage and find out I'm Jewish. This is good on many levels and important to make a statement not only to the society at large but to your own people.[87]

Playing a Brandwein or Tarras melody note for note with all the proper *klezmer dreydlekh* is enough to maintain the music on a cursory level, and that's fine for many musicians. But, as Zorn said to me, "The music is much more than a flat two and a sharp four." If you can "talk the talk" (Yiddish) you can really "walk the walk." The musician will bring a greater profundity to *klezmer* if he or she understands some portions of the history, folklore, and language.

The earliest descendants of today's *klezmorim* were the medieval Ashkenazic minstrels who played and sang in Yiddish. Thus, for the *klezmer bal-kulturnik* scene to continue to develop and flourish, whether it be neotraditionalists or avant-gardists, the Yiddish component will need to be explored, examined, and exploited. Old and new Yiddish songs will help us better understand the past, present, and future world of the *klezmer.*

---

[87] Interview with John Zorn, op. cit.

Musicologist and Yiddish folksong collector and performer Ruth Rubin once said, "To understand any aspect of the culture of a people, one should be familiar with its history and language.... Yiddish language, its song, its lore and literature, are living things.... When Yiddish is not spoken, it is not alive...when Yiddish folksong is not sung or heard it is lost...*zey vern farklungen* (they are drowned out).... Parts of the roots are broken."[88]

---

[88] Joel Shatzky, "The People's Voices: An Interview with Ruth Rubin," *Jewish Currents*, Vol. 39 No. 3, March 1985, pp. 15–17.

Klezmer Zikhroynes in di Yizker Bikher

•

(*KLEZMER* MEMORIES IN THE MEMORIAL BOOKS)

This appendix is collected from the *Yizker Bikher,* or Memorial Books in English. Over six hundred have been published, with new ones still being written. These books were written by Jews who survived the Holocaust, mainly to honor and memorialize those who perished from a particular town. The articles in these *Yizker Bikher* focus on the war years and at the end of each book is a list of the names of those who were murdered. However, most of the *Yizker Bikher* are also a kind of *pinkes* (Yid.: town chronicle). They not only include articles about the war years, but also a detailed history of the Jewish community in that particular town, with many entries about the various vicissitudes of city and *shtetl* Jewish life from the mid-nineteenth century (a few entries talk about events that are several decades earlier) to the eve of World War II.

Because they were never meant for mass consumption, only a small number of each book has ever been printed—primarily for those Jews who came from the places memorialized. A complete collection is housed at Hebrew University in Jerusalem; the second largest collection is at YIVO. The majority were written in Yiddish and Hebrew, but a few books were written in the national languages (Hungarian, Polish, Romanian) of the countries covered. Many of the *Yizker Bikher* have some English sections (usually introductions and summaries).

What makes these books—in essence, compilations of oral histories—unique is that they not only describe in detail the occupation and eventual destruction of each Jewish community, but how complex, interesting, and diverse Yiddish culture was. The author of each article grew up in the city or town that the *Yizker Bikh* memorializes. For *klezmer* enthusiasts and researchers, these first-person accounts (some told to the author by family and relatives) provide among the most accurate details available on the attitude of others toward the *klezmorim*, their daily lives, and their professions in the *shtetlekh* of Central and Eastern Europe. Entries deal with awkward situations (*klezmorim* being beaten up by their gentile employers), celebrations (the completion of a new *Torah* transcription; May Day), events (a wedding of two orphans in a cemetery during a typhus epidemic), and harsh realities of poverty and war. There are even references to certain kinds of dances (*kutner, larsey*) for which I was unable to find any definitions, and instruments (double-neck ten-string guitar, bass *bandura*, long-tube trumpet) that the *klezmorim* played that were not typical of *kapelyes* of the time.

The following is an annotated bibliography of all entries I found in the YIVO *Yizker Bikher* that mentioned *klezmer*. Most entries have been distilled down to a few sentences of description, because many display strong similarities—for example, a number of them describe a wedding from betrothal to *sheve brokhes*. The entries that are presented here in full are distinct and remarkable for their detail.

All the translations reflect the idiomatic expressions used by the authors. For example, when an author referred to *klezmers* rather than *klezmorim*, I retained his or her terminology. Similarly, I translated *muzikant* as musician and *orkestra* as orchestra but left *kapelye* as *kapelye*. Sometimes I used the exact words (indicated by quotation marks) used by the author because they were so unusual and rich in their content. Each location is spelled as it was spelled in the indigenous language of the region (this is how the books are catalogued at YIVO). In the body of the article I use the Yiddish spelling of the names of all Jews and non-Jews mentioned, unless they were already written in English. All non-English words are italicized and can be found in the glossary.

The bibliographic form follows the one compiled by Zachary M. Baker, used today for reference at YIVO. The names of the countries to which the towns belonged between the end of World War I and the eve of World War II are indicated in parentheses. An asterisk after the English title means the translated title was already given by the editors; otherwise the titles were translated by Baker. The *Yizker Bikher* are listed here in alphabetical order and under their official place-names. The Polish towns are listed as they were in 1938, and other localities as of 1913. The author's name of each article is spelled according to the YIVO system. The following abbreviations are used: (AH) Austro-Hungarian, (B) Belorussian, (L) Lithuanian, (P) Polish, (R) Romanian, and (U) Ukrainian.[1]

BARANOW (P). *Sefer Yizkor Baranow* (A Memorial to the Jewish community of Baranow*). Ed.: N. Blumenthal. Jerusalem, Yad Vashem, 1964. (Hebrew, Yiddish, English) "*Shtetl* Types" by Hirsh Fenster, pp. 155–56. (Yiddish)

The *klezmorim* performed at a wedding on *Simkhes Toyre* while Rabbi Yosefus joyfully danced for them.

BARANOWICZE (P). *Baranovitz; Sefer Zikaron* (Baranovitz Memorial Book). Tel Aviv, Assoc. of Former Residents of Baranovitz in Israel, 1953. (Hebrew, Yiddish) "The *Klezmer* Family Solomovitch," p. 447. (Photo caption: Mikhl the *Klezmer* and his students) (Yiddish)

Mikhl the *klezmer* performed for the Russian aristocracy and members of the Czar's court in 1914. The family *kapelye* included his daughter and some nonrelatives.

BEDZIN (P). *Pinkas Bendin* (Pinkas Bendin; A Memorial to the Jewish Community of Bendin*). Ed.: A. Sh. Stein. Tel Aviv, Assoc. of Former Residents of Bedzin in Israel, 1959. (Hebrew, Yiddish) "The 'Singing' City" by Der Shwartser (from the Zaglembye Newsaper, 1937) pp. 149–150. (Yiddish)

Klezmorim were prevalent and successful and played for both the Jews and Christians in town. Some Christians saw how the Jewish beggars were quite successful at their endeavors and decided to pretend to be disabled and beg for alms. The

---

[1] Jack Kugelmass and Jonathan Boyarin, *From a Ruined Garden: The Memorial Books of Polish Jewry* (New York: Schocken Books, 1983), p. 223.

Jewish beggars were not happy with this situation and organized, stating that no one would be allowed to mock and imitate them for money.

BIALA PODLASKA (P). *Sefer Biala Podlaska* (The Book of Biala Podlaska). Ed.: M. J. Feigenbaum. Tel Aviv, Kupat Gmilut Hesed of the Community of Biala Podlaska, 1961. (Hebrew, Yiddish) "Moshe Bass," p. 381. (Yiddish)

Decrepit old Moshe Bass played so tunelessly, his fellow *klezmorim* paid him *not* to play. But Moshe was determined and played without pay. Despite his physical weakness and blindness, he led afternoon Sabbath services with a strong, shrill voice.

BIALYSTOK (P). *Bialystok; Bilder Album...* (Bialystok Photo Album...*). Ed.: D. Sohn. New York, Bialystoker Album Committee, 1951. p. 132. (photo caption: A Family *Kapelye*) (Yiddish)

Lipa Perlstein's family *kapelye* from Washlikowa and his seven musical grandchildren (six girls and one boy) in 1930. One girl, Chana Godeloff, was currently a musician in Israel. They are shown playing violin, guitar, balalaika, and mandolin.

BILGORAJ (P). *Bilgoraj Yizkor-Bukh* (Bilgoraj Memorial Book). By Moshe Teitlboym. Jerusalem, 1955. (Yiddish) "Jewish Holidays," p. 42.

The night after *Yom Kiper,* gentile conscriptors interrupted a celebration with the *Rebe.* They took young Jewish boys to be registered. Ironically, the boys had to also pay a *ruble* for the privilege of being conscripted into the Czar's army.

BILGORAJ (*ibid.*) "Handworkers," p. 58. (Yiddish)

The *klezmorim* in town all descended from the Gimpel family and played at every celebration. Rising anti-Semitism among the Poles led to their replacement by the local gentile fireman's brigade band.

BILGORAJ (*ibid.*) "Interesting Types in Bilgoraj," p. 74.

The leader of the *kapelye* was the only one to take the train to a wedding. He traveled half the night while his *kapelye* played at the wedding. On the way home, his fellow *klezmorim* found him at the train station, worn out from his travels.

BOLECHOW (P). *Sefer Ha-zikaron Le-kodeshei* (Memorial Book of the Martyrs of Bolechow). Ed.: Y. Eshel. Assoc. of Former Residents of Bolechow in Israel, 1957. (Hebrew, Yiddish) "The Wedding by the Russian Rabbi," by Dvora Aykhler-Adler, pp. 267–68. (Yiddish)

The *klezmorim* played all week long for the wedding festivities of Rabbi Shlomo Perlov's daughter. The wedding was a lavish and important event in the *shtetl.*

BORSZCZOW (P). *Sefer Borszczow* (The Book of Borstchoff*). Ed.: N. Blumenthal. Tel Aviv, Assoc. of Former Residents of Borszczow in Israel, 1960. (Hebrew, Yiddish) "The Kowalkes," pp. 154–56. (Yiddish)

The Kowalkes were a wealthy and distinguished old family. They were generous patrons of Yiddish theatre and the synagogue. When one of them got married, it was a lavish celebration, no matter the time of year. They always hired *klezmorim* from another town.

BRICHEVO (R). *Pinkas Brichevo* (Memorial Book of Brichevo). Ed.: K. A. Bertini. Tel Aviv, Former Residents of Brichevo (Bessarabia) in Israel, 1970. (Hebrew, Yiddish) "An Orchestra in Town," by Moshe Mester, p. 285. (Yiddish)

Dudel Koyfman (first violin) built a successful *kapelye* with Shlomo and Fayvel Gelman. The members were: Koyfman, Shlomo Gelman (second violin), Morits Shekhter and Nionya Zisman (also violins), Moyshe Vaynshtayn (flute), and Fayvel Gelman and Sonya Levintal (guitars, mandolin, and sometimes violin). The *kapelye* disbanded when Koyfman immigrated to America.

BURSZTYN (P). *Sefer Bursztyn* (Book of Bursztyn). Ed.: S. Kanc. Jerusalem, The Encyclopedia of the Jewish Disapora, 1960. (Hebrew, Yiddish) "Rohatyner *Klezmorim*," p. 269 (photo and caption). (Yiddish)

The Rohatyner *klezmorim* were: Moyshele Faust, his sons Duvid, Itsik-Hirsh, Mordkhay-Shmuel, and Yankl, and others. For two generations they led brides and grooms to the *khupe*. The sons died by the hands of Hitler's murderers.

BYCHAWA (P). *Bychawa; Sefer Zikaron* (Bychawa; A Memorial to the Jewish Community of Bychawa Lubelska*). Ed.: J. Adini. Bychawa Organization in Israel, 1968. (Hebrew, Yiddish) "A Wedding in our Town Bychawa," by Aryeh (Leybele) Fik, pp. 256–57. (Hebrew)

Yerakhmiel *Klezmer*'s famous *kapelye* from Lublin played at the wedding of two prominent rabbis' children.

CHELM (P). *Sefer Ha-zikaron Le-kehilat Chelm; Shana Le-hurbana* (Yizkor Book in Memory of Chelem*). Ed.: Sh. Kanc. Tel Aviv, Chelm Society in Israel and the U.S., 1980/81. (Hebrew, Yiddish) "Once There was a Wedding in Chelm," by Moshe Lerer, pp. 317–18.

In Chelm, wedding preparations began with the signing of the engagement contract and ended after the celebration of the *sheve brukhes*.

CHELM (*ibid.*) p. 111. (photo and caption) (Yiddish)

The photo is of the *kapelye* from the "*Lines-Hatsedek*" organization.

CHMIELNIK (P). *Pinkas Chmielnik* (Memorial book of Chmielnik). Tel Aviv, Former Residents of Chmielnik in Israel, 1960. (Hebrew, Yiddish) "The Ruined Wedding on the Account of an Agreement between the Rabbi and *Klezmorim*," by Moshe Lyver Mints, pp. 212–16. (Yiddish) (picture of *klezmorim*, "Yidl with his Fiddle," p. 214)

One day Rabbi Abraham Yitskhok Silman, the rabbi of Chmielnik, asked Yosef-

Leyb Marshalik, the leader of the town's *klezmer* band, to his home. Rabbi Sil-man asked Yosef-Leyb to promise that he, his children, and his grandchildren would never play at a wedding where boys and girls danced together. "I promise you this," said Yosef-Leyb.

Almost all the *klezmorim* belonged to one large family. Yosef-Leyb played the bass and his son Sane played the violin. His daughter Chane's children also played in the *kapelye*. There was Notl, the oldest, on violin, Avraham on clarinet, and Yisroel on drum. Chane's husband Velvel also was a *klezmer* and played the trumpet, violin, and clarinet, sometimes with Yosef-Leyb. The youngest son, Elye, was too young to play in the band. Eventually he studied at the conservatory in Vienna and became a well-known cellist, giving concerts in Kielc, Lodz, and Kraków. He died young in Kielc. His only son survived the Holocaust and lived in America.

In 1895 there was a big wedding in town between Hirshl Stelmakher's son Yankl Rimazh and Yakhe Libe, Elye Penzel's daughter. The wedding took place in Yisroel Stolar's carpentry workshop. After the ceremony and customary Jewish dances, Shmuel Stelmakher, the groom's younger brother (a playboy of sorts), went up to Yosef-Leyb and asked him if he would perform more popular dances like the *kutner* and *larsey*, in which eight couples dance together. The first dance was the *kutner* dance, which cost Shmuel one *ruble*. The *ruble* was put into the tin can, which was tied to the belt of the youngest *klezmer*, the drummer. The tin can was locked and the key was left at Yosef-Leyb's home. After the wedding all the *klez-morim* went to his home where the can was opened, the money counted, and each *klezmer* received his proper share.

The music began and so did the dancing. Eventually Sane, who played first vio-lin, went to the front of the crowded room to see what one of the young boys wanted who was shouting at him. Apparently the *klezmorim* had begun to play the second section of the *kutner* dance before all the couples had completed their steps. When Sane got closer to the young man, he saw the boys dancing with the girls and quickly yelled something to Yosef-Leyb in *klezmer* slang. Suddenly the music stopped. It was explained to Shmuel that a promise had been made to the rabbi that mixed dancing would not take place at any wedding the Marshalik *klezmorim* played at. Shmuel insisted that he continue to play since he paid a *ruble* for the two dances. Yosef-Leyb refused, and at that very minute a fight broke out. Sane's violin was broken, along with the Yosef-Leyb's bass. While people were shout-ing, screaming, and running about, Yisroel the drummer quickly ran out with the tin can to save what little they had earned.

The next day Libe Elke Penzel, quite depressed, went to Yosef-Leyb's home to apologize and pay him the rest of his fee. He did not want to take it, but she insisted, knowing that several instruments had to be repaired. And this was how the play-boys of Chmielnik got back at the *klezmorim* for making the agreement with the rabbi.

CHMIELNIK (*ibid.*) "The Rich Man's Extravagant Wedding," by Leybl Fiemrikovski, p. 308. (Yiddish)

Tuvyeh Marshalik the *batkhn* entertained at a lavish wedding. They prepared the food six months before the wedding. There was so much food that a special train wagon brought the pepper for the fish, while ten cars were filled with salt just to kosher the meat. On the wedding day the family, neighbors, *batkhonim, shamasim,* and *klezmorim* arrived, all with a limitless hunger.

CHMIELNIK (*ibid.*) "A Wedding In Town," by Khane Fuks, pp. 309–12. (photo caption: A wedding with the Midlazh family, p. 312) (Yiddish)

A typical Jewish wedding in Chmielnik usually involved most of the Jews in town.

CHORZELE (P). *Sefer Zikaron Le-kehilat Chorzel* (Memorial Book of the Community of Chorzel). Ed.: L. Losh. Tel Aviv, Association of Former Residents of Chorzele in Israel, 1967. (Hebrew, Yiddish) "Yosef Tik Performs in the Theatre," by Menakhem Lanienter, pp. 201–02. (Yiddish)

A poor shopkeeper and violinist leaped at the chance to play the lead in a local play. Unfortunately his wife interrupted the performance for fear that he was losing money at the shop.

CZESTOCHOWA (P). *Tchenstokhover Yidn* (The Jews of Czestochowa). Ed.: R. Mahler. New York, United Czestochower Relief Committee and Ladies Auxiliary, 1947. (Yiddish) "A Courtyard off of Warsaw Street," by Y. Elkhanon Ply-Fileek, pp. 817–20.

The apartment house at Warshavskaya Street 5 was full of life and the noise from the Jewish residents, including several family *kapelyes.*

CZYZEWO (P). *Sefer Zikaron Czyzewo* (Memorial Book of Tshijewo*). Ed.: Sh. Kanc. Tel Aviv, Former Residents of Tshizhevo in Israel and the USA, 1961. (Hebrew, Yiddish) "A Wedding in Town," pp. 497–99. (Yiddish)

In Czyzewo there was no wedding without Yudl the *Batkhn.* After the wedding ceremony, the festivities took place in either a Christian teahouse or in one of two Jewish-owned homes. At the wedding, Yudl and the *kapelye* received a percentage of the *droshe geshank* according to the bride's parents' income and were still paid per dance by the women as well.

CZYZEWO (*ibid.*) "The Order of the Wedding Ceremony," by the groom, pp. 499–502.

A typical wedding in Czyzewo included throwing rotten food (or in the winter, snowballs) at the groom to signify that this should be the most painful time of his life.

CZYZEWO (*ibid.*) "Czyzewor *Klezmorim*," by Avraham Yosef Ritholz, pp. 579–80.

Avraham Yosef Ritholz had a large family. All of them comprised his *klezmer* orchestra and several other orchestras after he passed away. Before and after World War I, they experienced a lot of anti-Semitism when they played for gentiles. Eventually some family members immigrated to in America.

DABROWICA (P). *Sefer Dombrovitsa* (Book of Dabrowica). Ed.: L. Losh. Tel Aviv, Association of Former Residents of Dabrowica in Israel, 1964. (Hebrew, Yiddish) "The Next to Last Count," by Yitskhok Feyglshtayn, pp. 177–80. (Yiddish)

In Dabrowica, many Jews worked for the estate owned by Count Pliaster. They cleared his forests and built his new homes. All of the contractors were Jews. When he married, he hired the local *klezmorim* to play at his wedding. When Count Pliaster died, most of the town's Jews went to his funeral.

DEBICA (P). *Sefer Dembits* (Book of Debica). Ed.: D. Leibl. Tel Aviv, Association of Former Residents of Debica, 1960. (Hebrew, Yiddish) "Letsim," by Naftali Shnayer, pp. 53–54. (Yiddish)

In Dembica there were two Yehuda Leybs. One was Yehuda Leyb Dayn and the other was Yehuda Leyb Balbirer. People in town often got them mixed up. Balbirer was a businessman, while Dayn was an old-time doctor whose office was in the barbershop. He also was a *klezmer*. When he was not working he sat around with his fellow *letsim* friends and joked with the patrons.

DOBROMIL (P). *Sefer Zikaron Le-zekher Dobromil* (Memorial Book of Dobromil*). Ed.: M. Gelbart. Tel Aviv, The Dobromiler Society in New York and the Dobromiler Organization in Israel, 1964. (Hebrew, English, Yiddish) "Dobromiler Views and Ways of Life," by Sol Miler, pp. 70–74. (Yiddish)

In Dobromil there were four languages spoken: Yiddish, Polish, German, and Ruthenian. Though the Jews learned all four languages in the *folks-shule,* Yiddish was the language they spoke in the home and on the street. During weddings in Dobromil, the *muzikers* Yidl on violin and Leyb on bass performed.

DOBROMIL (*ibid.*) "*Klezmer*," by Z. Shtayn, pp. 223–24. (Yiddish)

Yidl Glozberg was the leader of the *kapelye*. Besides playing at Jewish and Christian weddings, he also gave the Christians music lessons. When Yidl wanted to get married, his prospective father-in-law at first did not agree to Yidl marrying his daughter because he did not want a *klezmer yung* for his daughter. Eventually Yidl prevailed and performed the *bazingen* for his own bride.

DOBRZYN (P). *Yizker Bletlekh* (Our Village*) by Shmuel Russak, Tel Aviv, 1972. (Yiddish, English) "The Old *Klezmer*," p. 47. (Yiddish)

Alter Nusbom was the *klezmer* at hundreds of Jewish weddings. When he was eighty it became too difficult to hold the violin. This caused Alter to be depressed. Sometimes one heard him playing by himself the sad melody *Kol Nidre.*

DOKSZYCE (P). *Sefer Yizkor Dokszyce-Parafianow* (Dokszyc-Parifianow Book*). Ed.: Shtokfish. Tel Aviv, Assoc. of Former Residents of Dokszyce-Parifianow in Israel, 1970. (Hebrew, Yiddish) "Weddings," by Kalman Shults, pp. 41–43. (Yiddish)

Two weeks before the wedding, the groom, who came from Dalhinov, said there was a problem with the dowry. He had not received the exact amount of the dowry that had been agreed upon. Quickly the *shatkhn* worked out the problem. On the day of the wedding, the whole town, including the poor, participated. Nakhum the Whistler led his *kapelye* on the violin while the *batkhn* and *lets* sang songs and rhyming poems.

DROHICZYN POLESKI (P). *Drohiczyn; Finf Hundert Yo Yidish Lebn* (Memorial Book Drohichyn*). Ed.: D. B. Warshawsky. Chicago, Book Committee Drohichyn, 1958. (Yiddish) (photo caption) "Nisn Saratchikis' Wedding in 1917," p. 31. (Yiddish)

The *khupe* was carried from Khaykl Milner's house to the synagogue courtyard with the *klezmorim* accompanying the wedding party.

DUBNO (P). *Dubno; Sefer Zikaron* (Dubno; A Memorial to the Jewish Community of Dubno, Wolyn*). By A. Boxer (Ben-Arjeh). Ed.: S. Eisenberg. Haifa, 1962. (Yiddish) "Jewish Weddings and *Klezmorim*," by Moshe Katshke, pp. 665–71. (Yiddish)

The *klezmer kapelye* in Dubno played at the weddings of Jews, peasants, and Polish princes. Some of the Dubno *klezmorim* were: Ruveyn Tsimering, Reb Eli Klezmer (Eli Struner), and Reb Mendl Klezmer (Mendel Katshke).

Ruveyn Tsimering was a clarinetist and composer. He was so good at writing music that he helped the *khazn* in the big synagogue. He read from the *Toyre* of the small synagogues. Reb Eli Klezmer played second violin and was the *gebe* in the Shoemakers' Synagogue. Reb Mendl Klezmer played the cornet. He was a fine musician who also wrote music. He was a sergeant in Nikolai's army and played in the military orchestra in Lutsk. During his four years of service he remained religious despite being in the military.

In the 1890s the *kapelye* numbered ten men (including a first violin) and a *batkhn*. They played not only in Dubno but also in the surrounding towns. About a month before a wedding, the representatives from the *kapelye* would visit the bride's father to make an agreement about their services and what they would be paid. Their salary was anywhere from ten to fifteen *rubles*. For this they had to do the following: Play at the *bazetsn* for the bride, lead her to the *khupe* in the synagogue, then lead the wedding party with *freylekhs* through only the streets where Jews lived. They were not permitted to go down the wide streets like Alexandrovka or Panienska, where the neighborhood was mixed. Anything that was part of the wedding ceremony was covered by the fees the *klezmorim* had earlier decided upon. But all of the dances during the party were paid for separately.

Up until World War I, the following dances were popular in Dubno: The quadrille, which was for four couples and cost four *kopeks*. The dance lasted about fifteen minutes and the tempo was slow. The *sherele*, which was danced by many couples, cost ten *kopeks* per couple. It started slowly and ended up in a strong gallop. The *freylekhs* was usually danced with one couple at a time, a man with his wife or two from the same sex. Sometimes four lined up, one across from the other. When the music began, one person would dance specific steps and figures opposite the other. Their hands were held down by their sides and they moved from side to side, back and forth. The dance lasted until one fell from fatigue. Then the other partner would grab hold of his tired partner's hands and they would begin to dance together with each other's hand on each of their shoulders, to the *freylekh*. Then the *klezmorim* would pick up the tempo while the in-laws all began to clap with great appreciation and ardor. Then the women would wave their handkerchiefs in the air, urging on each partner to surpass the other. Such a *freylekh* cost twenty *kopeks*. The *kozak* [*kozatchka*] the same amount. This dance was played for the in-laws and adolescents. The young danced waltzes, such as the Boston waltz, *krakowiaks*, a *lizginka*, and the *tsherkishn* dance, where the dancer held a knife in his hand. This dance received a big noisy applause. The majority of the dances took place before the *khupe* ceremony.

At about eleven P.M., the tables were set with various dishes, including sweets like honey cakes, fruit layer cakes, and sweet rolls. The main courses were *gefilte fish*, roast meat, *gildene yoyikh*, with baked *mandlen-broyt* and a compote. During the whole meal the *klezmorim* kept playing. Then they would play for the newlyweds a special *dobranotsh*. Before the melody began, the *batkhn* yelled: "This is for the distinguished couple, in-laws, etc." The *klezmorim* received a special fee for this tune. After the meal the *batkhn* began conducting the *droshe-geshank*. Afterward, the tables were pushed aside and the *klezmorim* played some more *freylekhs* or a polka. Then one of the *khasidim* would do the *mitsve tants* with the bride. Finally dawn was appearing and the *klezmorim* led the in-laws to their homes with music.

The police under the Czar and then later under the Poles were not ordered to watch such wedding ceremonies, but sometimes they came anyway, to see how everyone danced. Sometimes the police were invited in and offered a drink of whiskey. The *vlaste* came in and thanked the wedding couple for their hospitality. This always pleased the in-laws.

If the *klezmorim* were invited to play for a wealthy man or for the intelligentsia, then they polished their instruments and came in their very finest clothes. No one in the *kapelye* would miss such a rich wedding. If for some reason a *klezmer* could not be there, then they took a musician from their Czech neighbors. When the *klezmorim* played a wedding for a butcher, it was like being at a king's wedding. The butchers were generous and paid higher wages to the *klezmorim*. Plus there were a lot of extra dances. The butchers loved to dance a *freylekhs*. Their favorite *freylekh* was the *tsirele*. In this dance they would stomp with their boots and sing with the *klezmorim*. "Tsirele Mirele, take this sack, I will throw you a parsnip..."

From such butcher weddings the *klezmorim* made from fifty to sixty *rubles* outside of their guaranteed wages. When paid this amount, the *klezmorim* brought a box with a lock on it. They put the money into the box and gave it to a cashier. Then once a month they would divide it up in unequal parts. The better player usually was given a quarter of the proceeds and sometimes even half. Mendl Klezmer used to receive half the total amount while the bassist did not get more than a quarter and sometimes less. The cashier was usually ignorant but honest. After the money was divvied out to the last penny, the *klezmorim* bought a little whiskey and then brought home the rest, their *brukhe*. This *brukhe* was used to pay the businesses and stores where the *klezmer* had bought things on credit. It also paid the teacher and the landlord's rent.

The *klezmorim* also performed for the landowners and peasants in the surrounding area. Usually for a peasant wedding the *klezmorim* were paid twenty to thirty *rubles*. The gentile groom with his attendants came into town having already decided on the fee and picked up the *klezmorim* in a wagon and took them to the village. The *klezmorim* were skilled in the customs of the gentiles' weddings and played to their tastes. At the gentile wedding, whenever a distinguished guest stepped inside the groom's home, the *kapelye* played a march. Sometimes the guest interrupted the *klezmorim* and gave them a present. Often the gentile weddings ended with some kind of scandal or fight. When this happened, the *klezmorim* grabbed their instruments, jumped through the windows, and ran home.

When a circus came to town, the Dubno *klezmorim* played for them. Although the *klezmorim* were religious men, they still knew how to play for every situation. Unfortunately the livelihood of the *klezmorim* was economically very difficult. None of them left any inheritance for their children and their sons did not follow in their fathers' footsteps. The last Dubno *klezmorim* were all murdered by Hitler.

DUBOSSARY (R). *Dubossary; Sefer Zikaron* (Dubossary Memorial Book). Ed.: Y. Rubin. Tel Aviv, Association of Former Residents of Dubossary in America, Argentina and Israel, 1965. (Hebrew, Yiddish) "*Reb* Itsik Shargorodski the Dubossary *Klezmer*," by

Harry Shir, pp. 228–31. (Yiddish) (photo caption: Reb Itsik Shargorodski and his family. The young boy on the right is Hirshl [Harry Shir] photographed in 1897)

Itzik Shargorodski was a gifted composer. Some of his melodies were published by the musicologist Moshe Bik, who came from the same town. Hearing that *klezmers* in America played for the Yiddish theatre as well as for weddings, he left without his family but returned when his wife became ill with consumption. Back in Dubossary he became the leader again of the Dubossary *kapelye.*

DUSETOS (L). *Ayera Hayita B-Lite Dusiat Bi-re'I Ha-Zikhronot* (There Was a Shtetl in Lithuania; Reflected in Reminiscences). Ed.: Sara Weiss-Slep. Tel Aviv, the Society of Former Residents of Dusiat, 1989. (Hebrew) "A Wedding in the Town," by Rivke B., p. 92.

Weddings were always celebrated on *erev Shabes* in town. The *kapelye* consisted of a violin, flute, accordion, and drum.

DUSETOS (ibid.) "A Wedding in Town," By Henia B., p. 93.

The procession to the *khupe* was led by the *klezmer* violinist, then followed by everybody else holding lit candles. Behind the procession of people came the trumpet and drums.

FRAMPOL (P). *Sefer Frampol* (Frampol Book*). Ed.: D. Shtokfish. Tel Aviv (Book Committee), 1966. (Yiddish) "A Wedding in Town," pp. 160–65.

In Frampol there were *klezmorim,* but the *batkhn* was from Bilgoraj. Once the famous *batkhn* Shmuel Tsholnt was brought from Lublin, when the bride, an orphan, married an American. Weddings lasted all night until the last dance, the *gute-nakht,* was played.

FRAMPOL (*ibid.*) "*Reb* Leybish the Frampoler Composer," by Moyshe Likht Feld, pp. 233–39. (Yiddish)

Leybish was a *shokhet, mohel,* and composer of *khasidishe nigunim.* Sometimes a *klezmer* violinist accompanied him while he sang and other times he accompanied himself on the violin. Once the Trisker *Rebe,* Rabbi Moyshele Twerski, invited Leybish to lead the prayers during the Days of Awe in Trisk, but the Frampol Jewish community was upset. So instead Leybish wrote three marches for the Trisker *Rebe* that were sung in the Trisker synagogue.

GABIN (P). *Gombin; Dos Lebn un Umkum fun a Yidish Shtetl in Poyln* (The Life and Destruction of a Jewish Town in Poland*). Eds.: Jack Zicklin et al. New York, Gombin Society in America, 1969. (Yiddish, English) "*Klezmorim,*" by Yakov Rotbard, pp. 38–39. (Yiddish)

In Gombin, down one narrow street there were two stores. One was a grain store, the other a food store that was owned by Leybele-Khanon Klezmer. One always heard music at this corner. Sometimes it was wind instruments, other times a violin and a bass. Leybele-Khanon and his *kapelye* played many weddings.

GARGZDAI (L). *Sefer Gorzd (Lita); Ayara Be-hayeha U-be-hilayona* (Gorzd Book; A Memorial to the Jewish Community of Gorzd*). Ed.: Yitzhak Alperovitz. Tel Aviv, The Gorzd Society, 1980. (Hebrew, English, Yiddish) "Celebrations," by Arye Frank, pp. 126–27. (Hebrew)

Every seven years, after the completion of reading the *Talmud,* there was a great celebration fit for a king. The *klezmorim* played while the Jews ate cooked goose, fish, herring, *khales,* cakes, and fruit. Stories were told about Rabbi Shabatay and everyone had a good time. No one ever forgot this *siem* [Yid.: conclusion] celebration.

GLINOJECK (P). *Mayn Shtetele Glinovyetsk; Un di Vayterdike Vandlungen Plock-Wierzbnik, Zikhroynes* (My Town Glinojeck...,) by Shlomo Motskowits. Paris, 1976. (Yiddish) pp. 188–192.

The author remembers his aunt's joyous wedding. Only ten years after that, he was in the Starkhowitser concentration camp, remembering his aunt Dvore's beautiful rendition of *"Eli, Eli Lamo Azvasoni"* ("Oh, God, why have you forsaken me?")

GONIADZ (P). *Sefer Yizkor Goniadz* (Our Hometown Goniadz*). Ed.: D. Shtokfish. Tel Aviv, Association of Gniewashow in Israel and the Diaspora, 1971. (Hebrew, English, Yiddish) "A Wedding in Town," by Avraham Yap, pp. 501–02. (Yiddish)

Weddings were usually announced in the synagogue with music from the *klezmorim.* Since the town had no *kapelye,* one was brought from Trestyna. The wealthier weddings brought *klezmorim* from Stchutchin. The weddings were held in the market square. There the *batkhn* sang *zogekhts* and *muser* songs for the bride.

GROJEC (P). *Megilat Gritse* (Megilat Gritze*). Ed.: I. B. Alterman. Tel Aviv, Gritzer Association in Israel, 1955. (Hebrew, Yiddish) "The Gritzer Mama," by Avraham Fridman, pp. 175–77. (Yiddish)

In the town, Feygele Drayer the *Rebetsin* was called the "Gritzer Mama" because she took care of the sick, poor, and other sufferers. During World War I, a typhus epidemic hit the town. Feygele believed the only way to get rid of the plague was to have two orphans be married by their respective parents' gravesites. Yitskhok the Klezmer and his *kapelye* entertained in the cemetery.

GURA HUMORA (R). *Ayara Bi-derom Bukovina Koroteha Shel-kehila Yehudit (Gura Humora: Eine Kleinstadt in Der Sud Bokovina; Die Geschichte Einer Jüdischen gemeinde)* (A Small Town in South Bukowina; The History of Its Community). Eds.: Shraga Yeshurun, Zvi Wagner, Shlomo Apter. Tel Aviv, 1992. (Hebrew) "Music," by Shlomo Viniger, pp. 130–31.

The Buicăs were a Gypsy family that played at all the Jewish and non-Jewish celebrations, in the restaurants, and at the funerals in town. The band was in existence to World War I.

HIRLAU (R). *Der Khoyv Fun Zikorn; Mayn Moldevish Shtetl Harlau* (The Duty of Memory; My Moldavian Town Harlau) by Khayim Zaydman. Jerusalem, Yidishe Kultur-Gezelshaft, 1982. (Yiddish) "*Purim*," by Khayim Zaydman, pp. 240–243.

On *Purim* before lunch it felt like any other day. In synagogue we said *kroyvets* [Heb.: acronym for the voice of joy and salvation in the tents of the righteous] and the *megile* was read once more. In the street, all the Jewish shops were open and the artisans worked in the morning. They only began to celebrate the holiday in the afternoon.

There were many young boys and girls going around with covered saucers. The *shalakhmones* was being moved in both directions. One received from the households not only baked goods but also a coin with the *shalakhmones*. We also gave, but not a lot. We sent *shalakhmones* to the two rabbis, the old *shokhtim*, and to our good friends.

After lunch, one began to see disguises. Children wore disguises, but not in the evening, only at dusk. The older children wore some garment on the left side; then they would go around to the back door and go into the anteroom: "Mama, do you know who I am?" Then the mother began to laugh. "No, my child, who are you?" "I am Moyshele." "Oi, a blessing on your little head; I did not recognize you." The child was very happy, while the mother beamed with proud enjoyment and gave the child and the neighbor something.

We did the afternoon prayers early so we could go to the feast before sunset, while it was still *Purim*. The fathers wore their *shtrayml*s and Sabbath *kapotes*, while the mothers and their children were dressed in their best clothes and sat at the festive table. The dishes still leave me with a taste today. Such an atmosphere it was. The *koyletch* tasted like the Garden of Eden. Then there was the fish of the day, and the *gildene yoyikh;* everything was special for *Purim*. The mother made a sweet dish called *palave*. Just as one would never have a *seder* without a parsnip *tsimes*, one never had a *Purim* meal without *palave*. In the *palave* there were small raisins mixed in with a grain. We called it "kish-mish." There was also some rice and other things. The festive meal was cozy. And though it had started early, it ended late.

After the festive meal came all of the other *Purim* events, the *klezmers* and presentations to watch. There were no Jewish *klezmers* in our town. Our population was too small to have a permanent *klezmer kapelye*. You always had some entertainers at a wedding, but they were Jewish *klezmers* from the neighboring towns. For example, they came from Botoşani, who brought with them a *batkhn* as well, a necessary requisite at a Jewish wedding. So what would we do without *klezmers* for *Purim*? One wanted at least a little music.

In our town, there were three Gypsy families living in three different houses. In one of the houses lived some musicians who played the violin and other instruments. The Romanian Gypsies had a tradition of being musicians. They say that the great composer and pianist Franz Lizst from the previous century would occasionally visit the Romanian national poet Alexander Vassily in Moldova. Alexander had with him a Gypsy *kapleye* that included the famous Barbu Lautaru Brosh. They played for the guests at the table during the meal. Liszt enjoyed Barbu's playing. Barbu played so magically, even though he could not read music. Then Liszt played his composition, the *Second Hungarian Rhapsody*. At the end of the piece everyone applauded Liszt. Then Barbu asked him if he would repeat the rhapsody. Barbu then played the entire piece from memory. Liszt was thoroughly pleased with his performance.

I do not know if our Gypsies were the direct successors of Barbu, but they could play just as well. Every *Purim* they used to go around from afternoon into the evening with their violins throughout the whole town, playing Jewish and non-Jewish melodies at the Jewish homes. In return they received a few *groshen* and a treat. Along with the Gypsies, the *Purimshpilers* came around and sang the well-known "Haman Wanted to Hang All the Jews." They received some *homentashn*, other cookies, and some money.

There were also men and women who went around collecting *tsdoke* for the various charities while the beggars also went around from house to house. Then the young girls and boys, wearing different masks and original costumes, walked about the town visiting each others' homes. The weather was sometimes beautiful and sometimes not so beautiful, with rain and mud. Sometimes spring made a mistake and came early and it was nice to go out in the street and walk about under the full moon. In the late evening, couples, young men, and *klezmers* went around in the calm, homey atmosphere. In the homes people ate cookies, drank wine, sang "*Shoshanes-Yaakov*" [Heb.: The Rose of Jacob], and joked with the *Purimshpilers*. More or less this was *Purim* in Hirlau from the beginning of the century through the 1920s.

HORODENKA (P). *Sefer Horodenka* (The Book of Horodenka). Ed.: Sh. Meltzer. Tel Aviv, Former Residents of Horodenka and Vicinity in Israel and the USA, 1963. (Hebrew, Yiddish) "Jewish Weddings," by Sholom Kirshner, p. 105. (Yiddish)

The *Shabes* before the wedding was the *oyfruf,* when the groom was called to the *Toyre* for *mafter.* If the groom was weak in Hebrew, then *mafter* was a hardship rather than an honor. The town's *kapelye* was led by Kalman Rozenkrants and his son Hirsh-Kopl.

HOSZCZA (P). *Sefer Hoshtch; Yizker-Bukh* (The Book of Hosht—in Memoriam*). Ed.: R. Fink. New York and Tel Aviv, Society of Hosht, 1957. (Yiddish) "*Klezmer,* Gramophone and Movie Theatre," by Efrayim Yaron, pp. 176–79.

In Hoshch its eccentric *klezmorim* played for Jews but mostly for the gentiles.

HRUBIESZOW (P). *Pinkas Hrubieszow* (Memorial Book of Hrubieshov*). Ed.: B. Kaplinsky. Tel Aviv, Hrubieshov Associations in Israel and the USA, 1962. (Hebrew, Yiddish, English, Polish) "The Dance Plague," pp. 333–34. (Yiddish)

During the years 1918–20, dancing was a popular activity. The *khasidim* in town tried to prevent this, but many Jewish organizations held dances as successful fundraisers.

IWIE (P). *Sefer Zikaron Le-kehilat Iwie* (Ivie; In Memory of the Jewish Community*). Ed.: M. Kaganovich. Tel Aviv, Association of Former Residents of Ivie in Israel and "United Ivier Relief" in America, 1968. (Hebrew, Yiddish) "A Wedding in Iwie," by Osne Brand (Katshker) p. 378. (Yiddish)

In a poem, a wedding is described. The wedding took place on Friday before *Shabes.* On Saturday night after *Shabes* the dancing began and lasted all night. Today one does not see such a wedding.

IWIENIEC (P). *Sefer Iwieniec, Kamien Ve-ha seviva; Sefer Zikaron* (The Memorial Book of Iwieniec, Kamien and the Surrounding Region). Tel Aviv, Iwieniec Societies in Israel and the Diaspora, 1973. (Hebrew, Yiddish) "A Wedding in a Poorhouse," pp. 132–35. (Yiddish)

In the Iweiniecer poorhouse lived two families. One was Guta, who was blind in one eye, with her daughter Yente, the *meshugena.* In another room lived a mute woman with her son Yenkl, who was a cripple. When Yenkl's mother died, the town decided that he should marry Yente. The town provided everything for the wedding including the *klezmer* music.

IWIENIEC (*ibid.*) "A Wedding in Iwieniec," by Yitskhok Kuznits, p. 179–81.

The author described his sister's wedding with all the preparation and celebration in 1923.

JAROSLAW (P). *Sefer Jaroslaw* (Jaroslaw Book*). Ed.: Yitzhak Alperwitz. Tel Aviv, Jaroslaw Society, 1978. (Hebrew, English, Yiddish) "The Musical and Entertainment Life," by Arne Zilberman, p. 265. (Hebrew)

The musical and entertainment life in Jaroslaw was connected with the Gayger family. There was no event in the theatre or movie house that David Gayger's *kapelye* did not have an active role in. They also ran a dance and music school.

JAWOROW (P). *Matsevet Zikaron Le-kehilat Jaworow Ve-ha-seviva* (Monument to the Community of Jaworow and the Surrounding Region). Ed.: Michael Bar-Lev. Haifa, Jaworow Society in Israel and the United States, 1979. (Hebrew, Yiddish) "Weddings in the Town," by B. Maur, pp. 176–77. (Hebrew)

In Jaworow there was a wedding where Mordkhay *Marshalik,* Melekh Klezmer, and Meyer the *Khazn* all participated. After the wedding feast, the bride sat with her new husband at the table only for the men. At the table the *sheve brukhes* were recited, and then if the groom was a *yeshive* student, he gave a speech.

KALARASH (R). *Sefer Kalarash; Le-hantsahat Zikhram Shel Yehudei Ha-ayara She-nehreva Bi-yemei Ha-shoa* (The Book of Kalarash: In Memory of the Town's Jews, Which was Destroyed in the Holocaust). Eds.: N. Tamir et al. Tel Aviv, 1966. (Hebrew, Yiddish) "*Reb* Yoel Melamed the *Klezmer,*" by A. Kharuvi, p. 305. (Hebrew)

Reb Yoel's daughter Khayke was engaged to Itsik Klezmer. When the wedding day came, the wedding celebration was held in the horse stables after the floors were cleaned and the walls were covered with white sheets. Itsik played some memorable *doynes* at his own wedding.

KALISZ (P). *Sefer Kalish* (The Kalish Book*). Tel Aviv, The Israel-American Book Committee, 1964. (Hebrew, Yiddish) "At A Jewish Wedding," by Yakov Meshulam, pp. 483–484. (Yiddish)

At a wedding held in Kalisz the author sat near the groom, because the nearer you sat, the larger the portion of food you received. On the table were twelve cans all for putting in money meant for the groom. Money was also given to receive the first pieces of *khale* and fish, for Eli *Batkhn* to continue playing, and for all the other workers at the wedding.

KALUSZ (P). *Hayeha Ve-hurbana Shel Ha-kehile* (Kalusz: The Life and Destruction of the Community). Eds.: Shabatai Ynger, Moshe Ettinger. Tel Aviv, Kalusz Society, 1980. (Hebrew, Yiddish, English) "The *Klezmer* in the Night," (poem), p. 459. (Yiddish)

Mutsika the poor *klezmer* played the song "*Shir-Hamalos*" with great passion as he walked the streets from night to morning.

KALUSZ (*ibid.*) "Life in Kalusz—An Oral History," p. 572. (English)

In Kalusz, May Day and Polish Constitution Day (May 3rd) were celebrated by a brass band dressed in ornate black uniforms and hats of the miners. However, all weddings were celebrated with music from Itsikl Gutenplan's *kapelye.*

KALUSZYN (P). *Sefer Kaluszyn; Geheylikht der Khorev Gevorener Kehile* (Memorial Book of Kaluszyn). Eds.: A Shamri, and Sh. Soroka. Tel Aviv, Former Residents of Kaluszyn in Israel, 1961. (Yiddish) "Moshe-Ruvn the *Klezmer,*" pp. 249–52.

The *kapelye* in town was led by Moshe-Ruvn Ayzenshtayn, who played trumpet and violin. If there was a second wedding in town at the same time, the inferior *kapelye* was hired. If both *kapelyes* were occupied, then Asher-Motl, the violinist, was hired. After Poland defeated the Bolsheviks, three Jews in the town were accused of collaboration and sentenced to death. Moshe-Ruvn and his brothers were hired to play Chopin's Death March after they were executed. Later, Moshe-Ruvn and his brothers were killed by the Nazis.

KALUSZYN (*ibid.*) "Kaluszyner *Klezmorim*," by Shmul Ayzershtayn, pp. 253–254. (Yiddish)

The Ayzenshtayn family was the town's *kapelye*. The first leader of the *kapelye* was the virtuoso violinist Asher, who was succeeded by violinist, composer, and conductor Moshe-Ruvn. In 1916, when Kaluszyn was occupied by Kaiser Wilhelm's army, the Jews and Germans lived together fairly well. The Germans invited the Kaluszyner *kapelye* to play for the soldiers, who were gloomy and needed music to cheer them up. Once it was ten P.M. and everyone had to be inside their locked homes. The whole *kapelye* stood on a veranda while Asher, who was the soloist, stood on a veranda across from them and played with great heart and affection Wieniaski's "Legend," accompanied by his *kapelye*. The German soldiers with rapt attention stood below and listened to Asher's violin. The entire event was mystical in the late night. Eventually the Kaluszyner *kapelye* went to Warsaw, where they continue to play even in the Warsaw ghetto. There they played with tears and sadness Gebirtig's "Our Town is Burning."

KALUSZYN (*ibid.*) "Rabbi Naftali's Big Wedding," by Shlomo Kuperhand, p. 286. (Yiddish)

Rabbi Naftali, a widower, needed some money from the Charity for Brides organization when he made his daughter's wedding. The groom arrived by train and was met by Jews on horseback dressed as Cossacks and Circassians. Then Moshele Aynbinder (the head of the Charity for Brides organization) sang a special song accompanied by the orchestra.

KAMIEN-KOSZYRSKI (P). *Sefer Ha-zikaron Le-kehilat Kamien Koszrski Ve-ha-seviva . . .* (Kamin Koshirsky Book; In Memory of the Jewish Community*). Eds.: A. A. Stein et al. Tel Aviv, Former Residents, Kamin Korshirsky and Surroundoings in Israel, 1965. (Hebrew, Yiddish) "A Wedding in Town," by Mina Solovaytshik, pp. 523–24. (Yiddish)

A week before the wedding, the *shames* and his assistant Chane went from house to house and invited people to the wedding. Food and clothes were also prepared that week. The *kapelye* came from Ratne since Kamien did not have any *klezmorim*. The *kapelye* was led by Itsl Klezmer, who played violin and jazz clarinet.

KAMIEN-KOSZRSKI (*ibid.*) "The Town's New *Toyre* Scroll," by Yaakov (Ben Moshe) Plot. pp. 537–38. (Yiddish)

Milke never graduated from midwife's school but nearly all the women in the town went to her when they were in labor, even on *Shabes*. Since she did not have any of her own children, she decided to commission a new *Toyre* scroll to be donated to the Stepiner synagogue. The scribe was a Stepiner *khasid*. When the *Toyre* was completed, the whole town celebrated with Milke. After sundown, the community paraded through the streets with the *Toyre* under the *khupe* while the *klezmorim* played and everyone danced and sang.

KAZIMIERZ (P). *Pinkas Kuzmir* (Kazimierz–Memorial Book*). Ed.: D. Shtokfish. Tel Aviv, Former residents of Kazimierz in Israel and the Diaspora, 1970. (Hebrew, Yiddish) (A drawing of a *klezmer* playing the violin with the town behind him) by Kh. Goldberg.

KLECK (P). *Pinkas Kleck* (Pinkas Kleck ; A Memorial to the Jewish Community of Klezk-Poland*). Ed.: E. S. Stein. Tel Aviv, Former Residents of Klezk in Israel, 1959. (Hebrew, Yiddish) (photo caption: The *Kapelye* (1928)), p. 59.

Asher Waynger (bass), Efrayim Shpilberg (violin), Yosef-Leyb Waynger (violin from Russia), Yozik Marshinkovsky (clarinet, Christian), and a Christian. (bagpipe)

KLOBUCKO (P). *Sefer Klobutsk; Mazkeret Kavod Le-kehila Ha-kodosha She-hushmed* (The Book of Klobucko; In Memory of a Martyred Community which was Destroyed). Tel Aviv, Former Residents of Klobucko in Israel, 1960. (Yiddish) "Klobucker Wedding Customs," by Barukh Shimkovitch, pp. 58–59.

There was no *kapelye* in Klobutsko, so either the Zaloshner or Vloyner *kapelyes* were hired for celebrations. The Vloyner *kapelye* had five persons; the Zaloshner only four, so the Zaloshner *kapelye* cost two less *rubles* than the other *kapelye*. In town, the Zaloshner *klezmorim* were known as *grimplers*.

KOBYLNIK (P). *Sefer Kobylnik* (Memorial Book of Kobilnik*). Ed.: I. Siegelman. Haifa, Committee of Former Residents of Kobilnik in Israel, 1967. (Hebrew, Yiddish) "The Wedding Ceremony," by Dvora Bakhman, pp. 53–56. (Hebrew)

At the wedding feast everyone ate, drank, and danced. The *kapelye* played everything from a *sherele* to a tango. The dancing lasted to dawn.

KOIDANOVO (P). *Koydenov; Zamlbukh tsum Ondenk fun di Koydenover Kedoyshim* (Koidanov; Memorial Volume of the Martyrs of Koidanov) Ed.: A. Raisen. New York, United Koidanover Assn., 1955. (Yiddish) "At Poor Weddings," pp. 98–103.

Lagboymer was very important for the *klezmers* because they could not play while it was *sfire*. When it was *Lagboymer* the klezmers, under the leadership of the violinist Kaldunya, often split up so they could play at two weddings and then divvy out the total earnings according to the usual percentage each *klezmer* received.

KOIDANOVO (*ibid.*) "A Guest in My Town Koydenov," by M. Slovin, pp. 198–207.
The author wrote about his trip back to his town in ten years after having left it
in 1917. He visited the Koydenover *shtibl* and found out that the rabbi's daughter
was getting married. Many *khasidim* came to the wedding.

KOLKY (R). *Fun Ash Aroysgerufn* (Summoned from the Ashes). By Daniel Kac. Warsaw, Czytelnik, Zydowski Instytut Historyczny w Polsce, 1983. (Yiddish) "The Transfor-
mation of a *Nign*," by Daniel Kac, pp. 69–77. (photo caption: *klezmer* Peysekh Shnitser)
Peysekh the *Klezmer* was the leader of the town's *kapelye*. He met his tragic fate
at the hands of the Nazis and Ukrainian police. He was shot while he stood
naked in front of an open grave and played the violin. Legend has it that farmers
have said they have heard violin music coming from the Jewish cemetery.

KOLOMYJA (P). *Pinkas Kolomey* (Memorial Book of Kolomey). Ed.: Sh. Bickel. New
York, 1957. (Yiddish) (poem) "Yosl Klezmer Who Saved the Town From a Fire," by Naftuli Gros, pp. 251–52.
One night a large blaze lit up Kolomyja. As the firemen worked to extinguish the
fire, Yosl Klezmer played his violin in the middle of the market square. He played
until the fire was out. Afterward he went to the tavern, played some more, and
drank the whole night.

KOLOMYJA (*ibid.*) "The Speech Is Affirmed at the Funeral—Thursday April 10th," by
Shlomo Bikl, pp. 262–63.
The author praised and spoke about his friend Naftuli Gros, who was a known
poet throughout Galicia. Gros's alter ego was the character Yosl Klezmer.

KORZEC (P). *Korets (Wolyn); Sefer Zikaron Le-kehilatenu Sh-ala Aleha Ha-koret* (The
Koretsm Book; In Memory of Our Community that is No More*). Ed.: E. Leoni. Tel
Aviv, Former Residents of Korets in Israel, 1959. (Hebrew, Yiddish) "This Is How Someone Destroyed Our Town," by Dov Bergel, pp. 338–44. (Hebrew)
Dov Bergel was one of the few survivors of the town and in his memoirs he
mentioned the people he knew who perished. Among the many was Aron, who
was a religious Jew. He was the son in-law of Peysekh Klezmer.

KOPRZYWNICA (P) *Sefer Pokshivnitsa* (Memorial Book of Koprzywnica). Ed.: E. Erlich.
Tel Aviv, Former Residents of Koprzywnica in Israel, 1971. (Hebrew, English, Yiddish)
"Two Weddings in the Town," by Samuel Kozinsky, pp. 37–44. (English)
The author remembered a large *khasidic* wedding in town where two *batkhonim*,
one for the bride and one for the groom, were hired, along with a *kapelyes* from
Apt and Clementov. In contrast to this wedding, there was the wedding of the poor
orphans. To pay for the poor wedding, the rich households were taxed to raise the
necessary funds. However, there was not enough money to hire a *kapelye*, so two

brothers played some violin while some young boys were given whistles and tin covers and asked to be the percussionists.

KOSOW (East Galicia). *Sefer Kosow-Galicia Ha-mizrahit* (Memorial Book of Kosow, Kosow Huculski). Ed.: E. Kresel. Tel Aviv, Former Residents of Kosow and Vicinity in Israel, 1964. (Hebrew, Yiddish) "Music in Kosow," pp. 138–39. (Hebrew)

Kosow was a musical town. The local *klezmers* were known to everyone, even those who lived as far away as Kolomyja. They played for the Jews and Poles. Many youth in the town studied violin with one of the *klezmers*, Yekl Khayim Nakhmanes.

KOSOW (P). *Megiles Kosow* (The Scroll of Kosow). By Yehoshua Gertner. Tel Aviv, Amkho, 1981. (Yiddish) "The Kosower Mountain Merchants," by Yakov (Buzia) Raykher, pp. 193–95.

Life in the Carpathian Mountains was exciting but difficult. There were Jews who traded in cattle and others who went to the synagogue to *bentch gomel* [Yid.: blessing said by Jews after escaping any kind of danger] after having survived a bear or wolf attack. The weddings were lively with *klezmer* music and a lot of drinking.

KOSTOPOL (P). *Sefer Kostopol; Hayeha U-mota Shel Kehila* (Kostopol; The Life and Death of a Community*). Ed.: A. Lerner. Tel Aviv, Former residents of Kostopol in Israel, 1967. (Hebrew) "Matchmakers and Weddings," pp. 43–44.

Sometimes there was a wedding in town without any festivities and *klezmorim*. This happened when the groom was getting remarried because his first wife died. Other times it was because the respective in-laws from both sides did not like each other. But most times, weddings were celebrated with *klezmorim*.

KOZIENIEC (P). *Sefer Zikaron Le-kehihat Kozieniec* (Memorial Book of the Community of Kozieniec). Ed.: B. Kaplinski. Tel Aviv, Former Residents of Kozieniec in Israel..., 1969. (Hebrew, Yiddish) "The *Kapelye*," p. 215. (Yiddish)

Itsik had three sons. He played the violin while his oldest son Shloymele played on several different instruments. Besides just playing in their father's *kapelye*, the sons also played in the Fireman's Orchestra. Shloymele was the conductor of the Fireman's Orchestra. The second son, Yekl, had a barber business. Meyer, the third son, was twelve years old and played the violin.

KOZIENIEC (*ibid.*) "Itsik Klezmer (Nodelman)," p. 253.

Itsik Klezmer and his sons had a good reputation in town. He was the leader and first violinist in the *kapelye*. Nearly everyone in his *kapelye* was a family member or relative.

There was Shmerl on bass, Meyer-Shakhnes on flute, Yisroel the Tall with the long trumpet, his son Elal on bass drum, and Khamia on violin. They played at Jewish weddings and celebrations, gentile landowners' weddings, in towns, and in villages. They were the only *kapelye* in the Kozieniecer district. When Itsik played for the *badekns,* the wives and men swayed their heads as they all cried. Itsik played with great strength and was an immense artist.

During the Holocaust, Itsik's son Shloyme worked in the gas chambers in Treblinka. He played with the orchestra at the entrance as people were being led into the gas chamber. While he stood, he saw his nine-year-old son was being led inside. Suddenly Shloyme grabbed his son and pulled him out of the line. An SS officer saw this, kicked the boy in the stomach, and laughed. At that very moment, Shloyme smashed his violin over the SS officer's head and marched with his only child into the gas chamber.

KOZIENIEC (*ibid.*) "The Gabe's Wife Celebrates a Wedding," pp. 283–284.

The *gabes'* wives helped the poor with food, clothing, and shoes. Sometimes they also helped to make a *shidukh.* Once they helped Shamey the blind water porter's daughter get married. They prepared everything for the wedding, including hiring the *klezmorim.*

KRZEMIENIEC (P). *Kremenits, Vishgorodek un Pitshayev; Yizker-Bukh* (Memorial Book of Krzemieniec). Ed.: P. Lerner. Buenos Aires, Former residents of Kremenits and Vicinity in Argentina, 1965. (Yiddish) "Jews Celebrate a Wedding," pp. 322–323.

A typical Jewish wedding in Krzemieniec had music provided by Hirsh the *Klezmer.* His *kapelye* consisted of his three sons, Moyshe on violin, Yankl on trumpet, Mikhl on bass, and a drummer who also played cymbal. The music included such dances as the *broyges tants,* polka, quadrille, and *sher.* The gentile neighbors were very curious and crowded around the windows of the house to watch the celebration.

KRZEMIENIEC (P). *Pinkas Kremenits; Sefer Zikaron* (Memorial Book of Krzemieniec). Ed. A. S. Stein. Tel Aviv, Former Residents of Krzemieniec in Israel, 1954. (Hebrew, Yiddish) "Hirsh Klezmer," by M. Karnits, p. 403. (Yiddish)

Hirsh Klezmer's real family name was Komediant. Children would call him Komediant, but the town's Jews called him Hirsh Klezmer. His whole family made up the *kapelye* except for the drummer, who was also the water porter.

KRZYWICZE (P). *Ner Tamid; Yizkor Le-Krivitch* (Kryvitsh Yizkor Book*). Ed.: Matityahu Bar-Ratzon. Tel Aviv, Krivitsh Societies in Israel and the Diaspora, 1977. (Hebrew, Yiddish) "Customs and Traditions—A Wedding in Town," by Yosef Shmir, pp. 121–23. (Yiddish)

A wedding in the town was a happy affair for everyone, Jews and Christians alike. Yankl Klezmer played *vulekhls,* quadrilles, and other dances. While this happened, Christian men lined up two rows of pails full with water. This signified that the newlyweds' life should be as full of happiness as these pails were with water. As people walked by, they threw coins in the pails.

KUROW (P). *Yizker-Bukh Koriv; Sefer Yizkor Matsevet Zikaron La-ayaratenu Koriv* (Yizkor Book in Memoriam of Our Hometown Kurow*). Ed.: M. Grossman. Tel Aviv, Former Residents of Kurow in Israel, 1955. (Yiddish) "The Grandfather Made a Quiet Wedding Without *Klezmorim*," by Tuvia Gutman, p. 726.

The bride was only thirteen years old and already a mother. The wedding was not an official act, was not publicized, and *klezmorim* were not hired. Only the bride's and groom's families and relatives were at the *khupe*.

KUROW (*ibid.*) "The Mother's Head and the *Mitsve-Tants*," by Tuvia Gutman, p. 727.

The morning of the wedding, the mother (of the bride) shaved her head and put a kerchief on her head. The next morning, she put on the traditional head covering. During the *mitsve tants*, everyone dance a *korohod* with the bride. Afterward, everyone sat down to a good meal.

KUTY (P). *Kitever Yizker-Bukh* (Kitever Memorial Book). Ed.: E. Husen. New York, Kitever Sick and Benevolent Society in New York, 1958. (Yiddish) "Family Celebrations with the Kitever Jews," pp. 60–62.

In the town there were many family celebrations. There was a *bris* for a baby boy and a festive meal for a baby girl. When there was a wedding, the whole town celebrated with music from the *klezmers* and a special *khupe nign* by the *shames*.

LACHOWICZE (P) *Lachowicze; Sefer Zikaron* (Memorial Book of Lachowicze). Ed.: J. Rubin. Tel Aviv, Assoc. of Former Residents of Lachowicze, 1959. (Hebrew, Yiddish) "*Reb* Itche the Painter, Limestone Miner, Shoemaker, Glazier, *Klezmer* and Gravestone Engraver," by Shimshl Bagin Kaprisin, pp. 155–56. (Yiddish)

Reb Itche was an old skinny man with a white beard, youthful eyes, and a constant smile across his face. No matter what he was doing, he was always prepared to stop and tell a joke, riddle, or funny story. Though *Reb* Itche the painter, limestone miner, shoemaker, glazier, *klezmer,* and gravestone engraver had a many professions, he still was poor.

LACHWA: (P) *Rishon La-Mered; Lachwa* (First Ghetto Revolt, Lachwa*). Eds.: H. A. Malachi et al. Jerusalem, The Encyclopedia of the Jewish Diaspora, 1957. (Hebrew, Yiddish) "Shlomo Muzikant," by A. Faynberg. p. 54. (Hebrew)

Shlomo Muzikant was born in Luniniec into a family of *klezmorim*. After high school he went into the Polish army and became an officer. That was unusual for a Jew at that time. Eventually he moved to Lachwa and became a teacher in the Polish public school, where he taught Judaism.

LASK (P). *Lask; Sefer Zikaron* (Memorial Book Lask). Ed.: Z. Tzurnamal. Tel Aviv, Assoc. of Former Residents of Lask in Israel, 1968. (Hebrew, English, Yiddish) "*Klezmorim,*" by Yekhil Naymen, pp. 96–97. (Yiddish)

Though Khayml Klezmer's whole life was spent in poverty, he and his fellow *shpilmans* enjoyed playing at weddings. At poor weddings Khayml and his *kapelye* played for free but were given all the whiskey they wanted to drink. Once the *kapelye* traveled to play for a gentile landowner. Along the way they all tragically died in a fire.

LASK (*ibid.*) "Short Stories," by Zav, pp. 106–113. (Yiddish)

In Lask there was no theatre or movie house, but there were some holy institutions like the big synagogue, a large *besmedresh,* two Gerer *shtiblekh,* one Alexander *shtibl,* and a row of buildings that housed several organizations including the Charity for Unmarried Women. Once Khayml Klezmer and his *kapelye* performed for an old maid and her groom who got married with help from the Charity for Unmarried Women.

LENIN (P) *Kehilat Lenin; Sefer Zikaron* (The Community of Lenin; Memorial Book). Ed.: M. Tamari. Tel Aviv, Former Residents of Lenin in Israel and in the USA, 1957. (Hebrew, Yiddish) "The Status of Culture in Our Town," by Avraham Yitskhok Slutski, pp. 253–55. (Yiddish)

There was a bookbinder from Pinsk who started a theatre troupe in the town. All winter they rehearsed, and on *Purim* they presented their plays. On *Purim* all the actors in their costumes and many of the townspeople including Christians paraded through the streets led by a *kapelye.* Once, after the play was performed, the police came looking for the director. They were suspicious that he might be a revolutionary.

LESKO (P). *Sefer Yizkor; Mukdash Le-yehudei Ha-ayarot She-nispu Ba-shoa Be-shanim 1939–44, Linsk, Istrik . . . Ve-ha-seviva* (Memorial Book; Dedicated to the Jews of Linsk, Istrik . . . and Vicinity Who Perished in the Holocaust in the Years 1939–44). Eds.: N. Mark and Sh. Friedlander. Tel Aviv, Book Committee of the "Libai" Organization, 1965. (Hebrew, Yiddish) "Town Celebrations," by Shimon Friedlander, pp. 161–66. (Yiddish)

Linsk was a small town and maintained some of its own customs. Customs like when the bride walked to the *khupe,* she carried two hard-boiled eggs in her bosom that meant she should breed well. The town had no *kapelye* so they brought in *klezmers* from Istriker. The day after the wedding the attendants checked the sheets of the newlyweds. If there was a problem there was blushing among the wives and gossip for a week. The wedding then was known as *treyf* and spoiled.

LESKO (*ibid.*) "Three Village Weddings," by Noson Mark, pp. 293–98. (Yiddish)

The author described three different weddings. At one wedding two people were shot dead. Two gentiles were caught and justice was meted out. This wedding was known as the "black wedding." Another wedding was of a Polish and Ruthenian Jewish couple. And the third wedding employed two *batkhonim*. One who spoke in Yiddish and the other in Polish.

LIPNO (P). *Sefer Lipno; B-hotsat Irgun Yotsay Lipno V-haseviva* (Memorial Book Lipno). Ed.: Shmuel Alon (Domb). Tel Aviv, 1988. (Yiddish) "A Wedding in the Shtetl," by Domzinski, pp. 156–58.

Two *shamesim* carried lanterns borrowed from the *khevre-kedishe* and led the bride and groom to the synagogue courtyard. The *kapelmayster* was a bum, but polite and played with a sweet and fascinating tone.

LOSICE (P). *Loshits; Lezeykher an Umgebrakhte Kehile* (Losice; In memory of a Jewish Community Exterminated by Nazi Murderers*). Ed.: M. Shener. Tel Aviv, Former Residents of Losice in Israel, 1963. (Hebrew, Yiddish) "Yokl Poyker," by Duvid Rozl, p. 188. (Yiddish)

Yokl was a small, solidly built man and his drum was nearly as big as he was. He and his two sons played for the town's poor weddings. Rich weddings brought in *klezmers* from Semiatycze or from Siedlice with Izikl *Batkhn* (from Siedlice). However, all the Losicers insisted that Yokl had to be the drummer at these weddings.

LUBLIN (P). *Lublin* (Lublin Volumn*). Eds.: N. Blumenthal and M. Korzen. Jerusalem, The Encyclopedia of the Jewish Diaspora, 1957. (Hebrew, Yiddish) "Yuntil Klezmer Plays for His People," by M. Sh. Gashori, pp. 591–98. (Hebrew)

Both Jews and non-Jews of Lublin and Warsaw remember Yuntil Klezmer's violin music, which he played at weddings and balls. His name was surrounded in stories and legends about his virtuosity. He was also a noted composer who wrote *batkhones, khazones,* and *klezmer* music. He was born in Mezritsh in 1827 and died in Warsaw in 1892.

LUNINIEC (P). *Yizkor Kehilot Luniniec/Kozhanhorodok* (Memorial Book of the Communities of Luniniec/Kozhanhorodok). Eds.: Y. Zeevi (Wilk) et al. Tel Aviv, Assoc. of Former Residents of Luniniec/Kozhanhorodok in Israel, 1952. (Hebrew, Yiddish) "*Klezmorim,*" by Moshe Akerman, pp. 204–205.

When there was a wedding or a *bris* in town, Yakov the *Klezmer* and his family *kapelye* played. Before the wedding they played either a polka or quadrille for the bride and her girlfriends. For the in-laws they played a *mazltov* dance and at the end of the *droshe-geshank* the *kapelye* received a percentage of the money that was given.

LUNINIEC (*ibid.*) "The *Klezmer,*" by Yosef Zabi, pp. 220–21. (photo of Yakov Muzikant and his wife.)

The local *klezmer kapelye* was the Muzikant family. The leader Moshe Leyb eventually immigrated to America, followed by several other *klezmorim.*

MAKOV-MAZOWIECKI (P). *Sefer Zikaron Le-kehilat Makow-Mazowiecki* (Memorial Book of the Community of Makow-Mazowiecki). Ed.: J. Brat. Tel Aviv, Former Residents of Makow-Mazowiecki in Israel, 1969. (Hebrew, Yiddish) "My Town Makov," by Doba Gudes Kalina, pp. 154–57. (photo caption: A group youths celebrating with members of the Makover *klezmorim.* Shlomo Modrikamyen and his son Zalmen Fodl in 1919) (Yiddish)

> *Shabes* was an idyllic time in the town. Nearly every Friday evening a bride was led to the *khupe* as the townspeople rejoiced. When the elderly rabbi finally decided to immigrate to Israel, the town saw him off with lowered heads and heavy hearts.

MAKOV-MAZOWIECKI (*ibid.*) "The Kosker Rebe Asks a *Klezmer* From Makov to Play at Jewish Weddings," by Yehuda Rozenthal, pp. 433–34. (Yiddish)

> The father of the *khasid Reb* Yehoshua Yakov from Makov was a simple Jew who made a living playing at weddings. The rules of the Makover Jewish community stated that no other *klezmer* could play at weddings in the town except for this *klezmer,* as it was his only means for a livelihood. When he died, the town made his son Yehoshua-Yekl the town *klezmer.* However, he could not decide if he should play at weddings where women danced, so he went to the Kosker *Rebe* for advice. The *Rebe* advised him that one needs to enjoy himself after much toil but this enjoyment should be engaged in a spiritual way. So Yehoshua-Yekl went home and played at the weddings with his face turned to the wall so he could not see the women dancing. When the Kosker *Rebe* was married to his second wife, the Makover *klezmer* played at the wedding.

MIELNICA (U). *Melnitza, Pelakh Volyn-Ukrainah Sefer Hantsaha 'edot Ve-zikaron Lekehilat Melnitza* (Melnitza; In memory of the Jewish Community*). Ed.: Joshua Lior. Tel Aviv, Melnitza Survivors in Israel and the Diaspora, 1994. (Hebrew, Yiddish, English) "Yidl With His Fiddle . . . ," p. 150. (Drawing of *klezmorim*) (Yiddish)

> This poem was about two *klezmers,* Yidl and Berl, who used to play Yiddish songs on the streets. "They were devoured by wild beasts. Now the streets are silent."

MIKULINCE (AH). *Mikulince; Sefer Yizkor* (Mikulince Yizkor Book*). Ed.: Haim Preshel. The Organization of Mikulincean Survivors in Israel and in the U.S.A., 1985. (Hebrew, English) "The *Klezmorim* of Mikulince," by Yitzhak Schwartz, pp. 192–94. (English)

> The *kapelye* was made up of all family members except for the clarinetist, drummer, another violinist, and a Pole who played accordion. Outsiders were never considered as equal partners. The *klezmorim* had to work two jobs to make ends meet. Once, after a hard day's work, Naftuli Bass fell asleep while playing his bass.

This angered the *kapelmayster,* who awoke Naftuli, who then immediately played at a faster tempo. This angered the *kapelmayster* even more.

MINSK (B). *Minsk; Ir Ve-em* (Minsk, Jewish Mother City; Memorial Anthology*). Ed.: Shlomo Even-Shushan. Israel, Minsk Society, Ghetto Fighters' House, ha-Kibbutz ha-Meuhad, 1975-v. 1. (Hebrew) "Melodies of the *Klezmer,*" by Tsvi Gordon, pp. 528–29.

At the end of the nineteenth century, all weddings in town were done according to the *Shulkhn Orekh* [Heb.: the collection of laws and prescriptions governing the life of an orthodox Jew]. The *klezmorim* played and the *batkhn* Eliakum Zunser sang songs. Itche Duvid was the leader of the *kapelye.* After the *bazetsn,* he played a *nign* he called *shteyger.* Sometimes, to entertain the guests, he played his violin behind his back without missing a note.

MINSK-MAZOWIECKI (P). *Sefer Minsk-Mazowiecki* (Minsk-Mazowiecki Memorial Book*). Ed.: Ephraim Shedletzky. Jerusalem, Minsk-Mazowiecki Societies in Israel and Abroad, 1977. (Hebrew, English, Yiddish) "Streets and People," by Yisroelke Himlfarb, pp. 328–33. (Yiddish)

After revisiting Minsk after World War II, the author remembered the differences in the town from his boyhood days. The local *klezmer* band, the son, and the clarinetist were all close friends of the author.

MIR (P). *Sefer Mir* (Memorial Book of Mir). Ed.: N. Blumenthal. Jerusalem, The Encyclopedia of the Jewish Diaspora, 1962. (Hebrew, English, Yiddish) "Childhood," by Mendl Tabashnik, pp. 537–38. (Yiddish)

The Polish government officials, priests, and other dignitaries came to visit the schools. The gentile schools purposely failed to tell the Jewish schools they had also been invited. Nevertheless, Mendl Tabashnik took matter in his own hands and led the Jewish children in exercises (to the accompaniment of the local *klezmer* orchestra), so they could have their own celebration.

MLYNOW-MARVITS (P). *Sefer Mlynow-Marvits* (Mlynow-Muravica Memorial Book*). Ed.: J. Sigelman. Haifa, Former Residfents of Mlynow-Muravica in Israel, 1970. (Yiddish, Hebrew) "A Wedding in Mlynow," by Sylvia Barditch-Goldberg, pp. 27–29.

There was a big *khasidic* wedding in town that hired two *kapelyes.* One came from Loystk and the other from Alyk. The Alyker *kapelye* was led by Lazar the *batkhn,* while Itsik the *Klezmer,* who was deaf, led the Loystker *kapelye* on the violin. When the bride and groom were each led to the *khupe,* the rabbi greeted them in Hebrew, Russian, and Yiddish. During the festivities the *kapelye* played for the guests a variety of dances such as *padespans, wingerkas,* quadrilles, *mazurkas, krakowiaks, freylekhs, a sher,* and a *lancer.*

MLYNOW-MARVITS (*ibid.*) "The Groom Is Coming," pp. 172–74. (Yiddish)

For several generations, the wedding customs of the town remained the same: *klez-morim* accompanied the groom into town, played for the *batkhn*, and accompanied the bride and groom to and from the *khupe*. The *batkhn* was responsible for entertaining everyone all evening. After the formal ceremony, the *klezmorim* played all night long.

MLYNOW-MARVITS (*ibid.*) "A Bris," p. 174. (Yiddish)

A *bris* was a special event even though it was smaller than a wedding celebration. The *klezmorim* were hired to help celebrate the occasion.

MLYNOW-MARVITS (*ibid.*) "Other Celebrations," pp. 175–77. (Yiddish)

When there was either a new *Sefer Toyre* or *Ornkoydesh* dedicated, it was celebrated with as much joy as a wedding. The *Sefer Toyre* was carried under a *khupe* while the Alyker *klezmers* played and people danced. The celebration lasted all day.

MOGIELNICA (P). *Sefer Mogielnica-Bledow* (Book of Mogielnica-Bledow). Ed.: Yisrael Zunder. Tel Aviv, Mogielnica and Bledow Society, 1972. (Hebrew, Yiddish) "*Klez-morim*," by Yisroel Zonder, pp. 321–23.

The *kapelye* consisted of the *kapelmayster*, who played the trumpet, his sons, and two nonfamily members. After they got paid, each *klezmer* got a percentage of the payment according to the hierarchy of the *kapelye*. The *kapelmayster* got the largest percentage; then the first and then the second violinist, etc. After the wedding, arguments in *klezmer-loshn* were heard from the *kapelmayster*'s home about who was paid what percentage and why.

NOVOSELITSA (L) *Novoselitsa.* Ed. Shalom Dorner. Tel Aviv. Irgun Yotse Novoselitsa be-Yisrael, 1983. (Hebrew, Yiddish) "The Jewish Orchestra That Almost Was," by R. Yehoshua Markus, p. 62. (photo of *kapelye*)

In the town the Gypsy band played at all the Jewish occasions. However, once they refused to play a request at a celebration. So some Jews who played in the Russian bands decided to put together their own *kapelye*. They went to play a wedding when the Gypsies heard this and begged them not to compete with their band. The Gypsies promised to behave, so the *kapelye* took pity on them and disbanded.

NOWY SACZ (P). *Sefer Sants* (The Book of the Jewish Community of Nowy Sacz*). Ed.: R. Mahler. New York, Former Residents of Sants in New York, 1970. (Hebrew, Yiddish) "The Beginning of Yiddish Theatre in Naysants," by Khayim Flaster, pp. 519–23.

In the summer of 1898, the Yiddish Theatre came to Naysants. The leader of the troupe was Vaynberger. He was a good actor and director and his wife, Mrs. Shvarts, had a beautiful voice. In this troupe were the famous Weisenfrainds from Lemberg, with their two small children. The boy was Phillip, who was a good character actor and comedian, and the daughter, Sala, was a soubrette with a good voice. Besides them there were twelve others in the troupe. While in Naysants, the two children learned with Rabbi Shabatay in *kheder*. Phillip later on became the famous actor known as Paul Muni.

Since Naysants did not have a theatre hall, the troupe performed in horse tables owned by Mordkhay Landau. Soon the stalls looked like a regular theatre. The stalls were thoroughly cleaned, limestone was put on the walls, the footbaths were filled with sand, and a stage and gallery were constructed from wood. The troupe made their own decorations with a red curtain that had a blue harp on it. They planned to present some Goldfaden operettas and other plays, but they first had to get this accepted by the censor, Meshulam Shater. And after him, it had to be accepted by one of the local Polish authorities.

The orchestra was composed of the local *klezmorim* that played at all the weddings. The leader of the orchestra was Lazar, who had a beard and *peyes* and wore a *kapote* and *shtrayml* on *Shabes*. It was his first time leading a theatre orchestra. There was also Nahum Goldberger on clarinet, his two brothers, Hershel on flute and Meyer on bass, and their children Wolf on the drum and cymbal, and Solke on trumpet. Then there was Mendl Tsimbler and his two sons, Zanvil and Leybush, plus Herman and Shmuel his brother. They all played wind instruments. Finaly there was Safir on violin and his two sons Yidl and Oskar. In this group Hirshele Folger played the violin as well.

Folger was not a known musician but a *Talmud* scholar. Some years later he played for *khasidic* weddings and made a living. In the beginning he was bashful to play in *Reb* Lazar's theatre orchestra because he was a religious Jew. He kept company with religious Jews and visited the *Rebe* on the Jewish holidays. But gradually he began to wear nice clothes and enjoyed playing in the orchestra. But he still stayed religious.

The theatre performed four times a week: Saturday night, Sunday, Tuesday, and Thursday. The crowd was always large and even included the Austrian officers who were serving their military duty in Naysants. They enjoyed hearing the *Daytshmerish*, which was spoken by the actors. They understood quite a bit. It was very difficult for these itinerant Yiddish theatre troupes to make a living. By the years 1904–05, the repertoire of these Yiddish theatre troupes included works by Sholom Aleichem, Dimov, Gordin, Gutzikov, and others. However, it was a constant struggle for them to earn enough just to pay their expenses, so many of the actors had several other jobs to help earn a living.

OLYKA (P). *Pinkas Ha-kehila Olyka; Sefer Yizkor* (Memorial Book of the Community of Olyka). Ed.: Natan Livneh. Tel Aviv, Olyka Society. 1972. (Hebrew, Yiddish) "*Klezmer*," pp. 206–07. (Hebrew)

The local *klezmer kapelye* was known for its expertise and hired by gentiles as well as by Jews to play for all kinds of celebrations.

OPATOW (P). *Apt (Opatow); Sefer Zikaron Le-ir Va-em Be-Yisrael* (Apt; A Town Which Does Not Exist Anymore*) Ed.: Z. Yasheev. Tel Aviv, The Apt Organization in Israel, USA, Canada and Brazil, 1966. (Hebrew, English, Yiddish) "A Black Wedding in Apt," by Pinye Titl, pp. 106–07. (Yiddish)

There was a terrible cholera epidemic and the local rabbis decided to end the scourge with a "black wedding." They arranged for two orphans to be married in the local cemetery. The town turned out to celebrate as the *klezmorim* and the *batkhn* urged the guests to give gifts to the newlyweds.

OPATOW (*ibid.*) "A Wedding," By Eliezer Glat, p. 108. (Yiddish)

Weddings in the town were attended by all. They were tragicomedic events, especially when Aryesh *Klezmer* led the *kapelye* in a *nign* or *sher* and everyone cried.

OPATOW (*ibid.*) "The Economic Structure Among Jewish Workers—*Klezmers*," p. 133. (Yiddish)

The *kapelye*s in Opatow were the Lustig and Lewak families.

OPATOW (*ibid.*) "*Klezmorim*," Pinye Titl, pp. 137–39. (photos of Khayimke Klezmer and Arish Lustik) (Yiddish)

Khayimke Klezmer lived in the 1880s. He was a talented musician and was the leader of the *kapelye*. He and his son were called "the Lewaks." His son Moshele was a very good player and later on played second violin in the Lodzer philharmonic. His second son, Yakov-Simkhe, finished the conservatory studying the cello. Later on he played in the Warsaw symphony orchestra. From all these capable musicians, there was Aryesh Lustik.

Lustik returned from serving in the Czar's army in the 1880s. When he was in the army, his commander asked who wanted to be in the music corps. Since Aryesh loved music, he joined. The commanding officer (who had the rank of surveyor) told him to try the clarinet. Slowly he brought it to his lips and blew; a note came out. After a few more toots his commanding officer was pleased and told him to continue. Later on he learned the fingerings and soon became one of the best clarinetists in the music corps.

Yosef Lustik was Aryesh's older brother and Khayimke's brother-in-law. He was a talented violinist with good technique and played in the *kapelye* as well. But Aryesh who learned the clarinet was also a violinist and his specialty was Jewish music. After Khayimke's death he became the first violinist in the *kapelye*.

At a wedding when it was time for the *badekn*, Aryesh listened to the *batkhn*'s song "*Y'hi Ratson*" [Heb.: let it be his will] and knew exactly what to play. His violin spoke words that went to God in heaven and pleaded with him that he should watch over the bride as she went into her new life. Everyone had some tears in their eyes. Then, after the *khupe,* Aryesh stood by the wedding table while people were being served and began to play some more, sliding his hand back and forth on the long strings.

Another *klezmer* that played the violin was Meyer Wolf, Khayimke's son. He was the last of the Lewaks to play in the *kapelye.* He played with his eyes closed and often kept playing when the *kapelye* was quiet. When Aryesh played, his violin spoke of Jewish experiences. He did not play at all the Jewish weddings, so when he did, many people gathered outside the windows to listen and watch him.

During the winter the modern Yiddish theatre in Warsaw was closed, so some of the actors came to Apt and created a Yiddish theatre. The actors were amazed by Aryesh's musical talents. When he led the *kapelye* from the stage, they were like any Yiddish theatre, whether it was in Warsaw or Lodz.

There was a tradition in Apt to bless the new moon every month and bless the sun every twenty-eight years. In 1925, eight days before Passover, at six A.M., everyone gathered for the blessing of the sun ceremony. The rabbis had received permission to gather and greet the sunrise with music. People waited for Aryesh because they knew he had written a new melody for this special occasion. Then all of a sudden everyone heard this beautiful march. A thousand Jews gathered around the synagogue. At five A.M. the chief rabbi, Rabbi Khayim Yosef, dressed in his holiday clothes with a *shtrayml,* came out along with the other rabbis. The *klezmorim* played the Polish national anthem, then the *Hatikvah.* Then the public walked to the music along the wide street to the open field near the *shokhtim* houses. There Rabbi Khayim Yosef pointed his arm towards the east where the first rays of the sun were appearing. Everyone waited for the sign from the rabbi that told them they could now bless the sun. Then simultaneously the *klezmorim* took out the music that Aryesh composed and began to play. This melody written just for the blessing of the sun was talked about and remembered for a long time.

When the First of May came, the Jewish Workers Party prepared for demonstrations. The whole *kapelye* came with their wind instruments. They marched to the middle of the square, played the "Marsellaise" and then the "Internationale" to celebrate the workers' holiday. By the union house stood Moyshe Miler's house. Moyshe, a member of the Bund, stood on his balcony and gave a speech. At the end of it he yelled: "Long live the First of May!" Then Aryesh gave a sign to the *kapelye* by putting his clarinet to his mouth to play. Meyer Wolf stood with his violin under his chin with the peak of his cap down over his closed eyes while he took a nap. Then all of a sudden there was this was a loud shout, "Death to the bourgeoisie!" from the huge crowd below. Immediately Meyer Wolf woke up and began to play.

Aryesh enjoyed all kinds of music, so he often went to the home of the city's organist, who was also a singer and pianist, to play music. Aryesh played with him the necessary cultured music in town; thus the doors of all the distinguished Christian manors were always opened to Aryesh. From time to time a landowner's carriage came and picked up Aryesh, who was going to play at a Christian party. When there was a Christian ball in the city or at the manor, Aryesh brought his whole *kapelye.*

Aryesh gave his whole life to music and had a big heart. When other *klezmorim* would just shrug their shoulders when asked to play at a poor wedding, Aryesh would play for free. At these weddings Aryesh took his son or his son-in-law or his brother-in-law Leybush Poyker and made the wedding beautiful.

In 1925, there was a mining accident that buried five Polish miners. The mine was owned by a Jewish contractor, which gave the farmers in the villages an opportunity to go after the Jews. They proclaimed that "a Jewish sand contractor killed our brothers. Poles, your conscience cannot be calm. We must expel these parasites from our Polish land!" For three days the farmers came to town to visit the two who died as they lay in their coffins. The Jewish community knew that nothing good would come of it if the Poles came. Quickly some friends went to Aryesh to see if he could organize something with the church and the priests so that they would calm down this terrible situation and prevent any riot from taking place. The priests looked at each other and nodded in agreement that they would do something. Aryesh and his *kapelye* came and played a variety of tunes appropriate for the mourning of the two miners who were killed.

Off the wide main street lived the Lustik family. One always could hear music coming from their home. So a part of the street was called the "*klezmorim* street." In Aryesh's later years he played more of his own compositions. Of his eight children, all five of the boys were musicians, with Yankl and Leybush becoming the most known. One daughter, Tobele, became a skilled musician as well. Duvid, the only son who lived in Toronto, was the last of the Lustiks to play the violin. Duvid's son (Aryesh's grandson) Nosn played the piano.

OPATOW (*ibid.*) "Khayim Borekh Batkhn," by Sh. Mitsmakher, pp. 141–42.

In Kielce and the surrounding towns the most known *batkhonim* were: Yankl Krakowski, Yosl Keltser, Tuvia Marshalik from Staczow, and Khayim-Borekh, who came from a family of artists. Between the *batkhonim* and the *klezmorim,* the town was well served at wedding celebrations.

OSTROG (P). *Pinkas Ostra; Sefer Zikaron*...(Ostrog-Wolyn; In Memory of the Jewish Community*). Ed.: H. Ayalon-Baranick. Tel Aviv, Association of Former Residents of Ostrog, 1960. (Hebrew, Yiddish) "A Wedding in Town," by Mikhl Grines, pp. 359–66.

After the wedding meal, everyone danced. Each dance had a designated price. If the hall had dance leaders, they would not allow the *klezmers* to be paid separately. They led everyone in a *khasidishe rikudl* or a something else. However, the *klezmorim* would ask for a better price "under the table" for the dance tunes they played. The dance leaders were competition for the *klezmorim* and both performed until daybreak.

OSTROLENKA (P). *Sefer Kehilat Ostrolenka* (Book of Kehilat Ostrolenka*). Ed.: Y. Ivri. Tel Aviv, Association of Former Residents of Ostrolenka, 1963. (Hebrew, Yiddish) "*Klezmorim,*" by Yitzhak Ivri, pp. 92–93. (Yiddish)

In this religious town and the neighboring towns, *klezmorim* were able to make a good living. They played for weddings, where the local belief was, "Life went like the playing of the music." However, the wealthy families hired *klezmorim* from Łomża.

OSTROW MAZOWIECKA (P). *Ostrow Mazowiecka* by Judah Loeb Levin, Jerusalem-Tel Aviv, Yad Yahadut Polin, 1966. (Hebrew) "A Wedding in the City," by Mikhl Grins, pp. 299–303. (Hebrew)

At weddings children gathered around the *klezmorim* while they tuned. When the *klezmorim* were not looking, the children loved to play the instruments without getting caught. The *klezmorim* played an assortment of dances, including one called a *tush*.

OSTROW-MAZOWIECKA (P). *Sefer Ha-Zikaron Le-kehilat Ostrov-Mazovyetsk* (Memorial Book of the Community of Ostrow-Mazowiecka). Ed.: A. Margolit. Tel Aviv, Association of Former Residents of Ostrow-Mazowieck, 1960. (Hebrew, Yiddish) "*Klezmorim,*" pp. 373–74. (Yiddish) (photo of Shlomo Klezmer)

The *klezmorim* in town were poor but "purified" because their hearts and souls were full of music. They played for all the Jewish celebrations, as well as for balls held by the gentile landowners, who loved Jewish music and Jewish fish.

OSTROW-MAZOWIECKA (*ibid.*) "The Wedding Canopy," pp. 379–80 (drawing of a wedding with *klezmorim*) (Yiddish)

For a winter wedding celebration, the *klezmorim* played joyous music while the people, in all their finery, danced and played in the snow. The *batkhn* entertained as well.

OSZMIANA (P). *Sefer Zikaron Le-kehilat Oshmana* (Oshmana Memorial Book*) Ed.: M. Gelbart. Tel Aviv, Oshmaner Organization in Israel and the Oshmaner Society in the USA, 1969. (Hebrew, English, Yiddish) (photo caption: The production of Shulamis led by the drama circle. Photo includes the actors and *klezmorim*) p. 60e. (Hebrew, Yiddish)

OTWOCK (P). *Yizker-bukh; Otvotsk-Kartshev* (Memorial Book of Otvotsk and Kartshev*). Ed.: Sh. Kanc. Tel Aviv, Former Residents of Otvotsk-Kartshev, 1968. (Hebrew, Yiddish) "Batkhonim and Klezmorim," pp. 107–110. (Yiddish)

Two *batkhonim* and the *klezmorim* gave beauty and joy to Jewish weddings in Otwock.

OTWOCK (*ibid.*) "A Wedding in Otwock," by Yoel Mastboym, pp. 677–82. (Yiddish)

The news that the Czar was dead and that Piltzuki, who was sitting in prison, was released caused an outbreak of celebration with music in town. Later on a local man who was an orphan got married with the help of a gentile woman friend, who arranged everything. The townspeople laughed at the absurdity of the groom's nervousness, as he was not a young man.

OZAROW (P). *Memories of Ozarow; A Little Jewish Town That...* Ed.: Hillel Adler and Translator William Fraiberg. Montreal, Ozarow Press, 1997. (English) "The Musicians," by H. Czechowski, pp. 84–86.

When the *klezmorim* were not playing music then they worked as hairdressers, healers, and sometimes as tailors. One of the violinists was also the *batkhn,* who was married three times. Another *klezmer,* Moshe Lustig, owned a beauty salon with his wife. He had a radio, which was rare in town, and connected it to a speaker so passersby could hear the music. That same radio announced when Germany attacked Poland.

OZAROW (*ibid.*) "A Marriage in Lasocin," pp. 144–45. (English)

Two old friends decided to have their children marry each other. The bride came from the village and the groom from town. The wedding took place in Lasocin complete with a *batkhn* and *klezmorim.* The *kapelye* consisted of two violins and an accordion.

PARYSOW (P). *Sefer Porisov* (Parysow; A Memorial to the Jewish Community of Parysow, Poland*). Ed.: Y. Granastein. Tel Aviv, Former Residents of Parysow in Israel, 1971. (Hebrew, Yiddish) "A Wedding in Town," by Melekh Poskinski, pp. 152–53. (Yiddish)

In Parysow there were different wedding customs that were observed. One included hiring a gentile called the "red *sheygets,*" who led the mixed dances.

PARYSOW (*ibid.*) "A Wedding in Town," by Aron Zaygelman, pp. 178–180. (Hebrew)

Hirshele Sobiner from Sobin was a sought-after bandleader, who was known even to the Polish Congress. One had to arrange a wedding far in advance to hire him.

PINSK (P). *Pinsk Sefer Edut Ve-zikaron Le-kehilat Pinsk-Karlin* (Pinsk*). Ed.: N. Tamir (Mirski). Tel Aviv, Former Residents of Pinsk-Karlin in Israel, 1966–77. 3 Vols. (Hebrew, Yiddish) "The *Purim* Actors," by L. Morgontoy, pp. 235–36.

The *shtetlekh* loved to celebrate *Purim*. During *Purim,* actors and *klezmorim* made a good living going from house to house, despite the town's poverty.

PODHAJCE (P). *Sefer Podhajce; Dos Religize un Gezelshaftlekhe Lebn* (Podhajce Book; This Religious and Community Life). Ed.: M. S. Geshuri. Tel Aviv, Podhajce Society, 1972. (Hebrew, English, Yiddish) "The Religious and Community Life," by M. Pomerants, pp. 168–70. (Yiddish)

In Podhajce, weddings were held in the halls of the hotels. Sometimes the Faust *kapelye* was brought in from Rohatyn to play.

PRUZANA (P). *Pinkas Me-hamesh Kehilot Harevot...* (Memorial Book of Five Destroyed Communities...) Ed.: M/ W. Bernstein. Buenos Aires, Former Residents of Pruzana..., 1958. (Yiddish) "A Wedding in Malch," pp. 482–83.

There were many weddings in Pruzana. Sometimes the *klezmorim* from Kartuz-Bereza were hired to play at them. Once there was a lavish wedding for the daughter of a wealthy Jew. He was eventually forced by the Czar to sell his vast estate, because no Jews were allowed to own forests.

PRUSZKOW (P). *Sefer Pruszkow, Nadzin Ve-ha-seviva* (Memorial Book of Pruszkow, Nadzin and Vicinity). Ed.: D. Brodsky. Tel Aviv, Former Residents of Pruszkow in Israel, 1967. (Hebrew, Yiddish) "Berl Dukhnitser (Birnboym)," by Ruveyn Postolski, pp. 181–186. (Yiddish)

A wealthy Jewish landowner's most prized possession was the watch given to him at his wedding by his father-in-law. At weddings, he listened to the *klezmorim* and rubbed his watch.

PRZEDBORZ (P). *Sefer Yizkor Le-kehilat Radomsk Ve-ha-seviva* (Memorial Book of the Community of Radomsk and Vicinity). Ed.: L. Losh. Tel Aviv, Former Residents of Radom..., 1967. (Hebrew, Yiddish) "The *Purim* Ball," pp. 183–84. (Yiddish)

When there was a *Purim* ball in the town, the musicians came from Radomsk. At the ball the young people from many different organizations including *Poale-Tsion, Betar,* and *Tsair Mizrakhi* attended. Once some Polish youth came to the party who became drunk and tried to dance with the Jewish girls. Soon there was a big fight and they were eventually expelled from the ball. The following *Purim* ball these same Polish youth were not allowed in. That night when some of the young Jews walked home, they were hit over their heads with irons. But this time these Polish youth were quite astonished when some Jewish youths from Lodz came out of the ball and defended themselves.

PRZEDBORZ (*ibid.*) "Gershon Klezmer," pp. 219–20. (Yiddish)

Gershon Klezmer and his sons made up the *kapelye* with Kopl Blokhotzsh, who played bass. None of them were trained musicians.

PRZEDBORZ (*ibid.*) "A Wedding in Przedborz," by Sara Hamer-Jaklin, pp. 245–52. (Yiddish)

The author went to her cousin's wedding when she was eleven years old and remembered everything in sharp detail.

PRZEDBORZ (*ibid.*) "The Tragic Wedding," by Malke Alfisher-Vishinsk, pp. 285–87. (Yiddish)

On the day of the wedding the future in-laws came to meet the bride. The groom's mother had never seen her and did not know she was a hunchback. She decided that she and her son would go home. But the groom refused and married his intended mate. That night, while everyone danced, the mother, who was still upset, stayed outside in the cold air. Shortly after she became ill and died.

PRZYTYK (P). *Sefer Przytyk.* Ed.: David Shtokfish. Tel Aviv, Przytyk Societies in Israel, France and the USA, 1973. (Hebrew, Yiddish) "Portraits and Events," by Hillel Shtross-man, pp. 105–09. (Yiddish)

Every wedding processional was accompanied by music and a hundred people carrying lit torches.

PRZYTYK (*ibid.*) "A Wedding in Town," by Duvid Zitni Boymlgrin, pp. 146–50. (Yiddish)

The author described the wedding of *Reb* Yekl the wealthy furrier's daughter.

PULAWY (P). *Yizker-bukh Pulawy* (In Memoriam—The City of Pulawy*). Ed.: M. W. Bernstein. New York, Pulawer Yiskor Book Committee, 1964. (Yiddish) "Nosn the *Klezmer*," by Moyshe Rubenshteyn, p. 99.

Nosn the *Klezmer* had such a patriarchal mien. He was indispensable at weddings, even though he was not a very good musician.

PULTUSK (P). *Pultusk; Sefer Zikaron* (Pultusk Memorial Book). Ed.: Yitzhak Ivri. Tel Aviv, Pultusk Society, 1971. (Hebrew, Yiddish) "My Musical Memories," by Dan Aronovitsh, pp. 263–67. (Yiddish) (music examples)

I was born in 1909 in a small town near Mlawa. When I was four, my father Tsvi Aronovitsh and his family moved to Pulusk because he was hired as the town's *khazn-shokhet*. My father formed a large choir in which I sang that accompanied him when he prayed on *Shabes.*

My father was my first music teacher. During the long winter nights I sat on one side of my father and my younger brother Wolf on the other side as he taught us to read music notes. If my brother or I made a mistake when telling my father what note it was, he hit us. I cried so loud that our neighbor could hear.

When I was *Bar-Mitsve,* my father took me to Tuvia Bzshezhener. He took out of a closet a violin and gave it to me as a present for my *Bar-Mitsve.* The first lessons were from my father from the book "The King's Methods." Soon after he took me to Leybke Klezmer, who then became my teacher. Leybke Klezmer gave me my first piano lessons and taught me the scales. In his house he had a "Winged Clavier" (Forte-Piano). Once during a lesson he gave me a gift of one of his own compositions. It had the Jewish nuances and spirit. He sat there and wrote it with his shaking hands. Regretfully I lost the music. At weddings and other celebrations, Leybke would play with his son, who was deaf. Everyone wondered how his deaf son was able to become so musical.

In the synagogue my father led his twenty-two-member choir with four instrumentalists. The *klezmorim* were Leybke Skarzhepitse on first violin, his deaf son on contrabass, Leybke's grandson on flute, and on second violin it would either be Leybke's son-in-law or other grandson. Leybke's grandchildren became known musicians in Warsaw playing light music at cafés. One of the grandsons, Henekh Skarzhepitse, composed for the revue called Black and White staged at the Warsaw theatre Nowósci. The most famous piece from the revue was the fox-trot "Spring Spring."

The second performance that was with choir and orchestra was when a new *Toyre* had just been written for my father's synagogue. My father had a good relationship with his fellow artists. Leybke used to play his violin at my father's *Khanike* concerts and other religious presentations, like the dedication of a new building.

When I went for my violin lesson, I carried my violin under my housecoat so no one would know I was learning to play. Later on I went to another teacher who came from Odessa. When he came to Pultusk, he played in the movie theatre with Leybke's daughter, who played the piano. Eventually I went to the music conservatory in Warsaw and studied at the teachers' seminary at the same time. I graduated the conservatory in singing and composition. I was in France fighting in the underground in the winter of 1944 when I heard the terrible news on the radio, broadcast from London, about the murder of the Jews in Poland by the Nazis. I was immediately moved to create my *Kol-Nidre* for orchestra and choir. I never forgot my years growing up in Pultusk and my father's words: "A man must achieve something in his life."

PULTUSK (*ibid.*) "Leybke Skarzhepitse," by Raphael Moshe Shakh, pp. 340–41. (Yiddish)

> Leybke Klezmer was such a virtuoso that he was offered to play in the Warsaw opera orchestra. But he refused and said "I won't be able to eat any *tsholnt* then." When the famous *khazn* Gershon Sirotta and his daughter visited Pultusk, they were guests of Leybke's. When Menakhem Kipnis [famous musicologist and collector of Yiddish folksong—y.s.] heard Leybke play, he wrote an enthusiastic article in the Warsaw newspaper *Haynt* [Yid.: today] about him.

PUKSZIBNICE (P). *Sefer Pokshivnitsa* (Memorial Book of Koprzywnica). Ed.: E. Erlich. Tel Aviv, Former Residents of Koprzywnica in Israel, 1971. (Hebrew, Yiddish) "A Wedding in Town," by Bluma Gershteyn, pp. 100–02. (Yiddish)

Royanen Marshalik, the town's *batkhn,* was always hired to entertain at the weddings.

RACHOV-ANNOPOL (P). *Rachov-Annopol; Pirkei Edut Ve-zikaron* (Rachov-Annopol; Testimony and Remembrance*). Ed.: Shmuel Nitzan. Israel, Rachov/Annopol and Surrounding Region Society, 1978. (Hebrew, English, Yiddish) "A Wedding in Town," by Yekhil Mekler, pp. 369–70. (Yiddish)

The *klezmorim* were brought from Azsharow for a wedding. It was the custom to play for the scholars in the *besmedresh* before the ceremony. The musicians refused to play for them, which offended the Talmud scholars. They then threatened to break the *klezmorim*'s violins with the drum. The *kapelye* played for the young men in the *besmedresh.*

RACIAZ (P). *Galed Le-kehilat Raciaz* (Memorial Book of the Community of Racionz*). Ed.: E. Tsoref. Tel Aviv, Former Residents of Raciaz, 1965. (Hebrew, Yiddish, English) "A Wedding in Raciaz," by Avraham Yosef Klayner, pp. 42–43. (Hebrew)

The local *kapelye* consisted of two Jews and a gentile. The gentile was a very good violinist and the town's violin teacher for all the rich children.

RADOMSKO (P). *Sefer Yizkor Le-kehilat Radomsk Ve-ha-seviva* (Memorial Book of the Community of Radomsk and Vicinity). Ed.: L. Losh. Tel Aviv, Former Residents of Radomsk…, 1967. (Hebrew, Yiddish) "A Wedding in the Cemetery," by Zev Sobotowski, pp. 154–55.

In the spring of 1916 during World War I there was a typhus epidemic in the town. Finally, after trying everything, the town's rabbi decided to marry an orphan girl to the son of the town's water porter with the wedding ceremony held in the cemetery.

RADOMYSL WIELKI (P). *Radomysl Rabati Ve-ha-seviva; Sefer Yizkor* (Radomysl Wielki and Neighborhood; Memorial Book*) Eds.: H. Harshoshanim et al. Tel Aviv, Former Residents of Radomysl and Surroundings in Israel, 1965. (Hebrew, Yiddish, English) "My Wedding," by Yosef Margoshes, pp. 461–63. (Yiddish)

The author recounts her wedding festivities. Her father-in-law, a wealthy and generous man, held three wedding feasts: The first was for the poor, the second for the town's officials, and the third was on the wedding day for 250 wealthy friends and family members.

RADZIN (P). *Sefer Radzin* (The Book of Radzin). Ed.: I. Siegelman. Tel Aviv, Council of Former Residents of Radzin (Podolsky) in Israel, 1957. (Hebrew, Yiddish) "Musicians—A Radziner Motif," by Moshe Apelboym, p. 132. (Yiddish)

An illustration of two Jewish musicians playing the mandolin and violin, by Moshe Apelboym (1886–1931).

RADZYMIN (P). *Sefer Zikaron Le-kehilat Radzymin* (Le Livre Du Souvenir De La Juive De Radzymin*). Ed.: Gershon Hel. Tel Aviv, The Encyclopedia of the Jewish Diaspora, 1975. (Hebrew, Yiddish, French) "A Wedding in Town!" by Helen Milgrom, pp. 130–31. (Yiddish)

The author remembered traveling from Warsaw to Radzymin to celebrate the finishing of a new *Toyre*. The town celebrated as the *Toyre* was led under the *khupe*, led by *klezmorim*.

RADZYMIN (*ibid.*) "Khayim Shepsl Kaluski," pp. 139–40. (Yiddish)

The Poles established a school for Jewish children. Their teacher, Khayim-Shepsl Kaluski, loved music. This love came from his family's *klezmer* roots. During singing studies he accompanied himself and the children on the violin. His bass voice drowned out all the voices of the children. Eventually, the Polish ministry of education made Khayim-Shepsl leave the community state elementary school because they said he did not have the proper certificate from a teacher's seminary. He died in Treblinka with the rest of the Jews from Radzymin.

ROHATYN (P). *Kehilar Rohatyn Ve-ha-seviva* (Rohatyn; The History of a Jewish Community*). Ed.: M. Amihai. Tel Aviv, Former Residents of Rohatyn in Israel, 1962. (Hebrew, Yiddish, English) "Rohatyner Ways," by Dr. Yitskhak Leventer, p. 91. (Yiddish)

Every Jew in Rohatyn knew of the friendly Faust family *kapelye*. They were: Moyshe, Duvid, Itsik-Hirsh, Mordkhay-Shmuel, and Yakov.

ROHATYN (*ibid.*) "The Kapelye in Our Town," by Yehoshua Shpigel, p. 140. (photo caption: Sitting: Moyshe Faust, Wolf Tsimbler (Shwarts). Standing left to right: Morkhay-Shmuel Faust, Mendl Bas, Yankl Faust, Alter Marshalik, Itsik Hirsh Faust, and Duvid Faust) (Hebrew)

ROWNE (P). *Rowne; Sefer Zikaron* (Rowno; A Memorial to the Jewish Community of Rowno, Wolyn*). Ed.: A. Avitachi. Tel Aviv, "Yaljut-Wolyn"—Former Residents of Rowno in Israel, 1956. (Hebrew) "*Klezmorim* and Weddings," by Shmuel Yisraeli, pp. 338–39.

The two main *klezmer* families in Rowno were the Krasnes and Skolnes. They were like one big family. They married among themselves, worried about each other, and spoke *klezmer loshn* together at weddings. *Reb* Zindl was the leader of the two and died while playing his violin at a wedding.

ROZWADOW (P). *Sefer Yizkor Rozwadow Ve-ha-seviva* (Rozwadow Memorial Book*).

Ed.: N. Blumental. Jerusalem, Former Residents of Rozwadow in Israel..., 1968. (Hebrew, Yiddish, English) "Playing on *Purim* in Grandfather's House," by Menakhem Izik, p. 56. (Yiddish)

The author remembered *Purim* celebrations with *klezmer* music at his grandfather's house.

ROZYSZCZE (P). *Rozyszcze Ayarati* (Rozyszcze My Old Home*). Ed.: Gershon Zik. Tel Aviv, Rozyszcze Societies in Israel, the United States, Canada, Brazil and Argentina, 1976. (Hebrew, Yiddish, English) "A Wedding in Rozhishch," pp. 22–23. (photo caption: The Rozhishcher *Kapelye* before World War I) (English)

The wedding preparations began six months before the date of the wedding. Then the week before the *khupe,* the dowry was negotiated. Finally came the celebration with the family, guests, and *kapelye.*

ROZYSZCZE (*ibid.*) "The Klezmer," by Yosef Kriva, pp. 79–80. (photos and captions: *Reb* Moyshe Beckerman the *Kapelmayster,* the Roziezer *Kapelye,* Yosef Hofn, Violinist, a Banquet with Berl Klezmer, and a painting of three *klezmorim*) (Yiddish)

In Boyrekh (Beckerman) Klezmer's *kapelye* there was Moyshe, who played the violin. Moyshe was blessed with many beautiful daughters but unfortunately he had no dowry for them. Then one day he befriended the coachman's son Berele, who was an orphan without a mother. When Berele was thirteen years old, he gave an oath to Moyshe that he would marry his daughter Dvorele. When it was time for the wedding, Moyshe was seriously sick, so the *khupe* was by his bedside.

RUDKI (P). *Rudki; Sefger Yizkor Le-Yehudei Rudki Ve-ha-seviva* (Rudki Memorial Book: The Jews of Rudki and Vicinity*). Ed.: Joseph Chrust. Israel, Rudki Society, 1978. (Hebrew, Yiddish, English) "Weddings," p. 221. (Hebrew)

At weddings it was customary for the *batkhn* to divide his program into two parts, one before the *khupe* and one after. After the *khupe* and the meal, the *klezmorim* played many different dance melodies including the Charleston, local waltzes, the Vienna waltz, fox-trots, and the tango.

RUDKI (*ibid.*) "The Music in Rudki," p. 221. (Hebrew)

The best *kapelye* was led by Moyshe Durkhshnit. Moyshe had four daughters and his oldest played percussion in the *kapelye.* Moyshe's *kapelye* also accompanied the silent films in the movie house in town.

RYKI (P). *Yizker-bukh Tsum Fareybikn Dem Ondenk Fun Der Khorev-Gevorener Yidisher Kehile Ryki* (A Memorial to the Community of Ryki, Poland*). Ed.: Shimon Kanc. Tel Aviv, Ryki Societies in Israel, Canada, Los Angeles, France and Brazil, (photo caption: Moyshe Yudl Walman and his Family on the Day they Leave for Israel Entertained by Shlomo the *Klezmer*), p. 13.

RYKI (*ibid.*) "The Wedding of Hirsh Leyb," pp. 236–37. (Hebrew)

At Hirsh Leyb's wedding, the *klezmer's khevre* included Dudl the *batkhn,* his son Fishl on violin, and Butshele Droshkes on cello. After the ceremony, Hirsh and his wife went to *yikhed,* where some of his friends played a joke on him by putting water and straw on the bed. When they came out, everyone could tell by looking at them and their clothes what had transpired.

RYKI (*ibid.*) "Weddings," by Moyshe Taytboym, pp. 322–23. (Yiddish)

Dudl *Batkhn* was a *batkhn* and the leader of the *kapelye* that consisted of violin, two second violins, bass, and his son on trumpet.

SEMIATYCZE (P). *Kehilat* Semiatycze (The Community of Semiatich*). Ed.: E. Tash. (TurShalom). Tel Aviv, Assoc. of Former Residents of Semiatich in Israel and the Diaspora, 1965. (Hebrew, Yiddish, English) "Shepsl Klezmer and Anshel the *Batkhn,*" p. 142. (Hebrew)

The leader of the *kapelye* in our town was Shepsl the Barber, who was loved by all the women. They would say: "When Shepsl takes the violin, the feet are already dancing by themselves." Anshel the *batkhn* was also loved by all, but especially by the women as well.

SEMIATYCZE (*ibid.*) "Semiaticher *Klezmorim,*" by Yasha Halperin, p. 346. (Yiddish)

Semiatycze had its own *kapelye* and *batkhn.* They were the only one in the province. All the fancy weddings hired them. If they were not hired, then the wedding was considered second-rate. The main *klezmer* was Shepsl the Barber.

SHPOLA (U). *Shpola; Masekhet Hayei Yehudim Ba-ayara* (Shpola; A Picture of Jewish Life in the Town). By David Cohen. Haifa, Association of Former Residents of Shpola (Ukraine) in Israel, 1965. (Hebrew) "Weddings," pp. 165–69.

Most weddings were in the summer after *Shvues.* Before the actual wedding day, there was the *farshpil* on the Saturday night before the wedding, where the *klezmorim* played at the bride's home. A lot of future matches were made there. Another custom was for the bride to walk accompanied by the *klezmorim* carrying a new dress that she brought to a very special female friend or relative. The *kapelye* consisted of Refaylke, his four sons, and a gentile.

SIERPC (P). *Kehilat Sierpc; Sefer Zikaron* (The Community of Sierpc; Memorial Book). Ed.: E. Talmi (Wloka). Tel Aviv, Former Residents of Sierpc in Israel and Abroad, 1959. (Hebrew, Yiddish) "Jewish Weddings and Jewish *Klezmorim* in Sierpe," I. A. Liebzon, pp. 267–68. (Yiddish)

In Sierpc they had their own customs for a wedding. One was that during the *badekn,* the bride's hair was only covered with a scarf and not cut. Then during the

wedding feast, after the *mitsve* dance, the bride had her hair cut. Then she put
on her *sheytl.*

SKIERNIEWICE (P). *Sefer Skierniewice* (The Book of Skierniewice). Ed.: J. Perlow. Tel
Aviv, Former Residents of Skierniewice in Israel, 1955. (Yiddish) "Three Beautiful Masters: The Baker With His Violin, The Tinsmith With His Trumpet and The Cottonmaker With His Drum, Played at a Poor Wedding...," by Yisroel Heler, pp. 356–58.
(photo caption: Skierniewicer *Klezmorim,* The Zhiradover *Marshalik,* Yerakhmil Grin-
berg, Yosele Klezmer, Lipman Lentshner, Shmuel with his bass, Lipman Karp and
Tshvirtshok)

   In Skierniewice there were three dear Jews: Nison the Baker, Lipman the Tinsmith,
   and Berl the Cottonmaker. All three performed as *letsim* at *Purim-shpils, brises,*
   and weddings to help raise money for poor brides and grooms so they could still
   have a wonderful celebration. Once there was wedding where the bride and groom
   could not pay the town's *kapelye.* The local *kapelye* refused to play for them, so the
   three *letsim* got their instruments, formed their own *kapelye,* and played the wedding. This angered the town's *kapelye.*

SKUODAS (L). *Kehilat Skhkud; Kovets Zikaron* (Memorial Book of Skuodas). Tel Aviv,
Former Residents of Skuodas, 1948. (Hebrew, Yiddish) "The Women's Benevolent Society," p. 11. (Hebrew)

   The women of Skuodas made sure that a poor bride's wedding would be fine.
   Monies for the institution came from monthly contributions and pledges that
   were made just before the reading of the *Toyre* and the calling of the *alies.*

SLUTSK (B). *Pinkas Slutsk U-benoteha* (Slutsk and Vicinity Memorial Book*). Ed.: N.
Chinitz ans Sh. Nachmani. Tel Aviv, Yizkor-Book Committee, 1962. (Hebrew, English,
Yiddish) "The Wedding Dress," by Khayim Zaydes, pp. 365–66. (Yiddish)

   Once there was a wedding where the water porter had promised two hundred
   rubles for his daughter's dowry. Then a special dress was made for her that cost
   fifty *rubles.* On the day of the wedding, the mother-in-law did not want to go to
   the *khupe* because the dowry was not the full two hundred *rubles* as ag ed upon
   in the contract. Luckily the butcher gave his wife's jewelry as collateral until the
   extra fifty was paid. The *kapelye* consisted of violin, flute, and bass bandura.

SMORGONIE (P). *Smorgon Mehoz Vilno; Sefer Edut Ve-zikaron* (Smorgonie, District
Vilna; Memorial Book and Testimony). Tel Aviv, Assoc. of Former Residents of Smorgonie in Israel and USA, 1965. (Hebrew, Yiddish) "Shloymele the Magid and His Beautiful Melodies," by Beyle Ber, p. 357. (Yiddish)

   Shloymele who played *klezmer* gave private lessons, played for celebrations, and for
   the silent films to earn money for the school. After the conservatory in Vilna he

became a composer. His Jewish and classical music was heard throughout the concert halls of Vilna.

SMORGONIE (*ibid.*) "This Violin," by Tsvi-Hirshele Levin, pp. 358–60. (A poem about Shloymele. However, pages 359–60 are missing in the Memorial Book) (Yiddish)

SOCHACZEW (P). *Pinkas Sochaczew* (Memorial Book of Sochaczew). Eds.: A. Sh. Stein and G. Weissman. Jerusalem, Former Residents of Sochzczew in Israel, 1962. (Hebrew, Yiddish) "From the Book: Poland," by Y. Y. Trunk, pp. 342–50. (Yiddish)

Weddings were never during the day in the Kotsker synagogue courtyard. Everyone waited under the *khupe* until the *havdole* candle was completely burned out. Then the Kotzker *Rebe* came out of his room to the *khupe*. In Sochaczew, weddings were during the day, but *klezmorim* and *batkhonim* were not supposed to entertain. Once the *batkhn* sang his rhymes, and *Reb* Shmuel yelled: "Enough! These rhymes come off your tongue so dryly like an unfortunate *marshalik.*"

SOFIYIVKA AND IGNATOVKA (U) *Ha-ilan Ve-shoreshava; Sefer Korot T L Zofiowka-Ignatowka* (The Tree and the Roots; The History of T. L.-Sofyovka and Ignatovka*). Eds.: Y. Vainer, T. Drori, G. Rosenblatt, A. Shpilman. Beit-Tal Givatim, 1988. (Hebrew, Yiddish, English) "Weddings," by Eliezer Barkay, pp. 74–77.

At some weddings, a gentile band played at the Jewish weddings, but generally it was the Jewish *kapelye* led by Fasel Kalker, who played the violin.

SOKOLOW (P). *Sefer Ha-Zikaron; Sokolow-Podlask* (Memorial Book of Sokolow-Podlask). Ed.: M. Gelbart. Tel Aviv, Former Residents of Sokolow-Podlask in Israel and... in the USA, 1962. (Hebrew, Yiddish) "A Wedding," by Boyrekh Rozenboym, pp. 128–29.

The Sokolow *kapelye* had six musicians. Two of the *klezmers* were barbers. One cut the hair of the children and the poor while the other cut the hair of the young people.

SOKOLY (P). *Sefer Zikaron Le-kedoshei Sokoly* (Memorial Book of the Martyrs of Sokoly). Ed.: M. Gelbart. Tel Aviv, Residents of Sokoly, 1962. (Yiddish) "Musicians," by Khayim Alshe, p. 366. (List by profession of those who died).

Klezmorim: Both sons of *Reb* Mikhl Eliyahu, the former *shames* and gravedigger. And Yisroelke Pizok and Moyshe Meyer both died in America.

STASZOW (P). *Sefer Staszow* (The Staszow Book*). Ed.: E. Erlich. Tel Aviv, Former Residents of Staszow in Israel... and in the Diaspora, 1962. (Hebrew, Yiddish, English) "Birth and Childhood in Staszow," by Yekhazkil Kirshenboym, pp. 221–23. (photo caption: Zisl Fanfe playing the violin) (Hebrew)

The poor children in Staszow helped their parents by doing whatever work they found. One boy every *Peysekh* played a sad melody about spring coming. It reminded everyone about the pogrom that happened in Kishinev. There were some happy moments in Staszow, for example when a new *Toyre* was brought out or when a bride and groom were led to the *khupe* by *klezmorim*.

STASZOW (*ibid.*) "The Synagogue and *Beysmedreshim*," by Hershel Pomerantsblum, pp. 251–53. (photo caption: The *Shames* and his helper putting up the *khupe*) (Yiddish) The Staszower *klezmorim* were led by *Reb* Yisroel Ber and his family. The most gifted child was Rafayel, who eventually played first violin in the Berlin and Vienna orchestras.

STASZOW (*ibid.*) "Musicians, Cantors and Music Enthusiasts," by Moshe Rotenberg, pp. 295–98. (music) (Yiddish) Yakov Tsimerman was the local *klezmer*. Eventually he moved to Warsaw, where he began to make violins. His name became so well known as a violin maker that violin virtuosi like Huberman, Szigeti, Kreisler, and others came to his workshop for his opinions and violins.

STAVISCHE (U). *Stavisht*. Ed.: A. Weissman. Tel Aviv, The Stavisht Society, New York, 1961. (Hebrew, Yiddish) "A Wedding Ceremony," by David Kohn, pp. 145–48. (Yiddish) When the parents of a bride made a betrothal party where the engagement agreements were written, the dowry was left with a trusted person. The groom felt more comfortable with this arrangement and this was proof for the bride's father the wedding was on.

STEPAN (P). *Ayaratenu Stepan* (The Stepan Story; Excerpts*). Ed.: Yitzhak Ganuz. Tel Aviv, Stepan Society, 1977. (Hebrew, English) "*Klezmer*," by Yeshiahu Fray, p. 82. (Hebrew) In Stepan there was the Klinikas family *kapelye*. Two of the *klezmorim* supplemented their income by giving music lessons to the rich.

STOLIN (P). *Stolin; Sefer Zikaron Le-kehilat Stolin Ve-ha-seviva* (Stolin; A Memorial to the Jewish Communities of Stolin and Vicinity*) Eds.: A. Avatichi and Y. Ben-Zakkai. Tel Aviv, Former Residents of Stolin and Vicinity in Israel, 1952. (Hebrew) "Workers," by Aryeh Avatikhi, p. 134. There were many handicraft workers in town. There were tinsmiths, roofers, woodcutters, painters, seamstresses, hatmakers, butchers, coachmen, *klezmorim*, etc. Among the *klezmorim* there were several barbers, woodcutters, and a porter. After the Russian Revolution, many of the men lost jobs due to industrialization.

SUCHOWOLA (P). *Sefer Suchowola* (Memorial Book of Suchowola). Eds.: H. Steinberg et al. Jerusalem, Thre Encyclopedia of the Jewish Diaspora, 1957. (Hebrew, Yiddish) "Two Weddings," by Simkhe Lazar, pp. 379–82. (Yiddish) The author remembered two weddings he attended. At one wedding the Dombrover *klezmorim* joined the Suchowoler *klezmorim* and entertained the guests.

At the second wedding after the prayer "Grace After Meals" was said, the older folks got up and danced. One deaf man got up on a table and with his cane did the *shtek tants.* Afterward, the men studied the *Gemore* and sang *"Avinu Malkeynu."*

SUCHOWOLA (*ibid.*) "Suchowola Tales," by Sore Rukhl Bura, pp. 379–82. (Yiddish)
After Khane Nisl returned to town after her medical mishap, she decided she needed to have her sins pardoned, so she commissioned to have a *Sefer Toyre* written. When the *Toyre* was completed, she celebrated with a party. The *Toyre* was carried under the *khupe* while the Dubrovy *klezmorim* played music as they walked to the *shtibl.*

SUWALKI (P). *Yizker-bukh Suwalk* (Memorial Book of Suwalk). Ed.: B. Kahan. New York, The Suvalk and Vicinity Relief Committee of New York, 1961. (Yiddish) "Artists," by Berl Kohn, pp. 243–44.
In Suvalk and the surrounding areas, there were a few artists who went to America and became Yiddish actors. One was Jenny Atlos, who performed with Adler, Kessler, and Thomashevsky. Another was Bernard Gelling, who went to America in 1914. His father was a tailor and *klezmer.*

SWIECIANY (P). *Sefer Zikaron Le-esrim Ve-shalosh Kehilot She-nehrevu Be-zor Svintzian* (Svintzian Region; Memorial Book of the Twenty-Three Jewish Communities*). Ed.: Sh. Kanc. Tel Avivi, Former residents of Svintzian District in Israel, 1965. (Hebrew, Yiddish). "A Wedding in Town," by Sholom Yitskhok Tyts, pp. 845–48. (Yiddish)
When there was a wedding, the *shames* gave out the invitations. As a hobby, the children collected them. Different color invitations were worth different kinds of buttons. On the day of the wedding, the *klezmorim* arrived early before they led the groom and bride to the *khupe.* The *kapelye* was a quartet with violin, flute, bass, and *tsimbl.*

SWIR (P). *Ayaratenu Swir* (Our Townlet Swir*). Ed.: Ch. Swironi (Drutz). Tel Aviv, Former Residents of Swir in Israel and... in the United States, 1959. (Hebrew, Yiddish) "Family Artists," p. 190. (Yiddish)
Elikum the Barber was known as the Paganini of the town. Elikum also had a beautiful voice and sang and played at weddings. However, his main profession was as a barber. He worked even on *Shabes,* because many of his customers were leftists and did not keep the *Shabes.*

SZCZUCZYN (P). *Sefer Zikaron Le-kehilot Szczuczyn, Waliszki...* (Memorial Book of the Communities of Szczuczyn, Walsilszki...). Ed.: L. Losh. Tel Aviv, Former residents of Szczuczyn, Wasiliszki..., 1966. (Hebrew, Yiddish) "Wasilishker Musicians," p. 201. (Yiddish)
The Jewish shoemakers in Szczuczyn were also *klezmorim.* They had all learned to

play music while in the Czar's army. The leader of the *kapelye* was Yankl the Cossak. He played clarinet while his sons played cornet and baritone.

SZCZUCZYN (*ibid.*) "A Wedding in Town," Tsipora Berkovitsh and Yosef Bayer, pp. 210–11. (Yiddish)

After the wedding ceremony and celebration on Friday, the bride was taken to the synagogue on *Shabes*. Then that evening the *sheve brukhes* began, with music from the Shuster *kapelye*. Their first piece was a *freylekh* called "*Gut Vokh*."

SZUMSK (P). *Szumsk ... Sefer Zikaron Le-Kedoshei Szumsk ...* (Szumsk ... Memorial Book of the Martyrs of Szumsk ...). Ed.: H. Rabin. Tel Aviv, Former Residents of Szumsk in Israel, 1968. (Hebrew, Yiddish) "A *Khupe* in the Cemetery," by M. Khazn, pp. 382–86.

Over seventy years ago, there was a cholera epidemic throughout the world that killed over twenty million people. Our town Szumsk was also affected. The doctor and his two assistants could do nothing to relieve the sick and dying. Every day people woke up with fear of contracting the disease. Then the Russian government had all the *besmedreshim* and churches post instructions on how to stay clean and tidy. There was no way to get rid of sewage in our town. The water from our river was filthy with fecal matter and other stuff and there was no other water to drink. Without clean water, the disease spread faster.

So the doctor ordered everyone to wash all their fruit, heat the milk before drinking, and to boil all water before drinking it. The pharmacist gave people lime to spread in the outhouses and streets to keep them cleaner. Then the doctor and the Russian police commissioner walked through the town making sure people listened to the orders. But the epidemic raged on.

The people not only had to contend with the disease, but it was *Tamez* [Heb.: the tenth month in the Jewish calendar] and they could not get any relief from the oppressive heat. People went to the rabbi for answers. He answered them by reciting more psalms. The women went to the cemetery asking the dead for answers, while Rabbi Bereniv told people not to fast on *Tishebov* if they felt weak. Finally it was decided that a possible remedy for the epidemic was to make a wedding in the cemetery with an orphan bride. The public would be there along with *klezmorim*, hoping the epidemic would heed their offering.

Immediately the *shatkhn* went out looking for candidates. For the groom he found Perets the Fool, who was blind in one eye, lame in one foot, and a stutterer. He was at least thirty and had a sick mother. He went around every Friday with a sack collecting *khale* and other bread for the whole week. People give him a coin, a piece of meat or fish, and this is how he and his mother lived weekly. When he came to a house for bread, the girls asked him if he wanted to marry. Proudly with joy he answered yes and tried to kiss the girls. With a scream they ran away while he chased them, holding his coin in his hand. This was the spectacle every Friday when Perets the Fool came around for his bread.

The girl destined to be the bride limped a little with her left foot, was paralyzed in her right hand, was a tiny bit deaf, and had two red eyes. The groom immediately fell in love with her and the preparations for the wedding began. Perets's mother said it was not fair for her son to marry and not receive a dowry. But the orphan bride had no dowry, so the town collected one hundred rubles, the wedding clothes, and all the other equipment that was needed to make a wedding.

The wedding was set for Friday afternoon. All the people prepared themselves while the *shnaps* [Yid.: liquor, whiskey] flowed like water. Then everyone gathered in the square opposite the home where the wedding feast would be. All the young girls were dressed up and the *klezmorim* played music. Then at two P.M., with everyone gathered in the square, the groom and bride were led to the *khupe* at the cemetery, with the *klezmorim* leading the way, playing. The ceremony took place an hour before lighting the *Shabes* candles. Afterward, the *klezmorim* led the groom and bride back to his mother's home while everyone else prepared to welcome the *Shabes*. Perhaps the wedding helped as a remedy, but as soon as cooler weather came, there was less and less illness. Unfortunately because of the mother-in-law the couple's home did not have peace and quiet for too long.

SZYDLOWIEC (P). *Shidlovtser Yizker-bukh* (Yizkor Book Szydlowiec*). Ed.: Berl Kagan. New York, 1974. (Yiddish, English) "*Klezmorim* and *Batkhonim*," by Dvora Blonder, p. 155. (Yiddish)

The Gayger brothers and their relatives formed the *kapelye*. The *batkhonim* were Yudele Vinonski, a religious man, and Yitskhok Moyshe Rafalovitsh, the drummer in the *kapelye*. Rafalovitsh was more worldly and knew the modern songs.

TARGOWICA (P). *Sefer Trovits* (Memorial Book of Targovca*). Ed.: I. Siegelman. Haifa, Former Residents of Targovica in Israel, 1967. (Hebrew, Yiddish) "Weddings in the Town," by David Marants, pp. 24–25. (photo caption: The Wedding of Benyomin ben-Mikhl and Sara Koyfman) (Hebrew)

Everyone went to the wedding even if you were not invited, just to see the latest fashions, shoes, jewelery, etc. Mlotsek on his trumpet and Yidl on his violin were the *klezmers* and led everyone to the bride's house.

TARNOGROD (P). *Sefer Tarnogrod; Le-zikaron Ha-kehila Ha-yehudit She-nehreva* (Book of Tarnogrod; In Memory of the Destroyed Jewish Community). Ed.: Sh. Kanc. Tel Aviv, Organization of Former Residents of Tarnogrod and Vicinity in Israel, United States and England, 1966. (Hebrew, Yiddish) "The Black *Khupe* in the Cemetery," by Nakhum Krumerkop, pp. 95–99. (Yiddish)

In the summer of 1916 there was a cholera epidemic that raged in the towns near us. The rabbi decided to marry a hunchback and an old maid under a black *khupe* in the Jewish cemetery. This was an old remedy they had used before against various other epidemics. The *klezmorim* accompanied the couple and others with music to the cemetery.

TARNOPOL (P). *Tarnopol* (Tarnopol). Ed.: Ph. Korngruen. Jerusalem, Encyclopedia of the Jewish Diaspora, 1955. (Hebrew, Yiddish, English) "To the *Khupe!*" by Meyer Khartiner, pp. 321–30. (poem and *khupe* march music) (Hebrew and Yiddish)

The poem speaks about the joy, laughter, music, and general din of the wedding celebration. The *klezmorim* led the bride and groom to the *khupe*. After the *khazn* sang and the *havdole* candle burned out, the glass was broken and the *klezmorim* played a *freylekhs*. The *mizinke* [Yid.: youngest daughter] got married.

TELECHANY (P). *Telekhan* (Telekhan Memorial Book*) Ed.: Sh. Sokoler. Los Angeles, Telekhan Memorial Book Committee, 1963. (Hebrew, Yiddish, English) p. 314g. (photo caption: Telekhaner *Klezmorim,* 1908).

Hirshl Melnik, Nisl Melnik, and Fayvl Arkes Kagan. Fayvl lived in Hollywood and was a noted person in the musical world there.

TLUMACZ (P). *Tlumacz-Tolmitsh; Sefer Edut Ve-zikaron* (Memorial Book of Tlumacz*). Ed.: Shlomo Blond et al. Tel Aviv, Tlumacz Society, 1976. (Yiddish, Hebrew, English) "*Klezmorim* and Weddings," by Efrayim Shrayer, pp. 320–21, 68, XLIX–L. (Hebrew, Yiddish and English)

Weddings were held next to the big synagogue, while the wedding feasts were held either at the tavern or at the railroad station. The boisterous feasts were at the tavern and the quieter ones were at the railroad station. If the wedding was more prestigious, then the *klezmers* and *marshalik* from Stanislow were brought in and joined the local *kapelye*.

TLUSTE (P). *Sefer Tluste* (Memorial Book of Tluste). Ed.: G. Lindenberg. Tel Aviv, Association of Former Residents of Tluste and Vicinity in Israel and USA, 1965. (Hebrew, Yiddish) "Our Town," by Dr. A. Stup, pp. 69–71. (Yiddish)

Once a year the children dressed up as Hussars on *Purim.* They came inside the house and entertained with song and music. On *Purim,* even singing a Ukrainian song at a *khasidishe* table was not inappropriate. Afterward, dessert and whiskey was given to the children and the *kapelye*.

TLUSZCZ (P). *Sefer Zikaron Le-kehilat Tluszcz* (Memorial Book of the Community of Tluszcz). Ed.: M. Gelbart. Tel Aviv, Association of Former Residents of Tluszcz in Israel, 1971. (Hebrew, Yiddish) "The Tlusher *Kapelye* and their *Klezmorim,*" by Khenekh Perl, pp. 73–75. (Yiddish)

The Tluszczer *klezmorim* were the only *kapelye* in the Radziminer region with a good reputation. They were led by Hirshl Postalski on violin. When he died, his brother Yidl became the first violinist. To keep up their reputation, they employed a trumpeter from Warsaw who was also the local ballet teacher. During weddings, this handsome young man helped the religious women by calling out the dance steps.

TOMASZÓW-LUBELSKI (P). *Tomashover* (Lubelski) *Yizker-bukh* (Memorial Book of Tomaszów Lubelski). New York, Tomashover Relief Committee, 1965. (Yiddish) "The Big Wedding," by Asher Reyz, pp. 441-45. (photos and captions of the rabbis, groom, and guests dressed as Cossacks)

There was a lavish *khasidic* wedding where the Sayshinover *Rebe*'s daughter got married to the Hentshiner rabbi's son. The groom lived in another town and was met by three regiments of fifty *khasidim,* all dressed as Cossaks. Some carried swords and others carried guns as they were accompanied by two orchestras.

TOMASZÓW-LUBELSKI (*ibid.*) "Yoyl Batkhn and his War Experiences," by Yakov Shwarts, pp. 709-11. (photo caption Yoyl Batkhn at a wedding in Berlin immediately after the war)

Everyone in town knew Yoyl Handlesman, the teacher and *batkhn.* He spread his humor, jokes, and happiness to all weddings, even if it was a *shtile* wedding (one with no *klezmorim*).

TOMASZÓW-MAZOWIECKI (P). *Sefer Zikaron Le-kehilat Tomaszow Mazowiecki* (Tomashow-Mazowieck; A Memorial Book to the Jewish Community of Tomashow-Mazowieck*). Ed.: M. Wajsberg. Tel Aviv, Tomashow organization in Israel, 1969. (Hebrew, Yiddish, English, French). "Yosef Marshalik," pp. 322-23. (Yiddish)

The town's *batkhn* was Yosef Marshalik, who was known throughout Tomaszów and the surrounding areas."With Yosef's death the town lost an interesting typical Jewish character, authentic—and one of the most famous—*batkhonim.*"

TOMASZÓW-MAZOWIECKI (*ibid.*) "Shulik Klezmer," pp. 332-34. (Yiddish)

The famous *klezmer* Shulik Klezmer was revered throughout Poland for his beautiful violin playing.

TUCZYN: *Sefer Zikaron Le-kehilat Tuczyn-Krippe* (Tutchin-Krippe, Wolyn; In Memory of the Jewish Community*). Ed.: B. H. Ayalon. Tel Aviv, Tutchin and Krippe Relief Society of Israel..., 1967. (Hebrew, Yiddish) "A Wedding in Town," by Rivke Khamut, pp. 135-36. (Yiddish)

During the wedding feast the bride's in-laws crowded into the kitchen to tell the waiters that the groom's in-laws should be served first, so as not to insult them. After the *droshe geshank,* the *klezmorim* played a *sher.* Then the adults danced the *koyfn tants* and demonstrated to their children how it went.

TURKA (P). *Sefer Zikaron Le-kehilat Turka Al Nehar Stry Ve-ha-seviva* (Memorial Book of the Community of Turka on the Stry River and Vicinity). Ed.: J. Siegelman. Haifa, Former Residents of Turka (Stry) in Israel, 1966. (Hebrew, Yiddish) "The *Klezmorim* Are Arriving in Town," by Khayim Feler, pp. 137–39. (Yiddish) (photo caption: The Oferman *Kapelye*)

> In 1870, a *klezmer kapelye* (Shmuel Oferman and his family) arrived in town, because there were no *klezmorim*. From that point on, they were very successful in Turka and throughout Galicia as well.

TURKA (*ibid.*) "The Orchestra in the New Times," by Moshe From, pp. 139–43. (Yiddish) (photo caption: The Amateur Orchestra Under the Leadership of Pinkhus Shwarts)

> The next generation of Ofermans formed the nucleus of a *klezmer kapelye,* which became even more successful than the first *kapelye.* They were even brought to Mukács (across the Czechoslovakian border) for the marriage of the Mukácser *Rebe's* daughter.

TURKA (*ibid.*) "Rozele's Wedding," by Khayim Pelekh, pp. 168–70. (Yiddish)

> A slightly addled storyteller named Rozele was much beloved by the town. A young man came to Turka and fell in love with her. The whole town turned out for her wedding. She was led to the *khupe* by the townspeople and the Oferman *kapelye.*

TYSZOWCE (P). *Pinkas Tishovits* (Tiszowic Book*). Ed.: Y. Zipper. Tel Aviv, Association of Former Residents of Tiszowic in Israel, 1970. (Hebrew, Yiddish) "The Tishovitser Klezmorim," by Moyshe, pp. 179–80. (photo caption: Tishovitser *Klezmorim*) (Yiddish)

> The town *kapelye* was the Borukh family. They were so liked that they even played for the Christians for their special state celebrations. Now "everything is still because the Tyszowcer *klezmorim* are not here."

UHNOW (P). *Hivniv (Uhnow); Sefer Zikaron Le-kehila* (Hivnov (Uhnow); Memorial Book to a Community). Tel Aviv, Uhnow Society, 1981. (Hebrew, English) "Merrymaking at a Wedding in Uhnow," pp. 54–55. (English)

> If the groom was from out of town, then the bride's relatives went to the railroad station to meet him with the *kapelye.* Since there was no wedding hall in Uhnow, the festivities were held at the bride's house.

UTENA (P). *Yisker-bukh Utyan Un Umgegnt* (Memorial Book of Utyan and Vicinity). Tel Aviv, Nay Leben, 1979. (Yiddish) "A Wedding in Malyat," by Hadasa Fisher, pp. 124–25.

> Sore-Beyle, an older woman, got married to a considerably younger man from somewhere, but it did not matter. Her parents were rich and gave whatever amount for the dowry for their one and only daughter. During the wedding feast, the *klezmorim* sat in a corner and waited while the bride sat on her throne beaming as the guests came to give her a hearty *mazltov.*

WARKA (P). *Vurka; Sefer Zikaron* (Vurka Memorial Book). Tel Aviv, Vurka Societies in Israel, France, Argentina, England and the United States, 1976. (Hebrew, Yiddish) "Types and Figures in My Town," by Sh. Rozentsvayg, pp. 122–24. (Yiddish)

Pertshe, an older woman, finally found a husband, and the town rejoiced. They hired an important *batkhn* from Warsaw, and the Kozieniecer *kapelye*.

WARSAW (P) *Warsaw* (Warsaw Volume*). Ed.: J. Gruenbaum. Jerusalem, The Encyclopedia of the Jewish Diaspora, 1953–73. 3 vols. (Hebrew, Yiddish) "*Klezmorim, Jews,*" by M. Sh. Geshuri, pp. 473–79. (Hebrew)

The author gave a detailed description of the history of the *klezmer* in Poland from the end of the Middle Ages through the end of the nineteenth century.

WARSAW (*ibid.*) "Mixed Marriage," by Yekhiel Huper, pp. 479–88. (Hebrew)

There was a wedding between an orthodox groom and a bride who was from a non-orthodox family. The wedding was held at the Tłomackie Synagogue, where bankers, businessmen, and intellegentsia were all invited. The Vaghalter *klezmorim* performed at the wedding. Their talents were known wide and far. Their grandfather played with Paganini.

WARSAW (*ibid.*) "The Wedding of a Daughter of a *Khasid* to the Groom, a Modern Jew, in 1910." pp. 483–88. (Hebrew)

At this extravagant wedding there were two *kapelyes*. One played waltzes for the nonorthodox guests in one room, while the other played Moditser *nigunim* for the *khasidim* in another room. A *khasid* found out about the mixed waltz dancing and quickly had the *kapelye* stop playing. All the nonorthodox guests went home while the *khasidim* continued to celebrate.

WARSAW (P). *Pinkes Varshe* (Book of Warsaw). Eds.: P. Katz et al. Buenos Aires, Former Residents of Warsaw and Surroundings in Argentina, 1955. (Yiddish) "The Music and Musical Life of Warsaw," by J. Stutschefsky, pp. 572–88. (photo captions: Zimre Zeligfeld, M. Kipnis, Z. Shnyer, Gregor Fitelberg, David Baygelman)

The author wrote about the importance of the *batkhonim, klezmorim, khasidic nigunim,* and Yiddish folk and theatre songs, which all helped undeniably to create a national folk character for Jewish life in Eastern Europe. He also wrote brief biographies on several famous Polish Jewish musicians, such as Landowska, Huberman, Rubenstein, and many more.

WARTA (P). *Sefer D'Vart.* Ed.: Eliezer Estrin. Tel Aviv, D'Vart Society, 1974. (Hebrew, Yiddish) "*Klezmers,*" by Khanon Shutin, pp. 111–12. (Yiddish)

The wedding was planned and Yitskhok Klezmer was hired to play. He was especially known for his playing of polonaises.

WARTA (*ibid.*) "A Wedding in Town," by Mordkhay Mitus, pp. 349–55. (Hebrew)

The *klezmorim* in town were the Prukh family. "Their name in Polish meant dynamite, and they played with such great intensity it was as if they were going to explode." Each one of the members of the family *kapelye* was quite unique.

WEGROW (P). *Kehilat Wegrow; Sefer Zikaron* (Community of Wegrow; Memorial Book). Ed.: M. Tamari. Tel Aviv, Former Residents of Wegrow in Israel, 1961. (Hebrew, Yiddish) "Engagements, Weddings and *Sheve Brokhes,*" by Sh. Zabludovitsh, pp. 259–60. (Yiddish)

On the first *Shabes* after the wedding, it was the custom to bring the bride a gift of food like noodle or potato *kugl,* wine, beer, or fruit.

WISZNIEW NOWY (P). *Wisniowiec; Sefer Zikaron Le-kedoshei Wisniowiec She-nispu Be-shoat Ha-Nazim* (Wisniowiec; Memorial Book of the Martrys of Wisniowiec Who Perished in the Nazi Holocaust). Ed.: H. Rabin. Tel Aviv, Former Residents of Wisniowiec, 1970. (Hebrew, Yiddish) "Weddings," pp. 441–42. (Yiddish)

The whole town enjoyed the weddings, which were accompanied by the Haritske family *kapelye.* Before the newlyweds entered the hall to celebrate the wedding feast, a young boy from either the bride or groom's side entertained the couple with a poem either in Yiddish, Russian, or Hebrew. During World War I, the oldest son Duvid led a *kapelye* and discovered that the real family name was not Haritske but Mandelboym.

WISZNIEW (*ibid.*) "A Tragic Wedding," pp. 442–41.

On the day of the wedding, the groom's little brother drowned. The rabbi was asked whether they should proceed with the wedding. He determined they should, but without *klezmorim.*

WISZNIEW (*ibid.*) "A Wedding in Town," p. 456. (Yiddish)

After the *khupe* many youngsters went to the window of the home where the wedding feast took place and watched the festivities. The *klezmer* and *batkhn* Avromchik entertained the guests while he played the trumpet and sang rhymes.

WISZNIEW (*ibid.*) "The Pagentry of Avromchik's *Batkhones,*" pp. 457–59. (Yiddish)

This is the *batkhones* Avromchik recited while the other *klezmorim* accompanied him.

WLODAWA (P). *Yizker-bukh Tsu Vlodave* (Yizkor Book in Memory of Vlodava and Region Sobibor*). Ed.: Shimon Kanc. Tel Aviv, Wlodawa Societies in Israel and North and South America, 1974. (Hebrew, Yiddish, English) "The Wedding in Town," by Avraham Barnholts, pp. 529–33. (Yiddish)

Toward the end of World War I, the author's father prepared a lavish wedding for his daughter, who was marrying the grandson of the Bialy *Rebe*. He obtained permission from the German authorities so many rabbis could attend. The wedding lasted a week, with the *klezmorim* and *batkhn* accompanying throughout.

WLODAWA (*ibid.*) "*Klezmer*," pp. 551–52. (Yiddish)
The Wlodawer *klezmers*, the Shpilman and Fidlman families, played at weddings in and around Wlodawa. Besides weddings, they performed for the theatre, movie house, and for vacationers during summer in the country villages. If it was a rich wedding, they brought a *batkhn* from Lublin.

WLODZIMIERZEC (P). *Sefer Vladimeretz* (The Book of Vladimeretz). Ed.: A Meryerowitz. Tel Aviv, Former Residents of Vladimeretz in Israel, (196–). (Hebrew, Yiddish, English) "One Wedding," by Yaakov Bas, pp. 102–104. (Hebrew)
Pici Mkulak was a *klezmer* violinist known throughout Volyn. Once he gave a benefit concert in the Stoliner synagogue for the poor people in town. Everyone attended, even the Polish and Russian intelligentsia. Though gentiles came to the concert as well as Jews, the Stoliner *khasidim* were not angry. Music teachers were astonished at the artistry of this self-taught old man.

WOJSLAWICE (P). *Sefer Zikaron Voislavitze* (Yizkor Book in Memory of Voislavize*). Ed.: Shimon Kanc. Tel Aviv, Former Residents of Voislavitze, 1970. (Hebrew, Yiddish) "A Wedding and *Sheve Borukhes*," by Yaakov Tenenboym, pp. 156–60. (Yiddish)
The *klezmorim* played from the time of the *oyfrufn* through the last day of the *Sheve Brukhes*. The week that led up to the *oyfrufn* was called the silver week and the week from the *oyfrufn* to the wedding was called the golden week.

WOJSLAWICE (*ibid.*) "The *Batkhn*'s Rhymes," pp. 260–61. (Yiddish)
The author remembered his brother's engagement party and wedding. He said: "Since that time I have been to so many weddings, but there was none compared to my brother's. Those old traditions have disappeared like the Jews of my town."

WOJSLAWICE (*ibid.*) "The *Kapelye* and the Rabbi," by Fayvl Hokhe, pp. 365–66. (Hebrew)
In order to ensure that the *klezmorim* would show up for a local wedding, the town's butcher volunteered to walk to their town on *shabes* to secure a deposit (a trumpet). The rabbi was displeased that he walked so far and carried the trumpet on *shabes*, and banned him from selling meat for a month.

WOLKOWYSK (P). *Volkvisker Yizker-bukh* (Wolkovisker Yizkor Book*). Ed.: M. Einhorn. New York, 1949. (Yiddish) "The *Klezmorim* Accompany the Groom and Bride," by Dr. Moshe Einhorn, pp. 57–58. (photo caption: A *Khupe* in Wolkowysk)
The custom in town was to celebrate a wedding on Friday after lunch. The *kapelye*

consisted of two first violins, *sekund,* clarinet, trumpet, cornet, and flute. They paraded down the street playing *freylekhs* as they led everyone to the *khupe.*

WYSZKOW (P). *Sefer Wyszkow* (Wishkow Book*). Ed.: Sh. Shtokfish. Tel Aviv, Association of Former Residents of Wishkow Israel and Abroad, 1964. (Hebrew, Yiddish) "The Wishkower *Kapelye,*" by Yitskhok Markusmakher, pp. 55–57. (Yiddish)

At the meeting of the Wyszkower historians, Rabbi Harry and Rabbi Khayim discussed when there was a wedding without *klezmorim.* They spoke about the beautiful nature that surrounded their town. The Sonower forest, meadows, the wide and deep Bug River, and the big fruit orchards. Orchards filled with plums, apples, white pears, and red cherries. They remembered how the youth loved to play in the country and how on every *Shabes* and Jewish holiday you heard singing from nearly every home. And at celebrations you heard Metsh with his violin and Nosele on clarinet.

Then once there was this wedding where the bride, Leya-Eta, who was quite rude and stubborn, did not want to bring the whole Pultusker *kapelye* with the *batkhn* to the *khupe.* She said: "Father Metsh and his friend Nosele, they are not enough? They have to make a living. So why should there be *klezmorim* from another town?" The bride's father then told Metsh what she wanted and Metsh said not to worry, he would get a *kapelye* with a *batkhn.* Metsh went to his son Nosele and told him what they had to do. "Father, who will play the bass, drum, and violin?" "Well, I will get Isirel. His playing will capture all the wives." "But Isirel won't play in the *kapelye* for a few pieces of parsley and rotten apples. What will his wife cook? He needs some real earnings. For a few *rubles* he will play!" And what about the bass, drums, and a *batkhn*?" "We will get Palukhl to play bass." "Palukhl, father, he has no ear!" "It doesn't matter; we will still take him, and for a drummer I will get Yidl, he has a drum!" "What!" screamed Nosele, "Yidl who washed flasks? Oi, woe is me, what a *kapelye* we will have with Yidl on the drum and Palukhl on bass!" "And I have a *batkhn,* too," said Metsh, "Our young boy Khayim-Henekhl. I will send him immediately to Warsaw to the great Yosl and in one day he will learn to be a *batkhn.*"

The wedding day came and the Wyszkower *kapelye* played for the rude bride. It was quite a wedding. People stood head to head, young and old, Jews and gentiles, not to see the groom and bride but to hear the newly formed *kapelye.* Metsh, a pale, tall, broad-shouldered Jew, spoke to Nosele: "My child, when you play, really play! You know what I mean. They should play in the key of F on B. They should really take the spirit!" "Palukhl, the spirit of your father's father will be within you if you make true art with your bass. Come in with everyone and end with everyone, otherwise the wedding will end immediately. Yidl, how you wash and slurp from the flasks! This is not my way. I will show you how to do this properly just as I am a *klezmer*! Isirel, I have nothing to say to you. Nosele will keep an eye on you. And Khayim-Henekhel, my child—" (he was crying) "go and show what you know and capture them with your speaking."

Khayim-Henekhel put on his hat, stood on the bench, and began reciting *Toyre*. His words were sharp and rhymed. The wives wiped their eyes and the bride looked straight at the *batkhn* and gave a laugh. He stopped his speech and said the following: "Oi, bride, bride, cry, cry. From your mother you have a lot of charm, and when your groom will look upon you, he will break out in a great wail. And we all say Amen!" Then he shouted to his father and Nosele to play a *freylekhs* for the bride.

What a tumult it was with Metsh and Nosele playing and everyone dancing. Isirel played the violin but with a thin tone, but lyrical. Palukhl played the bass, but it was a low grating sound. Yidl hit the drum while snowballs thrown by a gang of youngsters were hitting it as well. Yidl was so angy that he gave an extra hit to the drum and screamed: "It will be like cholera for you when we meet again after I finish!"

It was pitch-black out while a small wind blew and the snow fell. The *khupe* candles were all extinguished and in the middle of this there was a scream: "Crazy Leya's shawl is burning!" A candle she carried caught her shawl on fire. What a scene this was. Yidl and Palukhl took this opportunity to jump to the kitchen and make a *l'khayim*. "Ai, ai, Yidl, Yidl," said Palukhl, "if only God would send us to such a fat wedding every week." "Yes," said Yidl, "the rolls, the fish, this great *yoyikh* with soup nuts. A ghost should take some of this." "You know what?" said Palukhl, "let us divide this up—a couple of rolls for you, and a couple for me. My children have not seen such rolls in a long time." "Let's run, Palukhl!" shouted Yidl.

At the *khupe* they had just broken the *kidesh* glass and now they were about to begin the *khupe* march. Palukhl ran back to his big bass, two times bigger than he was, and began to play. Yidl had his drum attached to him and could barely run. The *khupe* march was played and everyone was reveling. The Jews who lived near the wedding never forget how the Wyszkower *kapelye*, without any musical knowledge, brought joy to this celebration.

WYSZOGROD (P). *Wyszogrod; Sefer Zikaron* (Vishogord; Dedicated to the Memory...*). Ed.: H. Rabin. Tel Aviv, Former Residents of Vishogrod and..., 1971. "Kalman Agrodnik, the Musician and Conductor," by Motl Valfish, pp. 226–27. (photo by Kalman Agrodnik)

Kalman was such an accomplished violinist that at age twelve he was invited to lead the *kapelye*. He taught the rest of the band to read music and about basic music theory. He himself read, composed, and arranged. He changed the town's perception of *klezmorim* for the better. Eventually he went on to have a distinguished musical career, until he died in the Bialystoker ghetto.

YAMPOL (U). *Ayara Be-lehavot; Pinkas Yampola, Pelekh Volyn* (Town in Flames; Book of Yampola, District Wolyn). Ed.: L. Gelman. Jerusalem, Commemoration Committee for the Town with the Assistance of Yad Vashem and the World Jewish Congress, 1963. (Hebrew, Yiddish) "The Yampoler Water Carrier," by David Rubin, pp. 120–21. (Yiddish)

> The Shabse family *kapelye* aspired to get out of the water carrying business and become full-time *klezmorim.*

YAMPOL (*ibid.*) "Yampol's Own Music *Kapelye,*" by David Rubin, pp. 121–22. (Yiddish)

> The Yampoler *kapelye* (comprised of the Shabse family) was of adequate ability, and played mostly for poorer families. They themselves had to supplement their income by carrying water and fishing. They got by until the town was struck by cholera. After that they barely made a living.

YAMPOL (*ibid.*) "A *Khupe* in the Cemetery," by David Rubin, pp. 122–25. (Yiddish)

> The town arranged a wedding in a cemetery to offset the cholera epidemic. The Shabse family *kapelye* played for the wedding. Years later, the *kapelye*'s leader, Elynka, was murdered by a Ukrainian gangster.

YEDINTSY (R). *Yad Le-Yedinitz; Sefer Zikaron Le-yehudei Yedinitz-Bessarabia* (Yad L'Yedinitz; Memorial Book for the Jewish Community of Yedintzi, Bessarabia). Eds.: Mordekhai Reicher, Yosef Magen-Shitz. Tel Aviv, Yedinitz Society, 1973 (Hebrew, Yiddish) "A Wedding in Town," by Golde Gutman-Krimer, pp. 447–50. (Yiddish)

> At the *khupe* the *batkhn* and *klezmers* entertained. Later on everyone danced a *bulgarish* in the bride's home. Then there was more music during the feast and finally the *droshe-geshank,* where Alter Peltsnmakher and his wife Kantshe gave one hundred *lei* [Rom.: money].

YUSTINGRAD (U). *Yustingrad-Sokolivka; Ayara She-nihreva* (Yustingrad-Sokolivka; A Town that was Destroyed). Eds.: Leo and Diana Miller, Kibbutz Mashabei Sadeh, New York, 1972, 1983. (Hebrew, English) "*Klei-Koydesh,*" pp. 28–29. (drawing of a *kapelye*) (English)

> The Sokolivka orchestra was well known and played in the nearby towns for the Jews and for the landed gentry.

ZABLOTOW (P). *Ir U-metim; Zablotow Ha-melea Ve-ha-hareva* (A City and the Dead; Zablotow Alive and Destroyed). Tel Aviv, Former Residents of Zablotow in Israel and the USA, 1949. (Hebrew, Yiddish) "*Klezmorim,*" by Avraham Kish, pp. 178–79. (Yiddish)

> In Zablotow the Shiplman family were the *klezmorim.* The second son became a bandit and was caught. He was sentenced to twenty years' hard labor in a severe prison, where he later died. It was rumored that he dug a hole under the prison wall and disappeared.

ZABLUDOW (P). *Zabludow yizker-bukh* (Zabludowo; In Memoriam*). Eds.: Sh. Tsesler et al. Buenos Aires, Zabludowo Book Committee, 1961. (Yiddish) "Theatre, Culture and Entertainment in Zabludow," by David Zabludowski, pp. 272–81. (drawing of a wedding)

> Inspired by traveling theatre troupes, the author's father formed his own local theatre company. And since there was no local *kapelye,* they had to be brought from Bialystock whenever there was a wedding.

ZAGLEMBIE (P). *Pinkes Zaglembye* (Memorial Book Zaglembie). Ed.: J. Rapaport. Melbourne, Zaglembie Society and Zaglembie Committee in Melbourne; Tel Aviv, Hamenorah, 1972. (Yiddish, English) "The Jewish Musician," by Ruven Braynen, pp. 241–42. (Yiddish)

> I visited Bedzin, where I was wrote a report on various aspects of Jewish life in Poland. I was befriended by Dr. Maximillan Vasertsvayg, who took to me to the Jewish section where the poor lived. The doctor brought me to the home of a Jewish musician who played at weddings. It really was not a home but just a lair, one room and a window.
>
> When I walked into the *klezmer*'s filthy home, I saw poor forlorn children who wore dirty *tsitsim.* They ran and jumped, making a great racket. They looked at me with curiosity, as if I were a rich landowner. I wanted to ask the children some questions and pat their pale faces, but they did not stand still. Then one boy answered all my questions without any fear. With this kind of *khutspe* I could see this young boy becoming a millionaire or a baron.
>
> Inside the home it was quite horrible and shocking. Nothing I ever read or saw in a photo prepared me for this. The narrow room with black walls had two uncleaned beds in it. Straw was strewn across the beds with a cloth covering the straw. There was a table with weak uneven legs and a broken stool on the damp floor. The floor was full of mud and excrement. The smell was so foul it made me sick to my stomach. In a corner of the room there was a barren woman who sat in a puddle with twins barely a year old. Both struggled and cried, obviously from hunger.
>
> In one bed there was a girl about seventeen years old who was sick and moaning like an animal from hunger. In the other bed were two more children who were also sick from extreme hunger and two more who crawled on the floor. By the door stood a boy of about twenty who suffered from a lung malady. The doctor told me that this boy played the clarinet at weddings but his health condition made it difficult for him.
>
> The head of the family was forty-five years old and had nine children. He was sick with consumption and looked at his instrument with longing, unable to play. All eyes were on us in hopes that we would cure them of their sickness and hunger.

The doctor explained that he was a professor from Berlin. When the man heard this, he jumped up with happiness, hoping that the doctor could give him a prescription that would cure him so he could play at weddings again and earn some bread for his wife and children. The man explained how for several years it was difficult to play the clarinet because he had no breath and was too weak to blow. And when he was healthy he still hardly earned anything from the poor weddings. There seldom were rich weddings where he could earn more. And now he was a wreck, a broken tool. His son had played until he became sick. Now the instrument sat in the corner, rusting away. And with tears in his eyes he asked us what did he and his wife do to deserve this curse form God? What sins could the youngest have possibly done? Then the children's eyes looked at their father in hopes that he would save and cure them. I stood there shaken, feeling helpless. There was no end to my sorrow. There was nothing I could do to help these unfortunate people. I took out a silver coin and said: "Here, take this and buy some candy." When the mother heard this, she became angry and said: "God forbid you take this money from the professor!"

ZAGLEMBIE (*ibid.*) (painting) "Musicians," by Moshe Apelboym, pp. 278–79. (Yiddish) Moshe Apelboym was born in Amshinov in 1886 and died in Katowice in 1931. He painted various subjects of Jewish life including the *klezmorim*. In his last years he also painted many pictures depicting the lives of the coal miners that were prevalent in and around Katowice.

ZAMBROW (P) *Sefer Zambrow; Zambrove* (The Book of Zambrov*). Ed.: Y. T. Lewisky. Tel Aviv, The Zambrower Societies in USA, Argentina and Israel, 1963. (Hebrew, Yiddish, English) "The Broygez Dance," pp. 393–94. (Yiddish) (photo caption: Goldetchke son, a talented *klezmer* and hairdresser and part of the intellectual circle standing at his mother's gravestone) (Yiddish)

The author's grandmother really was angry when she danced the *broyges tants* with her son's mother-in-law at his wedding. But she followed the song and made peace by its end.

ZAMBROW (*ibid.*) "Yisroelke the Drummer," p. 548. (Yiddish)

The drummer in the town's *kapelye* was also a grocer.

ZAWIERCIE (P). *Sefer Zikaron; Kedoshei Zawiercie Ve-ha-seviva* (Memorial Book of the Martyrs of Zawiercie and Vicinity). Ed.: Sh. Spivak. Tel Aviv, Former Residents of Zawiercie and Vicinity, 1948. (Hebrew, Yiddish) "Avrahamele's Wedding," p. 188. (Yiddish)

The famous Zawiercie *klezmorim* played at a big wedding in town.

ZDZIECIOL (P). *Pinkas Zhetl* (Pinkas Zetel; A Memorial Book to the Jewish Community of Zetel*). Ed.: B. Kaplinski. Tel Aviv, Zetel Association in Israel, 1957. (Hebrew, Yiddish) "*Klezmer* and *Batkhonim,*" p. 92. (Yiddish)

The *kapelye* played while the *batkhn* Medvetski walked around and entertained the guests. He carried a parasol in one hand while a red handkerchief stuck out from his back pocket.

ZDZIECIOL (*ibid.*) "The Last *Batkhn,*" by Yakov Indershtayn, pp. 276–77. (Yiddish)

Moshe the Ox, later called *Reb* Moshe, was the *batkhn.* He was also a full-time shoemaker.

ZELECHOW (P). *Yizker-bukh Fun Der Zhelekhover Yidisher Kehile* (Memorial Book of the Community of Zelechow). Ed.: W. Yassni. Chicago, Former Residents of Zelechow in Chicago, 1953. (Yiddish) "The Typhus Epidemic and a Wedding at the Cemetery," by Moyshe Borukhovitsh.

In the Zelechow ghetto there was a terrible typhus epidemic that affected the Jews. Dr. Shkap was popular among the Jews and dedicated to the sick. He was sent by the *Judenrat* to another town because he headed the Jewish Social Self-Help organization.

Instead of Dr. Shkap, they brought in two doctors who controlled the whole hospital. To avoid disinfection and four weeks' quarantine, one had to bribe the doctors. The typhus epidemic continued to take many victims. Finally it was decided to arrange a wedding in the cemetery as well as a ceremony to bury whatever scraps of Jewish holy books remained in the *shtibl.*

A bride and a groom were found, and on the day of the wedding the community led the couple to the cemetery. Following behind them was a wagon filled with old Jewish books. The whole procession was accompanied by the *klezmorim.* Then the books were buried and the wedding took place. Afterward, the festivities were held at the *Judenrat*'s office with food, music, and small contributions of money for the newlyweds.

ZYRARDOW (P). *Pinkas Zyrardow, Amshino un Viskit* (Memorial Book of Zyrardow, Amshinov and Viskit). Ed.: M. W. Bernstein. Buenos Aires, Association of Former Residents in the USA, Israel, France and Argentina, 1961. (Yiddish) "Moyshe Apelboym," pp. 412–13. (photo: Moyshe Apelboym and a picture of a painting of a *klezmer kapelye.*)

Moshe Apelboym, born in Amshinov April 15, 1887 (d. January 3, 1931), was a well-known painter. Among his subjects, *klezmorim* figured prominently.

Klezmer Loshn

•

(*KLEZMER* SLANG)

The *klezmorim,* like other workers, had their own jargon. This professional argot provided a sense of camaraderie and secretiveness. The *klezmorim* often traveled far from their hometowns for gigs, stopping at inns or taverns to eat, drink, or sleep, so conversing in *klezmer-loshn* allowed them a certain privacy, particularly when among other Jews who spoke Yiddish. When the *klezmorim* performed for non-Jews (who often became drunk, leading to fights among themselves and with the *klezmorim*), using *klezmer-loshn* again provided a certain amount of security, particularly when they spoke about their employers and payment (usually in derogatory terms). For example, one *klezmer* told me, "Once when we were playing for the gentiles I remember hearing the leader of the *kapelye* speak about the bride's sister and how she had nice firm *krelikes* [breasts]. He said sleeping with her would be great and that it would cost less than five dances. I really didn't understand all of what he had said but I laughed with the rest of the musicians so I wouldn't feel left out."[1]

---

[1] Interview with David Kagan (originally from Bedzin, Poland) in Wrocław, Poland, December 7, 1984.

Since weddings formed the backbone of most earnings it is not surprising to find many words in *klezmer-loshn* about money and wedding guests. "Indeed the income of the musicians was largely dependent on the largesse of wedding guests, who had to be encouraged to pay for tunes. This often required the machinations of the musicians."[2]

The following saying sums it up: "*Yeder vus tantst met der kale · ·ft arayn in tsimbl far di klezmer shabes*" (Everyone who danced with the bride paid the *tsimbler* because there was no dancing with her on the Sabbath).[3]

Being able to speak *klezmer-loshn* allowed one to be an insider in the world of the *klezmer*, accepted by one's professional peers. This was similar to jazz musicians in America who created their own slang terms to be used among themselves. However, slang, unlike a professional argot, was less specific to one particular group and became known and used by the general public. The following piece of conversation could have been heard almost anywhere during the bebop era of the 1950s: "Dig this, man. This cool cat really blew his ax and earned a bill for the gig" (Understand this, man. This smooth musician really played his instrument and earned a hundred dollars for the job).

According to Dr. Robert A. Rothstein, a specialist in Slavic and Yiddish linguistics and folklore, the *klezmer-loshn* derives many of its words from the criminal's argot, the most international language in Europe. It incorporates words from many different languages, including Yiddish. Traveling the highways and byways of Eastern Europe (with stops at inns and taverns along the way) brought the *klezmer* into contact with the criminal element, which only reinforced the negative stereotype some Jews already had of the *klezmorim*. For example, take the following remark: "In the *klezmer* language we observe many words that in the first place are of sinners. It is a language only used by debauched males."[4]

---

[2] Robert A. Rothstein, "Klezmer-Loshn," in *Judaism,* Vol. 47, No. 185, Winter 1998, p. 25.
[3] I. Rivkind, "Notitsn: Tsu Klezmer-Loshn," in *Yidishe Shprakh,* Vol. 19, July 1959, p. 64.
[4] Avrom-Yitskhok Trivaks, "Klezmer-Loshn: Di Yidishe Zhargonen," in *Bay Undz Yidn,* edited by M. Vanvild (Warsaw: Pinkes Graubard, 1923), p. 167.

In *klezmer-loshn* there are many words that can be directly traced to criminal argots, including *Rotwelsch* (Ger.: thieves' Latin) and *Gaunersprache* (Ger.: thieves' language), *blatnoi* (Rus.: thieves' language), and *ganovim-loshn* (Yid.: thieves' language). Some of the loan words from the German thieves were *bash, biberen, stromer,* and *shwarts;* from the Russian thieves, *kitsh, stirkes,* and *warsukhe;* from the Polish, *mente, orshe,* and *keren;* and from the Yiddish, *drizhblen, smasan, reftiak,* and *tamukh.* Since most *klez-morim* played music primarily for Jews, they had to find languages other than Yiddish for creating their argot. Most of the words in *klezmer-loshn* originated from Russian or Ukrainian, with some Polish and Hebrew. Then there are a smattering of words derived from Czech, French, Greek, Hungarian, Latin, Romanian, and Romani. Some words did come directly from Yiddish but were turned into anagrams, like *shit* from *tish* (Yid.: table) and *bizen* from *ziben* (Yid.: seven). Some Yiddish words had a completely different meaning in *klezmer-loshn.* However, upon careful examination, one can see the logic. For example, *vorsht* (Yid.: sausage) in *klezmer-loshn* meant *clarinet, tshaynik* (Yid.: teapot) meant *trumpet,* and *shwarts* (Yid.: black) meant *night.*

Just as *klezmer-loshn* was infused with vocabulary from criminal argot, so was criminal argot infused with Yiddishisms. While doing research in Poland I met a couple of men who had spent time in prison. They spoke a prison argot they called *Gryps* or *Grpsera.* Some of the Yiddishisms they used are now part of regular Polish. For example, *dintojre,* "kangaroo court" (Yid.: *din-toyre,* lawsuit in rabbinical court), *trefny,* "stolen merchandise" or "hot goods" (Yid.: *treyf,* not kosher), *bachor,* "obnoxious boy" (Yid.: *bokher,* unmarried young Jewish man), *mojre,* "fate" (Yid. *moyre,* fear), *geszeft,* "make business" (Yid.: *gesheft,* business), *git,* "a redneck" (Yid. *git* or *gut,* good), *cymes,* "not a big deal" (Yid.: *tsimes,* fuss), and *mecyje,* "very cheap goods" (Yid.: *metsie,* bargain).

The Yiddish philologists who researched the *klezmer-loshn* before 1930 found that younger *klezmorim* were already forgetting much of the vocabulary. They also found that many of the Jewish waiters, cooks, cantors, and *batkhonim* who worked at Jewish weddings spoke *klezmer-loshn,* as did some Jewish actors and most of the Jewish barbers and barber-surgeons.[5] Thus it is no surprise to find out that many *klezmorim* were also barbers.

Klezmer-loshn was an important part of *klezmer* lore in the *shtetl,* and found its way into literature and song, including the works of Yiddish writers such as Sholom Aleichem (in his novel *Stempenyu*), Mendl Mokher Sforim (in his story "Fishker der Krumer"), and Irme Druker (in his novel *Klezmer*) and songwriters such as Shloyme Prizament and Moyshe Broderzon.

When Samuel Weissenberg did his *klezmer* field research in southern Ukraine in 1913, he was only able to collect some two hundred *klezmer-loshn* words because most of the *klezmorim* had forgotten the argot. Seventy-one years later, when I did my *klezmer* field research, I was only able to find seventeen *klezmer-loshn* words that were still remembered among these former *klezmer* informants. The usage of *klezmer-loshn* had disappeared.

The following glossary was put together from these sources and regions:

  I. (B) Bernshteyn, Mordkhay. "A Bintl Verter Fun Klezmer-Loshn," in
      Yidishe Shprakh, Vol. 19, NY. July 1959, pp. 22–25. (Bessarabia)
 II. (D) Dushman, Leon. *"Fakh-Leshones,"* *Tsaytshrift,* Minsk 2–3. 1928,
      pp. 875–877. (Belarus)
III. (E) Elzet, Yehuda. *"Melokhes un Bale-Melokhes,"* in *Der Vunder-Oytser*
      fun der Yidisher Shprakh. (four parts) Warsaw, Bracia Lewin-Epsztein,
      Part 2, 1918, pp. 32–44. (Poland)
 IV. (L) Landau, Alfred. *"Zur Russisch-Jüdischen 'Klezmer' Sprache."* in
      Mitteilungen der Anthropologischen Gesellschaft in Wien. Vol. 43, 1913,
      pp. 143–49. (Ukraine)
  V. (P) Prilutski, Noyekh. *"L'shon ha-Klezmorim b'Polonia,"* in *Reshumot.*
      Odessa, Moriah, 1918, pp. 272–91. (Poland)
 VI. (T) Trivaks (op. cit). pp. 167–71. (Poland)

---

[5] In Yiddish the barber-surgeon was called *feldsher.* In the *shtetl,* when speople had minor injuries like burns, sprains, cuts, or broken bones, they went to the *feldsher* if no doctor was available. Most often the *feldsher* was the barber, and was already equipped with a certain amount of first-aid knowledge.

VII. (W) Weissenberg, Samuel. *"Die Klesmer Sprache,"* in *Mitteilungen der Anthropologischen Gesellschaft in Wien.* Vol. 43, 1913, pp. 126-41. (Ukraine)

I also include words I found myself in Poland and Romania. In each of these sources are many of the same words; if the spelling is exactly the same then I include it only once in the glossary. The letters following each word represent the source collection.

alte bibi (Strom): aunt.[6]

altifkes (T): potatoes.

amayi (T): home.

antkhilen (W): runaway.

aney (T): absent, gone.

araynterkhenen (T) (sim. *araynterkhinen* [P]): to stick in, put in, to place, to insert.

arimkhilen (W): walking, walk around.

avekhilyen (T) (sim. *agkhilyen* [T], *agtrolen* [T], *hokn* [D], *khilen* [W], *avekhilin* [P], *aveglikhen* [W]): to leave, go away, depart.

aynkliven (W): to fall in love.

baker (T): two *groshen.*

baker (T) (sim. *baka* [P], *bak* [P], *bake* [P]): two.

baker-baker (T): four (2+2).

baker-baker-bakerlekh (D): four *kopecks.*

baker-detsem (T) (sim. *baki-detsem* [P], *baker-dezen* [W]): twenty (2×10).

baker-baker-spem (T): nine (2+2+5).

baker-baker-smalyer (D): four *rubles.*

baker-baker-strom (T) (sim. *bizen* [T], *bezin* [P]): seven (2+2+3).

baker-fikslekh-mit-baker-smalyer (D): eight *rubles.*

baker-fikslekh-mit-a-smalyer (D): seven *rubles.*

baker-fikslekh-smalyer (D): six *rubles.*

baker-smalyer (D): two *rubles.*

baker-strom (T): six (2×3).

bakernik (T) (sim. *bakerl* [D], *popike* [W]): one *kopeck,* two *groshen.*

baki-khashmil (T) (sim. *baker-bakerlekh* [D]): two *kopecks.*

baki-detsem (P) (sim. *masanke* [W]): ten *kopecks.*

baki-detsem (P) (sim. *rantsik* [D], *baki-detsen* [P]): twenty.

balani (T): 15 *kopecks* or 30 *groshen.*

baliva (W): you.

baliven (W): your, you (formal *you, your* in Ger.).

balives (W): their.

balni (P): one *groshen.*

baro (Strom): big.[7]

barok (W): cello.

baryal (T) (sim. *baryalik* [P]): hungry.

baryalnik (T): an eater, a glutton.

---

[6] Interview with Cili Svarț (originally from Moineşti, Rom.) in Iasi, Romania, March 16, 1996. The word *bibi* means *aunt* in Romani.

[7] Ibid. The word *baro* means *large* in Romani.

baryalnik (T): this mouth.

baryalnik (T) (sim. *beryalnik* [W]): spoon.

baryanske (T) (sim. *baryanski* [P]): mouth, face.

baryen (T) (sim. *bery* [T], *beryen* [T], *beryalen* [T], *bari* [P], *baryalen* [P], *barin* [P], *pape* [L]): to eat.

bash (T) (sim. *tshop* [T], *shab* [T], *tshap* [P], *shab* [P], *shap* [P], *babki* [W], *lova* [Strom]): money.[8]

basviden (T) (sim. *basmiden* [T], *basvizin* [P], *basvidet* [P]): to seat, to occupy (to *bazetsen* the bride).

baverben (T): to besmirch, to arrange.

baverzin (P): to pollute, dirty, make filthy.

baverziti-yoldin (P): filthy *khasidim.*

beryalne (E): restaurant.

beryalnitse (D): a meal.

beryet linkes (E): to eat nonkosher food.

beygele (L): a circle dance.

bezin-detsem (P): seventy (7×10).

bibern (T): to pray, to learn.

bibernik (T): a prayerbook (a *sider*).

bibernik (E): a learned man.

bibernik (P) (sim. *bibralnik* [D]): a small *sider,* small book.

birgolen (T) (sim. *spyokhes* [T], *ukriles* [W], *krelikes* [D]): breasts.

bis (T): twenty.

bisapans (T): twenty-five.

blads (W): non-Jewish male farmer.

bladsen (W): baptize.

bladsikhe (W): non-Jewish female farmer.

blate (Strom): "made" man (meaning he works with or has connections to the criminal underworld), he knows what is happening.[9]

bolben (W): to call.

borl (T) (sim. *berel* [T], *shvaler* [T], *smalyer* [W]): a *ruble.*

borukher (W): gigolo.

bos (W): sugar.

bosnik (W): cake.

botshkar (T) (sim. *smaryan* [T], *sahan* [P]): a *khasid.*

boytse (E): fear.

boytse hobn (E): be afraid.

bozhnik (T): gingerbread, ginger cake.

bozhnik (P): honey cake.

brak (P): bass, *pandura.*

bratan (T) (sim. *bratanek* [P], *bratvo* [P]): brother.

bratanek (P): nephew.

bratanikha (P): girlfriend, pal, buddy.

bratanikhe (P) (*sbramikhe* [W]): sister.

bratanitse (P): niece.

bratenyek (P) (sim. *bratul* [P], *sbram* [W]): little brother.

bratenyek (P): nice person.

buye (T): prostitute.

delovke (W) (sim. *kapure* [L]): married woman.

des (T) (sim. *detsem* [T], *dezmus* [W]): ten.

desapans (T): fifteen.

detsem-khashmil (T) (sim. *detsem-mit-a-khashmil* [P], *dezmus-mit-a-berel* [W]): eleven (10+1).

---

[8] Interview with Berko Gott in Dorohoi, Romania, February 25, 1985. The word *lova* is a slang term used among the Rom to mean *money.*

[9] Interview with Marty Levitt, January 25, 2002.

detsem-mit-pshat (P) (sim. *baker-fik-slekh-detsen* [D]): sixteen.

detsem-mit-seven (P): seventeen.

detsem-mit-spem (P): fifteen.

detsem-mit-strom (P): thirteen.

detsimer (T) (*detsemnik* [P]): ten groshen, 5 kopecks.

detsim-detsim (T) (sim. *dos* [T], *detsem-detsem* [P], *sotnye* [P], *detsen-detsener* [D]): one hundred (10×10).

detsim-mit-ptye (sim. *detsem-mit-srom* [P], *detsem-mit-ptye* [P], *baker-baker-detsen* [D]): fourteen.

detsmer (B) (sim. *spenyak* [W]): five kopecks.

dokoren (L) (sim. *dokoret* [L]): person.

doyl (T) (sim. *deyl* [W]): a man, married man.

doyl (B): a *yold*.[10]

doylevke (T) (sim. *dolivki* [P], *doylivki* [P], *delovke* [W]): a woman.

drapatsh (from Druker's novel *Klezmer*): a scraper, scratcher (on his instrument).[11]

dzhokhen (T) (sim. *zhokhen* [T]): to laugh.

drizhblen (T) (sim. *drizhblen* or *drizhben* [E], *drizhbelen* [B], *drushfen* [D], *drushpen* [W]): to sleep.

farkeret (T) (sim. *farkerit* [P]): drunk, drunkard.

finkel (E): burning.

flis (T) (sim. *shuha* [D]): *mikve*.

flisen (E) (sim. *brinslen* [W]): crying.

fliser (E): water.

fliseren (T) (sim. *shulen* [D]): to urinate.

fotyashnik (W): father (generally of the groom).

foyatshnitse (W): mother (generally of the groom).

fyol (E): gate.

grabishke (T) (sim. *zaberes* [T], *rabishke* [T], *rabishki* [P], *grabishki* [P], *grabishkis* [P], *grablyukhi* [W], *grabishkes* [pl.]): a hand.

hakhtlign (T) (sim. *hartlign* [E]): knife.

hoker (D): peddler, tramp, hiker.

hopsen (L): a kind of dance.

kadrol (T) (sim. *dulyen* [E], *dultser* [E], *finkel* [E], *ritsel* [E], *roykh* [E], *kudralnik* [D]) cigarette.

kanayen (D): understand.

kapure (L): married woman.

kasvenen (P): written.

kasvener (P): to write.

katrishki (T) (sim. *katerukhe, katre* [D]): a hat.

katroshnik (T): hatmaker.

karyalekhts (T): liquor, brandy, beer.

kef (P): medical assistant.

kep (T): cupping-glass.

keralnik (T) (sim. *keresh* [D]): a drunk man.

kerashim (D): a drunk woman.

keraze (D): to make a drink.

keren (T) (sim. *keryen* [B], *kerin* [P], *keren* [W], *keresh* [W]): to drink whiskey.

keren (T): to become drunk.

kero (T) (sim. *kerol* [T], *krozhe* [T], *kere* [P], *kerazh* [P], *orzhe* [D]): whiskey, liquor.

---

[10] *Yold* (Yid.): A Jewish male without a profession, son of a wealthy man, a simpleton, fop, chump, sucker.

[11] Robert A. Rothstein, "Klezmer-Loshn," *Judaism* Vol. 47, No. 1 (Winter 1988), p. 29.

keryalnye (E): saloon.

kez (T) (sim. *kes* [W]): six.

kilbes (E) (sim. *krelnik* [D], *lipki* [P]): a roll.

khamen (W): to make.

khayalnikes-raglayim (P) (sim. *khayalnikes* [W]): underpants, panties.

khashmil (T): (sim. *snopik* [D]): a *groshen*.

khashmil (T) (sim. *berel* [W]): one.

khat (T) (sim. *khad* [W]): eight.

khatsi-shvaler (P) (sim. *ful-smalyer* [D]): half a *ruble*.

khayalnikes (D): boots.

khayalnikes (W) (sim. *khilnikes* [P], *tsif* [W]): legs.

kheshtel (T): girl.

kheshtelekh (B) (sim. *shekht* [W]): girls.

khidke (T) (sim. *antkhilyay* [W]): disappear quickly, get away.

khidke (W): fast, quick.

khilnik (T) (sim. *khilyal* [W]): foot, shoe.

khilnikis (P) (sim. *khiyaln* [W]): shoes.

khilnik-makher (T) (sim. *khilyalnik* [W]): shoemaker.

khilyen (T) (sim. *khulyen* [B], *khilin* [P], *khilen* [W]): going, walking.

khiskhem (W) (sim. *reykhuldik* [W]): not normal.

khlis (W): go!

khone (T) (sim. *rashvyalnitshke* [T], *buye-t tchovalnitse* [E], *khuni* [P], *khune* [W], *borukhe* [W]): prostitute, licentious woman.

kipriven (T) (sim. *kompriven* [W], *kimpernyen* [E]): to buy.

kitsh (T) (sim. *kutshement* [P], *kutshementel* [P], *kutshment* [D]): jail, prison.

kitsh (P): jailer, warden.

klift (T): outer garment, coat.

kliften-shtiker (T) (sim. *kliftshtikmakher* [T], *klivtshikmakher* [P], *kropalnik* [W], *kliftentchiker* [E]): a tailor.

klinger (T) (sim. *maskhes* [W]): *shames, servant.*

klinger (D): police.

klis (T) (sim. *klisalnik* [T], *kliser* [T], *saynte(n)* [pl., D]): a thief.

klisalnitse (W): female thief.

kliv (T) (sim. *klivetse* [B], *kliva* [P], *kliver* [P], *klive* [W]): good, beautiful.

kliv (T): many.

kliven (W): love.

kliver-sahan (P): in-law, villain, ugly.

klivets (T): a rich man, good man, clever man.

klivetse (B): beautiful (woman).

klivts (P): garment, clothing.

kluntevne (D): brothel.

klyav (E): clever.

klyaver (E): a wise man.

klyunt (D): female.

kmizhe (E): shirt.

knasen (T): to see, look, know, recognize.

knasen (P): can, may, be able.

kolpan (T) (sim. *kolpa* [P]): a rabbi, important man, noted person, chief of police, aristocrat, landowner.

korpen (W): to sew.

krist (W) (sim. *roshti* [T]): city.

krokodil (L): quadrille.

ksive (T) (sim. *ksive* [P], *kasiber* [P], *kasive* [P], *ksiverl* [P], *stirke* [W], *skripalnye* [E]): document, letter, paper, ticket, passport.

kudren (T) (sim. *kudreven* [D], *finklen* [E]): smoking tobacco.

kutshemay (W): slow, quiet, unnecessary.

kvitsh (D): pig.

labren (T) (sim. *laben* [W], *labin* [P], *labern* [P]): to play cards.

labren (T) (sim. *labin* [P], *labern* [P]): to play music.

labeshnik (W): klezmer, cardplayer.

labushinske (T) (sim. *labrashnik*): the *klezmer* language.

labushnik (T) (sim. *balishnik, labishnik* [P], *labeshnik* [P], *labrashnik* [P], *lobeshnik* [B]): a *klezmer*.[12]

lap (T) (sim. *lvit* [E], *lyav* [D], *lyap* [W]): a rabbi.

lapekhe (T) (sim. *lapikhi* [P], *lyabikhe* [D]): a *rebetsn* (rabbi's wife).

lapsgrir (P): pouring rain.

las (W): dance hall.

lashen (W): to be angry.

lashen-sekh (W): to fight with words.

lazaye-soble (D): herring.

lazh (T) (sim. *lash* [W], *lashe* [W], *lazher* [P]): terrible, evil, wicked.

lazh (T) (sim. *lazhe* [B]): ugly.

lazhornik (T) (sim. *lazhuk* [P]): a poor person.

lazhin (P) to quarrel, curse, insult, blaspheme.

lazhor (T) (sim. *lozhuk* [T], *lazhuk* [P], *lashuk* [W]): not a honest person.

lazhikes (P): the poor.

lazshutshke (P) (sim. *lashutshke* [W]): poor woman, not an honest woman.

lazshutshke (D) (sim. *lazhornik* [T], *lazhuk* [P]): a bad person.

leter (W): plate.

leynen blat (Strom): to read music.[13]

likhalnik (W) (sim. *stromnik* [W]): coachman, driver.

linke-skhoyre (E): stolen goods.

linker-lvit (E): judge.

links (E): not kosher.

lipke (T) (sim. *okril* [T], *okrel* [T], *krel* [T], *ukril* [B], *kril* [W]): white bread, khale.

lipki (P): loaf of bread.

livake di kruke (L): very bad.

loben (B): to play in the theatre.

lobeshnik (B): actor.

lokt (W): cold.

loybish (T): Polish.

lyakike (W): cripple.

lyap (W): reverend.

marmulke (D): cow.

masikanke (T): women's clothes.

masinke (W): small.

maskatnyes (T) (sim. *likhalnikes* [W]): pants.

maskokles (T) (sim. *maskoklis* [P]): eggs.

matam (B): there.

matid (B): here.

matkhen (T) (sim. *matkhenen* [T], *matkhine* [P]): to see, to look, to gaze.

---

[12] *Labushnik* originates from the Belorussian *labukhi,* slang for a musician who traveled and generally played for parties. *Labukh* is slang in Belorussian for band. Yefim Gribow, originally from Mozir, Belarus, told me about this word.

[13] Interview with Itzil Fyer (originally from Przemysl) in Kraków, Poland, December 12, 1984.

matrinitse (T): mirror.

maslyanke (W): butter.

mehetam (W) (*mehitin* [Strom]): who.[14]

mente (T): a policeman, a soldier.

mentes (T): police, soldiers.

mhtam (T): who is she?

motre (B): look at this, to ogle.

motren (W): to see, to show.

motrenitse (W): mirror.

moyshe (B): public.

nakidke (B): cape.

natkhinen (T): stinks, smells.

natkhint (P): not good, spoiled, broken.

neske (Strom): do not talk.[15]

neskem (E): quiet

neskem-mtit (E): he is not there.

neskem (B) (sim. *neskim* [P], *neskin* [P]): no, do not.

neskim (T) (sim. *nesken* [W], *pitiuk* [B]): no, none, nothing.

noves-reykhldiker (D) (*novesreykhul* [W]): ne'er-do-well, failure, washout, good-for-nothing, stupid.

nune (W): nine.

obtoken (T): to give, hand, serve.

onmatkhinen (T): to look at, eye, gaze.

onverzen (T) (sim. *onverzin* [P], *balan* [P], *basamblen* [B], *balen* [W], *labern* [L]): to play.

onverzin (P) (sim. *verzin* [P]): to laugh at.

onverzin (P) (sim. *verzin* [P]): to blow hot air, to bullshit.

orshe (W) (sim. *svino* [W]): wine, brandy.

orzhe (T): to take a bit, a snack.

oysproben (T): to learn, to be informed.

ozne (T) (sim. *klinger* [P], *geyzer* [W]): watch, clock.

pans (T): five.

pedak (T) (sim. *perdyak, perdak* [P]): old-time barber surgeon, surgeon's assistant, dresser.

pekho (W): wedding ceremony.

pintak (D) (sim. *pintok* [L]): a rich man.

pintatshke (D): a rich woman.

pirakhes (W): poultry.

pityuk (T) (sim. *petyuk* [T], *ptyukhl* [P], *petyukl* [W]): small boy, child, youngster.

piv (W): one-half.

poben (T) (sim. *pribiren* [T], *proben* [T], *pobin* [P], *probin* [P]): his.

potshakhyen (T) (sim. *potshekhnyen* [T], *pritshakhnen* [W], *pritshakhnen-b pot- shakhnin* [P], *potshekhnin* [P]): die.

pribiven (W): to have.

pritshakhnet (D): dead.

proben (T): to explore, find, investigate.

probet (B): it is not available.

pshat (T): six.

pshat-detsem (T): sixty (6×10).

---

[14] Interview with Leopold Kozlowski (originally from Peremišljani, Ukraine), December 12, 1984.

[15] Interview with Marty Levitt, January 25, 2002. Marty learned this *klezmer* argot from his father. He remembered a few other words that were still in use among *klezmorim* up through the 1950s. These words were: *arzhe* (orzhe-whiskey), *bash, verzak,* and *yold.* During prohibition many a *klezmer* who played in a "speakeasy" could often be heard saying at the end of a gig: "*Legt avek di arzhe*" (Put away the whiskey), "*Bahalten di arzhe*" (Hide the whiskey), and "*Ver brengt aheym di arzhe?*" (Who's bringing home the whiskey?)

pshikhilyen (T) (sim. *pshilekhen* [T], *pshilekhin* [P], *prilikhen* [W]): to arrive, to come, to come in.

petyuk (W): son.

ptire (T) (sim. *ptye* [T], *ptye* [P], *ptire* [W]): four.

ptire (T) (sim. *ptye* [T]): four *groshen*.

ptirenik (T) (sim. *revtsirker* [T]): 40 *groshen*.

ptye-detsim (T) (sim. *ptye-detsem* [P]): forty (4×10).

ptyuk (B): shrimp (*fig.*), urchin.

ptyuk (P) (sim. *shvizhak* [P], *shivzik* [P]): boy, lad, youth.

rabukha (E): goose.

rafsh (E): borsht.

rapikhis (P): socks, stockings.

rantsik-spen (D): twenty-five.

rapkh (D): rat, stingy person.

reftele (W): a twenty-five *ruble* coin.

reptyak (T) (sim. *shpalt* [T], *perdzhak* [D], *reftyak* [W]): a doctor.

rib (W): beer.

ripke (T) (sim. *ktute* [W], *salepnitse* [E], *sakhme* [D]): vagina.

rishkes (E): wages.

rol (T): wagon.

rolen (T) (sim. *strazhen* [D]): to travel.

rolnik (T) (sim. *strazhman* [D]): coach-man, driver.

romk (W): market.

roshti (T): house, room.

roshvinen (T) (sim. *tshoben* [E], *tshoven* [P], *klunteven* [Strom]): to have sexual intercourse.

rubt (W): beard.

sbram (W): brother.

sbram-fotyashnik (W): uncle.

sbram-fotyashnitse (W): aunt.

sahan (T): bride or groom's father.

saksom (W): all.

salep (T) (sim. *saleb* [P]): head.

salep (T): buttocks.

salep (T) (sim. *sop* [D], *shmuren* [W]): penis.

salepnik (T) (sim. *salepnyok* [P], *shumren* [P]): fool, silly, stupid.

samen (P): to end, be completed.

sares (T) (sim. *svas* [D]): hair.

sargnik (Strom): horseman.[16]

savri (T) (sim. *sarvi* [T], *savli* [W]): fish.

savri (D): wine.

sek (W): cheese.

seven (T) (sim. *besen* [W]): seven.

seven-detsem (P): seventy.

shakhte (P) (sim. *shekhtil* [P], *shakhtil* [P], *shakhtivki* [P], *shekhtes* [pl., P]): virgin.

shekhen (W): to laugh.

shekhte (T) (sim. *shekhtel, shakhte*): woman, girl.

shit (T): table.

shlamen (T): to sleep.

shmarocer (L): wedding guest.

shnyotshke (T) (sim. *shnyotshki* [P]): a piece, bit, lump.

shnyotshke (T) a woman (*vulgar*).

shnosker (L): drinker.

shverzak (L): capitalist.

shoyfer (T) (sim. *tshaynik* [Strom]): trumpet.[17]

---

[16] Interview with Berko Gott in Dorohoi, Romania, February 25, 1985. *Sarg* is an anagram of the Romani word *gras,* which means *horse.*

[17] Ibid.

shtolfer (P): oboe
shtolper (Strom): flute.[18]
shpenerel (T) (sim. *shpeneril* [P]): a five-
ruble banknote.
shpilyakhe (W): meat, roasted meat.
shpyoshnik (E): butcher.
shudnikes (Strom): pranks.[19]
shuster (T): a stingy man.
shvantsiven (T) (sim. *shmalziven* [W],
smalziven [W], *shantseven* [D]): to
dance.
shvarts (T): night.
shvarts mit vays (E): coffee.
shvitshnik (E): candle, lamp.
shvizhik (T): a young man.
sikren (W): to light.
sikrenitse (W): brandy.
simpelman (L): virtuoso.
skalen (W): to cook.
skalnik (T): a waiter for a wedding.
skalnik (W): wood for burning.
skalnitshke (T) (sim. *skalnitse* [P],
skavlenitshikhe [D]): waitress.
skalnitshke (T) (sim. *skolnitse* [E]):
female cook.
skavlenik (D): waiter.
skelkha (W): drinking glass.
skolen (E): to cook.
skolnik (E): a male cook.
skripalnik (T): pencil, feather.
smar (T) (sim. *smarik* [D]): an old man.
smar (W): old.
smare fotyashnitse (W): grandmother.
smarer fotyashnik (W): grandfather.
smarikhe (T) (sim. *smaritshke* [D]): an
old woman.

smasanke (T) (sim. *smisanke* [T], *bsanke*
[T], *lakl* [T], *shvisanske* [T], *bsamka*
[E], *msanka* [E], *samsanytse* [E], *sim-
sonkele(kh)* [B], *smansanke* [P], *shiv-
sanke* [P], *lakme* [D]): bride.
smukhen (W): to hear.
smuryan (T) (sim. *sahan* [T], *siryak*
[W]): dog.
smoken-zikh (E) to kiss.
smosan (T) (sim. *shmotshan* [T], *bsan*
[T], *shvisan* [T], *msan* [E], *samsan*
[E], *smasan* [P]): groom.
snoske (D): small person, short, inferior.
snotshke(s) (B): play(s) (drama).
sobanen (T) (sim. *sokhbanen* [E], *sobane*
[P], *skharbanyen* [D]): hide, conceal.
sokhar (W): pig (as used to describe
someone).
sove (D) (sim. *tshove* [W]): he.
sovey (D) (sim. *tshoves* [W]): she.
spem (T) (sim. *shpen* [W]): five.
spem-detsem (T) (sim. *sen-dtsen* [D]):
fifty (5×10).
spen-detsen-baker-baker-detsen (D):
ninety.
spen-dtsen-mit-ransik (D): seventy.
spen-dtsen-mit-strom (D): eighty.
spem-dtsim (T) (sim. *spem-detsem* [P],
spen-smalyer [D]): five *rubles*, a five-
ruble banknote.
spyokhe (T) (sim. *shplyokhe, spyokhi* [P]
shplyakhe [W]): meat.
spyoshnik (E) butcher, *shokhet* (ritual
slaughterer).
sreyg (W): big.
srom (T): four.

---

[18] Ibid.

[19] Interview with Leopold Kozlowski, op. cit. (He also remembered the word *neskem*.)

srom-detsem (T): forty (4×100).

srom-detsim (T): forty *groshen,* twenty *kopecks.*

stakhnyen (T) (sim. *stekhnyen* [T], *shtakhmen* [D]): to set, put, place.

stakhnitse (W): inn, tavern.

starkes (T) (sim. *storkis* [P], *stirkes* [W]): cards.

stis (E): a louse.

stos (W): one thousand.

strakhan (W): soldier.

strakhanes (W): army

strashi (T) (sim. *strashil* [T], *strislye* [W], *verdreyung* [L]): a wedding.

strom (T): horse.

strom (T): three.

strom-bakerlekh (D): three *kopecks.*

strom-detsem (T) (sim. *strom-detsen* [D]): thirty (3×10).

stromer (T) (sim. *stromnik* [T], *strom-strom-stromnik* [P], *stromerl* [W]): three *groshen,* three-*ruble* bill.

strom-fikslekh (D): nine *rubles.*

stromubel (T) (sim. *strom-smalyer-ayn-fiksl* [D]): a three-*ruble* bill.

strom-strom-strom (T): nine (3+3+3).

sukhe (W) (sim. *suha* [L]): tea.

suzenitshe (L): these.

svidalnik (T) (sim. *serdalnik* [E]): a *batkhn.*

sviden (T) (sim. *smiden* [T], *smiden* [W], *svizen* [E]): to sit.

svidonye (E): pledge, pawn.

svizekhts (T) (sim. *rim* [D], *rashli* [W]): home, house, an apartment.

svizenye (E): a bank.

tablatir (L): music notes.

tamukh (D): son-in-law's/daughter-in-law's father.

tamushke (D) (sim. *tamukhte* [W]): son-in-law's/daughter-in-law's mother.

tentlen (T) (sim. *tintlen* [T], *skripen* [T], *lakhmenyen* [D]): to write, scribble.

tentler (T) (sim. *tintler* [T]): a writer, a secretary.

terkhenen (T) (sim. *terkhinen* [P]): to shave.

terkher (T): poor man, beggar.

terin (T) (sim. *tiren* [T], *teren* [B], *tarin* [P], *geteredik* (Strom): to speak, say, tell.[20]

token (T) (sim. *tokin* [P]): to give, to put in the hand.

tos (W): one hundred.

toyr (W): red.

treyfene skhoyre (E): contraband.

treters (B): shoes.

tsamen (T): to count.

tshakhnen (W): to be sick.

tshek (T) (sim. *tshiken* [T], *tsheken* [P], *tshik* [P],): to hit, smack, knock, slap (also: to commit a terrible act).

tshekal (T) (sim. *tshikal* [P], *tshukalnik* [D]): a bass drum.

tshekal (T) (sim. *tshikal* [P]): scissors.

tshekalnye (T) (sim. *tshikin* [P]): a hair-dresser's, a barbershop.

tsheker (B) (sim. *tshkene* [W]): pocket.

tshikalnik (T): a shaver, a barber.

tshikalnik (E): *shoykhet* (ritual slaughterer).

tshikalnik (Strom): drummer.[21]

---

[20] Interview with David Kagan (originally from Bedzin, Poland) in Wrocław, Poland, December 7, 1984. (He also remembered the words *kliv, neskem,* and *tshizhe.*)

[20] Interview with Berko Gott, op. cit.

tshizhe (E) (sim. *tshizhes* [E]): this.

tshizhe-tsuze (T): a man who does not belong in that job.

tshiken (E): to quarrel.

tshos (W): I.

tshosenen (W): me, myself, us.

tshosens (W): we.

tshoven (T) (sim. *drizhblen* [T], *klunteven* [D]): unsatisfactory intercourse.

tshoven (W): him, his.

tshvi (W): lamp.

tshvyen (W): to kiss.

tsito (T) (sim. *tsiter* [T], *khidke* [W]): hurry, quick, fast.

tsmutshenizes (W): ears.

tson (W): nose

tsuze (T): that one, this man, this person.

tsuzi (T) (sim. *tsuzenikhe* [T]): this woman, that woman.

ubiren (W): to take.

ufsmiden (W): to get up, to stand up.

unterhalter (T): second violin, *sekunde*.

uriben (W): to give.

usi (T): available, present.

uztsi-shvaler (T): half a *ruble*.

varzak (T) (sim. *verzak* [T], *versak* [W], *warsukha* [W]): the buttocks, behind, rear.

varem (T) (sim. *varim* [P]): leech.

varplye (T) (sim. *varplie* [T], *verplye* [P], *verplist* [P], *verplis* [P], *verpe* [P], *verpem* [P], *verfli* [W]): violin.

varsmiden (W): to arrest.

verbel (B): bass.

verbel (T) (sim. *verbil* [P]): drum.

verdreyen zikh (L): getting married.

verzalnik (P): unclean, impure, defile.

verzen (T): to pass gas.

verzen (T): playing too loudly, playing badly.

verzet (E): stink.

verzet (E): scorn, contempt.

vitshen (W): to wish.

vurst (Strom) (sim. *foyal* [W]): clarinet.[22]

yatl (E): child (also: a bastard).

yokhm (E) (sim. *yokhe*): wine.

yold (T) (sim. *tshizhe-yold* [T], *yolden* [P]): a Jewish male without a profession, the son of a wealthy man, not a *klezmer*, not a barber, a husband, simpleton, fop, chump, sucker.

yoldevke (T) (sim. *yoldivki* [P], *yoldes* [P], *yoldavke* [P], *doylevke* [B], *daylovke* [P]): fashionable woman, the wife of a *yold*, chump, sucker, etc.

yoldish (T): Jewish, simple-minded, foppish.

zaboren (T) (sim. *zbyaren* [T], *zaborin* [P], *zabyeren* [P]): to take.

zakidriven (T): to smoke, to light the tobacco pipe.

zarke (T): pocket, handbag.

zbram (T) (sim. *batvo* [W]): father (generally of the bride).

zbram-zbram (T) (sim. *fotyashnik* [W], *smarer-fotyashnitse* [W]): grandfather.

zbramikhe (T) (sim. *br'makhe* [T], *bramikhe* [E], *zbramilekhi* [P], *batvikhe* [W]): mother (generally of the bride).

zerkalnik (T) (sim. *zhilkalnik* [T], *zikralnik* [D]): a candlestick, *menorah*.

---

[22] Interview with M. Segal (originally from Iaşi, Romania) in Haifa, Israel, June 11, 1985. (In Yiddish, *vurst* means sausage.)

zevi (W): something to drive.

zhetshes (B) (sim. *tshvi* [W]): things.

zhlob (T) (sim. *zhlobukhe-elzet*): a male gentile, a peasant, yokel, hick, boor.

zhlobevke (T) (sim. *zlobike* [D]): a female gentile, a peasant, etc.

zhokhen (T) (sim. *zhokhin* [P]): to sing (also: to laugh, to cry).

zhokhalnik (T): a *khazn*, singer, choirboy.

zikres (T) (sim. *materyalnik* [T], *mareryalnikes* [pl., P], *zhikretsn* [B], *sikres* [W]): eyes.

zikres (D) (*sikre* [W]): candle.

zokher (W): pork.

Klezmer Nigunim

◆

(*KLEZMER* TUNES)

The following melodies are from my personal field-recording archives, which I have compiled over the last twenty years during trips to Central and Eastern Europe. This selection represents various kinds of *klezmer* melodies.

There has been a longstanding misconception that most *klezmer* informants are men, while female informants were reliable sources only for Yiddish songs, lullabies, and the like. My own research belies this impression; in fact, two of the informants of the music in this section were women. All of the music here comes from informants mentioned in the previous chapters.

"A Alt Yidishe Lid" (Yid.: "An Old Yiddish Song") came from Dumitru Bughici in Bucharest. His father was very famous throughout Moldavia as the leader of a well-known *kapelye*. The father had a vast repertoire, but rarely composed his own music; however, one of the *kapelye*'s most celebrated tunes was this one, which he had written.

A Alt Yidishe Lid

AVRAM BUGHICI

"Baveynen Di Kale" (Yid.: "The Bride's Lament") is from Izu (Itskhok) Gott of Iași. This is the only *baveynen* I ever collected. It's in an unusual key, and when he played it for me on his accordion, it had an improvisational feel (he never played it the same way twice). Despite its mournful air, it concludes with an upbeat *freylekhs*.

Baveynen Di Kale

IZU GOTT

I learned "Bessarabian Bulgar" from the Rom *klezmer* Nikolai Radu in Chişinău. He played so many wonderful *klezmer* tunes that it was hard to choose which one to include here. But this is one of my favorites.

Bessarabian Bulgar

NIKOLAI RADU

I learned "Bialystoker Tish Nign" (Yid.: Bialystocker Table Melody) from my friend Ludmilla Pollock in Warsaw; she had learned this plaintive ballad from her father, who had been interned in a gulag in World War II, where he learned it from a Jew from Bialystock.

Bialystoker Tish Nign

Cili Goldenzweig Svarț, wife of Itsik Kara Svarț, was born in Moinesti, Romania. She was the source for two pieces here: "Bosnian Waltz" and "Bukoviner Nign" (Yid.: Melody from Bukovina). I chose the former because it is unusual to associate *klezmer* with Bosnian Jewish culture, which was primarily Sephardic. Cili learned this waltz from her uncle, who owned a lumber mill in a small Bosnian village. "Bukoviner Waltz" is the melody I always associate with Cili—when I first went to Iaşi to interview her husband, I heard her cooking in the kitchen and humming this melody.

Bosnian Waltz

CILI GOLDENZWEIG SVART

Bukoviner Nign

CILI GOLDENZWEIG SVART

"Freylekh 7:50" was taught to me by the Rom *klezmer* Paul Babici of Iasį. Of all the tunes in this appendix, this is the best known. I actually knew the song before Paul played it for me; but what I had never heard was the C section. The apocryphal story behind the title is that the 7:50 train from Odessa was the common transportation for Jews traveling to Kiev. On this train, *klezmorim* were known to busk, moving from car to car. This was the most frequently requested tune.

Freylekh 7:50

PAUL BABICI

I learned "Khupe March" (Yid.: "Wedding Canopy March") from Simkhe Wajc, who lived in Warsaw. Of all the melodies I've collected over the decades, very few were wedding marches. Simkhe remembered this from his boyhood.

Khupe March

"Mey'en Nign" (Heb.: "The Refusal Melody") is the only one of the group that I found in archival sources, and, further, is the only one to come from Germany. The custom was that a bride and groom could be standing under the *khupe* and still have the opportunity to refuse the marriage. I suspect this rarely happened, but the custom was to sing this *nign* before the vows began to express relief that the wedding was going forward.

Mey'en Nign

I learned "Mitsve Tants" (Yid.: "The Good Deed Dance") from Aaron Tinichigiu, who lived in Iaşi. Aron had vivid memories of this tune, because as a young boy he'd been honored to dance it with the bride, his first cousin.

Mitsve Tants

ARON TINICHIGIU

"The Ukrainian Cakewalk" is from the *klezmer* Asher Wainshteyn, who came from Stolin. Before he passed away, Asher gave me his manuscript of the *klezmer* tunes he and his *kapelye* played in and around Stolin before and after World War I. The provenance of this tune represents the nomadic nature of *klezmer* music—Asher told me he'd originally learned it from a member of his band who'd learned it during a brief visit to America. (I recorded this tune with my band, Zmiros, on our *Cholent with Huckleberry* CD).

Ukrainian Cakewalk

FROM THE MANUSCRIPT OF ASHER WAINSHTEYN

Glossary

•

Adonoi-Molokh: the lord is king (name of a *klezmer* mode).

Ahava-Raba: a great love (name of a *klezmer* mode).

Akaydes Yitskhok: the story about the sacrifice of Isaac.

Akheshveyrosh Shpil: Ahashuerus play.

alie: to be called up to the *Toyre*.

alter heym: old home; this is how immigrant Jews referred to their birthplaces.

Avinu Malkeynu: Our Father, Our King; a prayer recited on the High Holidays.

badekn: the veiling of the bride.

bale'basim (pl.): the followers of the *rebe*.

bale zemer: master of the music.

bal-kulturnik (bale-kulturniks pl.): owner or master of the culture.

bar mitsve: the religious ceremony whereby a thirteen-year-old Jewish boy becomes a young adult in the Jewish community.

bandura: Ukrainian/Russian plectrum instrument.

batkhn: wedding bard or jester.

batkhones: witty rhyming songs sung by the *batkhn*.

baveynen: the lamenting of the bride.

bazetsn: the seating of the bride.

bazingen: literally, the singing of the bride. The musicians sing to her about the pains and joys of marriage.

beknbroyt: bread given to *klezmorim* by the groom's family as a gift.

besmedresh: small orthodox house of worship.

bezem tants: broom dance; the same as the *shtekn tants*.

Blatnoi: Russian thieves' language.

bobe-mayse: a tale, story.

bratsche: viola, second violin.

bris: covenant; the act and ceremony of circumcision.

brokhe: blessing; *klezmer* slang for extra money; a tip.

broyges tants: angry dance.

brummbass: buzz bass.

bulgar (bulgarish): an up-tempo dance.

cobza: Romanian plectrum instrument.

czardas: Hungarian dance that starts slowly and gradually increases in tempo.

Daytshmerish: German words or phrases sporadically used in Yiddish.

davenen: synagogue praying.

Di Dorfishe Shil: the rural synagogue.

Di Klezmer Shil: the *klezmer* synagogue.

dobranotsh: good-night dance.

dobridyen: good-morning dance.

doyne: a display piece that is semi-improvised.

drek: dirt, filth, excrement.

dreydlekh: *klezmer* ornamentation.

dveykes: religious ecstasy.

drash: sermon, speech.

droshe geshank: the announcing of the gifts.

dudlezack: German version of the French bagpipe called a *musettet.*

dibek: evil spirit.

emune-shtarkung: literally, faith-strengthening; renewal.

essen teg (pl.): days of the week poor *yeshive* students were given a free meal.

fandanca: a Russian dance that originated from the Spanish fandango.

fantazi: (Yid: fantasy) nondance tune often played at the wedding table.

farshpil: prelude.

feldsher: barber-surgeon.

flageoletts: harmonic notes.

folks-shule: public school.

freygish: another name for the Ahava-Raba mode.

freylekhs: most common upbeat *klezmer* dance.

gabe: trustee or warden of a synagogue.

gaguyim-nigunim (pl.): Khasidic spiritual vocal songs.

gaje: non-Rom.

Ganovim-Loshn: Yiddish thieves' language.

gartl: belt or sash worn by orthodox and *khasidic* Jews.

gas-nign: street song.

Gaunersprache: German thieves' language.

Gemore: the Talmud, the part that comments on the *mishne.*

gildene yoyikh: chicken soup, the bride and groom's first meal after the ceremony and after having fasted all day.

glitsh (glitshn pl.): glissando note in *klezmer* music.

Goldene Midine: golden country; what Jews in Central and Eastern Europe called America.

graf: count.

grimpler: a person who hums or whistles clumsily, usually out of tune.

gute-morgn tants: good-morning dance.

gute-nakht tants: good-night dance.

gute-vokh: good week; a greeting one says after the Sabbath has ended.

hackbrett: a kind of hammer dulcimer.

hakbreydl: a kind of hammer dulcimer.

hakht: chop; to annoy.

halutzim: Zionist pioneers in Israel.

Hatikvah: Israeli and Zionist national anthem.

haskole: the Age of Enlightenment.

Havdole: the ceremony performed at the end of the Sabbath.

haynt: today.

hetman: a cossack chief.

hislayves: ardor.

homentash (homentashn pl.) triangular Purim cookie filled with fruit or poppyseeds.

honga: Bessarabian line dance in 2/4 time.

hora: Romanian-Jewish dance.

hoyf (hoyfn pl.): courtyard.

husle: Ukrainian stringed instrument played with a bow.

Judenharfe: Jew's harp.

Judenleier: Jewish hurdy-gurdy.

Judenrat: Jewish Council appointed by the Nazis to represent the Jewish community. They were responsible for enforcing Nazi orders affecting the Jews.

Juden Spielhaus: Jewish concert/dance hall.

Juden Tanzhäuser: Jewish dance halls.

Judentantz: Jewish dance.

Jüdische Zigeunerkappellen: Jewish Gypsy orchestras.

kahal: Jewish community organization.

kale: bride.

kapelmayster: conductor; leader of the band.

kapelye: music band.

kapote: caftan.

kashrut: Jewish dietary laws.

katzenmusik: cat music; irritating music.

khale: challah bread.

khaluts (khalutsim pl.): Jewish pioneer to Palestine.

Khanike: Jewish festival commemorating the purification of the Temple in Jerusalem after the defeat of the Assyrian-Greeks.

khaper (khapers pl.): the man who seized Jewish boys to serve in the Czar's military.

kharpe-shpilers: literally, shameful players; musicians who played the Jew's harp, or *guimbard*.

khasid (khasidim pl.): a follower of the kabbalistic and spiritual philosophy begun by the Ba'al Shem Tov in the eighteenth century.

khazn (khazonim pl.): cantor.

khazones: the art of the cantor.

kheyder: traditional Jewish elementary school class.

kheyrem: ban, excommunication.

khevre: a gang, bunch.

khevre kedishe: the holy congregation, the burial society.

khevrisa: a gang, a music group.

khosn: groom.

khosn's tish: The groom's table, where he presides and is feted by his fellow male guests.

khupe: wedding canopy.

khusidl: a dance similar to the *freylekhs*, often danced by the *khasidim*.

khutspe: nerve, impertinence.

kidesh: benediction over the wine; the small meal served after Sabbath morning prayers.

kitl: white linen robe worn by orthodox Jewish men as a sign of purification.

klezmer (klezmorim pl.): Jewish musician.

klezmer loshn: the *klezmer*'s argot.

kneytsh (kneytshn pl.): short, squeezed note used in klezmer music.

kokhaleyn: small bungalow where people did their own cooking.

Kol Nidre: a very reverent prayer recited on Yom Kiper.

kolomeyke: Carpathian circle dance.

kopeks: Russian monetary unit.

korohod: circle dance.

kosher kikh (kosher kikhn pl.): kosher kitchen.

kosher tants: the wedding dance done with the bride, signifying that she is not menstruating and is hence fit to dance with men.

koyfn tants: buying dance.

koyletch: a special large round *khale* baked for holidays and weddings.

krakowiak: Polish dance popular among the upper class.

kreplekh: pockets of dough stuffed with meat or vegetables.

krentsl: *khasidic* circle dance.

krekht (krekhtsn pl.): moaning long notes in *klezmer* music.

kugl: pudding.

kumpanye: company, music group.

kvetch: complaint; a squeezed note.

landmanshaft (landsmanshaftn pl.): organization of expatriate Jews from the same town.

Legboymer: a Jewish festival in the spring.

lets (letsim pl.): clown, jester, buffoon.

l'khayim: to life! (one says this when making a toast).

maftir: one who reads the weekly selection of the Prophets after reading from the *Toyre*.

Magen-Avos: the guardian of our fathers (name of a *klezmer* mode).

Maharil: head man, leader.

mandlen-broyt: almond bread, cookie.

maralne: a rubato display piece.

marshalik: wedding jester or master of ceremonies.

mashke: liquor.

maskil (maskilim pl.): a follower of the enlightenment or *haskole* movement.

mazltov tants: congratulations dance.

mazurka: up-tempo Polish dance.

medresh: Homilies consisting of biblical exegesis and rabbinical literature.

megile: scroll; lengthy document read on certain holidays.

mekheteneste tants: in-laws dance.

meshugene: crazy man, lunatic.

mignon: French waltz.

mikve: pool for ritual immersion; ritual bath.

Misheberakh: he who blesses (name of a *klezmer* mode).

misnaged (misnagdim pl.): orthodox opponent to the *khasidim*.

mishne: the collection of postbiblical laws and rabbinical discussions of the second century that forms part of the Talmud.

mitsve: a good deed.

mitsve tants: good deed dance.

moyel: circumciser.

muser: The study of strict ethical behavior according to Jewish law.

muzikant (muzikantn pl.): musician.

nai: Romanian panflute.

nar (narim pl.): fool, clown.

nadn: dowry.

navenadnike: migrant; wanderer; a homeless traveler.

nign (nigunim pl.): generally a wordless melody, often sung by the *khasidim*.

nusekh: musical version.

oberek: Polish dance popular among the peasantry.

ornkoydesh: the holy ark where the synagogue *Toyres* are kept.

oyfrufns: the calling up of the groom to read the *Toyre* on the Sabbath preceding the wedding.

Ov-Horakhamim: father of mercy; name of a *klezmer* mode.

padespan: a Russian waltz based upon Spanish themes.

patsh tants: clap dance.

peye (peyes pl.): earlock, side curl.

Peysekh: Jewish holiday commemorating the release of the ancient Hebrew people from slavery in Egypt.

polka: up-tempo dance in 2/4 time.

portamento: continuous gliding from one note to another.

pozharne komande: fire brigade.

positiv: a fixed organ.

possenmaker: jester, buffoon.

possenreiser: jester, buffoon.

primas: the leader of the band; first violinist.

proste goy (proste goyim pl.): coarse, rude gentile.

Purim: Jewish festival commemorating the defeat of Haman.

Purim Shpil: a play commemorating Haman's defeat, performed on *Purim.*

pushke: alms box.

rabbi: teacher, Jewish religious leader.

reb: mister; traditional honorific preceding a man's first name.

rebe (rabeim, pl.): spiritual leader of a particular *khasidic* sect.

rikudl: a *khasidic* circle dance.

Rosheshone: the beginning of the Jewish New Year.

rosh kahal: leader of the Jewish community.

Rosh Khoydesh Elul: the first day of the sixth month.

Rotwelsch: German thieves' language.

schutzjuden: protected Jews.

scodatura: untuned.

Seder (Sederim pl.): the festive meal celebrated during the first and second nights of Passover.

sekund: second violin.

severs tants: server's or waiter's dance.

seyfertoyre: scroll of the *Toyre.*

Sfire: seven weeks of mourning between *Peysekh* and *Shvues.*

Shabes: the Sabbath.

shalakhmones: presents exchanged by friends on *Purim.*

shames (shamosim pl.): sexton.

shande: shame.

shatkhn: matchmaker.

sher (sherele): a *klezmer* square dance with couples.

sheygets: gentile boy; impudent lad.

sheytl: wig worn by orthodox women.

sheve brokhes: the seven blessings said at the end of the first day of the wedding celebration; the seven days of celebrating the wedding.

shidekh (shidukhim pl.): match, marriage.

Shir-Hamalos: Song of Ascents; a psalm recited on holidays, Sabbaths, and at weddings.

shmues: talk, conversation.

shnaps: liquor, whiskey.

Shnayders' Shil: tailors' synagogue.

Shnayders' Vaybers' Shil: tailors' wives' synagogue.

shoyfer: the ram's horn blown in synagogues on Rosheshone and Yom Kiper.

shoykhet (shokhtim pl.): Jewish ritual slaughterer.

shpielleuter: one of several terms, including shpilman, spilman, and spielleute, for wandering musicians.

shpilman: gleeman; wandering musician.

shtibl (shtiblekh pl.): small *khasidic* house of worship.

shtile khasene: a wedding without *klez-morim.*

shtiler tants: quiet dance.

shtetl (shtetlekh pl.): small town.

shtetl kahal: Jewish community organization.

shteyger: musical mode; similar to a scale.

shtek tants: stick dance.

shtey-gramen: literally, stand-up rhymes. Like *batkhones,* these are improvised rhyming poems.

shtrayml (shtraymlekh pl.): fur-edged hat worn by *khasidic* Jews on the Sabbath and holidays.

shtroyfidl: straw fiddle; Belorussian folk instrument similar to a xylophone.

Shulkhan Orekh: the collection of laws and prescriptions governing the life of an orthodox Jew.

shul-klopper: the synagogue striker.

shund: literary trash.

Shvues: a Jewish holiday celebrating the giving of the *Toyre* and gathering of first fruits.

sider: prayer book.

simkhe (simkhes pl.): celebration.

Simkhes *Toyre:* the eighth day of the Feast of Tabernacles (*Sukes*).

sirba: Romanian circle or couple dance.

skotshne (Polish, hop): hopping dance

or sometimes an instrumental display piece.

spielleute: itinerant German minstrel.

Sukes: the Jewish harvest holiday.

taksim: slow display piece that uses improvisation mixed with *fioritura.*

Talmud: The basic body of Jewish oral law consisting of the interpretation of laws contained in the *Toyre.*

tanz-un-spielhaus: dance and playhouse.

tales (taleysim, pl.): prayer shawl.

tats (tatsn, pl.): cymbal.

taytsh: Yiddish version of the *Toyre.*

tshoks: bent notes.

tsholnt: traditional stew made with beans, potatoes, meat, and spices eaten on Sabbath afternoon.

Terkisher gebet: Romanian display piece with Turkish influence.

tikhl tants: handkerchief dance.

tish: table.

Tishebov: A Jewish day of fasting and mourning to commemorate the destruction of the first and second Temples in Jerusalem.

tish nign: table song; wordless *khasidic* melody sung at the table.

tnay (tnoyim pl.): s., a condition or term of an engagement; pl., the engagement contract and party.

Toyre: the Five Books of Moses.

tsdoke: charity, alms.

treyf: not kosher; contaminated.

treyger: porter.

trop: musical accent.

tsadek: *khasidic* leader.

tsimbl: hammer dulcimer.

tsimes: vegetable and/or fruit stew.

tsitse (tsitsim pl.) one of the four tassels on the *tales*, or the undergarment worn by orthodox Jews; also the garment itself.

tzuica: strong Romanian plum or pear liquor.

Unesane-Tokef: first prayer recited on *Rosheshone*.

vivat: an upbeat dance similar to the *freylekhs*.

vlaste: a representative from the local gentile government.

vulekhl: a semi-improvised piece similar to the *doyne*. Could also be an up-tempo piece similar to a *freylekhs*.

wingerka: Hungarian-sounding dance popular among the Russian and Polish upper classes.

yenuka: baby.

yeshive (yeshives pl.): school for Talmud study.

Yidish kayt: Judaism.

yikhes: pedigree, lineage.

yikhed: a private room the bride and groom immediately went to after the wedding ceremony.

Yizker Bikher: memorial books.

Yinglish: words that combine Yiddish and English.

Yom Kiper: The Day of Atonement.

Yosef Shpil: The play about Joseph.

yungatsh: rascal.

zhok: same as *gas-nign;* street song.

zink: cornet.

zinkenisten: cornetists.

zogekhts: a plaintive display piece.

Bibliography

•

BOOKS

Aleichem, Sholom. *Stempenynu: Ale Verk fun Sholom-Aleykhem.* (New York: Sholom Aleykhem Folksfond, 1919)

Alpert, Michael, Rothstein, Robert A., and Slobin, Mark, eds. *Jewish Instrumental Folk Music: the Collection and Writings of Moshe Beregovski.* (Syracuse University Press, 2001)

Ausubel, Nathan. *The Book of Jewish Knowledge.* (New York: Crown Publishers, 1968)

Baines, Anthony, ed. *Musical Instruments Through the Ages.* (London: Penguin Books, 1973)

Beregovskii, Moises. *Folklider: Naye Materyaln Zamlung.* Edited by Z. Skuditzki. (Moscow: Emes, 1933)

Bick, Moshe. *Khatunot Yehudit: Niginot v'Zikhronot.* (Haifa, Israel: Haifa Music Museum and AMLI Library, 1964)

Blue, Brian, and Strom, Yale. *The Last Jews of Eastern Europe.* (New York: Philosophical Library, 1987)

Bonanni, Filippo. *Antique Musical Instruments and Their Players: 152 Plates from Bonanni's 18 Century "Gabinetto Armonico".* (New York: Dover Publications, Inc., 1964)

Braun, Joachim. *Jews in Soviet Music* (research paper No. 22). (Jerusalem: Hebrew University of Jerusalem, June 1977)

Castello, Elena Romero, and Kapon, Uriel Macias. *The Jews and Europe: 2000 Years of History.* (New York: Henry Holt & Company Inc., 1994)

Dawidowicz, Lucy S. *The Golden Tradition: Jewish Life and Thought in Eastern Europe.* (Boston: Beacon Press, 1967)

Dawidowicz, Lucy S. *The War Against the Jews 1933–45.* (London: Penguin Books, 1975)

Dobroszycki, Lucjan, and Barbara Kirshenblatt-Gimblett. *Image Before My Eyes: A Photographic History of Jewish Life in Poland 1864–1939.* (New York: Schocken Books Inc., 1977)

Druker, Irme. *Klezmer.* (Moscow: Sovietskii Pisatali, 1976)

Druker, Irme. *Mikhele Yosele Guzikov.* (Moscow: Sovietskii Pisatali, 1990)

Dvilianskii, Arkadii. *Muzykal'nyi Evereiskii Folklor Belarusi.* (Mogilev, Belarus: Belfort, 1996)

Eisenstein, Judith Kaplan. *Heritage of Music: The Music of the Jewish People.* (New York: Union of American Hebrew Congregations, 1972)

Eliach, Yaffa. *There Once Was a World: A Nine-Hundred-Year Chronicle of the Shtetl of Eishyskok.* (Boston: Little, Brown and Company, 1998)

Erik, Max. *Geshikhte fun der Yidishe Literatur.* (Warsaw, Poland: Pinkas Farlag, 1928)

Fater, Issacher. *In Der Velt Fun Muzik un Muzikers.* (Tel Aviv: Israel Book Publishing House, 1998)

Fater, Issacher. *Yidishe Muzik in Poyln Tsvishn Beyde Velt-Milkhomes.* (Tel Aviv: Velt Federatsia fun Poylishe Yidn, 1970)

Fuks, Marian. *Muzyka Ocalona.* (Warsaw, Poland: Wydawnictwa Radia I Telewizji, 1989)

Goldin, Max. *On Musical Connections Between Jews and Neighboring Peoples of Eastern and Western Europe.* Translated by Robert R. Rothstein. (Amherst, Massachusetts: International Area Studies Program University of Massachusetts, 1989)

Gruber, Ruth Ellen. *Virtually Jewish: Reinventing Jewish Culture in Europe.* (University of California Press, 2002)

Harkavy, Alexander. *Yidish-English-Hebreisher Verterbukh/Yiddish-English-Hebrew Dictionary,* 4th ed. (New York: Hebrew Publishing Co., 1928)

Herzog, Elizabeth, and Zborowski, Mark. *Life Is with People: The Culture of the Shtetl.* (New York: Schocken, 1952)

Hoberman, J. *Bridge of Light: Yiddish Film Between Two Worlds.* (New York: Museum of Art/Schocken Books Inc., 1991)

Holde, Arthur. *Jews in Music: From the Age of Enlightenment to the Mid-Twentieth Century.* (New York: Bloch Publishing Company, 1974)

Howe, Irving. *World of Our Fathers: The Journey of the East European Jews to America and the Life They Found and Made.* (New York: Schocken, 1990)

Kammen, Jack and Joseph. Edited and compiled. *Kammen International Dance Folio No. 1.* (Carlstadt, New Jersey: J & J Kammen Music Co., 1924)

Kammen, Jack and Joseph. Edited and compiled. *Kammen International Dance Folio No. 9.* (Carlstadt, New Jersey: J & J Kammen Music Co., 1934)

Katz, Mickey, and Coons, Hannibal. *Papa, Play for Me.* (New York: Simon & Schuster, 1977)

Kostakowsky, Wolff N. *International Hebrew Wedding Music.* (Brooklyn, New York: Nat Kostakowsky, 1916)

Kugelmass, Jack, and Boyarin, Jonathan. Edited and translated. *From A Ruined Garden: The Memorial Books of Polish Jewry.* (New York: Schocken, 1983)

Kun, Josh. *The Most Mishige: The Music and Comedy of Mickey Katz.* (unpublished manuscript, 1994)

Liptzin, Sol. *Eliakum Zunser: Poet of His People.* (New York: Behrman House Inc., 1950)

Loeffler, James Benjamin. *A Gilgul fun a Nigun: Jewish Musicians in New York, 1881–1945.* Harvard Judaica Collection Student Research Papers No. 3. (Cambridge, Massachusetts: Harvard College Library, 1997)

McCagg, William O., Jr. *A History of Habsburg Jews 1670–1918.* (Bloomington, Indiana: Indiana University Press, 1989)

Nettl, Paul. *Alte Jüdische Spielleute und Musiker.* (Prague, Czechoslovakia: Dr. J. Flesch, 1923)

Nettl, Paul. *Forgotten Musicians.* (New York: Philosophical Library, 1957)

Neugroschel, Joachim. Edited and translated. *The Shtetl: A Creative Anthology of Jewish Life in Eastern Europe.* (Woodstock, New York: The Overlook Press, 1989)

Nulman, Macy. *Concise Encyclopedia of Jewish Music.* (New York: McGraw-Hill, 1975)

Perlman, Robert. *Bridging Three Worlds: Hungarian-Jewish Americans, 1848–1914.* (Amherst, Massachusetts: The University of Massachusetts Press, 1991)

Pryzament, Shlomo. *Broder Zingers-Los Cantares di Brody.* (Buenos Aires: Union Central Israelita Polacca en la Argentina, 1960)

Rabinovitch, Israel. *Jewish Music, Ancient and Modern.* (Montreal: Book Center Montreal, 1952)

Rabinowicz, Harry M. *Hasidism: The Movement and Its Masters.* (Northvale, New Jersey: Jason Aronson, 1988)

Rivkind, Isaac. *Klezmorim: Perek b'Toldot ha'Amanot ha'Amamit.* (New York: Futuro Press Inc., 1960)

Rogovoy, Seth. *The Essential Klezmer: A Music Lover's Guide to Jewish Roots and Soul Music, from the Old World to the Jazz Age to the Downtown Avant-Garde.* (Chapel Hill, North Carolina: Algonquin Books of Chapel Hill, 2000)

Rosenfeld, Lulla. *Jacob Adler and the Yiddish Theater.* (New York: Thomas Crowell, 1977)

Roskies, Diane K., and Roskies, David G. *The Shtetl Book.* (New York: KTAV, 1975)

Rothmueller, Aron Marko. *The Music of the Jews: A Historical Appreciation.* Translated by H. C. Stevens. (South Brunswick, New Jersey: Thomas Yoseloff, 1967)

Rubin, Ruth. *Voices of a People: The Story of Yiddish Folksong.* (New York: McGraw-Hill, 1963)

Saculet, Emil. *Yidishe Folks-Lider.* (Bucharest, Romania: Editura Muzicala, 1959)

Saleski, Gdal. *Famous Musicians of Jewish Origin.* (New York: Ganis and Harris, 1949)

Sandrow, Nahma. *Vagabond Stars: A World History of the Yiddish Theater.* (New York: Harper and Row, 1977)

Sapoznik, Henry. *The Compleat Klezmer.* (Cedarhurst, New York: Tara Music, 1987)

Sapoznik, Henry. *Klezmer! Jewish Music from Old World to Our World.* (New York: Schirmer Books, 1999)

Schöenfield, Joachim. *Shtetl Memoirs: Jews in Galicia Under Austria and in the Reborn Poland 1898–1939.* (Hoboken, New Jersey: KTAV Publishing House, Inc., 1985)

Schudt, Johann Jacob. *Jüdische Merkwürdigkeiten.* (Frankfurt am Main and Leipzig, Germany: Samuel Tobias, 1922)

Svarţ, Itzik Kara. *Yungen Yorn un. . . . Veyniker Yunge.* (Bucharest, Romania: Editura Kriterion, 1980)

Sendrey, Alfred. *Bibliography of Jewish Music.* (New York: Columbia University Press, 1951)

Sendrey, Alfred. *The Music of the Jews in the Diaspora (up to 1800): A Contribution to the Social and Cultural History of the Jews.* (Cranbury, New Jersey: Thomas Yoseloff, 1970)

Sharvit, Uri. *Chassidic Tunes From Galicia.* (Jerusalem: Renanot-Monsa Press, Bar Ilan University, 1995)

Shatsky, Jacob. *Simhat Hanefesh: A Book of Yiddish Poems by Elhanan Kirchan.* (facsimile) (New York: Max N. Maisel Publisher, 1926)

Slobin, Mark. *Fiddler on the Move: Exploring the Klezmer World.* (New York: Oxford University Press Inc., 2000)

Slobin, Mark. Edited and translated. *Old Jewish Folk Music: The Collections and Writings of Moshe Beregovski.* Edited by Mark Slobin. (Philadelphia: University of Pennsylania Press, 1982)

Strom, Yale. *A Tree Still Stands: Jewish Youth in Eastern Europe Today.* (New York: Philomel Books, 1990)

Strom, Yale. *The Hasidim of Brooklyn: A Photo Essay.* (Northvale, New Jersey: Jason Aronson, 1993)

Strom, Yale. *Uncertain Roads: Searching for the Gypsies.* (New York: Four Winds Press, 1994)

Stutschevsky, Joachim. *Di Muzik un dos Muzikalishe Lebn in Poyln.* (Warsaw, Poland: 1956)

Stutschevsky, Joachim. *Ha-Klezmorim: Toldotehem, Orakh-Hayehem, v'Yezirotehem.* (Jerusalem: Bialik Institute, 1959)

Wallace, Lady, translator. *Mendelssohn's Letters from 1833–1847,* 2nd ed. (Philadelphia, Pennsylvania: Frederick Leypoldt, 1865)

Weinreich, Uriel. *Modern English-Yidish Yidish-English Verterbukh/Modern English-Yiddish-English Dictionary.* (New York: YIVO/McGraw-Hill, 1968)

Werner, Eric. *A Voice Still Heard: The Sacred Songs of the Ashkenazic Jews.* (Philadelphia: Pennsylvania State University Press, 1976)

Zylbercweig, Zalman. *Lektsikon fun Yidishn Teater.* (New York: 1934)

ARTICLES

Beregovski, Moshe. "Yidishe Instrumentale Folks-Muzik," *Kabinet far Derlernen di Yidishe Sovietishe Literatur, Shprakh un Folklor,* Nos. 1–3 (Kiev, Ukraine: Folklor-Sektsyse, 1937)

Berliner, Abraham. "Aus Dem Leben der Juden Deutschlands im Mittelalter," *Gesellschaft für Jüdische Volkskunde in Hamburg.* Edited by Ismar Elbogen. (Berlin, Germany: Schocken Verlag, 1927)

Berliner, Abraham. "Aus Dem Leben der Deutschen Juden im Mittelalter," *Gesellschaft für Jüdische Volkskunde in Hamburg.* (Berlin, Germany: M. Poppelauer's Buchhandlung, 1900)

Bernshteyn, Mordkhay. "A Bintl Verter fun Klezmer-Loshn," *Yidishe Shprakh,* vol. 19. (New York: July 1959)

Bordowitz, Hank. "Klezmer Rocks: Yiddish Music is on a Roll," *B'nai Brith Jewish Monthly.* (February/March 1993)

Dion, Lynn. "Klezmer Music in America: Revival and Beyond," *Jewish Folklore and Ethnology Newsletter.* (June 8, 1986)

Dushman, Leon. "Fakh-Leshones," *Tsaytshrift,* Nos. 2–3. (Minsk, Belorussia: 1928)

Elzet, Yehuda. "Melokhes un Bale-Melokhes," *Der Vunder-Oytser fun der Yidisher Shprakh,* part 2. (Warsaw, Poland: Bracia Lewin-Epsztein, 1918)

Gidman, M. "Yidishe Kultur: Geshikhte in Mitlalter," *Yidn in Daytshland dos XIV un XV Yahrhundert.* (Berlin, Germany: Klal-Verlag, 1922)

Glantz, Rudolf. "A Berikht fun a Ben-Dor Vegn Fayerlikher Protsesia fun dem Prager Yidn dem 24tsn April 1741," *Arkhiv far der Geshikhte fun Yidishn Teater un Drama,* vol. I. (Vilna–New York: 1930)

Glantz, Rudolf. "Der Kamf Kegn Batkhonim un Klezmorim in Daytshland Onheyb 19tsn Yohrhundert," *YIVO Bleter,* vol. 28. (New York: 1948)

Kahn, Henekh. "Yidish Muzik in Poyln," *Di Tsukunft,* vol. 48. (New York: July 1943)

Kirshenblatt-Gimblett, Barbara. "Sounds of Sensibility," *Judaism: A Quarterly Journal of Jewish Life & Thought,* vol. 47, No. 185. (Winter 1998)

Kon, Pinkhes. "A Khasone-Farshtelung un Klezmorim in Slutsk mit 100 Yorn Tsurik," *YIVO Bleter,* vol. 18, No. 2. (New York: 1941)

Landau, Alfred. "Zur Russisch-Jüdischen 'Klezmer' Sprache," *Mitteilungen der Anthropologischen Gesellschaft in Wien,* vol. 43. (Vienna, Austria: 1913)

Levy, Joseph B. "Jüdische Hochzeitsgebräuche Im Alten Frankfurt," *Ost und West: Illustrirte Monatsschrift fur das Gesamte Judentum,* vol. XIV. Edited by Leo Winz. (Berlin: Verlag Ost und West Leo Winz, June 1914)

Lewin, Louis. "Geschichte der Juden in Lissa," *Herausgegeben mit Unterstutzung der Gesellschaft zur Forderung der Wissenschaft des Judentums.* (Pinne, Germany: Verlag N. Gundermann, 1904)

Lifschitz, I. "Batkhonin un Leytsim bay Yidn," *Arkhiv far der Geshikhte fun Yidishn Teater un Drama,* vol. 1. Edited by Dr. Jacob Shatsky. (Vilna–New York, 1930)

Lifschitz, I. "Yidishe Farvayler af di Leiptsiger Yaridim," *Arkiv far der Geshikhte fun Yidishn Teater un Drama,* vol. I. (Vilna–New York, 1928)

Norman, Bob. "Echoes from the Shtetl: Reviving Jewish Klezmer Music," *Sing Out! The Folk Song Magazine,* vol. 28, No. 4. (July/August 1980)

Prilutski, Noyekh. "L'shon Ha-klezmorim b'Polonia," *Reshumot.* (Odessa, Ukraine: 1918)

Rivkind, Isaac. "Notitsn: Tsu Klezmer-Loshn," *Yidishe Shprakh,* vol. 19. (New York: July 1959)

Rothstein, Robert A. "Klezmer-Loshn," *Judaism: A Quarterly of Jewish Life & Thought,* vol. 47, No. 185. (Winter 1998)

Rubin, Joel. "Rumenishe Shtiklekh: Klezmer Music Among the Hasidim in Contemporary Israel," *Judaism: A Quarterly of Jewish Life & Thought,* vol. 47, No. 185. (Winter 1998)

Sandler, Boris. "The Paradox of Yiddish," *Forward.* (December 1, 2000)

Schlosz, Lehrer L. Von. "Jüdisches Zigeunerkappelle in Ungarn," *Mitteilungen zur Jüdischen Volkskunde,* vol. XXIII, No. 3. Edited by Max Grunwald. (Berlin: Verlag S. Calvary Co., 1907)

Shatsky, Jacob. "Muzik-Kultur Bay Yidn" *YIVO Bleter,* vol. 25. (New York: 1951)

Shatsky, Jacob. "Purim-Shpiln un Letsim in Amsterdamer Getto," *YIVO Bleter,* vol. 19. (New York: 1942)

Shatzky, Joel. "The People's Voices: An Interview with Ruth Rubin," *Jewish Currents,* vol. 39, No. 3. (March 1985)

Shepard, Richard F. "Klezmer Music Makes Leap to Carnegie Hall," *New York Times.* (February 18, 1983)

Shepard, Richard F. "Whether Klezmer or Classical, It's Music for This Man's Clarinet," *New York Times.* (November 14, 1987)

Shulgod, Marc. " 'Ghetto' Sounds: The Song of a Survivor," *Los Angeles Times.* (November 29, 1986)

Trivaks, Avrom-Yitskhok. "Kley-Zemer-Loshn: Di Yidishe Zhargonen," *Bay Undz Yidn.* Edited by M. Vanvild. (Warsaw, Poland: Pinkas Graubard, 1923)

Wall, Alexandra J. "Rhythm and Jews: Post-Klezmer Music—A Ride to Everywhere," *Moment,* vol. 24, No. 4. (August 1999)

Watrous, Peter. "Remember Mickey Katz? No? Well, Just Listen to This," *New York Times.* (January 19, 1990)

Weissenberg, Samuel. "Die Klesmer Sprache," *Mitteilungen der Anthropologischen Gesellschaft in Wien*, vol. 43. (Vienna, Austria: 1913)

Weissenberg, Samuel. "Eine Jüdische Hochzeit in Sudrussland," *Mitteilungen zur Jüdischen Volkskunde*, vol. XV, No. 1. (Berlin: 1905)

Wolf, Albert Von. *Fahrende Leute bei den Juden, Mitteilungen zur Jüdischen Volkskunde*, vols. 25–32. Edited by Max Grunwald. (Leipzig, Germany: M. W. Kaufman, 1908–09)

LINER NOTES

Feldman, Walter Zev. *Khevrisa: European Klezmer Music.* (Smithsonian Folkways Recording, 2000)

Schlesinger, Michael. *Jakie Jazz 'em Up: Old Time Klezmer Music 1912–1926.* (Global Village Music, 1984)

Schlesinger, Michael. *Klezmer Music 1910–42.* (Global Village Music, 1996)

Strom, Yale. *Cholent with Huckleberry.* (Global Village Music, 1988)

Strom, Yale. *Garden of Yidn.* (Naxos World, 2001)

FILMS

Broughton, Simon. *Fiddlers on the Hoof.* (London, England: distrib. British Broadcasting Corporation, 1989)

Daum, Menachem. Rudavsky, Oren. *A Life Apart: Hasidim in America.* (New York: distrib. First Run Features, 1997)

DuBose, Glee. Lenzer, Don. *In the Fiddler's House.* (New York: distrib. Public Broadcasting Corporation, 1995)

Goldman, Michal. *A Jumpin' Night in the Garden of Eden.* (New York: distrb. First Run Features, 1988)

Schwietert, Stefan. *A Tickle in the Heart.* (Berlin, Germany: distrib. Kino Video, 1996)

Strom, Yale. *Carpati: 50 Miles, 50 Years.* (New York: distrib. New Yorker Films, 1996)

Strom, Yale. *The Last Klezmer: Leopold Kozlowski: His Life and Music.* (New York: distrib. New Yorker Films, 1994)

Discography

•

The following discography gives good examples of the different styles of the artists interviewed in this book as well as others.

MOSHE BERLIN (Israel) *Klezmer Music From Tel Aviv* (live *klezmer* concert in Berlin). Wergo (1990).

MOSHE BERLIN (Israel) *Mazl Tov-Moshe Berlin and Friends* (*klezmer* and Carlebach at a live concert). Gal-Paz (2001).

NAFTULI BRANDWEIN (New York) *King of Klezmer* (essential Brandwein archival recordings from 1922–26 and four selections from his last recording session in 1941). Rounder 1127 (1997).

BRAVE OLD WORLD (U.S.) *Beyond the Pale* (traditional *klezmer doynes* and *horas* mixed with new Yiddish songs). Rounder 3135 (1994).

BRAVE OLD WORLD (U.S.) *Blood Oranges* (new Jewish art music). Red House RHR 134 (1999).

DON BYRON (New York) *Plays the Music of Mickey Katz* (Katz's tunes heard once again). Elektra/Nonesuch 79313–2 (1993).

URI CAINE (New York City) *Primal Light* (arrangements and improvisations of music by Mahler including *klezmer* version of the third movement from Mahler's First Symphony). Winter and Winter 910 004–2 (1997).

DAVKA (San Francisco) *Judith* (Old world *klezmer* trio sound). Tzadik TZ 7135 (1999)

DI NAYE KAPELYE (Hungary) *Di Naye Kapleye* (Hungarian, Romanian, and Rom-influenced *klezmer* from field recordings). Oriente RIEN CD 17 (1998).

EPSTEIN BROTHERS ORCHESTRA (Florida) *Kings of Freylekh Land: A Century of Yid-dish-American Music* (a *klezmer* repertoire of theatre, cabaret, *khasidic* tunes from post–World War II to the early 1970s). Spectrum/Wergo SM 1611–2 (1995).

MARTY EHRLICH'S DARK WOODS ENSEMBLE (New York) *Sojourn* (jazz mixed with Jewish motifs on several tunes). Tzadik TZ 7136 (1999).

FLYING BULGAR KLEZMER BAND (Toronto) Agada: *Tales From Our Ancestors* (*klez-mer* mixed with jazz). Traditional Crossroads TCRO 4294 (1993); *Tsirkus* (original Yiddish songs mixed with jazz). Traditional Crossroads TCRO 4292 (1999).

HASIDIC NEW WAVE (New York) *Kabalogy* (avant-garde jazz, improvisations, *khasidic nigunim* and singing). Knitting Factory KFR 239 (1999).

HASIDIC NEW WAVE (New York) *From the Belly of Abraham* (*khasidic* motifs mixed with jazz improvisation and Senegalese percussion). Knitting Factory KFR 294 (2001).

HOLLYWOOD KLEZMER (Los Angeles) *From L.A. to Odessa* (traditional *klezmer* with classical guitar and clarinet). Brandeis-Bardin Institute (1999).

JAKIE, JAZZ'EM UP (New York City) *Old-Time Klezmer Music 1912–1926* (archival recordings from the "golden age" of *klezmer,* including Hoffman, Kandel, Schwartz, and others). Global Village Music 101 (1984).

JASCHA LIEBERMAN TRIO (Kraków) *Remembrance of Kazimierz* (European *klezmer* violin mixed with new world harmonies). Universal Music Polska 157 060–2 (1999).

JOEL RUBIN JEWISH MUSIC ENSEMBLE (Germany) *Beregovski's Khasene* (Beregov-ski's Ukrainian *klezmer* fieldwork arranged for a sextet). Weltmusik SM 1614–2 (1997).

KAPLEYE (New York) *On the Air: Jewish-American Radio* (vintage archival Yiddish radio mixed with new arrangements of new versions). Shanachie 67005 (1995).

KHEVRISA (New York City) *European Klezmer Music* (traditional *klezmer* violin and *tsimbl* music from the nineteenth and early twentieth centuries). Smithsonian Folk-ways Recordings SFW 40486 (2000).

DAVID KRAKAUER (New York) *A New Hot One* (clarinet *klezmer* modes mixed with rock 'n' roll and jazz improvisations). Label Bleu LBLC 6617 HM83 (2001).

KLEZMATICS (New York City) *Jews with Horns* (*klezmer* modes mixed with new arrangements, new Yiddish lyrics, and improvisation). Xenophile 4032 (1995).

KLEZMATICS (New York) *Possessed* (*klezmer* modes mixed with new Yiddish and English poetry set to music). Xenophile 4050 (1997).

KLEZMER CONSERVATORY BAND (Boston) *Touch of Klez!* (big *kapelye* sound with tight arrangements of instrumentals and vocals of Yiddish classics, theatre, and Mickey Katz). Vanguard VMD–79455 (1985).

KLEZMER CONSERVATORY BAND (Boston) *The Thirteenth Anniversary Album* (Yiddish revue with a big *kapelye* sound). Rounder 3125 (1993).

KLEZMORIM (Berkeley, California) *First Recordings 1976–78* (includes "East Side Wedding," *klezmer* and traditional Yiddish songs and instrumental pieces, and "Streets of Gold," which is also traditional *klezmer* with only clarinet and all brass instruments). Arhoolie CD 309 (1989).

KOL SIMCHA (Switzerland) *Symphonic Klezmer* (*klezmer* with symphonic arrangements). Claves CD 50–9627 (1996).

KROKE (Poland) *Trio* (traditional *klezmer* mixed with chamber music arrangements for a trio). Oriente RIEN CD 04 (1996).

FRANK LONDON (New York) *Nigunim* (*khasidic* vocals mixed with trumpet and keyboard). Tzadik TZ7129 (1998).

FRANK LONDON'S KLEZMER BRASS ALLSTARS *Di Shikere Kapelye* (*klezmer* brass ensemble). Piranha Records PIR 1467 (2000).

MAXWELL STREET KLEZMER BAND (Chicago) *You Should Be So Lucky!* (Yiddish theatre, vaudeville, and folksongs played by a large *kapelye*). Shanachie 67006 (1996).

MUZIKAS (Hungary) *The Lost Jewish Music of Transylvania* (traditional Hungarian Transylvanian *klezmer* instrumentals and Yiddish vocals). Hannibal HNCD 1373 (1993).

NAFTULE'S DREAM (Boston) *Smash Clap!* (*klezmer* modes mixed with rock, free jazz, and electric guitar). Tzadik TZ7125 (1998).

PARADOX TRIO (New York) *Source* (*klezmer* mixed with Balkan motifs and rhythms). Knitting Factory KFR 237 (1999).

REBBE SOUL (Los Angeles) *Common Tongue—Step Into My World* (Jewish motifs mixed with rock, worldbeat sounds, and vocals). RebbeSoul Music (2000).

ABE SCHWARTZ (New York) *Master of Klezmer Music Vol. One—The First Recordings –1917* (78 LP recordings of a traditional *kapelye*). Global Village Music 126 (1988).

ALICIA SVIGALS (New York) *Fidl Klezmer Violin* (traditional *klezmer* violin). Traditional Crossroads TCRO 4286 (1997).

ANDY STATMAN (New York) *Jewish Klezmer Music* (traditional *klezmer* repertoire for clarinet, bass, and *tsimbl*). Shanachie 21002 (1978).

ANDY STATMAN (New York) *Songs of Our Fathers* (Hebrew prayers, *nigunim,* and *klezmer* for two mandolins and clarinet). Acoustic Disc ACD-14 (1995).

ANDY STATMAN (New York) *Between Heaven and Earth: Music of the Jewish Mystics* (*khasidic nigunim* played with free improvisational expression). Shanachie 64079 (1997).

YALE STROM (New York) *Hot Pstromi: With A Little Horseradish on the Side* (*klezmer* mixed with *khasidic,* Turkish, Cajun, flamenco, and Russian original tunes). Global Village Music CD 158 (1993).

YALE STROM (San Diego) *Leopold Kozlowski: The Last Klezmer* (Polish *klezmer* sound track for film directed by Strom; includes only field recording of *klezmer* lesson). Global Village Music CD 168 (1994).

YALE STROM (San Diego) *Carpati: 50 Miles, 50 Years* (Carpathian *klezmer* and Rom folk film sound track for film directed by Strom). Global Village Music CD 173 (1996).

YALE STROM (New York/San Diego) *Tales Our Fathers Sang: New Jewish Music with Tam* (original *klezmer* tunes composed for National Public Radio series: Jewish Short Stories: From the Old World to the New). Global Village Music CD 180 (1999).

YALE STROM (New York/San Diego) *Garden of Yidn* (old and new Yiddish and Ladino vocals with innovative arrangements). Naxos World 76005-2 (2001).

DAVE TARRAS (New York City) *Master of Klezmer Music Vol. 1, Original Recordings 1929–1949* (Tarras playing with several different *kapelyes*). Global Village Music 105 (1989).

JOSHUA WALETZKY (New York) *Crossing the Shadows* (original Yiddish songs and music). Waletzky Music WM001CD (2000).

JOHN ZORN (New York) *Kristallnacht* (Jewish modes mixed with loud free jazz improvisations). Tzadik TZ 301 (1993).

JOHN ZORN (New York) *Circle Maker* (string trio and sextet renditions of Zorn's Jewish-inspired composition Masada). Tzadik TZ 7106 1995.

JOHN ZORN'S MASADA (New York) *Live at Tonic* (Jewish modes fused with free and jazz improvisations). Tzadik TZ 7334-2 (2001).

Index

•